Selected Literary Essays

SELECTED LITERARY ESSAYS

by C. S. LEWIS

Edited by
WALTER HOOPER

CAMBRIDGE
At the University Press
1969

Published by the Syndics of the Cambridge University Press
Bentley House, 200 Euston Road, London N.W.1
American Branch: 32 East 57th Street, New York, N.Y.10022

PR
6023
E926
A16
1969

Printed in Great Britain
at the University Printing House, Cambridge
(Brooke Crutchley, University Printer)

Contents

Preface

This book contains all C. S. Lewis's essays on literature, with the exception of his *Studies in Medieval and Renaissance Literature* and four other essays which I am unable to reprint here. All have been published before either in periodicals or collections of essays by various hands. As a good many are out of print, however, and the cost of owning the volumes in which the others are contained would be prohibitive, it has seemed to me a good time to gather them into one volume. Before mentioning each in turn, I hope to throw some light on the background out of which these essays arose.

From his schooldays Lewis's major ambition was to be a great poet, and what appeared to be his first step in that direction came early in his life. In 1919, a few months after his return from the war to read Honour Moderations at University College, Oxford, he published his first book, *Spirits in Bondage: A Cycle of Lyrics*, under the pseudonym of Clive Hamilton—forty poems, most of which were written during his years at Malvern College (1913–14) and while he studied privately under W. T. Kirkpatrick at Great Bookham in Surrey (1914–17). Though Lewis's academic record at Oxford is most impressive—a First in 'Mods' (1920), a First in 'Greats' (1922), and a First in English (1923)—the diary he kept from 1919 to 1929 is anything but optimistic. It is, in the main, a chronicle of his efforts to write and publish his poems. Although his chief interest lay in the long narrative poems he was writing at the time, he sought to keep the name of Clive Hamilton before the public by posting one short poem after the other to the editor of such-and-such a magazine. With one exception,[1] all were returned. And though he continued to write narrative poems up to the middle 1930s, the only one ever published was *Dymer* in 1926. Most of the others were eventually lost or destroyed.[2] If we did not have Lewis's forty-odd books of literary criticism, literary history, theology, novels—as well as the volume or

[1] 'Joy', *The Beacon*, vol. III (May 1924), pp. 444–5.
[2] *Dymer* and three other narrative poems by Lewis are published together as *Narrative Poems*, ed. Walter Hooper (London, 1969).

essays in your hands at the moment—his diary would tell a very unhappy story indeed.

While Lewis was trying—and failing—to join the ranks of his favourite poets, he was at the same time anxious to defend them against the vogue for *vers libre* and the modern contempt for narrative poetry. Opportunities lay close at hand.

One was the Martlet Society, a literary society in University College limited to twelve undergraduate and former graduate members. The minute-books of the society are lodged in the Bodleian Library. And though the quality of the writing of the minutes varies over the years, there emerges from the pages a most lively account of Lewis's participation in the fortnightly meetings.

Lewis was elected Secretary of the Martlets at their 188th meeting on 31 January 1919. At the 191st meeting on 12 March 1919 (while Lewis was acting as scribe), a fellow-member read Lewis's paper on William Morris. It was by no means as thoughtful and developed a paper as that printed in this book, but some of the same ideas appear in both. At the 196th meeting on 15 October 1919 Lewis was elected President of the Martlets, and on 3 November 1920 Lewis (still President) read a paper at the 211th meeting, the basic ideas of which continued to be those he held for the rest of his life. The Secretary records that:

There being no further private business, the President commenced his paper on narrative poetry. He took up, from the first, a fighting attitude. In an age of lyrical activity he was come to defend the epic against the prejudice of contemporaries. Edgar Allan Poe had said that a long poem was impossible, but he was sufficiently answered by the extreme richness of our literature in good narrative poetry. The real objection of the moderns was based on the fact that they would not make the effort to read a long poem. That effort, the reader contended, was necessary to the true appreciation of the epic: for art demands co-operation between the artist and his audience. He went on to speak of the poetic 'fullness' of narrative poetry, illustrating the power for tragedy by a quotation from the Tenth Book of Paradise Lost, and mentioning Masefield's Jane in Reynard the Fox as an example of the portrayal of character. Quotations from Spenser showed to what advantage a great artist could use external surroundings as a background to develop a mood. After an interesting digression on the nature and value of 'simile', the President brought his paper to a close. It was as able a vindication of the narrative form as could well be constructed; and it was strengthened by a varied, though certainly not excessive, use of quotation.[1]

[1] Bodleian Library, MS. Top. Oxon. d. 95/3, fos. 108–9. I am indebted to Mr P. C. Bayley of the Martlet Society, University College, Oxford, for permission to quote from the Martlet Society minute-books.

After his examination in Greats, financial and domestic worries set Lewis hunting for a job. As he was unable to obtain a fellowship in any of the Oxford colleges to which he applied, his father offered to support him for another year. Lewis had already come to the conclusion that 'it is impossible to be a poet'[1] and so decided to read for the English School, hoping that by adding a second string to his bow he might be in a stronger position should a fellowship in philosophy fall vacant the next year. The English School was at first a disappointment. Up till now he had thought of English literature as something essentially private; it had now to be treated as a 'subject'. Besides this, the change from Greats to English seemed a step down and on returning from the first lecture in the English School he records (his diary for 16 October 1922) 'a certain amateurishness in the talk and look of the people'.[2]

His disappointment was not long-lasting. He was fortunate in having Professor F. P. Wilson for his tutor and on that same day he began an essay on Chaucer's debt to the *Filostrato*—the germ, no doubt, of the third essay in this book. The entry in his diary for the next day will, perhaps, come as a surprise to those of us who have long admired the beauty and clarity of Lewis's prose. 'From lunch till tea time', he wrote, 'I worked at an essay on Troilus. My prose style is really abominable, and between poetry and work [i.e. domestic chores] I suppose I shall never learn to improve it.'[3] His interest in the Martlets, which had flagged during his reading for Greats, was rekindled and he became a more regular and serious member.

Though Lewis continued to devote some time every day to his own poems, his interest in English literature flourished and broadened under the guidance of F. P. Wilson and his tutor in Anglo-Saxon, Miss Elizabeth Wardale. It is interesting to discover from his diary how many of the essays in this book had their origin in the weekly essays Lewis wrote for Professor Wilson. Besides the one on Chaucer, I find, for instance, him writing on 18 January 1923: 'I went on with Donne and read the Second Anniversary which is "a new planet": I

---

[1] *Lewis Papers: Memoirs of the Lewis Family 1850–1930*, vol. VII, p. 237. (The *Lewis Papers* consist of one set of eleven volumes of letters, diaries, and other family documents in typescript compiled by Major W. H. Lewis from original manuscripts. It is to Major Lewis, who owns the *Lewis Papers*, that I am indebted for permission to quote from them here.)

[2] *Ibid.*, p. 254. [3] *Ibid.*, p. 255.

never imagined or hoped for anything like it.'[1] And on 22 January:
'After tea ... I attacked my essay on the influence of Donne on the
17th century lyric.'[2] A few days earlier he had begun his paper on
Spenser for Professor George Gordon's discussion class.

It was at this class, held in an upstairs room in the Schools overlooking
High Street, that Lewis on 2 February 1923 first remembered seeing
Mr (now Professor) Nevill Coghill whose turn it was to read a paper
on 'Realism'. Lewis was immensely impressed by the man and his
paper, and was delighted when they met a few days later at a tea
given by Miss Wardale. 'Coghill', he wrote that evening, 'did most
of the talking, except when contradicted by me. He said that Mozart
had remained a boy of six all his life. I said nothing cd. be more
delightful: he replied (and quite right) that he could imagine many
things more delightful.'[3]

It had been decided at the outset that the minutes of Professor
Gordon's class were to be kept in Chaucerian verse, an inducement
in itself to Lewis and Coghill. Though Professor Coghill has told us
of the paper on Spenser which Lewis read to the class on 9 February
1923,[4] he omitted to say that it was he who wrote the minutes of this
meeting. As the minute-book of the discussion class was given to me
by Lewis,[5] I am able to offer the following extracts of the minutes
which Professor Coghill wrote at the time. Lewis's own manuscript
has not survived, but Professor Coghill, writing close on the heels of
the event, tells us in his notes as much as we shall probably ever know
of Lewis's paper:

> In Oxenford some clerkés of degree
> Were gadréd in a goodlye companye
> And I was oon, and here will yow devise
> Our felaweshipe that worthy was and wys ...
> Sir Lewis was ther; a good philosopher
> He hadde a noble paper for to offer.
> Wel couthe he speken in the Greeké tongue;
> And yet, his countenance was swythe yong ...
> Then to Sir Lewis turned the Professour
> (That was our tales juge and governour)

[1] Lewis Papers: Memoirs of the Lewis Family 1850–1930, vol. VIII, p. 17.
[2] Ibid., p. 25.   [3] Letters of C. S. Lewis, ed. W. H. Lewis (London, 1966), p. 85.
[4] 'The Approach to English', Light on C. S. Lewis, ed. Jocelyn Gibb (London, 1965),
pp. 51–2.
[5] Lewis's own description of Professor Gordon's discussion class is found in The Life
of George S. Gordon by M[ary] C. G[ordon] (Oxford, 1945), p. 77.

And cried unto hym "Now by Pigges bones,
"Thou shallt a noble tale for the nones,
"Somewhat to quite Daun Darlow and the Cogge.
"Rede us of Spenser, by Seint Jamés dogge.
"Lordynges, attend, and hear our philosópher
"That hath both wit and beauty in his coffer!"

Anon turned Lewis to a bluë boke
He swalwed thrice; hys dewy fingers shooke
And he bigan with right a myrie cheere
His tale anoon; and spake in this mannere.

Heere bigynneth Sir Lewis'
TALE
of
DAUN SPENSER.

"Desert the lesser groves of Poesy;
No more of Cuddie or the nuptial scene
All Spenser's magic and his melody
Find sweet perfection in the Faery Queene.
There, Elegy and Pastoral, I weene
And moral virtue chorus their full song;
The mind of Spenser grew not; it had been,
And still was, gentle; only a new throng
Of words more beautifully bear his verse along.

"And fifty years taught nothing more than this;
To bend his vowels to a gracious line;
Grandeur and thunder, magic and the bliss
Of Heavenly Music, and the inner shine
Of γάνος, or the gleaming of divine
Moist, quiet woodland things; all these he found
Distilled old myths and thoughts into new wine,
But not new thoughts; and though the Queene is crowned
With many beauties, oft she is most falsely gowned.

"But leave her faults admitted, leave his passion
Untrue, mere copy: Love, he did not know
But amorous reverie in a sensuous fashion
He well could sing, and make his verses grow
One to another, like a forest row
Of deepening trees; no drama, but a mood
Of queer archaic dream, and spacious flow
Of changing rhythms, till then not understood.
He was a pioneer, that did not cut, but plant a wood.

"And his sweet satisfying poesy
Offers no problem to the gnawing mind,
But pours the balm of pure simplicity
In allegories old as is mankind;

Vague and indefinite, they lie behind
The purpose of the poem; for all speech
Of men is allegory, ill-defined
Spenserian and dim: and who can teach
How fact and symbol are related each to each?

"So leave him, more than lovely, less than great;
He was a poet; he was nothing more:
Nay—but a poet's poet; and there sate
Milton and Keats within his forest door.
Young dreamy boys delight in Spenser's lore
And eat his satisfying faery food
And Wordsworth on his native mountain shore
Caught echoes from that dim enchanted wood;
Then enter ye who dare, ye who have understood."

There is not space enough here to reproduce Professor Coghill's verse-notes on the discussion which followed the reading of Lewis's paper. Lewis was, I expect, as delighted with the disagreement as with the agreement, and it may have been his habitual desire for 'rational opposition' which led him to read the same paper to the Martlets the following week. The discussion that followed the second reading may well have been one of the liveliest the Martlets had ever known. The Secretary tried to capture it in the minutes,[1] and Lewis recorded as much of it as he could remember in his diary. Most of the Martlets took the view that a work of art ought to be judged simply as an expression of the artist's experience whether it communicated anything to anyone else or not. Lewis, on the other hand, contended that 'taking art as an expression, it must be the expression of something: and one can't abstract the "something" from the expression'.[2] This may not seem of much importance as I have reduced it here, but my reason for mentioning it at all is because the discussion was probably a literary milestone for Lewis: he understood how differently others read and judge literature, and he was forced to defend what he loved and believed to be true. He argued his case more clearly years later in *An Experiment in Criticism*,[3] but he was already at work marshalling his ideas and trying them out in the cut-and-thrust debates with his fellow students.

Though Lewis attended the Martlets regularly, the next time he addressed the Society was on 18 June 1924. The Secretary records that:

[1] Bodleian Library, MS. Top. Oxon. d. 95/4, fos. 163–5.
[2] *Lewis Papers*, vol. VIII, p. 71.
[3] *An Experiment in Criticism* (Cambridge, 1961). See in particular chapter IV, p. 28.

The minutes of the last meeting were read and carried; the President then called upon Mr. Lewis to read his paper on James Stephens. Mr. Lewis began by congratulating himself on *his entire ignorance of biographical detail* and proceeded forthwith to a critical appreciation of his author's works . . .[1]

I italicise 'his entire ignorance of biographical detail' because the words illustrate how early in his life Lewis came to believe that a book ought to be judged on its own merits rather than as a means whereby one steeps oneself in the personality of the author. This may well have been the seed out of which eventually grew his famous essay on 'The Personal Heresy in Criticism'.[2]

We are so accustomed to thinking of Lewis as an English critic that we usually forget—if we ever knew, for it is not common knowledge—that at this time he considered himself a candidate for a fellowship in philosophy. Thus, it was quite natural that he be asked to deputise for E. F. Carritt (the philosophy tutor at University College) during 1924 when Carritt was teaching in the United States. At this time Lewis attended the meetings of the Oxford Philosophical Society and, despite his love for English literature, disapproved of English as a final honour school. Before the year was out he had applied for several fellowships, but the only one offered him was a fellowship in English language and literature at Magdalen College. This was not the work Lewis had been expecting to undertake and his reasons for accepting it are, I expect, quite honestly expressed in a letter to his father in which he says:

. . . I am rather glad of the change. I have come to think that if I had the mind, I have not the brain and nerves for a life of pure philosophy. A continued search among the abstract roots of things, a perpetual questioning of all that plain men take for granted, a chewing the cud for fifty years over inevitable ignorance and a constant frontier watch on the little tidy lighted conventional world of science and daily life—is this the best life for temperaments such as ours? . . . I am not condemning philosophy. Indeed in turning from it to literary history and criticism, I am conscious of a descent: and if the air on the heights did not suit me, still I have brought back something of value . . . At any rate I escape with joy from one definite drawback of philosophy—its solitude. I was beginning to feel that your first year carries you out of the reach of all save other professionals. No one sympathizes with your adventures in that subject because no one understands them: and if you struck treasure trove no one would be able to use it.[3]

[1] Bodleian Library, MS. Top. Oxon. d. 95/4, fo. 17.
[2] Later reprinted as the opening chapter of Lewis's and E. M. W. Tillyard's *The Personal Heresy: A Controversy* (London, 1939).
[3] *Lewis Papers*, vol. VIII, p. 299.

It is interesting to imagine how different Lewis's career might have been had he been offered, and accepted, a fellowship in philosophy. Would he, I wonder, have eventually found his way into the English School? If not, what sort of books (if any) would he have written? Though I never spoke with Lewis about this, he would, I expect, have reminded us that the 'road' not taken has no reality and, therefore, offers no answers.[1] What is abundantly clear in Lewis's writings, both critical and imaginative, is the influence of his foundation in philosophy and Greek and Latin literature. Speaking of Lewis's move from Greats to English, Professor Coghill says, 'Lewis ... was finding all that he knew of Greek and Latin poetry reflected in his English studies, and he was learning to illuminate the latter by the former with sudden comparisons and contrasts that sparkled and exploded in his conversation.'[2]

Not only was Lewis striking treasure-trove almost daily in his English studies, but he found that a large part of English literature, particularly the Anglo-Saxon, would give up its treasures only after one had dug deep and hard enough. But Lewis was never loath to do his 'prep'; indeed, he found satisfaction in tackling those problems in scholarship which often deter less determined men. I inherited from Lewis's library most of the texts he used while reading Greats and English. Every page has a running headline in the upper margin and he usually compiled an index at the back of each book. A lover of clarity, Lewis was impatient with authors whose books he considered needlessly obscure. One such text was H. C. K. Wyld's *A Short History of English* (London, 1921) which he used in the study of Old English. In his diary of 15 February 1923 he complained: 'I attempted to get some useful information out of Wyld's Short History (The Cad) which is full of facts most painfully collected but presented in a very muddled way and extraordinarily difficult to work on.'[3] A few years later, when he was teaching Old English to his pupils at Magdalen, he decided to 'find out what Wyld says in spite of all Wyld does to prevent me'.[4] For several weeks he worked with great enjoy-

---

[1] Nevertheless, I venture to guess that, if Lewis had become a philosopher, and if he had still been converted, the one most purely philosophical book of his we would still have had is *The Abolition of Man*. For several years prior to his appointment at Magdalen, he had been at work on a paper entitled 'Hegemony of Moral Values'. It was sent to *Mind* but never published, and, as far as I can discover, is no longer extant.

[2] Coghill, *op. cit.*, pp. 53–4.

[3] *Lewis Papers*, vol. VIII, p. 71.　　　　　　　[4] *Ibid.*, vol. IX, p. 142.

ment on turning the section on 'West Germanic to Primitive O.E.'
into a mnemonic poem. It began (and I omit Lewis's footnotes to the
poem):

I. From *W. GMNC* to *Primitive O.E.*
                Vowel Changes.

AU, AI, Ă, Ā, EU, IU.   When Hors and Hengist turned the prow
                From home, they brought germanic AU
                And AI from Baltic woods afar
                And short Ă and the longer Ā
                And EU and its companion IU;
                Through all whose fates I mean to see you.
A > Ǽ   The short Ă soon began to wag,
                WĂGAN turned WÆGN, DĂGS turned DǼG;
                Or, by a following nasal bitten,
                More often as an "O" was written;
                Ā nasalised (in some cold lough),
                Followed by X, became an ŌH;
                Said Hengist "BRĀXTA, DĀHTA ought-ter
                Be rather sounded BROHTE, Þ OHTE."
                To whom thus Hors replied with scorn . . .[1]

In the summer of 1925 Lewis's interest in becoming a poet was
given fresh encouragement. It had been seven years since he published
his first volume of verse, and he was now correcting the proofs of
Dymer, a long narrative poem in rhyme royal. At the same time, he
was annoyed at what he called 'the hectic theory of poetry as existing
in momentary lyrical impressions'.[2] Anxious to strike a blow at the
new *avant-garde* poets, he broached to his friends the idea of a literary
hoax: 'A series of mock Eliotic poems to be sent up to the Dial and
Criterion until sooner or later one of these filthy editors falls into the
trap.'[3] Of their first meeting a few days later he wrote (in his diary):

We all read our Eliotic poems and discussed plans of campaign. C—— thought
that if we succeeded it would always be open to Eliot to say that we had meant
the poems seriously and afterwards pretended they were parodies; his answer to
this was to make them acrostics and the ones he had composed read downwards
"Sham poetry pays the world in its own coin, paper money". Then came the
brilliant idea that we should be a brother and sister, Rollo and Bridget Considine.
Bridget is the elder and they are united by an affection so tender as to be almost
incestuous. Bridget will presently write a letter to Eliot (if we get a foothold)
telling him about her own and her brother's life. She is incredibly dowdy and

[1] From one of Lewis's notebooks in my possession.
[2] *Lewis Papers*, vol. IX, p. 105.
[3] *Ibid.*, pp. 107–8.

about thirty five. We rolled in laughter as we pictured a tea party where the Considines should meet Eliot: Y—— would dress up for Bridget and perhaps bring a baby. We selected as our first shot my "Nidhogg" (by Rollo) and H——'s "Conversation" and Y——'s "Sunday" (by Bridget). They are to be sent from Vienna where H—— has a friend. We think Vienna will decrease suspicion and is also a likely place for the Considines to live in. Our meeting broke up about 12. H—— and C—— are in it for pure fun, I from burning indignation.[1]

Whether because Lewis's indignation burnt itself out, or because the editors refused to publish their poems, I have never discovered in the *Dial* and the *Criterion* any poems by the Considines. It would, I feel, be unfair to Lewis to leave matters here. When he and Eliot met at Lambeth Palace where they worked together on the revision of the Psalter they became good friends. Speaking of this to me afterwards, Lewis said, 'You know that I never cared for Eliot's poetry and criticism, but when we met I loved him at once.'

Dymer was well received, but its reviewer in the *Sunday Times* expressed, I believe, the feelings of many readers when he said of the poem: 'It seems to us that Mr. Hamilton has mistaken his opportunity ... as a prose tale how splendidly it would have flowed!'[2] Perhaps Lewis agreed for he never attempted to publish any of his longer poems after this.[3] Not only was he certain that he would never be a great poet but he believed, as he wrote to his brother, that

there is no longer any chance of discovering a long poem in English which will turn out to be just what I want and which can be added to the *Faerie Queene*, the *Prelude*, *Paradise Lost*, *The Ring and the Book*, the *Earthly Paradise* and a few others—because there aren't any more.[4]

This sounds as though Lewis had come to the end of his own productivity. On the contrary, he seems at last to have begun. On 10 July 1928 he wrote to his father saying:

I have actually begun the first chapter of my book ... Of course like a child who wants to get to the painting before he has really finished drawing the outline, I have been itching to do some actual *writing* for a long time ... The actual book is about mediaeval love poetry and the mediaeval idea of love.[5]

The book is, of course, *The Allegory of Love*. A great milestone was to be reached and another book to be written before the publication

---

[1] *Lewis Papers*, vol. ix, p. 110.
[2] *Sunday Times* (19 September 1926), p. 9.
[3] Almost all the shorter ones are found in his *Poems*, ed. Walter Hooper (London, 1964).
[4] *Letters of C. S. Lewis*, p. 129.   [5] *Ibid.*, p. 127.

of *The Allegory of Love* in 1936. I mean Lewis's conversion in 1931 and the publication of his theological and semi-autobiographical *Pilgrim's Regress* in 1933. Lewis had long shared much in common with his favourite poets: he now shared with them that most binding of all beliefs. With his conversion, that little hard core of worldly ambition, evident on almost every page of his diary, seems to have dropped into oblivion. And with the dying of his old ambition he became more interested in *what* he wrote about than what *he* might become by writing. He continued to write short poems for the rest of his life but, beginning with 'What Chaucer really did to *Il Filostrato*' (1932), and later in his imaginative works, his poetic insight and his critical reason seem to have flowed together and expressed themselves in one activity. Despite his disagreements about some things, Lewis could at long last say, as he does in the fourteenth essay in this book, 'as Mr Eliot and I believe' (p. 208).

English scholars disagree on the proper method of editing the works of a modern author. In brief, some insist on printing exactly what the author wrote regardless of whether it contains errors or not. Others maintain that an editor's job is to print what he thinks the author *intended*. My method has been that of the latter.

Lewis had the most astonishing memory of any man I have ever met. I have heard him quote a hundred or so lines from, say, *Beowulf* or *Paradise Lost* without (so far as I could tell) making an error. Because he remembered almost everything he read, he usually quoted straight from memory without bothering to check the texts themselves. Because it is so easy for errors to creep into essays of this sort, whether they are the fault of the author or the publisher or both (as is usually the case), I have compared all the quoted material in these essays with the texts which (in most cases) I think Lewis used. All told, I have made about 500 corrections. As the majority of them, however, do not affect the sense of the essays, I have made my emendations silently. Though Lewis was quick to spot errors in logic and meaning, he was not in the least pedantic and was usually so interested in *what* he was writing about that he was often indifferent to the minutiae precious to strict pedants. He had, on the other hand, a high regard for accuracy and, had I pointed out to him the errors in his quotations, I feel certain he would have corrected them himself.

It will probably be noticed that I have added a good many footnotes of my own. Lewis usually assumed that his readers had read and remembered as much as he, but my own ignorance convinces me that such is not always the case. And as it sometimes took me several hours to locate the source of some of the lines he quoted—as for instance the poem 'On God Ureisun of Ure Lefdi' on page 56—I thought others would be as glad to have them in footnotes as I was to find them. Some method, however, was needed to distinguish my footnotes from Lewis's. As mine are far more numerous than his, I have used the symbols * † ‡, etc., to refer to Lewis's notes and superior arabic figures to refer to mine.

Before listing the essays in this book I wish to thank all the publishers of books and periodicals in which these essays first appeared. I am particularly grateful to the Oxford University Press for permission to reprint most of the essays which originally appeared under the title *Rehabilitations and Other Essays* (London, 1939). I am indebted to Geoffrey Bles Ltd. for permission to reprint the essays numbered 1, 7, 9, 15, 17 and 21 from *They Asked for a Paper* (London, 1962). As all the essays in this book were reprinted (some with slight alterations by Lewis) from various journals, I have chosen to list their original sources in the paragraphs which follow.

'*De Descriptione Temporum*', Lewis's inaugural lecture as the Professor of Medieval and Renaissance English Literature in the University of Cambridge, was first published by the University of Cambridge Press in 1955. 'The Alliterative Metre' appeared first in *Lysistrata*, vol. II (May 1935) and afterwards in *Rehabilitations*. 'What Chaucer really did to *Il Filostrato*' was first published in *Essays and Studies*, vol. XIX (1932) and 'The Fifteenth-Century Heroic Line' in *Essays and Studies*, vol. XXIV (1939). 'Hero and Leander', the Warton Lecture on English Poetry, was read to the British Academy in 1952 and was published in the *Proceedings of the British Academy*, vol. XXXVIII in that same year.

'Variation in Shakespeare and Others' was first read to the Mermaid Club and afterwards printed in *Rehabilitations*. 'Hamlet: The Prince or the Poem?', the Annual Shakespeare Lecture of the British Academy, 1942, was first published in the *Proceedings of the British Academy*, vol. XXVIII (1942). 'Donne and Love Poetry in the Seventeenth Century' originally appeared in *Seventeenth Century Studies Presented to Sir Herbert Grierson* (Oxford, 1938). 'The Literary Impact of the Authorised Version', the Ethel M. Wood Lecture, was delivered before the University of London on 20 March 1950 and was published by the Athlone Press in 1950. 'The Vision of John Bunyan' was first read over the B.B.C. and afterwards published in *The Listener*, vol. LXVIII (13 December 1962).

'Addison' was originally published in *Essays on the Eighteenth Century Presented to David Nichol Smith* (Oxford, 1945). 'Four-Letter Words' was first published in *The Critical Quarterly*, vol. III (Summer 1961) and 'A Note on Jane Austen' in *Essays in Criticism*, vol. IV (October 1954). 'Shelley, Dryden, and Mr Eliot' was read at Bedford College, London, and published afterwards in *Rehabilitations*. 'Sir Walter Scott' was read to the Edinburgh Sir Walter Scott Club at their Annual Meeting on 2 March 1956 and later published in *The Edinburgh Sir Walter Scott Club Forty-ninth Annual Report, 1956*. 'William Morris' was read to the Martlet Society on 5 November 1937 and later published in *Rehabilitations*.

'Kipling's World' was read to the English Association and then published in *Literature and Life: Addresses to the English Association*, vol. I (London, 1948). 'Bluspels and Flalansferes: A Semantic Nightmare' was read at Manchester University and afterwards published in *Rehabilitations*. 'High and Low Brows' was read to the English Society at Oxford and later published in *Rehabilitations*. 'Metre' originally appeared in *A Review of English Literature*, vol. I (January 1960). 'Psycho-Analysis and Literary Criticism' was read to a literary society at Westfield College and was afterwards published in *Essays and Studies*, vol. XXVII (1942). 'The Anthropological Approach' was originally published in *English and Medieval Studies Presented to J. R. R. Tolkien on the Occasion of his Seventieth Birthday*, ed. Norman Davis and C. L. Wrenn (London, George Allen and Unwin Ltd., 1962).

Now, having said which essays are contained in this book, it remains for me to name those which, for various reasons, I have not been able to include. They are—besides the *Studies in Medieval and Renaissance Literature*, ed. Walter Hooper (Cambridge, 1966)—Lewis's essay on 'The English Prose *Morte*', in *Essays on Malory*, ed. J. A. W. Bennett (Oxford, 1963); and the three remaining essays which make up *Rehabilitations*—'The Idea of an "English School"', 'Our English Syllabus' and 'Christianity and Literature'—the last of which can be found reprinted in Lewis's *Christian Reflections*, ed. Walter Hooper (London, 1967). These essays together with those contained in this volume comprise the total of C. S. Lewis's essays on literature.

PREFACE

My thanks to the friends who have helped me with this book are many and great. Professor J. R. R. Tolkien has given me much wise advice and permitted me to print part of a letter he wrote to me on page 18. So certain was I of receiving help from Professor I. Ll. Foster of Jesus College that I am as familiar with his college staircase as I am with my own. Professor John Lawlor, Dr and Mrs Austin Farrer, Mr Roger Lancelyn Green, Mr Owen Barfield, Mr Colin Hardie and Dr J. M. S. Tompkins have answered so many questions for me that I have almost come to regard them as my private information-bureau. Dr Warfield M. Firor of Baltimore, Maryland, sent Lewis food-packages during the war and came to my rescue with financial support to help me put this book together. Professor Nevill Coghill has kindly permitted me to make use of his verse-notes of Lewis's paper on Spenser. Lastly, Major W. H. Lewis, Miss Priscilla Tolkien, my parents —Mr and Mrs A. B. Hooper—and Dr and Mrs Fred R. Klenner have helped me in ways too numerous to recall but no less appreciated.

WALTER HOOPER

Jesus College, Oxford
September 1968

Note

Superior figures in the essays refer to editorial footnotes; the asterisk–dagger system is used to refer to C. S. Lewis's footnotes.

I

'De Descriptione Temporum'

Speaking from a newly founded Chair, I find myself freed from one embarrassment only to fall into another. I have no great predecessors to overshadow me; on the other hand, I must try (as the theatrical people say) 'to create the part'. The responsibility is heavy. If I miscarry, the University might come to regret not only my election—an error which, at worst, can be left to the great healer—but even, which matters very much more, the foundation of the Chair itself. That is why I have thought it best to take the bull by the horns and devote this lecture to explaining as clearly as I can the way in which I approach my work; my interpretation of the commission you have given me.

What most attracted me in that commission was the combination 'Medieval and Renaissance'. I thought that by this formula the University was giving official sanction to a change which has been coming over historical opinion within my own lifetime. It is temperately summed up by Professor Seznec in the words: 'As the Middle Ages and the Renaissance come to be better known, the traditional antithesis between them grows less marked.'* Some scholars might go further than Professor Seznec, but very few, I believe, would now oppose him. If we are sometimes unconscious of the change, that is not because we have not shared it but because it has been gradual and imperceptible. We recognise it most clearly if we are suddenly brought face to face with the old view in its full vigour. A good experiment is to re-read the first chapter of J. M. Berdan's *Early Tudor Poetry*.† It is still in many ways a useful book; but it is now difficult to read that chapter without a smile. We begin with twenty-nine pages (and they contain several mis-statements) of unrelieved gloom about grossness, superstition, and cruelty to children, and on the twenty-ninth comes the sentence, 'The first rift in this darkness is the Copernican doctrine'; as if a new hypothesis in astronomy would naturally make a man stop hitting his daughter about

---

* J. Seznec, *La Survivance des dieux antiques* (London, 1940), trans. B. F. Sessions (Kingsport, Tennessee, 1953), p. 3.
† New York, 1920.

the head. No scholar could now write quite like that. But the old picture, done in far cruder colours, has survived among the weaker brethren, if not (let us hope) at Cambridge, yet certainly in that Western darkness from which you have so lately bidden me emerge. Only last summer a young gentleman whom I had the honour of examining described Thomas Wyatt as 'the first man who scrambled ashore out of the great, dark surging sea of the Middle Ages'.* This was interesting because it showed how a stereotyped image can obliterate a man's own experience. Nearly all the medieval texts which the syllabus had required him to study had in reality led him into formal gardens where every passion was subdued to a ceremonial and every problem of conduct was dovetailed into a complex and rigid moral theology.

From the formula 'Medieval and Renaissance', then, I inferred that the University was encouraging my own belief that the barrier between those two ages has been greatly exaggerated, if indeed it was not largely a figment of Humanist propaganda. At the very least, I was ready to welcome any increased flexibility in our conception of history. All lines of demarcation between what we call 'periods' should be subject to constant revision. Would that we could dispense with them altogether! As a great Cambridge historian has said: 'Unlike dates, periods are not facts. They are retrospective conceptions that we form about past events, useful to focus discussion, but very often leading historical thought astray.'† The actual temporal process, as we meet it in our lives (and we meet it, in a strict sense, nowhere else) has no divisions, except perhaps those 'blessed barriers between day and day', our sleeps. Change is never complete, and change never ceases. Nothing is ever quite finished with; it may always begin over again. (This is one of the sides of life that Richardson hits off with wearying accuracy.) And nothing is quite new; it was always somehow anticipated or prepared for. A seamless, formless continuity-in-mutability is the mode of our life. But unhappily we cannot as historians dispense with periods. We cannot use for literary history the technique of Mrs Woolf's *The Waves*. We cannot hold together huge masses of particulars without putting into them some kind of

* A delicious passage in Comparetti, *Vergil in the Middle Ages*, trans. E. F. M. Benecke (London, 1895), p. 241, contrasts the Middle Ages with 'more normal periods of history'.
† G. M. Trevelyan, *English Social History* (London, 1944), p. 92.

structure. Still less can we arrange a term's work or draw up a lecture list. Thus we are driven back upon periods. All divisions will falsify our material to some extent; the best one can hope is to choose those which will falsify it least. But because we must divide, to reduce the emphasis on any one traditional division must, in the long run, mean an increase of emphasis on some other division. And that is the subject I want to discuss. If we do not put the Great Divide between the Middle Ages and the Renaissance, where should we put it? I ask this question with the full consciousness that, in the reality studied, there is no Great Divide. There is nothing in history that quite corresponds to a coastline or a watershed in geography. If, in spite of this, I still think my question worth asking, that is certainly not because I claim for my answer more than a methodological value, or even much of that. Least of all would I wish it to be any less subject than others to continual attack and speedy revision. But I believe that the discussion is as good a way as any other of explaining how I look at the work you have given me. When I have finished it, I shall at least have laid the cards on the table and you will know the worst.

The meaning of my title will now have become plain. It is a chapter-heading borrowed from Isidore.* In that chapter Isidore is engaged in dividing history, as he knew it, into its periods; or, as he calls them, *aetates*. I shall be doing the same. Assuming that we do not put our great frontier between the Middle Ages and the Renaissance, I shall consider the rival claims of certain other divisions which have been, or might be, made. But, first, a word of warning. I am not, even on the most Lilliputian scale, emulating Professor Toynbee or Spengler. About everything that could be called 'the philosophy of history' I am a desperate sceptic. I know nothing of the future, not even whether there will be any future. I don't know whether past history has been necessary or contingent. I don't know whether the human tragi-comedy is now in Act I or Act V; whether our present disorders are those of infancy or of old age. I am merely considering how we should arrange or schematise those facts—ludicrously few in com-parison with the totality—which survive to us (often by accident) from the past.[1] I am less like a botanist in a forest than a woman

* *Etymologiarum*, ed. W. M. Lindsay (2 vols. Oxford, 1911), v, xxxix.

[1] In his essay on 'Historicism' Lewis discusses at length the belief that 'men can, by the use of their natural powers, discover an inner meaning in the historical process'. The essay is found in his *Christian Reflections*, ed. Walter Hooper (London, 1967), pp. 100–13.

arranging a few cut flowers for the drawing-room. So, in some degree, are the greatest historians. We can't get into the real forest of the past; that is part of what the word *past* means.

The first division that naturally occurs to us is that between Antiquity and the Dark Ages—the fall of the Empire, the barbarian invasions, the christening of Europe. And of course no possible revolution in historical thought will ever make this anything less than a massive and multiple change. Do not imagine that I mean to belittle it. Yet I must observe that three things have happened since, say, Gibbon's time, which make it a shade less catastrophic for us than it was for him.

1. The partial loss of ancient learning and its recovery at the Renaissance were for him both unique events. History furnished no rivals to such a death and such a re-birth. But we have lived to see the second death of ancient learning. In our time something which was once the possession of all educated men has shrunk to being the technical accomplishment of a few specialists. If we say that this is not total death, it may be replied that there was no total death in the Dark Ages either. It could even be argued that Latin, surviving as the language of Dark Age culture, and preserving the disciplines of Law and Rhetoric, gave to some parts of the classical heritage a far more living and integral status in the life of those ages than the academic studies of the specialists can claim in our own. As for the area and the *tempo* of the two deaths, if one were looking for a man who could not read Virgil though his father could, he might be found more easily in the twentieth century than in the fifth.

2. To Gibbon the literary change from Virgil to *Beowulf* or the *Hildebrand*, if he had read them, would have seemed greater than it can to us. We can now see quite clearly that these barbarian poems were not really a novelty comparable to, say, *The Waste Land* or Mr Jones's *Anathemata*. They were rather an unconscious return to the spirit of the earliest classical poetry. The audience of Homer, and the audience of the *Hildebrand*, once they had learned one another's language and metre, would have found one another's poetry perfectly intelligible. Nothing new had come into the world.

3. The christening of Europe seemed to all our ancestors, whether they welcomed it themselves as Christians, or, like Gibbon, deplored it as humanistic unbelievers, a unique, irreversible event. But we have seen the opposite process. Of course the un-christening of Europe in

4

our time is not quite complete; neither was her christening in the Dark Ages. But roughly speaking we may say that whereas all history was for our ancestors divided into two periods, the pre-Christian and the Christian, and two only, for us it falls into three—the pre-Christian, the Christian, and what may reasonably be called the post-Christian. This surely must make a momentous difference. I am not here considering either the christening or the un-christening from a theological point of view. I am considering them simply as cultural changes.* When I do that, it appears to me that the second change is even more radical than the first. Christians and Pagans had much more in common with each other than either has with a post-Christian. The gap between those who worship different gods is not so wide as that between those who worship and those who do not. The Pagan and Christian ages alike are ages of what Pausanias would call the δρώμενον,† the externalised and enacted idea; the sacrifice, the games, the triumph, the ritual drama, the Mass, the tournament, the masque, the pageant, the epithalamium, and with them ritual and symbolic costumes, *trabea* and laticlave, crown of wild olive, royal crown, coronet, judge's robes, knight's spurs, herald's tabard, coat-armour, priestly vestment, religious habit—for every rank, trade, or occasion its visible sign. But even if we look away from that into the temper of men's minds, I seem to see the same. Surely the gap between Professor Ryle and Thomas Browne is far wider than that between Gregory the Great and Virgil? Surely Seneca and Dr Johnson are closer together than Burton and Freud?

You see already the lines along which my thought is working; and indeed it is no part of my aim to save a surprise for the end of the lecture. If I have ventured, a little, to modify our view of the transition from 'the Antique' to 'the Dark', it is only because I believe we have since witnessed a change even more profound.

The next frontier which has been drawn, though not till recently, is that between the Dark and the Middle Ages. We draw it somewhere about the early twelfth century. The frontier clearly cannot compete with its predecessor in the religious field; nor can it boast such drastic redistribution of populations. But it nearly makes up for these

---

* It is not certain that either process, seen (if we could see it) *sub specie aeternitatis*, would be more important than it appears to the historian of culture. The amount of Christian (that is, of penitent and regenerate) life in an age, as distinct from 'Christian Civilization', is not to be judged by mortals.

† *De Descriptione Graec.* II, xxxvii.

deficiencies in other ways. The change from Ancient to Dark had, after all, consisted mainly in losses. Not entirely. The Dark Ages were not so unfruitful in progress as we sometimes think. They saw the triumph of the *codex* or hinged book over the roll or *volumen*—a technical improvement almost as important for the history of learning as the invention of printing. All exact scholarship depends on it. And if—here I speak under correction—they also invented the stirrup, they did something almost as important for the art of war as the inventor of Tanks. But in the main, they were a period of retrogression: worse houses, worse drains, fewer baths, worse roads, less security. (We notice in *Beowulf* that an old sword is expected to be better than a new one.) With the Middle Ages we reach a period of widespread and brilliant improvement. The text of Aristotle is recovered. Its rapid assimilation by Albertus Magnus and Thomas Aquinas opens up a new world of thought. In architecture new solutions of technical problems lead the way to new aesthetic effects. In literature the old alliterative and assonantal metres give place to that rhymed and syllabic verse which was to carry the main burden of European poetry for centuries. At the same time the poets explore a whole new range of sentiment. I am so far from underrating this particular revolution that I have before now been accused of exaggerating it. But 'great' and 'small' are terms of comparison. I would think this change in literature the greatest if I did not know of a greater. It does not seem to me that the work of the Troubadours and Chrétien and the rest was really as great a novelty as the poetry of the twentieth century. A man bred on the *Chanson de Roland* might have been puzzled by the *Lancelot*. He would have wondered why the author spent so much time on the sentiments and so (comparatively) little on the actions. But he would have known that this was what the author had done. He would, in one important sense, have known what the poem was 'about'. If he had misunderstood the intention, he would at least have understood the words. That is why I do not think the change from 'Dark' to 'Middle' can, on the literary side, be judged equal to the change which has taken place in my own lifetime. And of course in religion it does not even begin to compete.

A third possible frontier remains to be considered. We might draw our line somewhere towards the end of the seventeenth century, with the general acceptance of Copernicanism, the dominance of Descartes, and (in England) the foundation of the Royal Society. Indeed, if we were considering the history of thought (in the narrower sense of the word) I believe this is where I would draw my line. But if we are considering the history of our culture in general, it is a different matter. Certainly the sciences then began to advance with a firmer and more rapid tread. To that advance nearly all the later, and (in my mind) vaster, changes can be traced. But the effects were delayed. The sciences long remained like a lion-cub whose gambols delighted its master in private; it had not yet tasted man's blood. All through the eighteenth century the tone of the common mind remained ethical, rhetorical, juristic, rather than scientific, so that Johnson could truly say, 'the knowledge of external nature, and the sciences which that knowledge requires or includes, are not the great or the frequent business of the human mind.'[1] It is easy to see why. Science was not the business of Man because Man had not yet become the business of science. It dealt chiefly with the inanimate; and it threw off few technological by-products. When Watt makes his engine, when Darwin starts monkeying with the ancestry of Man, and Freud with his soul, and the economists with all that is his, then indeed the lion will have got out of its cage. Its liberated presence in our midst will become one of the most important factors in everyone's daily life. But not yet; not in the seventeenth century.

It is by these steps that I have come to regard as the greatest of all divisions in the history of the West that which divides the present from, say, the age of Jane Austen and Scott. The dating of such things must of course be rather hazy and indefinite. No one could point to a year or a decade in which the change indisputably began, and it has probably not yet reached its peak. But somewhere between us and the Waverley Novels, somewhere between us and *Persuasion*, the chasm runs. Of course, I had no sooner reached this result than I asked myself whether it might not be an illusion of perspective. The distance between the telegraph post I am touching and the next telegraph post looks longer than the sum of the distances between all the other posts. Could this be an illusion of the same sort? We cannot pace the periods as we could pace the posts. I can only set out the grounds on which, after frequent reconsideration, I have found myself forced to reaffirm my conclusion.

[1] 'Life of Milton', in *Lives of the English Poets*, vol. I, ed. George Birkbeck Hill (Oxford, 1905), p. 99.

1. I begin with what I regard as the weakest; the change, between Scott's age and ours, in political order. On this count my proposed frontier would have serious rivals. The change is perhaps less than that between Antiquity and the Dark Ages. Yet it is very great; and I think it extends to all nations, those we call democracies as well as dictatorships. If I wished to satirise the present political order I should borrow for it the name which *Punch* invented during the first German War: *Govertisement*. This is a portmanteau word and means 'government by advertisement'. But my intention is not satiric; I am trying to be objective. The change is this. In all previous ages that I can think of the principal aim of rulers, except at rare and short intervals, was to keep their subjects quiet, to forestall or extinguish widespread excitement and persuade people to attend quietly to their several occupations. And on the whole their subjects agreed with them. They even prayed (in words that sound curiously old-fashioned) to be able to live 'a peaceable life in all godliness and honesty' and 'pass their time in rest and quietness'. But now the organisation of mass excitement seems to be almost the normal organ of political power. We live in an age of 'appeals', 'drives', and 'campaigns'. Our rulers have become like schoolmasters and are always demanding 'keenness'. And you notice that I am guilty of a slight archaism in calling them 'rulers'. 'Leaders' is the modern word. I have suggested elsewhere[1] that this is a deeply significant change of vocabulary. Our demand upon them has changed no less than theirs on us. For of a ruler one asks justice, incorruption, diligence, perhaps clemency; of a leader, dash, initiative, and (I suppose) what people call 'magnetism' or 'personality'.

On the political side, then, this proposed frontier has respectable, but hardly compulsive, qualifications.

2. In the arts I think it towers above every possible rival. I do not think that any previous age produced work which was, in its own time, as shatteringly and bewilderingly new as that of the Cubists, the Dadaists, the Surrealists, and Picasso has been in ours. And I am quite sure that this is true of the art I love best, that is, of poetry. This question has often been debated with some heat, but the heat was, I think, occasioned by the suspicion (not always ill-grounded) that those who asserted the unprecedented novelty of modern poetry

[1] 'New Learning and New Ignorance', *English Literature in the Sixteenth Century, excluding Drama*, The Oxford History of English Literature, vol. III (Oxford, 1954), p. 50.

intended thereby to discredit it. But nothing is farther from my purpose than to make any judgement of value, whether favourable or the reverse. And if once we can eliminate that critical issue and concentrate on the historical fact, then I do not see how anyone can doubt that modern poetry is not only a greater novelty than any other 'new poetry' but new in a new way, almost in a new dimension. To say that all new poetry was once as difficult as ours is false; to say that any was is an equivocation. Some earlier poetry was difficult, but not in the same way. Alexandrian poetry was difficult because it presupposed a learned reader; as you became learned you found the answers to the puzzles. Skaldic poetry was unintelligible if you did not know the *kenningar*, but intelligible if you did. And—this is the real point—all Alexandrian men of letters and all skalds would have agreed about the answers. I believe the same to be true of the dark conceits in Donne; there was one correct interpretation of each and Donne could have told it to you. Of course you might misunderstand what Wordsworth was 'up to' in *Lyrical Ballads*; but everyone understood what he said. I do not see in any of these the slightest parallel to the state of affairs disclosed by a recent symposium on Mr Eliot's 'Cooking Egg'.* Here we find seven adults (two of them Cambridge men) whose lives have been specially devoted to the study of poetry discussing a very short poem which has been before the world for thirty-odd years; and there is not the slightest agreement among them as to what, in any sense of the word, it means. I am not in the least concerned to decide whether this state of affairs is a good thing, or a bad thing.† I merely assert that it is a new thing. In the whole history of the West, from Homer—I might almost say from the *Epic of Gilgamesh*—there has been no bend or break in the development of poetry comparable to this. On this score my proposed division has no rival to fear.

3. Thirdly, there is the great religious change which I have had to mention before: the un-christening. Of course there were lots of sceptics in Jane Austen's time and long before, as there are lots of Christians now. But the presumption has changed. In her days some kind and degree of religious belief and practice were the norm: now,

---

* 'A Cooking Egg', *Essays in Criticism*, vol. III (July 1953), pp. 345–57.

† In music we have pieces which demand more talent in the performer than in the composer. Why should there not come a period when the art of writing poetry stands lower than the art of reading it? Of course rival readings would then cease to be 'right' or 'wrong' and become more and less brilliant 'performances'.

though I would gladly believe that both kind and degree have improved, they are the exception. I have already argued that this change surpasses that which Europe underwent at its conversion. It is hard to have patience with those Jeremiahs, in Press or pulpit, who warn us that we are 'relapsing into Paganism'. It might be rather fun if we were. It would be pleasant to see some future Prime Minister trying to kill a large and lively milk-white bull in Westminster Hall. But we shan't. What lurks behind such idle prophecies, if they are anything but careless language, is the false idea that the historical process allows mere reversal; that Europe can come out of Christianity 'by the same door as in she went' and find herself back where she was. It is not what happens. A post-Christian man is not a Pagan; you might as well think that a married woman recovers her virginity by divorce. The post-Christian is cut off from the Christian past and therefore doubly from the Pagan past.

4. Lastly, I play my trump card. Between Jane Austen and us, but not between her and Shakespeare, Chaucer, Alfred, Virgil, Homer, or the Pharaohs, comes the birth of the machines. This lifts us at once into a region of change far above all that we have hitherto considered. For this is parallel to the great changes by which we divide epochs of pre-history. This is on a level with the change from stone to bronze, or from a pastoral to an agricultural economy. It alters Man's place in nature. The theme has been celebrated till we are all sick of it, so I will here say nothing about its economic and social consequences, immeasurable though they are. What concerns us more is its psychological effect. How has it come about that we use the highly emotive word 'stagnation', with all its malodorous and malarial overtones, for what other ages would have called 'permanence'? Why does the word 'primitive' at once suggest to us clumsiness, inefficiency, barbarity? When our ancestors talked of the primitive church or the primitive purity of our constitution they meant nothing of that sort. (The only pejorative sense which Johnson gives to *Primitive* in his Dictionary is, significantly, 'Formal; affectedly solemn; imitating the supposed gravity of old times'.) Why does 'latest' in advertisements mean 'best'? Well, let us admit that these semantic developments owe something to the nineteenth-century belief in spontaneous progress which itself owes something either to Darwin's theorem of biological evolution or to that myth of universal evolutionism which is really so different from it, and earlier. For the two great imaginative

expressions of the myth, as distinct from the theorem—Keats's
Hyperion and Wagner's *Ring*—are pre-Darwinian. Let us give these
their due.[1] But I submit that what has imposed this climate of opinion
so firmly on the human mind is a new archetypal image. It is the
image of old machines being superseded by new and better ones. For
in the world of machines the new most often really is better and the
primitive really is the clumsy. And this image, potent in all our
minds, reigns almost without rival in the minds of the uneducated.
For to them, after their marriage and the births of their children, the
very milestones of life are technical advances. From the old push-bike
to the motor-bike and thence to the little car; from gramophone to
radio and from radio to television; from the range to the stove; these
are the very stages of their pilgrimage. But whether from this cause
or from some other, assuredly that approach to life which has left
these footprints on our language is the thing that separates us most
sharply from our ancestors and whose absence would strike us as
most alien if we could return to their world. Conversely, our assumption that everything is provisional and soon to be superseded, that
the attainment of goods we have never yet had, rather than the
defence and conservation of those we have already, is the cardinal
business of life, would most shock and bewilder them if they could
visit ours.

I thus claim for my chosen division of periods that on the first
count it comes well up to scratch; on the second and third it arguably
surpasses all; and on the fourth it quite clearly surpasses them without
any dispute. I conclude that it really is the greatest change in the
history of Western Man.

At any rate, this conviction determines my whole approach to my
work from this Chair. I am not preparing an excuse in advance lest
I should hereafter catch myself lecturing either on the *Epic of
Gilgamesh* or on the Waverley Novels. The field 'Medieval and
Renaissance' is already far too wide for my powers. But you see how
to me the appointed area must primarily appear as a specimen of
something far larger, something which had already begun when the
Iliad was composed and was still almost unimpaired when Waterloo
was fought. Of course within that immense period there are all sorts
of differences. There are lots of convenient differences between the

---

[1] Lewis pronounces a funeral oration over the 'myth of universal evolutionism' in his
essay 'The Funeral of a Great Myth', *Christian Reflections*, pp. 82–93.

area I am to deal with and other areas; there are important differences within the chosen area. And yet—despite all this—that whole thing, from its Greek or pre-Greek beginnings down to the day before yesterday, seen from the vast distance at which we stand today, reveals a homogeneity that is certainly important and perhaps more important than its interior diversities. That is why I shall be unable to talk to you about my particular region without constantly treating things which neither began with the Middle Ages nor ended with the end of the Renaissance. In that way I shall be forced to present to you a great deal of what can only be described as Old European, or Old Western, Culture. If one were giving a lecture on Warwickshire to an audience of Martians (no offence: Martians may be delightful creatures) one might loyally choose all one's *data* from that county: but much of what you told them would not really be Warwickshire lore but 'common tellurian'.

The prospect of my becoming, in such halting fashion as I can, the spokesman of Old Western Culture, alarms me. It may alarm you. I will close with one reassurance and one claim.

First, for the reassurance. I do not think you need fear that the study of a dead period, however prolonged and however sympathetic, need prove an indulgence in nostalgia or an enslavement to the past. In the individual life, as the psychologists have taught us, it is not the remembered but the forgotten past that enslaves us. I think the same is true of society. To study the past does indeed liberate us from the present, from the idols of our own market-place. But I think it liberates us from the past too. I think no class of men are less enslaved to the past than historians. The unhistorical are usually, without knowing it, enslaved to a fairly recent past. Dante read Virgil. Certain other medieval authors* evolved the legend of Virgil as a great magician. It was the more recent past, the whole quality of mind evolved during a few preceding centuries, which impelled them to do so. Dante was freer; he also knew more of the past. And you will be no freer by coming to misinterpret Old Western Culture as quickly and deeply as those medievals misinterpreted Classical Antiquity; or even as the Romantics misinterpreted the Middle Ages.† Such mis-

---

* On their identity see Comparetti, *Virgilio nel Medio Evo*, ed. G. Pasquali (Firenze, 1943), p. xxii. I owe this reference to Mr C. G. Hardie.

† As my examples show, such misinterpretations may themselves produce results which have imaginative value. If there had been no Romantic distortion of the Middle Ages,

interpretation has already begun. To arrest its growth while arrest is still possible, is surely a proper task for a university.

And now for the claim: which sounds arrogant but, I hope, is not really so. I have said that the vast change which separates you from Old Western has been gradual and is not even now complete. Wide as the chasm is, those who are native to different sides of it can still meet; are meeting in this room. This is quite normal at times of great change. The correspondence of Henry More* and Descartes is an amusing example; one would think the two men were writing in different centuries. And here comes the rub. I myself belong far more to that Old Western order than to yours. I am going to claim that this, which in one way is a disqualification for my task, is yet in another a qualification. The disqualification is obvious. You don't want to be lectured on Neanderthal Man by a Neanderthaler, still less on dinosaurs by a dinosaur. And yet, is that the whole story? If a live dinosaur dragged its slow length into the laboratory, would we not all look back as we fled? What a chance to know at last how it really moved and looked and smelled and what noises it made! And if the Neanderthaler could talk, then, though his lecturing technique might leave much to be desired, should we not almost certainly learn from him some things about him which the best modern anthropologist could never have told us? He would tell us without knowing he was telling. One thing I know: I would give a great deal to hear any ancient Athenian, even a stupid one, talking about Greek tragedy. He would know in his bones so much that we seek in vain. At any moment some chance phrase might, unknown to him, show us where modern scholarship had been on the wrong track for years. Ladies and gentlemen, I stand before you somewhat as that Athenian might stand. I read as a native texts that you must read as foreigners. You see why I said that the claim was not really arrogant; who can be proud of speaking fluently his mother tongue or knowing his way about his father's house? It is my settled conviction that in order to read Old Western literature aright you must suspend most of the responses and unlearn most of the habits you have acquired in reading modern literature. And because this is the judgement of a native, I claim that, even if the

we should have no *Eve of St Agnes*. There is room both for an appreciation of the imagined past and an awareness of its difference from the real past; but if we want only the former, why come to a university? (The subject deserves much fuller treatment than I give it here.)

* *A Collection of several Philosophical Writings* (Cambridge, 1662).

defence of my conviction is weak, the fact of my conviction is a historical *datum* to which you should give full weight. That way, where I fail as a critic, I may yet be useful as a specimen. I would even dare to go further. Speaking not only for myself but for all other Old Western men whom you may meet, I would say, use your specimens while you can. There are not going to be many more dinosaurs.

2

The Alliterative Metre

'Tis ignorance that makes a barren waste
Of all beyond itself.   KEATS

In the general reaction which has set in against the long reign of
foreign, syllabic metres in English, it is a little remarkable that few
have yet suggested a return to our own ancient system, the alliterative
line. Mr Auden, however, has revived some of its stylistic features;[1]
Professor Tolkien will soon, I hope, be ready to publish an alliterative
poem;[2] and the moment seems propitious for expounding the
principles of this metre to a larger public than those Anglo-Saxon
and Old Norse specialists who know it already.

I

Alliteration is no more the whole secret of this verse than rhyme is
the whole secret of syllabic verse. It has, in addition, a metrical
structure, which could stand alone, and which would then be to this
system as blank verse is to the syllabic.

2

Latin verse is based on quantity (= the length of time taken to
pronounce a syllable). Modern English is based on stress-accent
(= the loudness with which a syllable is pronounced). Alliterative
verse involves both.

[1] Readers will find numerous examples in two volumes of verse published by Auden
prior to the appearance of this essay. They are *Poems* (London, 1930) and *The Orators*
(London, 1932). The former contains 'Paid on both Sides' which is mentioned in
Herbert Howarth's *Notes on Some Figures behind T. S. Eliot* (London, 1965): '"Paid
on both Sides" and such a poem as "Doom is dark" [both by Auden] showed Eliot
how powerful the "consonantal rhymes" (so C. L. Wrenn, who tutored Auden, used
to call them), and the terse phrases they encourage, speak to the English ear. In 1934,
electing the story of Becket for his Canterbury play, he acted on Auden's example
and went to English alliterative poetry for a medium' (p. 338).

[2] Professor Tolkien tells me that Lewis was probably referring to his poem, 'The Fall
of Arthur', which has never been completed or published. Though Professor Tolkien's
alliterative poem, 'The Homecoming of Beorhtnoth Beorhthelm's Son', was in
existence when Lewis wrote this essay, Professor Tolkien does not recall showing it
to him before it was revised and published in *Essays and Studies*, vol. VI, new series
(1953), pp. 1–18.

3

In order to write alliterative verse it is therefore necessary to learn to distinguish not only accented from unaccented syllables, but also long from short syllables. This is rendered difficult by our classical education which allows boys to pronounce *ille* so that it rhymes with *silly*, and nevertheless to call the first syllable long, which, in their pronunciation, it is not. In dealing with English quantity the reader must learn to attend entirely to *sounds*, and to ignore spelling.

DEFINITION   A long syllable is one which contains *either* a long vowel (as *fath(er)*, *fame*, *seek*, *pile*, *home*, *do*); or, a vowel followed by more than one consonant (as *punt*, *wind*, *helm*, *pelt*).*

CAUTION (A)   It is here that the trouble from spelling occurs. In modern English spelling, for reasons which need not be discussed here, such words as *silly*, *pretty*, *merry*, *sorrow*, *attraction*, show a double consonant in spelling where there is no shadow of a double consonant in pronunciation. The reader can convince himself of this by comparing the pretended double T in *pretty* with the real double T in *hot toast*: and he will then hear how a real double consonant renders the first syllable of *hot toast* long, while that of *pretty*, though accented, is short. So, in *distiller* the pretended two L's are one, while in *still life* we have a real double L, disguised as a triple L. True double consonants can be heard in *palely* (*cf. Paley*), *fish-shop* (*cf. bishop*), *unnamed* (*cf. unaimed*), *midday* (*cf. middy*), *solely* (*cf. holy*).†

CAUTION (B)   In modern English many words, chiefly monosyllables, which end in a single consonant are pronounced differently according to their position in the sentence. If they come at the end of a sentence or other speech-group—that is, if there is a pause after them—the

---

* That two or more consonants make the *syllable* long is not a metrical rule but a phonetic fact; that they make the preceding *vowel* long, as some say, is neither a rule nor a fact, but false.

† -NG in English usually represents a single consonant (G nasalized), but sometimes it represents this consonant followed by a pure G in addition. Hence the first syllable is short in *singer*, *ringer*: long in *linger*, *finger*.

final consonant is so dwelled upon that the syllable becomes long. If the reader listens carefully he will find that the syllable *man* is short in

> 'Manifold and great mercies'
> or 'The man of property',

but long in

> 'The Invisible Man'
> or 'The Descent of Man'.

With this caution, the reader will be glad to hear, the serious difficulties in the re-education of our ear are over.

4

Each line consists of two half-lines, which are independent metrical organisms, connected only by the alliteration.

5

The half-line consists of *Lifts* and *Dips*.

DEFINITIONS

A Lift = either (a) one syllable both long and accented (as the first syllable of *ogre*, *mountain*, *Repton*); or (b) two syllables whereof the first is short but accented, and the second unaccented (as the first *two* syllables of *merrily*, *vigorous*, *melancholy*, *evident*). (Thus in *vary* the first syllable is a Lift: in *very* the whole word is a Lift.)
A Dip = any reasonable number of unaccented syllables whether long or short.

In the following sentences the syllables printed in capitals are Lifts, the rest Dips.

> Of COURSE we assUME.
> When a phiLOLOGist is a FOOL.
> RhadaMANTHus in his MISERy.

6

Every half-line must contain neither more nor less than two Lifts. (The ancient poetry sometimes introduces a three-lift type which stands to this metre much as the Alexandrine stands to decasyllabics: but the beginner will be wise to neglect it.)
The five different types of half-line depend on the five ways in

which Lifts and Dips are combined. Before learning these, however, the reader should 'work his ear in' with the following:

> We were TALKing of DRAGONS, | TOLKien and I
> In a BERKshire BAR. | The BIG WORKman
> Who had SAT SILent | and SUCKED his PIPE
> ALL the EVEning, | from his EMPTY MUG
> With GLEAMing EYE | GLANCED toWARDS us;
> 'I SEEN 'em mySELF', | he SAID FIERCEly.[1]

7

The 'A' type of half-line is arranged Lift-dip, Lift-dip.

> e.g. GREEN and GROWing.
> MERRY were the MINSTrels.
> COME from the COUNTry.

LICENCE   One or two unaccented syllables may be added before the first Lift, forming what is technically known as an Anacrusis.

> e.g. And green and growing.
> And so merry were the minstrels.
> He came from the country.

WARNING   But this licence should be very seldom used in the second half-line. In the first half-line (i.e. at the beginning of the whole line) it may be used freely.

8

B type = dip-Lift, dip-Lift.

> e.g. And NUMBED with NIGHT.
> Where MAIDS are MERRY.
> And to the PALACE of PRIDE.

---

[1] I have been asked by many people if these lines were part of a longer poem. The answer, I regret to say, is No. They were written simply for the purpose of illustrating the alliterative line. Professor Tolkien, when I asked if he knew the origin of these lines, kindly favoured me with the following note: 'The occasion is entirely fictitious ...A remote source of Jack's [C.S.L.'s] lines may be this: I remember Jack telling me a story of Brightman, the distinguished ecclesiastical scholar, who used to sit quietly in Common Room saying nothing except on rare occasions. Jack said that there was a discussion on dragons one night and at the end Brightman's voice was heard to say, "I have seen a dragon." Silence. "Where was that?" he was asked. "On the Mount of Olives", he said. He relapsed into silence and never before his death explained what he meant.'

WARNING   The first dip may contain 'any reasonable number' of unaccented syllables: but the second should normally consist of a *single* unaccented syllable. In all circumstances a predominantly 'anapaestic' movement is to be avoided.

9

C = dip-Lift, Lift-dip.

(NOTE   Here we reach a rhythm of daily occurrence in our speech (e.g. 'I can't stand him') which has been allowed no *metrical* recognition for centuries.)

> e.g. The MERRY MASTer.
> In the DARK DUNGeon.
> Through CLOUDS CLEAVing.
> It is EVER-OPen.
> And with GOD'S BENISon.

LICENCE   In this type a *single short, accented* syllable may serve as the second Lift, giving us:

> A cold kipper.
> But they're hard-headed.
> A proud palace.

10

D = Lift, Lift-dip.

Here there is only one dip, whereas A, B, and C have two. To compensate for this, in D types the dip must be strengthened by a syllable* nearly (but not quite) as strong as the Lifts.

(NOTE   This again rescues a genuine English speech rhythm from metrical non-existence.)

> e.g. HARD HAYmaking.

It will be heard that the syllable *mak* is as long as, but just less accented than, *hard* and *hay*.

> e.g. BRIGHT QUICKsilver.
> MAD MERRYmaking.
> SHODDY SHIPbuilders.
> GRIM GLADIator.
> HELL'S HOUSEkeeper.

---

* Or, of course, two syllables whereof the first is short. The rules for 'compensating elements' are, in this respect, identical with the rules for Lifts.

In all these examples the strengthening element of the dip stands first in the dip: e.g. in 'Hell's *housekeeper*', *keep-* comes before *-er*. Obviously the reverse order may be used, giving us:

> ALL UNDerclothes.
> MAD MULTitude.
> EATS ARTichokes.
> POOR DESTitude.

LICENCE 1   In D, as in C, a single short, accented syllable may serve as the second Lift, giving us, instead of *Hard haymaking*, such forms as:

> SHEER SHOTover.
> PURE PALimpsest.

LICENCE 2   The compensating element in the dip may also be a single short, accented syllable, giving us:

> MAD MELANCHOly.
> HEAV'N'S WAR-office.
> BORN BOOT-legger.

LICENCE 3   The sub-type *Mad multitude* may be extended by inserting a single unaccented (and preferably short) syllable between the two Lifts, so as to give:

> MAD the MULTitude.
> EATing ARTichokes.

II

E = Lift-dip-Lift.

Here again we have only one dip, and again the dip must contain a compensating element. E, in fact, is a rearrangement of D.

> e.g. HAYmakers HEARD.
> SHIPbuilders SHOW.
> GLADiator GRIM.

LICENCE   The compensating element in the dip may be a single short, accented syllable, giving us:

> NEW-College KNOWS.

12

For the reader's convenience, I add a recapitulation of the five types.

A   1   Green and growing.
      2   (With Anacrusis) The grass is growing.
B   And life runs low.
C   1   A dark dungeon.
      2   (With single short for 2nd Lift) The gray gravel.
D   1   Hell's housekeeper.
      2   (With compensating element last in dip) Earth's antidote.
      3   (With single short for 2nd Lift) East Abingdon.
      4   (With single short for compensating element in dip) Heav'n's war-office.
      5   (Extended) Evil antidote.
E   1   Shipbuilders show.
      2   (With single short for compensating element in dip) New-College knows.

13

In every line both the Lifts of the first half-line may, and one must, alliterate with the first Lift of the second half-line. As

> In a Berkshire Bar. The Big workman

(both Lifts in the first half alliterating with the first of the second) or,

> We were Talking of dragons, Tolkien and I

(one Lift of the first half alliterating with the first of the second).
    An alliteration on all four Lifts as in

> And walks by the waves, as winds warble

is regarded not as an added beauty, but as a deformity. (Its use in Middle English, it will be found, radically alters the character of the metre.)

14

Where only one Lift in the first half-line alliterates, it should normally be the first.

15

All vowels alliterate with one another.

> WARNING Do not be deceived by spelling. *Union* alliterates with *yeast, yellow,* &c., not with *uncle.*

16

No half-line of any type should end in a pure dactyl. *Noble Norbury, with trash and trumpery, glancing gloomily,* &c., are unmetrical.

17 *Structure*

(1) The medial pause which divides the first from the second half of the line must be strictly observed, so that the two halves fall apart as separate speech-groups.

(By speech-groups I mean those units—rhythmical, rhetorical, emotional, and to some extent syntactical, units—out of which our actual conversation is built up. Thus if the reader says 'The big workman who had sat silent and sucked his pipe all the evening', he will (I hope) find that the speech-groups coincide with the half-lines in the example given under para. 6. A good deal of re-education is here necessary, for the chief beauty of syllabic verse lies in a deliberate clash or contradiction between the speech-groups and the 'feet', whereas in alliterative verse the speech-group is both the metrical, and the aesthetic, unit. See below, para. 18.)

Examples. Thus, *he will stand as a stone till the stars crumble,* is metrically good. *The laugh of the lovely lady is silent* is bad. But *Lost is the laugh of the lovely damsel* is not a line at all: for it pretends metrically to be:

LOST is the LAUGH of the LOVEly DAMsel

(A-type + A with anacrusis): and in this the first half is so impossible as a speech-group that a poet could have written it only because he was really still thinking in feet and syllables, and not in speech-groups and half-lines.

(2) But while we cannot run across the medial break, we can run across the end of a line. In other words, the last half of a given line and the first half of the next are more intimately connected than the two halves of a single line. Hence we may write

There stands a stone. Still'd is the Lady's
Peerless laughter.

Corollary. Hence, though the poem begins and ends with a full line, yet within the poem a new paragraph or sentence should usually begin in the second half of a line.

18 *Aesthetics*

It follows that whereas syllabic poetry primarily uses the evocative qualities of words (and only secondarily those of phrases), alliterative poetry reverses the procedure. The phrase, coinciding with the half-line, is the poetic unit. In any English country tap-room the student may hear from the lips of labourers speech-groups which have a certain race and resonance in isolation. These are the elements of our native metre.

Such are the rules. Where no tradition—at least no modern tradition—exists it is rash to offer advice, but perhaps two counsels may be given. In the first place, if any one is attracted by the metre in general, but disposed to omit the rules of quantity and produce a merely accentual adaptation, I would like to save him disappointment by warning him that he will almost certainly produce rubbish. Torture the language, or the thought, as he will, the result will be *thin*. The thing to aim at is richness and fullness of sound, and this cannot be attained without quantity: with quantity, the metre opens possibilities of resonance which have not been exploited for a thousand years. In the second place, I would advise him to be on his guard against too many B types. His iambic training will probably be tempting him to them at every turn: but if he yields his poem will sound like octo-syllabics. And lastly, I would advocate to all who have a taste for such things some serious contention with the difficulties of this metre. A few successful specimens would be an excellent answer to the type of critic (by no means extinct) who accuses the moderns of choosing *vers libre* because they are not men enough for metre. For if syllabic verse is like carving in wood and *vers libre* like working with a brush, this is like carving in granite.

A man who preaches a metre must sooner or later risk his case by showing a specimen: and if the fate of Gabriel Harvey deters me, that of Campion invites. In order to avoid misunderstanding I must say that the subject of the following poem was not chosen under the influence of any antiquarian fancy that a medieval metre demanded medieval matter, but because the characters of the planets, as conceived by medieval astrology, seem to me to have a permanent value as spiritual symbols—to provide a *Phänomenologie des Geistes* which is specially worth while in our own generation. Of Saturn we know more than enough. But who does not need to be reminded of Jove?

THE PLANETS

Lady LUNA, in light canoe,	A : B
By friths and shallows of fretted cloudland	B : C
Cruises monthly; with chrism of dews	A : B
And drench of dream, a drizzling glamour,	B : B
Enchants us—the cheat! changing sometime	B : A
A mind to madness, melancholy pale,	A2 : E2
Bleached with gazing on her blank count'nance	A : C
Orb'd and ageless. In earth's bosom	A : C2
The shower of her rays, sharp-feathered light	B : E2
Reaching downward, ripens silver,	A : A
Forming and fashioning female brightness,	A : A
—Metal maidenlike. Her moist circle	D2 : C
Is nearest earth. Next beyond her	B : A
MERCURY marches;—madcap rover,	A : A
Patron of pilf'rers. Pert quicksilver	A : D
His gaze begets, goblin mineral,	B : A
Merry multitude of meeting selves,	D2 : B
Same but sundered. From the soul's darkness,	A : C
With wreathèd wand,* words he marshals,	B : A
Guides and gathers them—gay bellwether	A : D4
Of flocking fancies. His flint has struck	C : B
The spark of speech from spirit's tinder,	B : C
Lord of language! He leads forever	A : B
The spangle and splendour, sport that mingles	A2 : A
Sound with senses, in subtle pattern,	A : C2
Words in wedlock, and wedding also	A : C
Of thing with thought. In the third region	B : C
VENUS voyages . . . but my voice falters;	A : C
Rude rime-making wrongs her beauty,	D : A
Whose breasts and brow, and her breath's sweetness	B : C
Bewitch the worlds. Wide-spread the reign	B : E
Of her secret sceptre, in the sea's caverns,	A2 : C2
In grass growing, and grain bursting,	C : C
Flower unfolding, and flesh longing,	A : C
And shower falling sharp in April.	C : A

* Alliteration on second lift of the first half. The orthographic *w* in *wreathèd* has, of course, no metrical function.

The metal of copper in the mine reddens	B : C2
With muffled brightness, like muted gold,	C : B
By her finger form'd. Far beyond her	B : A
The heaven's highway hums and trembles,	C : A
Drums and dindles,* to the driv'n thunder	A : C
Of SOL's chariot, whose sword of light	C : B
Hurts and humbles; beheld only	A : C
Of eagle's eye. When his arrow glances	B : C
Through mortal mind, mists are parted	B : A
And mild as morning the mellow wisdom	A2 : C
Breathes o'er the breast, broadening eastward	E : A
Clear and cloudless. In a clos'd garden	A : C
(Unbound her burden) his beams foster	A2 : C
Soul in secret, where the soil puts forth	A : B
Paradisal palm, and pure fountains	E : C
Turn and re-temper, touching coolly	A : A
The uncomely common to cordial gold;	B : B
Whose ore also, in earth's matrix,	C : C
Is print and pressure of his proud signet	B : C
On the wax of the world. He is the worshipp'd male,	B : B
The earth's husband, all-beholding,	C : A
Arch-chemic eye. But other country	E2 : C
Dark with discord dins beyond him,	A : A
With noise of nakers, neighing of horses,	B : A
Hammering of harness. A haughty god	A : B
MARS mercenary,† makes there his camp	D2 : E
And flies his flag; flaunts laughingly	B : D
The graceless beauty, grey-eyed and keen,	A2 : E
—Blond insolence—of his blithe visage	D2 : C2
Which is hard and happy. He hews the act,	B : B
The indifferent deed with dint of his mallet	B : B
And his chisel of choice; achievement comes not	B : A2
Unhelped by him;—hired gladiator	B : D
Of evil and good. All's one to Mars,	B : E
The wrong righted, rescued meekness,	C : A
Or trouble in trenches, with trees splintered	A : C
And birds banished, banks fill'd with gold	C2 : E
And the liar made lord. Like handiwork	B : D2
He offers to all—earns his wages	B : A
And whistles the while. White-featured dread	B : E
Mars has mastered. His metal's iron	A : C
That was hammered through hands into holy cross,	B : B
Cruel carpentry. He is cold and strong,	D5 : B
Necessity's son.‡ Soft breathes the air	B : E

* Cf., Malory, v, ch. 8.   † -ary being the compensating element in the Dip.
‡ The c in necessity, being an s in pronunciation, carries the first alliteration.

Mild, and meadowy, as we mount further	A : C
Where rippled radiance rolls about us	C : A
Moved with music—measureless the waves'	A : E
Joy and jubilee. It is JOVE's orbit,	D5 : C
Filled and festal, faster turning	A : A
With arc ampler. From the Isles of Tin	C : B
Tyrian traders, in trouble steering	A : C
Came with his cargoes; the Cornish treasure	A : B
That his ray ripens. Of wrath ended	C : C
And woes mended, of winter passed	C : B
And guilt forgiven, and good fortune	B : C
Jove is master; and of jocund revel,	A : C2
Laughter of ladies. The lion-hearted,	A : A2
The myriad-minded, men like the gods,	A2 : E
Helps and heroes, helms of nations	A : A
Just and gentle, are Jove's children,	A : C
Work his wonders. On his wide forehead*	A : C2
Calm and kingly, no care darkens	A : C
Nor wrath wrinkles: but righteous power	C : B
And leisure and largess their loose splendours	A2 : C
Have wrapped around him—a rich mantle	A2 : C
Of ease and empire. Up far beyond	A2 : E
Goes SATURN silent in the seventh region,	C : C
The skirts of the sky. Scant grows the light,	B : E
Sickly, uncertain (the Sun's finger	A : C
Daunted with darkness). Distance hurts us,	A : A
And the vault severe of vast silence;	B : C
Where fancy fails us, and fair language,	A2 : C
And love leaves us, and light fails us	C : C
And Mars fails us, and the mirth of Jove	C : B
Is as tin tinkling. In tattered garment,	C : C
Weak with winters, he walks forever	A : B
A weary way, wide round the heav'n,	B : E
Stoop'd and stumbling, with staff groping,	A : C
The lord of lead. He is the last planet	B : C2
Old and ugly. His eye fathers	A : C
Pale pestilence, pain of envy,	D2 : A
Remorse and murder. Melancholy drink	A : E2
(For bane or blessing) of bitter wisdom	B : C
He pours for his people, a perilous draught	A2 : B
That the lip loves not. We leave all things	C : C
To reach the rim of the round welkin,	B : C
Heaven's hermitage, high and lonely.	D2 : A

* This is C 2 in my pronunciation because I pronounce *forehead* so as to rhyme with *horrid*. In the alternative pronunciation (which is now heard even among educated speakers) it would be C 1.

3

What Chaucer really did to '*Il Filostrato*'

A great deal of attention has deservedly been given to the relation between the *Book of Troilus* and its original, *Il Filostrato*, and Rossetti's collation[1] placed a knowledge of the subject within the reach even of undergraduate inquirers. It is, of course, entirely right and proper that the greater part of this attention has been devoted to such points as specially illustrate the individual genius of Chaucer as a dramatist and a psychologist. But such studies, without any disgrace to themselves, often leave singularly undefined the historical position and affinities of a book; and if pursued intemperately they may leave us with a preposterous picture of the author as that abstraction, a *pure* individual, bound to no time nor place, or even obeying in the fourteenth century the aesthetics of the twentieth. It is possible that a good deal of misunderstanding still exists, even among instructed people, as to the real significance of the liberties that Chaucer took with his source. M. Legouis, in his study of Chaucer to which we all owe so much, remarks that Chaucer's additions 'implied a wider and more varied conception' than those of Boccaccio; and again 'Chaucer's aim was not like Boccaccio's to paint sentimentality alone, but to reflect life'.[2] I do not wish to contradict either statement, but I am convinced that both are capable of conveying a false impression. What follows may be regarded as a cautionary gloss on M. Legouis's text. I shall endeavour to show that the process which *Il Filostrato* underwent at Chaucer's hands was first and foremost a process of *medievalization*. One aspect of this process has received some attention from scholars,* but its importance appears to me to be still insufficiently stressed. In what follows I shall, therefore, restate this aspect in my own terms while endeavouring to replace it in its context.

* *Vi{.* William George Dodd, *Courtly Love in Chaucer and Gower* (Boston, 1913).

[1] William Michael Rossetti, *Chaucer's Troylus and Cryseyde Compared with Boccaccio's Filostrato*, Chaucer Society, first series, vols. XLIV and LXV (London, 1875–83).

[2] Emile Legouis, *Geoffrey Chaucer*, trans. L. Lailavoix (London, 1913), p. 134.

Chaucer had never heard of a renaissance; and I think it would be difficult to translate either into the English or the Latin of his day our distinction between sentimental or conventional art on the one hand, and art which paints 'Life'—whatever this means—on the other. When first a manuscript beginning with the words *Alcun di Giove sogliono il favore* came into his hands, he was, no doubt, aware of a difference between its contents and those of certain English and French manuscripts which he had read before. That some of the differences did not please him is apparent from his treatment. We may be sure, however, that he noticed and approved the new use of stanzas, instead of octosyllabic couplets, for narrative. He certainly thought the story a good story; he may even have thought it a story better told than any that he had yet read. But there was also, for Chaucer, a special reason why he should choose this story for his own retelling; and that reason largely determined the alterations that he made.

He was not yet the Chaucer of the *Canterbury Tales*: he was the *grant translateur* of the *Roman de la Rose*, the author of the *Book of the Duchesse*, and probably of 'many a song and many a lecherous lay'.* In other words he was the great living interpreter in English of *l'amour courtois*. Even in 1390, when Gower produced the first version of his *Confessio Amantis*, such faithful interpretation of the love tradition was still regarded as the typical and essential function of Chaucer: he is Venus' 'disciple' and 'poete', with whose 'ditees and songes glade ... the lond fulfild is overal'. And Gower still has hopes that Chaucer's existing treatments of *Frauendienst* are only the preludes to some great 'testament' which will 'sette an ende of alle his werk'.† These expectations were, of course, disappointed; and it is possibly to that disappointment, rather than to a hypothetical quarrel (for which only the most ridiculous grounds have been assigned), that we should attribute Gower's removal of this passage from the second text of the *Confessio Amantis*. It had become apparent that Chaucer was following a different line of development, and the reference made to him by Venus had ceased to be appropriate.

It was, then, as a poet of courtly love that Chaucer approached *Il Filostrato*. There is no sign as yet that he wished to desert the courtly tradition; on the contrary, there is ample evidence that he still regarded himself as its exponent. But the narrative bent of his genius was already

* *C.T.*, I 1086. † *Conf. Am.*, VIII, 2941–58.

urging him, not to desert this tradition, but to pass from its doctrinal treatment (as in the *Romance of the Rose*) to its narrative treatment. Having preached it, and sung it, he would now exemplify it: he would show the code put into action in the course of a story—without prejudice (as we shall see) to a good deal of doctrine and pointing of the amorous moral by the way. The thing represents a curious return upon itself of literary history. If Chaucer had lived earlier he would, we may be sure, have found just the model that he desired in Chrétien de Troyes. But by Chaucer's time certain elements, which Chrétien had held together in unity, had come apart and taken an independent life. Chrétien had combined, magnificently, the interest of the story, and the interest of erotic doctrine and psychology. His successors had been unable or unwilling to achieve this union. Perhaps, indeed, the two things had to separate in order that each might grow to maturity; and in many of Chrétien's psychological passages one sees the embryonic allegory struggling to be born.* Whatever the reason may be, such a separation took place. The story sets up on its own in the prose romances—the 'French book' of Malory: the doctrine and psychology set up on their own in the *Romance of the Rose*. In this situation if a poet arose who accepted the doctrines and also had a narrative genius, then *a priori* such a poet might be expected to combine again the two elements—now fully grown—which, in their rudimentary form, had lain together in Chrétien. But this is exactly the sort of poet that Chaucer was; and this (as we shall see) is what Chaucer did. The *Book of Troilus* shows, in fact, the very peculiar literary phenomenon of Chaucer groping back, unknowingly, through the very slightly medieval work of Boccaccio, to the genuinely medieval formula of Chrétien. We may be thankful that Chaucer did not live in the high noon of Chrétien's celebrity; for, if he had, we should probably have lost much of the originality of *Troilus*. He would have had less motive for altering Chrétien than for altering Boccaccio, and probably would have altered him less.

Approaching *Il Filostrato* from this angle, Chaucer, we may be sure, while feeling the charm of its narrative power, would have found himself, at many passages, uttering the Middle English equivalent of 'This will never do!' In such places he did not hesitate, as he might have said, to *amenden* and to *reducen* what was *amis* in his author. The majority of his modifications are corrections of errors which Boccaccio

* *Viz. Lancelot*, 369–81, 2844–61; *Yvain*, 6001 *et seq.*, 2639 *et seq.*; *Cligès*, 5855 *et seq.*

had committed against the code of courtly love; and modifications of this kind have not been entirely neglected by criticism. It has not, however, been sufficiently observed that these are only part and parcel of a general process of medievalization. They are, indeed, the most instructive part of that process, and even in the present discussion must claim the chief place; but in order to restore them to their proper setting it will be convenient to make a division of the different capacities in which Chaucer approached his original. These will, of course, be found to overlap in the concrete; but that is no reason for not plucking them ideally apart in the interests of clarity.

I. Chaucer approached his work as an 'historial' poet contributing to the story of Troy. I do not mean that he necessarily believed his tale to be wholly or partly a record of fact, but his attitude towards it in this respect is different from Boccaccio's. Boccaccio, we may surmise, wrote for an audience who were beginning to look at poetry in our own way. For them *Il Filostrato* was mainly, though not entirely, 'a new poem by Boccaccio'. Chaucer wrote for an audience who still looked at poetry in the medieval fashion—a fashion for which the real literary units were 'matters', 'stories', and the like, rather than individual authors. For them the *Book of Troilus* was partly, though of course only partly, 'a new bit of the Troy story', or even 'a new bit of the matter of Rome'. Hence Chaucer expects them to be interested not only in the personal drama between his little group of characters but in that whole world of story which makes this drama's context: like children looking at a landscape picture and wanting to know what happens to the road after it disappears into the frame. For the same reason they will want to know his authorities. Passages in which Chaucer has departed from his original to meet this demand will easily occur to the memory. Thus, in I, 141 *et seq.*, he excuses himself for not telling us more about the military history of the Trojan war, and adds what is almost a footnote to tell his audience where they can find that missing part of the story—'in Omer, or in Dares, or in Dyte'. Boccaccio had merely sketched in, in the preceding stanza, a general picture of war sufficient to provide the background for his own story—much as a dramatist might put *Alarums within* in a stage direction: he has in view an audience fully conscious that all this is mere necessary 'setting' or hypothesis. Thus again, in IV, 120 *et seq.*, Chaucer inserts into the speech of Calkas an account of the quarrel between Phebus and

Neptunus and Lameadoun. This is not dramatically necessary. All that was needed for Calkas's argument has already been given in lines 111 and 112 (*cf. Filostrato*, IV, xi). The Greek leaders did not need to be told about Laomedon; but Chaucer is not thinking of the Greek leaders; he is thinking of his audience who will gladly learn, or be reminded, of that part of the cycle. At lines 204 *et seq.* he inserts a note on the later history of Antenor for the same reason. In the fifth book he inserts unnecessarily lines 1464–1510 from the story of Thebes. The spirit in which this is done is aptly expressed in his own words:

> And so descendeth doun from gestes olde
> To Diomede.   (v, 1511)

The whole 'matter of Rome' is still a unity, with a structure and life of its own. That part of it which the poem in hand is treating, which is, so to speak, in focus, must be seen fading gradually away into its 'historial' surroundings. The method is the antithesis of that which produces the 'framed' story of a modern writer: it is a method which romance largely took over from the epic.

II. Chaucer approached his work as a pupil of the rhetoricians and a firm believer in the good, old, and now neglected maxim of Dante: *quia omnis qui versificatur suos versus exornare debet in quantum potest.*[1] This side of Chaucer's poetry has been illustrated by Mr Manly* so well that most readers will not now be in danger of neglecting it. A detailed application of this new study to the *Book of Troilus* would here detain us too long, but a cursory glance shows that Chaucer found his original too short and proceeded in many places to 'amplify' it. He began by abandoning the device—that of invoking his lady instead of the Muses—whereby Boccaccio had given a lyrical instead of a rhetorical turn to the invocation, and substituted an address to Thesiphone (*Filostrato*, I, i–v; *cf. Troilus*, I, 1–14). He added at the beginning of his second book an invocation of Cleo and an apology of the usual medieval type, for the defects of his work (II, 15–21). Almost immediately afterwards he inserted a *descriptio* of the month of May (an innovation which concerned him as poet of courtly love no less than as rhetorician) which is extremely beautiful and appro-

---

* John Matthews Manly, 'Chaucer and the Rhetoricians', *The Proceedings of the British Academy*, vol. XII (1926), pp. 95–113.

[1] *De Vulgari Eloquentia*, II, i, 2 (17), in *Le Opere di Dante. Testo Critico della Società Dantesca Italiana*, ed. M. Barbi and others (Firenze, 1921), p. 337.

priate, but which follows, none the less, conventional lines. The season is fixed by astronomical references, and Proignè and Tereus appear just where we should expect them (II, 50–60, 64–70). In the third book the scene of the morning parting between the two lovers affords a complicated example of Chaucer's medievalization. In his original (III, xlii) Chaucer read

> Ma poich' e' galli presso al giorno udiro
> Cantar, per l'aurora che sorgea.

He proceeded to amplify this, first by the device of *circuitio* or *circumlocutio*; *galli*, with the aid of Alanus de Insulis, became 'the cok, comune astrologer'. Not content with this, he then repeated the sense of that whole phrase by the device *expolitio*, of which the formula is *Multiplice forma Dissimuletur idem; varius sis et tamen idem,** and the theme 'Dawn came' is varied with *Lucifer* and *Fortuna Major*, till it fills a whole stanza (III, 1415–21). In the next stanza of Boccaccio he found a short speech by Criseida, expressing her sorrow at the parting which dawn necessitated: but this was not enough for him. As poet of love he wanted his *alba*; as rhetorician he wanted his *apostropha*. He therefore inserted sixteen lines of address to Night (1427–42), during which he secured the additional advantage, from the medieval point of view, of 'som doctryne' (1429–32). In lines 1452–70 he inserted antiphonally Troilus's *alba*, for which the only basis in Boccaccio was the line *Il giorno che venia maledicendo* (III, xliv). The passage is an object lesson for those who tend to identify the traditional with the dull. Its matter goes back to the ancient sources of medieval love poetry, notably to Ovid, *Amores* I, 13, and it has been handled often before, and better handled, by the Provençals. Yet it is responsible for one of the most vivid and beautiful expressions that Chaucer ever used:

> A-cursed be thy coming in-to Troye,
> For every bore hath oon of thy bright yën!
> (III, 1452)

A detailed study of the *Book of Troilus* would reveal this 'rhetoricization', if I may coin an ugly word, as the common quality of many of Chaucer's additions. As examples of *apostropha* alone I may mention, before leaving this part of the subject, III, 301 *et seq.* (O tonge), 617

---

* Geoffroi de Vinsauf, *Poetr. Nov.*, 224–5.

et seq. (But O Fortune), 715 *et seq.* (O Venus), and 813 *et seq.* where Chaucer is following Boethius.

III. Chaucer approached his work as a poet of *doctryne* and *sentence*. This is a side of his literary character which twentieth-century fashions encourage us to overlook, but, of course, no honest historian can deny it. His contemporaries and immediate successors did not. His own creatures, the pilgrims, regarded *mirthe* and *doctryne,** or, as it is elsewhere expressed, *sentence* and *solas,*† as the two alternative, and equally welcome, excellences of a story. In the same spirit Hoccleve praises Chaucer as the 'mirour of fructuous entendement' and the universal 'fadir in science'‡—a passage, by the by, to be recommended to those who are astonished that the fifteenth century should imitate those elements of Chaucer's genius which it enjoyed instead of those which we enjoy. In respect of 'doctryne', then, Chaucer found his original deficient, and 'amended' it. The example which will leap to every one's mind is the Boethian discussion on free will (IV, 946–1078). To Boccaccio, I suspect, this would have seemed as much an excrescence as it does to the modern reader; to the unjaded appetites of Chaucer's audience mere thickness in a wad of manuscript was a merit. If the author was so 'courteous beyond covenant' as to give you an extra bit of 'doctryne' (or of story), who would be so churlish as to refuse it on the pedantic ground of irrelevance? But this passage is only one of many in which Chaucer departs from his original for the sake of giving his readers interesting general knowledge or philosophical doctrine. In III, 1387 *et seq.*, finding Boccaccio's attack upon *gli avari* a little bare and unsupported, he throws out, as a species of buttress, the *exempla* of Myda and Crassus.§ In the same book he has to deal with the second assignation of Troilus and Criseyde. Boccaccio gave him three stanzas of dialogue (*Filostrato*, III, lxvi–lxviii), but Chaucer rejected them and preferred—in curious anticipation of Falstaff's thesis about pitch—to assure his readers, on the authority of 'thise clerkes wyse' (III, 1691) that 'felicitee' is felicitous, though Troilus and Criseyde enjoyed something better than 'felicitee'. In the same stanza he also intends, I think, an allusion to the *sententia* that occurs elsewhere in the Franklin's Tale.‖ In IV,

---

* *Canterbury Tales*, B 2125. † *Ibid.*, A 798.
‡ *Regement of Princes*, 1963 *et seq.*
§ This might equally well have been treated above in our rhetorical section. The instructed reader will recognize that a final distinction between *doctrinal* and *rhetorical* aspects is not possible in the Middle Ages. ‖ *C.T.*, F 762.

197–203, immediately before his 'historial' insertion about Antenor, he introduces a *sentence* from Juvenal, partly for its own sake, partly in order that the story of Antenor may thus acquire an exemplary, as well as a 'historial' value. In IV, 323–28 he inserts a passage on the great *locus communis* of Fortune and her wheel.

In the light of this sententious bias, Chaucer's treatment of Pandarus should be reconsidered, and it is here that a somewhat subtle exercise of the historical imagination becomes necessary. On the one hand, he would be a dull reader, and the victim rather than the pupil of history, who would take all the doctrinal passages in Chaucer seriously: that the speeches of Chauntecleer and Pertelote and of the Wyf of Bath not only *are* funny by reason of their sententiousness and learning, but are intended to be funny, and funny by that reason, is indisputable. On the other hand, to assume that sententiousness became funny for Chaucer's readers as easily as it becomes funny for us, is to misunderstand the fourteenth century: such an assumption will lead us to the preposterous view that Melibee (or even the Parson's Tale) is a comic work—a view not much mended by Mr Mackail's suggestion that there are some jokes *too* funny to excite laughter and that Melibee is one of these. A clear recognition that our own age is quite abnormally sensitive to the funny side of sententiousness, to possible hypocrisy, and to dulness, is absolutely necessary for any one who wishes to understand the past. We must face the fact that Chaucer's audience could listen with gravity and interest to edifying matter which would set a modern audience sleeping or sniggering. The application of this to Pandarus is a delicate business. Every reader must interpret Pandarus for himself, and I can only put forward my own interpretation very tentatively. I believe that Pandarus is meant to be a comic character, but not, by many degrees, so broadly comic as he appears to some modern readers. There is, for me, no doubt that Chaucer intended us to smile when he made Troilus exclaim

> What knowe I of the quene Niobe?
> Lat be thyne olde ensaumples, I thee preye.
> (I, 759)

But I question if he intended just that sort of smile which we actually give him. For me the fun lies in the fact that poor Troilus says what I have been wishing to say for some time. For Chaucer's hearers the point was a little different. The suddenness of the gap thus revealed between Troilus's state of mind and Pandarus's words cast a faintly ludicrous air on what had gone before: it made the theorizing and the *exempla* a little funny in retrospect. But it is quite probable that they had not been funny till then: the discourse on contraries (I, 631–44), the *exemplum* of Paris and Oënone, leading up to the theme 'Physician heal thyself' (652–72), the doctrine of the Mean applied to secrecy in love (687–93), the *sentences* from Solomon (695) and elsewhere (708), are all of them the sort of thing that can be found in admittedly serious passages,* and it may well be that Chaucer 'had it both ways'. His readers were to be, first of all, edified by the doctrine for its own sake, and then (slightly) amused by the contrast between this edification and Troilus's obstinate attitude of the plain man. If this view be accepted it will have the consequence that Chaucer intended an effect of more subtility than that which we ordinarily receive. We get the broadly comic effect—a loquacious and unscrupulous old uncle talks solemn platitude at interminable length. For Chaucer, a *textuel* man talked excellent doctrine which we enjoy and by which we are edified: but at the same time we see that this 'has its funny side'. Ours is the crude joke of laughing at admitted rubbish: Chaucer's the much more lasting joke of laughing at 'the funny side' of that which, even while we laugh, we admire. To the present writer this reading of Pandarus does not appear doubtful; but it depends to some extent on a mere 'impression' about the quality of the Middle Ages, an impression hard to correct, if it is an error, and hard to teach, if it is a truth. For this reason I do not insist on my interpretation. If, however, it is accepted, many of the speeches of Pandarus which are commonly regarded as having a purely dramatic significance will have to be classed among the examples of Chaucer's doctrinal or sententious insertions.†

IV. Finally, Chaucer approached his work as the poet of courtly love. He not only modified his story so as to make it a more accurate representation in action of the orthodox erotic code, but he also went out of his way to emphasize its didactic element. Andreas Capellanus had given instructions to lovers; Guillaume de Lorris had given instructions veiled and decorated by allegory; Chaucer carries the

---

* *Cf. C.T.*, I 140–55.

† From another point of view Pandarus can be regarded as the *Vekke* of the *Romance of the Rose* (*cf.* Thessala in *Cligès*) taken out of allegory into drama and changed in sex, so as to 'double' the rôles of *Vekke* and *Frend*.

process a stage further and gives instruction by example in the course of a concrete story. But he does not forget the instructional side of his work. In the following paragraphs I shall sometimes quote parallels to Chaucer's innovations from the earlier love literature, but it must not be thought that I suppose my quotations to represent Chaucer's immediate source.

1. Boccaccio in his induction, after invoking his mistress instead of the Muses, inserts (I, vi) a short request for lovers in general that they will pray for him. The prayer itself is disposed of in a single line

> Per me vi prego ch' Amore preghiate.

This is a little more than a conceit, abandoned as soon as it is used: a modern poet could almost do the like. Chaucer devotes four stanzas (I, 22–49) to this prayer. If we make an abstract of both passages, Boccaccio will run 'Pray for me to Love,' while Chaucer will run 'Remember, all lovers, your old unhappiness, and pray, for the unsuccessful, that they may come to solace; for me, that I may be enabled to tell this story; for those in despair, that they may die; for the fortunate, that they may persevere, and please their ladies in such manner as may advance the glory of Love.' The important point here is not so much that Chaucer expands his original, as that he renders it more liturgical: his prayer, with its careful discriminations in intercession for the various recognised stages of the amorous life, and its final reference *ad Amoris majorem gloriam*, is a collect. Chaucer is emphasising that parody, or imitation, or rivalry—I know not which to call it—of the Christian religion which was inherent in traditional *Frauendienst*. The thing can be traced back to Ovid's purely ironical worship of Venus and Amor in the *De Arte Amatoria*. The idea of a love religion is taken up and worked out, though still with equal flippancy, in terms of medieval Christianity, by the twelfth-century poet of the *Concilium Romarici Montis*,* where Love is given Cardinals (female), the power of visitation, and the power of cursing. Andreas Capellanus carried the process a stage further and gave Love the power of distributing reward and punishment after death. But while his hell of cruel beauties (*Siccitas*), his purgatory of beauties promiscuously kind (*Humiditas*), and his heaven of true lovers (*Amoenitas*)† can hardly be other than playful, Andreas deals with the love religion

---

* *Zeitschrift für Deutsches Alterthum*, vii, pp. 160 *et seq.*
† Andreas Capellanus, *De Arte Honeste Amandi*, ed. Trojel (Copenhagen, 1892), i, 6 D² (pp. 91–108).

much more seriously than the author of the *Concilium*. The lover's qualification is *morum probitas*: he must be truthful and modest, a good Catholic, clean in his speech, hospitable, and ready to return good for evil. There is nothing *in saeculo bonum* which is not derived from love:* it may even be said, in virtue of its severe standard of constancy, to be 'a kind of chastity'—*reddit hominem castitatis quasi virtute decoratum.*†

In all this we are far removed from the tittering nuns and *clerici* of the *Concilium*. In Chrétien, the scene in which Lancelot kneels and adores the bed of Guinevere (as if before a *corseynt*)‡ is, I think, certainly intended to be read seriously: what mental reservations the poet himself had on the whole business is another question. In Dante the love religion has become wholly and unequivocally serious by fusing with the real religion: the distance between the *Amor deus omnium quotquot sunt amantium* of the *Concilium*, and the *signore di pauroso aspetto* of the *Vita Nuova*,§ is the measure of the tradition's real flexibility and universality. It is this quasi-religious element in the content, and this liturgical element in the diction, which Chaucer found lacking in his original at the very opening of the book, and which he supplied. The line

> That love hem bringe in hevene to solas
>
> (I, 31)

is particularly instructive.

2. In the Temple scene (Chaucer, I, 155–315. *Filostrato*, I, xix–xxxii) Chaucer found a stanza which it was very necessary to *reducen*. It was Boccaccio's twenty-third, in which Troilus, after indulging in his 'cooling card for lovers', mentions that he has himself been singed with that fire, and even hints that he has had his successes; but the pleasures were not worth the pains. The whole passage is a typical example of that Latin spirit which in all ages (except perhaps our own) has made Englishmen a little uncomfortable; the hero must be a lady-killer from the very beginning, or the audience will think him a milksop and a booby. To have abashed, however temporarily, these strutting Latinisms, is not least among the virtues of medieval *Frauendienst*: and for Chaucer as its poet, this stanza was emphatically one of those that 'would never do'. He drops it quietly out of its place, and thus brings the course of his story nearer to that of the

---

* *Ibid.*, i, 6 A (p. 28). † *Ibid.*, i, 4 (p. 10).
‡ *Lancelot*, 4670, 4734 *et seq.* § *Vita Nuova*, III.

Romance of the Rose. The parallelism is so far intact. Troilus, an unattached young member of the courtly world, wandering idly about the Temple, is smitten with Love. In the same way the Dreamer having been admitted by Ydelnesse into the garden goes 'Pleying along ful merily'* until he looks in the fatal well. If he had already met Love outside the garden the whole allegory would have to be reconstructed.

3. A few lines lower Chaucer found in his original the words

> il quale amor trafisse
> Più ch' alcun altro, pria del tempio uscisse.
>
> (I, xxv)

Amor trafisse in Boccaccio is hardly more than a literary variant for 'he fell in love': the allegory has shrunk into a metaphor and even that metaphor is almost unconscious and fossilized. Over such a passage one can imagine Chaucer exclaiming, *tantamne rem tam negligenter?* He at once goes back through the metaphor to the allegory that begot it, and gives us his own thirtieth stanza (I, 204–10) on the god of Love in anger bending his bow. The image is very ancient and goes back at least as far as Apollonius Rhodius.† Ovid was probably the intermediary who conveyed it to the Middle Ages. Chrétien uses it, with particular emphasis on Love as the avenger of contempt.‡ But Chaucer need not have gone further to find it than to the *Romance of the Rose*:§ with which, here again, he brings his story into line.

4. But even this was not enough. Boccaccio's *Amor trafisse* had occurred in a stanza where the author apostrophizes the *Cecità delle mondane menti*, and reflects on the familiar contrast between human expectations and the actual course of events. But this general contrast seemed weak to the poet of courtly love: what he wanted was the explicit erotic *moral*, based on the special contrast between the ὕβρις of the young scoffer and the complete surrender which the offended deity soon afterwards extracted from him. This conception, again, owes much to Ovid; but between Ovid and the Middle Ages comes the later practice of the ancient Epithalamium during the decline of antiquity and the Dark Ages: to which, as I hope to show elsewhere, the system of courtly love as a whole is heavily indebted. Thus in the fifth century Sidonius Apollinaris in an Epithalamium, makes the

---

* *Romance of the Rose*, 1329 (Chaucer's).
† *Argonautica*, III, 275 *et seq.*   ‡ *Cligès*, 460; *cf.* 770.
§ *Romance of the Rose*, 1330 *et seq.*; 1715 *et seq.*

bridegroom just such another as Troilus: a proud scoffer humbled by Love. Amor brings to Venus the triumphant news

> Nova gaudia porto
> Felicis praedae, genetrix. Calet ille *superbus*
> Ruricius.*

Venus replies

> gaudemus nate, *rebellem*
> *Quod vincis.*

In a much stranger poem, by the Bishop Ennodius, it is not the ὕβρις of a single youth, but of the world, that has stung the deities of love into retributive action. Cupid and Venus are introduced deploring the present state of Europe

> Frigida consumens multorum possidet artus
> Virginitas.†

and Venus meets the situation by a threat that she'll 'larn 'em':

> Discant populi tunc crescere diuam,
> Cum neglecta iacet.‡

They conclude by attacking one Maximus and thus bringing about the marriage which the poem was written to celebrate. Venantius Fortunatus, in his Epithalamium for Brunchild reproduces, together with Ennodius's spring morning, Ennodius's boastful Cupid, and makes the god, after an exhibition of his archery, announce to his mother, *mihi vincitur alter Achilles.*§ In Chrétien the rôle of tamed rebel is transferred to the woman. In *Cligès* Soredamors confesses that Love has humbled her pride by force, and doubts whether such extorted service will find favour.‖ In strict obedience to this tradition Chaucer inserts his lines 214–31, emphasising the dangers of ὕβρις against Love and the certainty of its ultimate failure; and we may be thankful that he did, since it gives us the lively and touching simile of *proude Bayard*. Then, mindful of his instructional purpose, he adds four stanzas more (239–66), in which he directly exhorts his readers to avoid the error of Troilus, and that for two reasons: firstly, because Love *cannot* be resisted (this is the policeman's argument—we may as well 'come quiet'); and secondly because Love is a thing 'so vertuous in kinde'. The second argument, of course, follows tradi-

---

* Sid. Apoll., *Carm.*, XI, 61. † Ennodius, *Carm.*, I, iv, 57.
‡ *Ibid.*, 84. § Venant. Fort., VI, i.
‖ *Cligès*, 682, 241.

tional lines, and recalls Andreas's theory of Love as the source of all secular virtue.

5. In lines 330–50 Chaucer again returns to Troilus's scoffing—a scoffing this time assumed as a disguise. I do not wish to press the possibility that Chaucer in this passage is attempting, in virtue of his instructional purpose, to stress the lover's virtue of secrecy more than he found it stressed in his original; for Boccaccio, probably for different reasons, does not leave that side of the subject untouched. But it is interesting to note a difference in the content between this scoffing and that of Boccaccio (*Filostrato*, I, xxi, xxii). Boccaccio's is based on contempt for women, fickle as wind, and heartless. Chaucer's is based on the hardships of love's *lay* or religion: hardships arising from the uncertainty of the most orthodox *observances*, which may lead to various kinds of harm and may be taken amiss by the lady. Boccaccio dethrones the deity: Chaucer complains of the severity of the cult. It is the difference between an atheist and a man who humorously insists that he 'is not of religioun'.

6. In the first dialogue between Troilus and Pandarus the difference between Chaucer and his original can best be shown by an abstract. Boccaccio (II, vi–xxviii) would run roughly as follows:

    T. Well, if you must know, I am in love. But don't ask me with whom (vi–viii).

    P. Why did you not tell me long ago? I could have helped you (ix).

    T. What use would *you* be? Your own suit never succeeded (ix).

    P. A man can often guide others better than himself (x).

    T. I can't tell you, because it is a relation of yours (xv).

    P. A fig for relations! Who is it? (xvi).

    T. (after a pause) Criseida (xx).

    P. Splendid! Love has fixed your heart in a good place. She is an admirable person. The only trouble is that she is rather *pie* (*onesta*): but I'll soon see to that (xxiii). Every woman is amorous at heart: they are only anxious to save their reputations (xxvii). I'll do all I can for you (xxviii).

Chaucer (I, 603–1008) would be more like this:

    T. Well, if you must know, I am in love. But don't ask me with whom (603–16).

    P. Why did you not tell me long ago? I could have helped you (617–20).

T. What use would *you* be? Your own suit never succeeded (621–3).

P. A man can often guide others better than himself, as we see from the analogy of the whetstone. Remember the doctrine of contraries, and what Oënone said. As regards secrecy, remember that all virtue is a mean between two extremes (624–700).

T. Do leave me alone (760).

P. If you die, how will she interpret it? Many lovers have served for twenty years without a single kiss. But should they despair? No, they should think it a guerdon even to serve (761–819).

T. (much moved by this argument, 820–6) What shall I do? Fortune is my foe (827–40).

P. Her wheel is always turning. Tell me who your mistress is. If it were my sister, you should have her (841–61).

T. (after a pause)—My sweet foe is Criseyde (870–5).

P. Splendid: Love has fixed your heart in a good place. This ought to gladden you, firstly, because to love such a lady is nothing but good: secondly, because if she has all these virtues, she must have Pity too. You are very fortunate that Love has treated you so well, considering your previous scorn of him. You must repent at once (874–935).

T. (kneeling) *Mea Culpa!* (936–8).

P. Good. All will now come right. Govern yourself properly: you know that a divided heart can have no grace. I have reasons for being hopeful. No man or woman was ever born who was not apt for love, either natural or celestial: and celestial love is not fitted to Criseyde's years. I will do all I can for you. Love converted you of his goodness. Now that you are converted, you will be as conspicuous among his saints as you formerly were among the sinners against him (939–1008).

In this passage it is safe to say that every single alteration by Chaucer is an alteration in the direction of medievalism. The Whetstone, Oënone, Fortune, and the like we have already discussed: the significance of the remaining innovations may now be briefly indicated. In Boccaccio the reason for Troilus's hesitation in giving the name is Criseida's relationship to Pandaro: and like a flash comes back Pandaro's startling answer. In Chaucer his hesitation is due to the courtly lover's certainty that 'she nil to noon swich wrecche as I be wonne' (777) and that 'ful hard were it to helpen in this cas' (836). Pandaro's original

> Se quella ch' ami fosse mia sorella
> A mio potere avrai tuo piacer d' ella
> (II, xvi)

is reproduced in the English, but by removing the words that provoked it in the Italian (*È tua parente*, xv) Chaucer makes it merely a general protestation of boundless friendship in love, instead of a cynical defiance of scruples already raised (Chaucer, 861). Boccaccio had delighted to bring the purities of family life and the profligacy of his young man about town into collision, and to show the triumph of the latter. Chaucer keeps all the time within the charmed circle of *Frauendienst* and allows no conflict but that of the lover's hopes and fears. Again, Boccaccio's Pandaro has no argument to use against Troilo's silence, but the argument 'I may help you.' Chaucer's Pandarus, on finding that this argument fails, proceeds to expound the code. The fear of dishonour in the lady's eyes, the duty of humble but not despairing service in the face of all discouragement, and the acceptance of this service as its own reward, form the substance of six stanzas in the English text (lines 768–819): at least, if we accept four lines very characteristically devoted to 'Ticius' and what 'bokes telle' of him. Even more remarkable is the difference between the behaviour of the two Pandars after the lady's name has been disclosed. Boccaccio's, cynical as ever, encourages Troilo by the reflection that female virtue is not really a serious obstacle: Chaucer's makes the virtue of the lady itself the ground for hope—arguing scholastically that the *genus* of virtue implies that *species* thereof which is *Pitee* (897–900). In what follows, Pandarus, while continuing to advise, becomes an adviser of a slightly different sort. He instructs Troilus not so much on his relationship to the Lady as on his relationship to Love. He endeavours to awaken in Troilus a devout sense of his previous sins against that deity (904–30) and is not satisfied without confession (931–8), briefly enumerates the commandments (953–9), and warns his penitent of the dangers of a divided heart.

In establishing such a case as mine, the author who transfers relentlessly to his article all the passages listed in his private notes can expect nothing but weariness from the reader. If I am criticized,

I am prepared to produce for my contention many more evidential passages of the same kind. I am prepared to show how many of the beauties introduced by Chaucer, such as the song of Antigone or the riding past of Troilus, are introduced to explain and mitigate and delay the surrender of the heroine, who showed in Boccaccio a facility condemned by the courtly code.* I am prepared to show how Chaucer never forgets his erotically didactic purpose; and how, anticipating criticism as a teacher of love, he guards himself by reminding us that

<blockquote>
for to winne love in sondry ages,
In sondry londes, sondry been usages.†
</blockquote>

(II, 27)

But the reader whose stomach is limited would be tired, and he who is interested may safely be left to follow the clue for himself. Only one point, and that a point of principle, remains to be treated in full. Do I, or do I not, lie open to the criticism of Professor Abercrombie's 'Liberty of Interpreting'?‡

The Professor *quem honoris causa nomino* urges us not to turn from the known effect which an ancient poem has upon us to speculation about the effect which the poet intended it to have. The application of this criticism which may be directed against me would run as follows: 'If Chaucer's *Troilus* actually produces on us an effect of greater realism and nature and freedom than its original, why should we assume that this effect was accidentally produced in the attempt to conform to an outworn convention?' If the charge is grounded, it is, to my mind, a very grave one. My reply is that such a charge begs the very question which I have most at heart in this paper, and but for which I should regard my analysis as the aimless burrowings of a thesis-monger. I would retort upon my imagined critic with another question. This poem is more lively and of deeper human appeal than its original. I grant it. This poem conforms more closely than its original to the system of courtly love. I claim to prove it. What then is the natural conclusion to draw? Surely, that courtly love itself, in spite of all its shabby origins and pedantic rules, is at bottom more

---

* A particularly instructive comparison could be drawn between the Chaucerian Criseyde's determination to yield, yet to seem to yield by force and deception, and Bialacoil's behaviour. *Romance of the Rose*, 12607–88: specially 12682, 12683.

† *Cf.* II, 1023 *et seq.*

‡ Lascelles Abercrombie, 'A Plea for the Liberty of Interpreting', *The Proceedings of the British Academy*, vol. XVI, Annual Shakespeare Lecture, 1930 (1930).

43

agreeable to those elements in human, or at least in European, nature, which last longest, than the cynical Latin gallantries of Boccaccio? The world of Chrétien, of Guillaume de Lorris, and of Chaucer, is nearer to the world universal, is less of a closed system, than the world of Ovid, of Congreve, of Anatole France.

This is doctrine little palatable to the age in which we live: and it carries with it another doctrine that may seem no less paradoxical—namely, that certain medieval things are more universal, in that sense more classical, can claim more confidently a *securus judicat*, than certain things of the Renaissance. To make Herod your villain is more human than to make Tamburlaine your hero. The politics of Machiavelli are provincial and temporary beside the doctrine of the *jus gentium*. The love-lore of Andreas, though a narrow stream, is a stream tending to the universal sea. Its waters move. For real stagnancy and isolation we must turn to the decorative lakes dug out far inland at such a mighty cost by Mr George Moore; to the more popular corporation swimming-baths of Dr Marie Stopes; or to the teeming marshlands of the late D. H. Lawrence, whose depth the wisest knows not and on whose bank the hart gives up his life rather than plunge in:

> Þaer maeg nihta gehwaem nið-wundor seon,
> Fyr on flode!

4

The Fifteenth-Century Heroic Line

It is a commonplace of literary history that English metre is bad from the age of Chaucer to the age of Surrey. At one time this was popularly attributed to the changing state of the language, and specially to the loss of that final -e on which the syllabic pattern of Chaucer's verse seems to depend. But this is an explanation which presupposes part of the phenomenon to be explained. If a man understands a metre he can fit it to the language he hears spoken in his own time: if he cannot do so, that means he does not understand it; just as, if a boy cannot repeat a geometrical proof when the master has changed the letters or turned the figure upside down, we know that he has not understood it. The master's change of the letters may, indeed, be described as the cause of the boy's failure in his lesson, but it is a cause that can become operative only on one condition—the boy's prior failure to understand the proof. In the same way, linguistic change can produce metrical chaos only on condition that the poets were already deaf to metre when the change overtook them. If they had clearly grasped a metrical Form they could have applied it unchanged to the changing Matter of language, as we, who understand the Form of Shakespeare's verse, do not, like Shakespeare, put *motion* where a trisyllable is required. If the explanation of fifteenth- and early sixteenth-century verse is to be found at all, it must not be sought in the history of the language.

We often speak carelessly as if 'metre' in general were bad in this period; but we are usually thinking only of the lines which we try to read as decasyllabics. The octosyllabics even of Lydgate are good enough; so are the carols and other lyrics, and so, in its way, is the loose ballad metre of *Gamelyn* and *Beryn*. Even in Wyatt the stumbling-blocks occur far more often in what seem to be decasyllabics than in his lyric metres. I say 'what seem to be decasyllabics' because that is precisely the point on which we must not begin by begging the question. In the following discussion I shall give the arbitrary name 'Fifteenth-Century Heroic' to the line which we find in *The Temple of Glas*, *The Pastime of Pleasure*, Barclay's *Eclogues*, Wyatt's *Complaint upon Love to Reason*, and, in general, all those poems which appear at first sight to attempt the decasyllabic line without success. The question I propose is whether the Fifteenth-Century Heroic is, in fact, an attempt at our decasyllable; and, if it is not, what else it may be.

At the outset we shall do well to remind ourselves that the modern decasyllable, as we have known it from Spenser to Bridges, is a very strange metre. In the first place it has an uneven number of beats, thus differing from the ancient hexameter, the *Kalevala* metre, and the old Germanic alliterative line. In the second place—and perhaps in consequence of this—it has no medial break, thus differing from the hexameter, the alliterative line, the Fourteener, and the Fourteener's ancestor, the line of *Ormulum*. This second characteristic is obscured by the unfortunate practice of calling any pause in a decasyllabic line its *caesura*, and thus suggesting that it is, like the ancient *caesura*, a metrical fact. It is nothing of the sort. It can occur anywhere the poet chooses and need not occur at all, and is therefore no part of the pattern, though it may be a very important part of the poet's handling of the pattern so as to move passion or delight. It is a rhetorical and syntactical fact, not a metrical fact. Hence Milton rightly tells us that 'musical delight' consists on the one hand 'in apt numbers' and, on the other, in 'the sense variously drawn out from one verse into another'[1]—that is, on the shifting relations between the metrical pattern (the 'numbers') and the rhetorical or syntactical units which are fitted into it. The very fact that the latter can be varied at will proves that they are not part of the pattern. To 'draw out variously' the true metrical *caesura* of the hexameter does not lead to 'musical delight'; it leads, or led, only to the birch—and rightly as far as metrical science is concerned.

Now the result of these two characteristics is that the decasyllabic line stands at a much farther remove than almost any other metre from the natural modes of rhythmical human behaviour, whether in song or dance or shout. One's feet trip it instinctively to a hexameter or an octosyllabic. The *Kalevala* metre, if not handled with great discretion, pounds in our ear like a heart-beat. A half-line of Anglo-Saxon verse, once metrically understood, can hardly be heard, even by the inner ear, as anything but what it is. But the decasyllable is no such thing. In all good metre, no doubt, there should be some degree of discrepancy, some room for play, between the pattern (the noise the words *pretend* to make) and the natural pronunciation: but the

---

[1] Note on 'The Verse' prefixed to *Paradise Lost*.

decasyllabic outstrips all others in the discrepancy it allows and even demands. The octosyllabic can do wonders in this direction by a skilful use of long words, but it cannot avoid many lines of the type 'The wynd was good, the Schip was yare',[1] in which the metrical pattern coincides exactly with the real, or with any imaginable, pronunciation. Compared with the decasyllable, which is all art and spirit, it remains mere nature. But the decasyllabic, even if it wishes, can hardly impose its rhythm in this way. Even 'The singing masons building roofs of gold'[2] hints a tiny difference between the ideal pattern and the real speech-rhythm—'building' counts for a shade more ideally than it does in natural reading. The ease with which our prose admits 'blank verse lines', and the difficulty which many find in detecting them, are further proofs of the same fact. Hence all poetry in this metre has to be read with what we may call 'double audition'.

Most of us have been so trained to this that we are now hardly conscious of it—though it is very significant that a generation is growing up which has already begun to lose the trick. We do not usually notice that the line 'While other animals unactive range' (*P.L.*, IV, 621) is pure *Beowulf* if we attend solely to the speech-rhythm; the first half being the C type with two disyllabic lifts, the second, type B. *While other animals* is, from this point of view, own brother to *se þe waeter-egesan* (*Beow.*, 1260), and *unactive range* to *be waepned-men* (1284). Still less do we notice the converse—how many admirable decasyllables we could dig out of *Beowulf* if we started with the assumption that it was a blundering attempt at our familiar modern line: as,

> Swaese gesiþas swa he selfa baed. (29)
> Gewat ða neosian syþðan niht becom. (115)
> In Caines cynne þone cwealm gewraec. (107)

But perhaps the truth can be put in its clearest light by an experiment. Read

> I have given no man of my fruit to eat,
> I trod the grapes, I have drunken the wine.
> Had you eaten and drunken and found it sweet,
> This wild new growth of the corn and vine;

and now read this:

> I comfort few and many I torment,
> Where one is spared a thousand more are spent;

---

[1] Gower, *Confessio Amantis*, v, 3299. [2] *Henry V*, I, ii, 198.

I have trodden many down beneath my feet,
I have given no man of my fruit to eat.

I conjecture that you have read the last line of my second example differently from the opening line of my first: yet as mere language, separated from the ideal pattern, they are identical. And this, let us notice in passing, is a strong and beautiful example of Aristotle's doctrine that the whole is 'naturally prior' to its parts.

The modern decasyllabic, then, is a metre which demands from those who are to write or read it a power of 'double audition' which must be the growth of long training and for which nothing in their previous poetical experience had prepared the Englishmen of Chaucer's time. If this is so, two questions arise: (1) Is it probable that Chaucer himself had caught the music of the modern decasyllabic and intended his countrymen to hear this music in his own verse? (2) Even if Chaucer did so intend, is it at all probable that they would have understood him? The first question I leave for the present unanswered.

To the second question only one consideration prevents me from answering 'No' at once. It may be urged that though the line of ten syllables was new in England it was old in France, and that French examples would have prepared the ears of Chaucer's educated audience to understand the music of the modern decasyllabic. This argument would be strong if the French ten-syllable line had, in fact, run to the same tune as our modern—that is, Spenserian—decasyllabic. But it does not. The French verse of Chaucer's immediate predecessors had parted company with stress-accent as a metrical element and was, in that respect, the same as French verse in the nineteenth century. A single line from Deschamps—

Angleterre, d'elle ce nom s'applique—[1]

should be enough to convince us. Here we have no 'drumming decasyllabon' but a mere ten syllables. If Chaucer was in fact introducing the tune of Spenser, Milton, and Tennyson, then he was introducing a new thing for which French poetry furnished only a hint, and to which French poetry would hardly at all have opened the ears of his contemporaries. Italian poetry would have helped them a great deal more: but we have not yet evidence that many of them knew it.

[1] 'Ballade adressée à Geoffroy Chaucer, en lui envoyant ses ouvrages', *Œuvres Complète de Eustache Deschamps*, vol. II, Société des Anciens Textes Français (Paris, 1880), line 15 (p. 139).

It seems to me, then, that we must answer the second question in the negative. If Chaucer meant his lines to be read as the modern scholar reads them, it is extremely likely that he was disappointed. Indeed, having begun his greatest poem with

> Whán that Áprille with his shóures sóte,

he was asking a good deal if he expected readers bred on the alliterative line, the octosyllabic, the *Horn* metre, and the metre of *Gamelyn*, to see at once that the poem was to go to the pattern of 'The singing masons building roofs of gold'.

Thus far we have argued *a priori*. It remains to be seen what Chaucer's successors actually did. In the interests of clarity I am going to give a purely static account of the Fifteenth-Century Heroic as I conceive it to be, neglecting for the present the history of its rise and its various modifications.

I believe that the modern reader can learn this metre most easily from William Allingham's 'The Fairies' (number 769 in the *Oxford Book of English Verse*).[1] This poem is printed in short lines which may equally well be treated as half-lines. I have never heard of any one who called it unmetrical or found a difficulty in reading it: but as soon as we attempt a metrical analysis we find ourselves in trouble. The first four lines,

> Up the airy mountain,
> Down the rushy glen,
> We daren't go a-hunting
> For fear of little men,

can be treated as lines of three stresses, the first two in falling, the last two in rising, rhythm. But the fifth ('Wee folk, good folk') can equally well be treated as two stresses. Yet we do not feel that the metre has changed either here or in such lines as 'High on the hill-top' and 'For seven years long'.[2] We may solve our problem in two ways. We can say that all the lines have three beats and explain away the apparent dimeters, pleading that the strong pause in 'Wee folk, good folk' compensates for a missing stress, that *years* carries a stress in 'For sév'n yeárs lóng', and *on* a phantasmal or theoretical stress in 'Hígh òn the híll-top'. On the other hand, we may say that all the lines have two full stresses and no more—the first syllable of *airy* being weaker than *up* or than the first syllable of *mountain*—but that

---

[1] Number 776 in the new, enlarged edition (1939).
[2] 'The Fairies', iii, 1; v, 2.

they admit a third half stress, like the D and E types in Anglo-Saxon verse. If we adopt the second explanation we may notice that the rhythm of *daedcene monn* is very close to that of 'Áll nìght awáke' and '(The) Óld Kìng síts'.[1] In the meantime, however, without awaiting a decision on the metrical problem, we have enjoyed the poem. We want a definition of what we have enjoyed that does not prejudge the ultimate metrical problem. I suggest the following: a long line divided by a sharp medial break into two half-lines, each half-line containing not less than two or more than three stresses, and most half-lines hovering between two and three stresses in a manner analogous to the Anglo-Saxon types D and E. When the scheme is thus stated in the abstract, we are at first tempted to say that something so vague as this cannot be called a metre at all: but against this I set the fact 'The Fairies' is felt to be metrical by every reader. Indeed its metre is not even an unfamiliar one. We heard something like it before we could read in 'Péase pudding hót' and 'Óld Mòther Slípper-Slapper'. We read something like it not many years since in Mr de la Mare's 'All That's Past'.* We find it in the famous carol—

> He cám àlso stýlle
> Þere his móder wás
> As déw in aprýlle,
> Þat fállyt òn þe grás.[2]

If such a metre is admitted, we may proceed to note that it must every now and then yield lines which can be read as decasyllables and which certainly will be read as such by any reader who starts with the assumption that the poem is attempting to be decasyllabic. Thus from 'The Fairies' we can get

> Some in the reeds óf the black mountain lake
> With frogs for their watch-dógs all night awake[3]

* Here the ideal norm seems to be *3* beats in the first half-line and *2* in the second ('Where snów sleeps cóld beneáth the ázure skíes'). But we also find in the first half-line only *2* beats ('Síng such a hístory') and *2½* ('Vèry óld are the wóods') and, in the second, what I take to be *3* ('Óh, nó man knóws'). It will be noticed that if we lineate the poem in whole lines these make rough decasyllabics, though the reader who treated them simply as such would be missing the real quality of the poem. *Cf.*, in the same poet, 'Song of the Mad Prince', 'Jim Jay', and 'Some One'.

[1] 'The Fairies', ii, 8; iii, 2.
[2] Entitled 'The Maiden Makeles' in *Religious Lyrics of the XVth Century*, ed. Carleton Brown (Oxford, 1939), lines 7–8 (p. 119).
[3] ii, 5.

and from the carol

> I syng of a myden þát is makëles . . .
> Moder and mayden was neuer non but che.[1]

It will also tend to produce lines that can be read as loose 'anapaestic' four-beats if we start with a misunderstanding. Thus in Allingham's poem,

> They stóle little Brídget for séven years lóng.[2]

If so read, poems in this metre will seem to consist of some deca-syllables, some 'anapaestic' four-beats, and some floundering lines that are neither one nor the other: but that is just what many of the 'bad' poems between Chaucer and Spenser sound like. Thus in the *Assembly of Gods* we can read as very stumbling decasyllables—

> His shéte from hís bodý down hé let fáll,
> And ón a rewde máner he salútyd áll the roút,
> Wíth a bóld voyse cárpyng wórdýs stoút.
> But he spáke all hólow ás hit hád be óon
> Had spóke in anóther wórld þat had wóo begóon.
>
> (437)

But the result is extremely ugly and the slurring of *rewde* in the second line is jaw-breaking. I think it more probable that the poet meant us to read,

> His shéte from his bódy
> Dówn he let fáll,
> And ón a rèwde máner
> He salútyd àll the róut,
> Wíth a bóld voÿse
> Cárpying wórdýs stoút.
> Bút he spáke all hólow,
> Ás hit hád be óon
> Had spóke in anóther wórld
> Þát had wóo begóon.

Even this may not seem very melodious to modern ears and *Wíth a bóld vòice* still gives trouble: but I believe it can be carried off by a reader who is thinking in terms of the nursery-rhyme metre which I am suggesting and who puts a strong accent on *with* and *bold*. The last four half-lines, in their new dress, seem to me good.

Applying the same treatment to Barclay's second *Egloge* (697 *et seq.*) we get

---

[1] 'The Maiden Makeles', *op. cit.*, lines 1, 9.   [2] 'The Fairies', v, 1.

> Then cáll for the priést
>   When Í refúse to drínke,
> This ále bréwĕd Béntly,
>   It máketh mè to wínke.
> Thou sáyest trúe Córnix,
>   Beléue me, bý the róod
> No hánd is so súre
>   That can álway make góod,
> But tálke of the coúrt
>   If thóu haste ány móre,
> Sét doẁne the bóttle,
>   Sàue some lícour in stóre.

Nothing will make Barclay a good poet; but I submit that such merits as this passage has will disappear if we give it back the usual lineation, and try to read it as decasyllabic verse. In the same way we can get a modicum of beauty out of Elyot's

> The blode becometh wanne, the eien firye bright,
> Like Gorgon the monstre appierynge in the nyght
>   (*Boke named the Gouernour*, II, vi)

by setting it to the country dance of

> The blode becómeth wánne,
>   The eíen fírye bríght,
> Like Górgon the mónstre
>   Appíerynge in the nýght.

And who would wish to stretch again on the bed of Procrustes these lines from Hawes?

> These daúnces trúely
>   Músyke hàth me toúght
> To lúte or daúnce,
>   But it auáyled noúght;
> For the fýre kyńdled
>   And wáxĕd móre and móre,
> The daúncynge bléwe it
>   With her beáute clére.
> My hért sékened
>   And begán wàxe sóre;
> A mýnute VI hoúres,
>   And VI hoúres a yére,
> I thoúght it wás,
>   So héuy wàs my chére.
> But yét fòr to cóuer
>   My gréte lòue arýght,

The oútwarde coúntĕnàuce
I máde glàdde and lýght.
(*Pastime of Pleasure*, 1595 *et seq.*)

A natural objection to my hypothesis may take the form of the question, 'Is there any verse, however decasyllabic, which could not, if we chose, be read as you want us to read Hawes and Barclay?' I must freely confess that there is very little decasyllabic verse which cannot be tortured into what I call the Fifteenth-Century Heroic. From the very nature of the decasyllable on the one hand and the Fifteenth-Century Heroic on the other, it must, on my view, follow that either metre will yield many lines which could occur in the other: indeed this fact is a necessary part of my case. But there remains a difference between lines which 'can, if we choose', be 'tortured' into the Fifteenth-Century Heroic and lines which can be read better and more naturally in that metre than in the decasyllabic. I think 'His shéte fròm his bodý · doẃn he let fáll' a true Fifteenth-Century Heroic not because it *can* be read thus but because this reading seems to me more natural, pleasing, and probable than 'His shéte from hís bodý down hé let fáll', and because the neighbouring line 'And on a rewde maner he salutyd all the rout' is quite intolerable as a decasyllabic. Conversely, I do not read Pope's line as 'A míghty máze! · but nót withoùt a plán',[1] though it would be possible to do so, because the alternative 'A míghty máze but nót withoút a plán' seems more probable and pleasing, and also because the neighbouring line 'Of all who blindly creep, or sightless soar'[2] is clearly a very good decasyllable and would be atrocious as

Of áll who blìndly créep,
Or síghtless soár.

Once again we meet Aristotle. The metre of a poem does not result from the metre of individual lines; it is the whole which determines the parts.

The distinction between what is best read according to my hypothesis and what can only be tortured into it must, of course, be applied to the late medieval poets whom we are now considering. I do not claim that all can be read as Fifteenth-Century Heroics. I find that *The Assembly of Gods* is my best example and that most of Hoccleve will not fit in at all. Such a line as 'No wight with me, in the, my sone, hath part'* would have to be 'murdered' if we tried to force it in.

---

* *Lamentation of the Green Tree*, 16.
[1] *An Essay on Man*, Ep. 1, 6. [2] *Ibid.*, 1, 12.

At this point no one will forget Hoccleve's own statement that he was the friend and pupil of Chaucer.* Have we here a real proof of this discipleship and, with it, a proof that Chaucer was writing true decasyllabics but that the tradition (for reasons I have suggested) was very soon lost?

My answer to this question is little more than a guess. There are lines in Chaucer which read much more naturally as Fifteenth-Century Heroics: 'Whan Zéphirus eék · with his swéte bréeth',† or 'Bút a góvernour · wýly and wýs'.‡ His licences at the middle of the line may not be incompatible with the true decasyllabic movement; but his habit of knocking off the initial unaccented syllable is so foreign to that movement that I question whether any decasyllabic poet from Surrey to the present day has dreamed of imitating it, though the corresponding licence in octosyllabics ('Towered cities please us then') is so common and natural that we hardly notice it. On the other hand, there are hundreds of lines in Chaucer that demand pure decasyllabic reading—'God woot no lussheburgyes payen ye',§ &c. And the pleasure which not a few generations have now had in Chaucer thus read is strong, though not conclusive, evidence that they have read him correctly.

Chaucer could not transport the rhythm of the French decasyllable directly into English, for that metre, being unaccentual, has no rhythm in the English sense. You cannot export snakes from Iceland.[1] Chaucer had run against this difficulty very early in his career when he was translating the *Roman de la Rose* and had sometimes adopted the desperate solution of writing English verses which have the right number of syllables and ignore accent. Such lines as

> With a thredë basting my slevis (104)
> And litel coude of norture (179)
> Upon any worthy man falle (255)

---

* *Regement of Princes*, 1960, 2077.
† *C.T.*, A 5.   ‡ *C.T.*, B 3130.
§ *C.T.*, B 3152.
[1] Iceland or *Ireland?* I am inclined to think Lewis meant the latter, referring to the well-known fact that there are no snakes in Ireland as they traditionally were driven out by St Patrick. On the other hand, Lewis was knowledgeable of Icelandic sagas and history and would have known that there are no snakes in Iceland either. Although we might think that Ireland would add more force to his statement, it is not certain that he thought so. I have examined Lewis's copy of *Essays and Studies* in which this essay first appeared: he made several corrections in it, but he did not change Iceland to Ireland.

would seem metrical to a Frenchman: to us they are not verse at all. When, in his maturity, he began to naturalize the ten-syllabled line he did not repeat this blunder. What exactly he did I doubt if we shall ever know; but it seems likely to me that he attempted a compromise. On the one hand, he followed the French in having (usually) ten syllables in a line, and sometimes he had five full stresses, thus attaining the modern decasyllabic tune. But the other tune—that which I have attempted to describe—was running in his head and he allowed it to intrude; he even welcomed it by having many strong medial pauses, by admitting hypermetrical syllables at the pause, and, above all, by sometimes dropping the unaccented first syllable of the whole line and thus forcing the first half-line into a more native rhythm. Such compromise was possible because, as all my examples show, the one metre slips easily into the other. I suspect that his verse was a precarious balance of different metrical forces. He himself knew how to read it aloud; but perhaps, even from the first, few others could read it exactly as he wished. Hoccleve and some of the poets of the *Chauceriana* may have learned the art, but in Lydgate the strong medial pause and the essentially undecasyllabic movement ('Írows and wóod ànd maléncolík') are already normal, and the fact that we usually have nine or ten syllables makes little difference.* In the poets who follow, down to, and partly including, Wyatt, the number of syllables ceases to matter and the rough metre which I call the Fifteenth-Century Heroic is established.

A glance at the earlier history of English verse will perhaps render my theory more acceptable. The starting-point of that history, and the key to some of its mysteries, is the alliterative metre of *Beowulf* and Pseudo-Caedmon. This consists of two sharply divided half-lines, of which each has normally two stresses. But what are called the D and E types of half-line show an all-important variation; they have two and a half—two full stresses and one medium stress. From the decay of the alliterative metre the metre of Laȝamon's *Brut* is engen-

---

* Lydgate's often-quoted admission that he took no heed 'nouther of shorte nor longe' is quite irrelevant to any discussion of his metre. To neglect 'short and long' in English verse either means nothing or means 'to make no distinction between accented and unaccented syllables'. If this were what Lydgate had done, we should find his verse either merely syllabic (like the lines quoted above from Chaucer's *Romaunt of the Rose*) or else tending to force metrical accents on to weak syllables. In fact, however, we find him comparatively heedless of the number of syllables and generally attentive to stress. His statement about 'shorte and longe' is therefore merely a piece of conventional medieval self-depreciation and throws no light whatsoever on his practice.

dered. In the *Brut* the type with two stresses ('Hórs and Héngest') is retained, and so, unless my ear plays me false, is a type with two and a half ('And Haéngest swíðe faeíre');[1] but we also find—and doubtless as a development of the old two and a half—a type with three full stresses—'Þá queð Héngest to þan kínge'.[2] The total result is that the formula for Laȝamon's metre is 'Two, *or* two-and-a-half, *or* three'.

Two different developments then follow. In *King Horn*, on the one hand, we find the type with three stresses erected into the norm, though lines that seem to have only two are still occasionally permitted ('Þe héued of wénte',[3] 'Réynild mi dóȝter'[4]). But in 'On God Ureisun' liberty is still allowed between two and three. Thus we can have two stresses in the first half and two in the second:

Pléieð and swéieð · and síngeð bitwéonen.[5]

Or three in the first, and two in the second:

Crístes mílde móder · séynte Maríe.[6]

Or three in both:

Mi líf and mí tohópe · min héale míd iwísse.[7]

Traces of similar variability can be found in the Middle English *Bestiary* and in the *Proverbs of Alfred*; and it has never been denied that in the later developments of the alliterative metre itself, in *Gawain and the Green Knight* for example, three-stressed and two-stressed types occur side by side in the first half of the line. If this background to Chaucer's metrical activities be remembered, and if it be also remembered that the French decasyllabic, being unaccented, was no metre at all to English ears, the hypothesis which I advance about the true nature of his verse will not be judged very improbable. Nor is it unlikely, if such a native rhythm were allowed a footing in Chaucer, that in his successors it would rebel, and rebel successfully, against its foreign and syllabic master, thus giving the Fifteenth-Century Heroic.

---

[1] Laȝamon, *Brut*, ed. Frederic Madden (3 vols. London, 1847), line 14061 (of MS Cotton Caligula A ix).

[2] *Ibid.*, 14077.

[3] *King Horn*, ed. Joseph Hall (Oxford, 1901), line 610 (of MS Gg. 4.27.2).

[4] *Ibid.*, 903.

[5] 'On God Ureisun of Ure Lefdi' in *Old English Homilies and Homiletic Treatises*, ed. Richard Morris, vols. xxix–xxxiv, first series, Early English Text Society (Oxford, 1868), line 28 (p. 193).

[6] *Ibid.*, line 1 (p. 191). [7] *Ibid.*, line 6 (p. 191).

When this also begins to decline, the Elizabethans, attending to one only of its many variations, try to read it as the rough four-beat line which Gascoigne apparently attributes to Chaucer and which Spenser uses in his February eclogue. To that tune Chaucer was read for centuries, and to such reading, perhaps, we owe the heavy over-emphasis which the older critics laid on his comic elements, since these best survived such treatment. Then came the beginnings of modern scholarship and the discovery of final -e. Critics whose ears had been trained on the Greek iambic and the modern decasyllable then learned to read the verse of Chaucer as if it were that of Milton or Pope. What could not be so read was quarantined as 'licence' or emended, and the metre of Chaucer's successors was dismissed as a blundering attempt at pure decasyllabics. But all this time the rhythm of the Fifteenth-Century Heroic had continued a humble existence in popular lyric and nursery rhyme: it had, perhaps, contributed in some degree to our choice of the Italian decasyllable as our principal metre; it had started from hiding to delight even learned readers in *The Shepherds Sirena*; and it survived to produce a few poems 'choice and light' in modern times. It is this survival which has now enabled us—if my theory is true—to recover the metrical history of the later Middle Ages in England.

5

Hero and Leander

Chapman's four books or sestiads on Hero and Leander are, I believe, very seldom read in conjunction with Marlowe's two. The whole temper of modern criticism, which loves to treat a work of art as the expression of an artist's personality and perhaps values that personality chiefly for its difference from others, is unfavourable to a poem by two authors.[1] It comes naturally to us to treat the total *Hero and Leander* as two separate works. Nor, of course, is there any reason why we should not do so. There are some composite works—for example, the *Romance of the Rose*—which are best dealt with in this way. But there are others such as our composite English *Morte Darthur*, where earlier English work and French work and Malory and Caxton so subtly grow together into 'something of great constancy' that the modern approach is baffled. I am not claiming that *Hero and Leander* is in that class. We know quite well which parts are by which poet, their styles are clearly distinct, there is no 'contamination' (in the textual sense), and pseudo-Musaeus is so far in the background that we can ignore him. Yet I think we shall be richly rewarded if we obey the apparent invitation of the old editions and read the poem, at least sometimes, as a whole. For here, as I shall try to persuade you, collaboration has produced an extremely fortunate result. Each poet has contributed what the other could not have done, and both contributions are necessary to a worthy telling of the story. For the difference in style and outlook here corresponds to the two movements of which that story consists. If we feel young while we read the first two sestiads and feel in the remaining four that youth has died away, our experience is very like Hero's. If Venus dominates Marlowe's narrative and Saturn that of Chapman, the same may be said of the

---

[1] In his essay on 'The Personal Heresy in Criticism' (*Essays and Studies*, vol. XIX (1934), pp. 7–28) Lewis attacked the belief that poetry is, or should be, the expression of the poet's personality. His attempt to supplant this 'personal heresy' with an objective or impersonal theory of poetry was challenged by E. M. W. Tillyard whose interpretation of *Paradise Lost* Lewis had questioned. So began an interesting series of exchanges between Lewis and Tillyard which were published as *The Personal Heresy: A Controversy* (Oxford, 1939) and are now reprinted in Oxford Paperbacks (1965).

events which each narrates. It is almost, as it ought to be, like passing
from a Song of Innocence to a Song of Experience.

Of course, when we speak of 'innocence' in connexion with the
first two sestiads we are using the word 'innocence' in a very peculiar
sense. We mean not the absence of guilt but the absence of sophistication, the splendour, though a guilty splendour, of unshattered
illusions. Marlowe's part of the poem is the most shameless celebration
of sensuality which we can find in English literature—unless we
extend the category of literature to include such works as the book-
sellers call 'curious'. It does not even keep within the bounds of what
might be called, either in the older or the modern sense, a 'kindly'
sensuality. It exults to see

> the gods in sundrie shapes,
> Committing headdie ryots, incest, rapes   (I, 143),

and the loves of Neptune in Sestiad II are what Saintsbury called
'Greek style'. The point need not be laboured. A critical tradition
which can stomach the different, but far worse, depravities of *Tamber-
laine*, can well put up with *Hero and Leander*. The question which
Marlowe's sestiads invite is not a moral one. They make us anxious
to discover, if we can, how Marlowe can write over eight hundred
lines of almost unrelieved sensuality without ever becoming mawkish,
ridiculous, or disgusting. For I do not believe this is at all easy
to do.

Marlowe's success is most easily seen if we compare him with other
sixteenth-century specimens of the erotic epyllion. Lodge's *Scillaes
Metamorphosis* is hardly good enough: despite its frequent beauties it
is too static and too lacrimose. Drayton's *Endimion and Phoebe* suffers
from discordant aims and even discordant styles. We shall have to
come to *Venus and Adonis*. And I must frankly confess that, in so far
as the two works are comparable at all, Marlowe seems to me far
superior to Shakespeare in this kind. *Venus and Adonis* reads well in
quotation, but I have never read it through without feeling that I am
being suffocated. I cannot forgive Shakespeare for telling us how
Venus perspired (175), how 'soft and plump'[1] she was, how moist
her hand,[2] how Adonis pants in her face,[3] and so forth. I cannot
conceive why he made her not only so emphatically older but even so
much larger than the unfortunate young man. She is so large that

---

[1] *Venus and Adonis*, 142.   [2] *Ibid.*, 143.   [3] *Ibid.*, 62.

she can throw the horse's rein over one arm and tuck the 'tender boy' under the other.[1] She 'governs him in strength'[2] and knows her own business so badly that she threatens, almost in her first words, to 'smother' him with kisses. The word 'smother', combined with these images of female bulk and strength, is fatal: I am irresistibly reminded of some unfortunate child's efforts to escape the voluminous embraces of an effusive female relative. It is, of course, true that there are touches of reality in Shakespeare's poem which cannot be paralleled in Marlowe's. But I am not sure that reality (in the sense of naturalism) is what a poem of this type demands: at any rate, naturalism such as Shakespeare gives. Shakespeare shows us far too much of Venus' passion as it would appear to a third party, a spectator—embarrassed, disgusted, and even horrified as any spectator of such a scene would necessarily be. No doubt this unwelcome effect comes in because Shakespeare is, in general, a far profounder and more human poet than Marlowe. His very greatness prevents his succeeding in the narrow and specialized world of erotic epyllion. But it suits Marlowe exactly. He does not see beyond the erotic frenzy, but writes from within it. And that, curiously enough, is his poetic salvation.

In reading *Venus and Adonis* we see lust: in reading Marlowe's sestiads we see not lust but what lust thinks it sees. We do not look at the passion itself: we look out from it upon a world transformed by the hard, brittle splendour of erotic vision. Hence all that sickly weight and warmth which makes unrestrained appetite in the real world so unpleasant to the spectator or even, perhaps, in retrospect to the principals themselves, does not appear at all. Instead of Shakespeare's sweating palms and poutings and pantings and duckings and 'lustful language broken'[3] and 'impatience' that 'chokes the pleading tongue'[4] we have a gigantic insolence of hyperbole. The real world, which Shakespeare cannot quite forget, is by Marlowe smashed into bits, and he makes glory out of the ruin. Hero has been offered Apollo's throne. The brightness of her neck makes a collar of pebbles shine like diamonds by reflection. The sun will not burn her hands. The ladies of Sestos, walking in procession, make the street a 'firmament of breathing stars'.[5] In that world there are boys so

---

[1] *Venus and Adonis*, 31.   [2] *Ibid.*, 42.
[3] *Ibid.*, 47.   [4] *Ibid.*, 217.
[5] *Hero and Leander: Begun by Christopher Marlowe; and finished by George Chapman*, I, 97–8.

beautiful that they can never drink in safety from a fountain: the water nymphs would pull them in.

If you compare these hyperboles with one of Shakespeare's you will easily see the difference. His Venus promises Adonis that her hand will 'dissolve or seem to melt' in his.[1] That, of course, is hyperbolical, but it is in touch with fact—with the fact that hands may be hot, moist, and soft. But Marlowe's hyperboles are so towering that they become mythopoeic. They have, none the less, their own wild consistency and co-operate in building up such a world as passion momentarily creates, a topsy-turvy world where beauty is omnipotent and the very laws of nature are her willing captives. This mythopoeic quality is reinforced by Marlowe's use of what may be called the aetiological conceit, as in his passage about Mercury and the fates at the end of I, or his explanation why 'Since *Heroes* time hath halfe the world beene blacke'.[2] Though the whole two sestiads celebrate the flesh, flesh itself, undisguised, rarely appears in them for long. Leander's beauty is presented half mythically: he is a prize like the golden fleece, his body is as 'straight as *Circes* wand',[3] and the description of him shines with the names of *Nectar, Pelops, Jove*, and the cold *Cinthia*.

With this style there go two other characteristics. One, of course, is the metre—a ringing and often end-stopped couplet, compared with which the stanza of *Venus and Adonis* is unprogressive and the enjambed couplets of *Endymion* invertebrate. I suspect that the masculine quality of the verse, in fruitful tension with the luxury of the matter, plays an important part in making so much pure honey acceptable: it is a beautiful example of Wordsworth's theory of metre. The other is the total absence of tenderness. You must not look in Marlowe for what Dryden called 'the softnesses of love'. You must, indeed, look for love itself only in the narrowest sense. Love here is not 'ful of pittie'[4] but 'deaffe and cruell':[5] his temple is a blaze of grotesques. Leander woos like 'a bold sharpe Sophister'.[6] The male and immortal lover who first tries to ravish him, ends by trying to kill him. Hero is compared to diamonds, and the whole work has something of their hardness and brightness. Marlowe sings a love utterly separated from kindness, *cameraderie*, or friendship. If female

---

[1] *Venus and Adonis*, 144.
[2] *Hero and Leander*, I, 50.
[3] *Ibid.*, I, 61.
[4] *Ibid.*, II, 287.
[5] *Ibid.*, II, 288.
[6] *Ibid.*, I, 197.

spiders, whose grooms (I am told) do 'coldly furnish forth the marriage tables', wrote love-poetry, it would be like Marlowe's. But, however shocking, this treatment is an artistic success. We know from some terrible scenes in Keats's *Endymion* how dangerous it is to attempt the mixture of tenderness and sensuality in verse. Licentious poetry, if it is to remain endurable, must generally be heartless: as it is in Ovid, in Byron, in Marlowe himself. If it attempts pathos or sweetness an abyss opens at the poet's feet. Marlowe never comes near that abyss. His poem, though far from morally pure, has purity of another sort—purity of form and colour and intention. We may feel, as we come to the end of the Second Sestiad, that we have been mad, but we do not feel that we have been choked or contaminated. And yet I believe that the final impression left on an adult's mind is not one of madness or even of splendour, but, oddly enough, of pathos. If we had caught Marlowe striving after that effect in such a poem we should perhaps have turned from him with contempt. But it is not so. What moves us is simply our knowledge that this passionate splendour, so insolent, so defiant, and so 'unconscious of mortality', is 'desperately mortal'.

That it was doomed, for Hero and Leander, to end in misery Marlowe of course knew well. He wrote only the first movement of the story, the ascending movement; how he would have handled the descent we do not know. If he was to do it successfully, he would have had to use powers not found in the first two sestiads: would have had to 'change his notes to tragic'. The necessity of this change, even had he lived, renders tolerable the still greater change, the change to another author, which now meets us at the beginning of the Third Sestiad. If ever one poet were to 'take over' from another, no happier juncture could be found. At the very moment when the theme begins to demand a graver voice, a graver voice succeeds.

In his Dedicatory Epistle Chapman describes himself as drawn 'by strange instigation' to continue Marlowe's work. From a line in the Third Sestiad (195), when he describes himself as 'tendering' Marlowe's 'late desires', some conclude that Marlowe had asked Chapman to finish the poem. But it is not at all clear why this should be called 'strange instigation'. Perhaps Chapman poetically feigned, or (quite as probable) actually believed, that he had been strangely instigated by Marlowe since Marlowe's death. I am certainly inclined to think that when, in the same passage, he sends his own genius

('thou most strangely-intellectuall fire') to 'confer' with Marlowe's
'free soule' in the 'eternall Clime', he is speaking seriously: believing,
like Scaliger and others, that a man's *genius* is a personal, immortal
creature, distinct from himself. But the question is not of great
importance. The poetic impulse which moved Chapman to write is
quite clear from his own sestiads as a whole, and especially from the
opening lines of the Third. And it was essentially an impulse to
continue, to finish. We cannot doubt that he had entered into
Marlowe's erotic poetry with the fullest (temporary) sympathy. But,
to his graver mind, it cried out for its sequel. As he says

> Joy grauen in sence, like snow in water wasts.
>   (III, 35)

It had fallen to Marlowe to tell of joy graven in sense, it fell to him
to tell of the wasting. Love, or such love as Hero's and Leander's, is
in Chapman's eyes 'a golden bubble full of dreames' (III, 231): he
will show how it burst.

I do not think we should regard this as a 'cauld clatter of morality'
officiously and unpoetically added to a poem which does not require
it. There are several reasons against doing so. The most obvious is
the fact, already mentioned, that the myth itself already contained a
tragic ending. The second is that the picture of headlong love presented
by Marlowe demands some nemesis poetically no less than morally.
Every man who sees a bubble swell, will watch it, if he can, till it
bursts. A story cannot properly end with the two chief characters
dancing on the edge of a cliff: it must go on to tell us either how, by
some miracle, they were preserved, or how, far more probably, they
fell over. I do not mean that Chapman would have put it to himself
quite like that. Conceiving poetry as a kind of philosophy, he would
have been content with a purely ethical justification for his sestiads. I
mean that even if we banish, as he would not have banished, all moral
considerations, our aesthetic interests would still demand a second,
downward, movement. Finally, we must remind ourselves that the
particular moral content which Chapman put into his part of the
poem was not nearly so platitudinous for him as it would have been
for a nineteenth-century poet.

Chapman's sestiads are a celebration of marriage in contrast to,
and condemnation of, the lawless love between Hero and Leander.
We are in danger of taking this as a thing of course. It was not so in

Chapman's day. When writers like Lyly and Greene fall into a fit of moralizing they are quite likely not to make a distinction between lawless and wedded love, but to attack love and women altogether in the old ascetic, misogynistic manner which goes back to St Jerome. When Sidney's heroes struggle against love they too are concerned less with the distinction between lawful and unlawful than with the baseness or unmanliness of the passion itself as something contrary to the heroic ideal. In taking the line he does, which is the same as Spenser's, Chapman is therefore doing something not without importance. It may have given him more trouble than it gave Spenser, for there are passages in his plays which suggest that the old conceptions of courtly love still come to life in his mind. His part of *Hero and Leander* is to be taken as the product of serious thought.

It is especially to be noted that his doctrine is no facile warning against enchantments which he could not feel. This is one of those things which a poet can show only by the actual quality of his writing, and Chapman does so. Time and again he writes lines of an extravagant sweetness which Marlowe could not surpass. As this:

> Musick vsherd th'odorous way,
> And wanton Ayre in twentie sweet forms danst
> After her fingers.   (v, 42)

Or when the Athenian maidens have been carried off by robbers and, at the same hour the stars are coming out,

> the yellow issue of the skie
> Came trouping forth, ielous of crueltie
> To their bright fellowes of this vnder heauen.
>   (v, 171)

When Hymen hands the lily to Eucharis,

> As two cleere Tapers mix in one their light,
> So did the Lillie and the hand their white.
>   (v, 221)

A girl's skin is 'softer than soundest sleep'.[1] Leander, dripping from his swim, runs to his sister 'singing like a shower',[2] and as the white foam drops off him

> all the sweetned shore as he did goe,
> Was crownd with odrous roses white as snow.
>   (iii, 81)

---

[1] *Hero and Leander*, iii, 39.   [2] *Ibid.*, iii, 74.

I am not saying that the quality in all these is exactly like Marlowe's. Chapman has his own slower movement and his own type of conceit; he is nearer than Marlowe to the metaphysical manner. But they are not less rapturous and exalted than Marlowe's. If Chapman does not permanently abandon himself to 'golden bubbles', it is not because he could not. He knows what he rejects.

This rejection is not in any way that I can discover based on Christian grounds. And this is not to be explained by the fact that the story is Pagan and involves the Pagan deities. That would have presented no difficulties to a medieval or Elizabethan poet if he had wished to christianize it. The gods and goddesses could always be used in a Christian sense, as they are in *Comus* or in *Reason and Sensuality*. If Chapman had wished to theologize, chastity embodied in Diana or divine reason in Minerva would have descended to rebuke Leander. The figure who actually appears to him is someone quite different—the goddess Ceremonie. To a modern Englishman, I suspect, no abstraction will seem less qualified for personification and apotheosis. We do not—at least that class of Englishmen who study literature do not—perform ceremonies gracefully, nor attend them with much enthusiasm, and we doubt whether any ceremony can modify the nature of the act which it accompanies. The Elizabethan sentiment was very different. About ceremonies in the Church there might be some dispute: but even there the Puritans objected to them not so much because they desired a pure, individual inwardness as because they thought that a Divine positive law excluded certain ceremonies. In secular life ceremony reigned undisputed. The chroniclers describe ceremonies at length as if they were equal in importance to the gravest political events. And so perhaps they were. Pageant, masque, tournament, and emblem book taught men to expect a visible and formalized expression of every rank, emotion, attitude, and maxim. One quarrelled, loved, dined, and even played by ceremonial rule. The Ciceronian in Latin and the Euphuist in English made prose a ceremony. The universe itself with its noble and base metals, its sublunary and translunary regions, and the nicely graded hierarchy of planetary intelligences, was a vast ceremony proceeding in all space and all time. It is in ceremony that Shakespeare's 'Degree' and Spenser's 'Concord' are manifested.[1]

[1] On iconography in Spenser, see the Introduction to Lewis's book *Spenser's Images of Life*, ed. Alastair Fowler (Cambridge, 1967).

Chapman condemns the loves of Hero and Leander not because the pair were ill matched, nor because they lacked the consent of parents, nor because he admires virginity, nor by the Christian law, but only because, being hasty and not waiting for marriage, they had defied *Time* and *Ceremonie*. *Time* must, of course, here be understood as meaning 'the right time', 'timeliness', the Latin *opportunitas*: it is very close to Elyot's virtue of *maturitie* (*Boke named the Gouernour*, I, xxii), and its connexion with Ceremonie becomes plainer if we remember that it is one of the virtues which, in Elyot's scheme, we learn from dancing. Chapman takes great pains to make us understand his point of view. Ceremonie, for him, is what distinguishes a fully human action from an action merely necessary or natural. As he says, no praise goes to the food which 'simply kils our hunger'[1] or the dress that 'clothes but our nakednes'.[2] We reserve praise for 'Beautious apparell and delicious cheere'.[3] Thus unexpectedly the goddess Ceremonie, who forbids lawless *luxuria*, is from another point of view almost the patroness of luxury—the ordered, humane luxury of evening dress, and choice wines, and good cookery. The embraces of Hero and Leander were, after all, only a coarse meal snatched by ravenous hunger 'with ranke desire' (III, 49). Here, as everywhere else, it is the humanised and 'orderd' procedure that 'still giues pleasure freenes to aspire'[4] and

> Vpholds the flowrie bodie of the earth
> In sacred harmonie.   (III, 61)

The whole 'bench of Deities'[5] (the planets) hang in the hair of this goddess. Devotion, Order, State, Reuerence, Societie, and Memorie, are her shadows. Chapman sees her as our defence against utter ruin and brutality: as Shakespeare sees Degree. And, as in the *Dunciad* the enemies are always creeping on, so here we see Confusion, and (close on her heels)

> *Barbarisme*, and *Auarice*,
> That followd eating earth, and excrement
> And humane lims.   (III, 138)

We are told that they would soon storm the palace of the gods 'were *Ceremonie* slaine'.[6] It is tempting to say that Ceremonie is simply Chapman's name for civilization. But that word has long been

---

[1] *Hero and Leander*, III, 50.   [2] *Ibid.*, III, 51.   [3] *Ibid.*, III, 54.
[4] *Ibid.*, III, 56.   [5] *Ibid.*, III, 115.   [6] *Ibid.*, III, 141.

prostituted, and if we are to use it we must do so with a continual reminder that we mean not town-planning, and plumbing and ready-cooked foods but etiquette, ball-rooms, dinner-parties, judges' robes and wigs, Covent Garden, and coronations in Westminster Abbey. In a word, we must realize that what we should regard as the externals of civilization are, for Chapman, essential and vital. The simplest way of doing this is not to use the word *civilization* at all but to retain his own word *ceremonie*, remembering what he meant by it.

It is early in the Third Sestiad that Ceremonie appears to Leander. The remainder of that sestiad and the whole of the next are concerned with Hero's remorse and deterioration—a passage to which I must presently return. Up to the end of the Fourth, Chapman is occupied with his negative theme, the condemnation of lawless, unceremonial, love. In the Fifth we have the positive side, the celebration of the lawful and ceremonial alternative, marriage. The contrast is pointed for us first by the fact that Hero (who has now resolved on a life of consistent hypocrisy) exercises her priestly function by marrying two young lovers and afterwards attending their marriage feast. To this feast, apparently unbidden, there comes a very curious person. She is called a nymph but has rather the characteristics of a sixteenth-century English fairy. She is a 'little Siluane',[1] known as Apollo's 'Dwarfe', a haunter of 'greene *Sestyan* groues',[2] a prophetess. Her name is Teras: that is *monstrum*, portent, prodigy. From that point of view she continues, in a personified form, the sinister omens which have harassed Hero in the preceding sestiad; and her function at the banquet is fulfilled when she left the company and

> the turning of her back
> Made them all shrieke, it lookt so ghastly black.
>
> (v, 489)

Seen from the front she had been beautiful: in other words, the one omen that had appeared to be good turns out to be bad, and Hero's fate is sealed. But between her pleasing entry and her terrifying exit she has exercised another function. Perched on an altar she has entertained the marriage party with the tale of another marriage, which marriage in its turn (this sestiad is constructed like a Chinese nest of boxes) was between Marriage himself, Hymen, and Eucharis, was in fact the archetypal marriage. Much of it is concerned with

---

[1] *Ibid.*, v, 77.   [2] *Ibid.*, v, 63.

mystical explanations of Pagan marriage ceremonies: a sort of learning dear to the Elizabethans. The only thing in it which calls for comment is the part played by the girl Adolesche—Garrulity, or Chatterbox, who had a face

> Thin like an iron wedge, so sharpe and tart,
> As twere of purpose made to cleaue *Loues* hart.
>
> (v, 299)

This unpleasant young woman hurried off to Athens to spread the news of the love between Hymen and Eucharis, but arrived just as their marriage feast was ending and found no market for her scandal. She sank beneath her disappointment and was promptly metamorphosed into a parrot. The meaning of this little fable is, I suppose, obvious. Adolesche tries to play the part played by the tale-bearer or *losengier* in an affair of courtly love, but fails because marriage comes in between her and her hopes. Chapman is pointing out that marriage settles the old problem of the *losengier*. From this tale Teras, her terrible back still hidden, turns to sing her Epithalamion: in a sense the heart, though not the climax, of Chapman's story, and perhaps the finest lyric he ever wrote. He never praised Night more deliciously:

> O come soft rest of Cares, come night,
> Come naked vertues only tire,
> The reaped haruest of the light,
> Bound vp in sheaues of sacred fire.[1]

This summary is intended to make clear that Chapman's part of *Hero and Leander* is, as we should expect, a doctrinal and philosophical poem, very seriously meant by the poet. Much invention has gone to the creation of a new mythology which embodies his doctrine. Venus' motive for treating so sternly an offence which she, of all goddesses, might be expected to have pardoned is too trivial and too merely mythological for so grave a story: but with that exception the 'plot' (if one may so call it) is watertight and enables Chapman to say what he wanted to say. But, of course, all this will be unavailing if the actual texture of the writing fails to please.

It must be admitted that Chapman has his bad moments. The worst is when, in Sestiad VI, 197, Neptune suddenly jumped up and 'for haste his forehead hit Gainst heauens hard Christall'. We might at least have been spared the adjective *hard*; it is for most of us too painfully, and therefore too comically, reminiscent. Of course, what

---

[1] *Hero and Leander*, v, 431.

Chapman means is to tell us, in conceited language, that the waves rose heaven-high. The influence at work here is, I have little doubt, that of Du Bartas. Chapman is trying the Bartasian technique which consists in representing things great and superhuman in the most humdrum and anthropomorphic terms. I do not think we should continue to laugh at that technique as our fathers did. The French poet, after all, bequeathed it to our admired Metaphysicals. Marvell's vigilant *patrol* of stars,[1] Donne's liberated soul that 'baits not at the Moone',[2] Herbert's representation of Christ as an innkeeper,[3] are all Bartasian in character. Elsewhere Chapman is more successfully Bartasian. To tell us that the moon rose, he says:

> The Saffron mirror by which *Phoebus* loue,
> Greene *Tellus* decks her, now he held aboue
> The clowdy mountaines.   (v, 407)

It should be noticed that the lines which I quoted a moment ago from the Epithalamion are really of the same sort:

> The reaped haruest of the light,
> Bound vp in sheaues of sacred fire.

The image, when we work it out, is Bartasian; daylight is mowed like a field at evening and the harvest is tied up into those sheaves which we call stars.

Of course, Chapman is not more conceited than Marlowe had been: he is conceited in a different way. His style admirably exemplifies the transition from the pure Elizabethan manner to that of the Metaphysicals. It can, as earlier quotations have perhaps shown, display on occasion all the old abandonment and sweetness. But in general it is slower, weightier, more difficult. And Chapman, when he first comes on the stage at the opening of Sestiad III, very wisely explains the difference so that, with a little goodwill, one may take it as a change arising from the story itself and not merely from change of authorship.

> More harsh (at lest more hard) more graue and hie
> Our subiect runs, and our sterne *Muse* must flie.
> Loues edge is taken off . . .[4]

The last phrase is curiously happy, for it applies not only to the experience of Hero and Leander but to that change in English poetry

---

[1] 'Upon Appleton House', XL, xi, 313.   [2] 'The second Anniversarie', 195.
[3] 'Christmas.'   [4] *Hero and Leander*, III, 3.

with which Chapman's succession to Marlowe coincides. The old love for a poetry of pure deliciousness was, indeed, losing its edge. Honey began to pall. That is why a movement either to the more violent and knotty poetry of Donne or to the harder and severer poetry of Milton was necessary. In that way the composite *Hero and Leander* is a kind of bridge. The English Muse herself loses her innocence in the process of telling how Hero lost hers.

The new effect 'more hard, more graue and hie' depends on several changes. The most obvious is that of metre. Marlowe uses some enjambment, but I think he is happiest, most irresistibly himself, when he is most end-stopped: here, as in his plays, the superb single line is his characteristic glory—'The sweet fruition of an earthly crowne',[1] 'To entertaine diuine *Zenocrate*',[2] 'Who euer lov'd, that lov'd not at first sight?'[3] When there is a run-over it seldom adds much music. But Chapman can write true verse paragraphs in couplets, and the pauses are well managed. There is also a far greater intrusion of philosophical and reflective matter: fifteen lines on optics in the Third (235 *et seq.*), nine on the nature of beauty (99 *et seq.*), and eighteen on the properties of numbers (323 *et seq.*) in the Fifth. These will be unwelcome to the modern reader, but the last is relevant to Chapman's intention, and if we cared as much as our ancestors did for Arithmo-sophy (so to call it), it might please. We can also find in Chapman passages of a saturnine realism which, in their own way, strengthen and, as it were, thicken the poem: the sketch of Adolesche has already been mentioned. You may add the description of women talking at a funeral in the tale of Teras (v, 185 *et seq.*). Yet after all, these detachable passages count for less than that habitual cast—by no means a pale cast—of thought, which mixes with the normal flow of the narrative. A phrase like 'forme-giuing *Cyprias* siluer hand' (v, 314) is typical. *Silver* connects it with the old style of Marlowe: but *forme-giuing* lets in the whole doctrine of the archetypal Uranian Venus and the influence of the third heaven. Chapman is taking his Venus more seriously than Marlowe would have done. When he has to describe a woman yielding to a wholly legitimate love, he says

> The bribde, but incorrupted Garrison
> Sung *Io Hymen*.   (v, 253)

[1] *Tamburlaine*, Pt. I, ii, vi, 880.   [2] *Ibid.*, Pt. II, ii, iii, 2985.
[3] *Hero and Leander*, I, 176.

There is a concentration of thought in 'bribde but incorrupted' which it would be hard to find in Spenser, Sidney, or the young Shakespeare. If we could purge the word 'cleverness' of the sneering overtones that it has unfortunately acquired, I should say that Chapman's poetry is almost everywhere cleverer than Marlowe's: his imagination not less stimulated by the senses but more stimulated by ideas. The following describes the moment at which Hero's remorse weakens and a reaction in favour of Leander begins.

> And all this while the red sea of her blood
> Ebd with *Leander*: but now turnd the flood,
> And all her fleete of sprites came swelling in
> With childe of saile, and did hot fight begin
> With those seuere conceits, she too much markt,
> And here *Leanders* beauties were imbarkt.
> He came in swimming painted all with ioyes,
> Such as might sweeten hell: his thought destroyes
> All her destroying thoughts.
>
> (III, 323)

The splendour of the first line and a half has been praised before. What I would rather draw your attention to is the manner in which, throughout, the ideas and images catch fire from one another: how the ebb leads to the flood, and then the flood no longer exists for itself but carries a fleet, and the swelling of its sails leads to 'with childe of saile' and thence to a sea fight, and thence back to Leander, now swimming again; but all this not for ornament, as it might be in a long-tailed epic simile, but closely presenting the movement of Hero's mind.

This passage comes among the lines—there are nearly five hundred of them—which Chapman devotes to Hero in her solitude, in the Third and Fourth Sestiads. This is on the whole the high-light of his poem. The process of her degeneration is well conceived. It begins in blank despair, at first neither hopeful nor desirous of concealment, then passes to a long stillness, then to the reaction which I have just quoted which leads at once to the delusive belief that all will yet (somehow) be well. After that comes the resolution to be a hypocrite. It is, as I say, well conceived: but it is presented not after the fashion of the novelist nor even as Chaucer would have done it. It reaches us through an intricate pattern of conceit, symbol, and myth, much commented on and generalized. The method seems to me highly successful. The first despair is expressed in a tragic conceit which could not be bettered—

> She was a mother straight and bore with paine
> Thoughts that spake straight and wisht their mother slaine.
>
> (III, 227)

The prolonged and static misery which follows is not directly described at all. What we are actually shown is simply Hero's dress and Hero's pose—the robe of black 'Cypres', 'exceeding large',[1] the left hand clasping it at her breast, the bent head, the knees 'Wrapt in vnshapefull foulds'.[2] It is a method proper to painting but equally proper to narrative poetry: we respond to it with our muscular as well as with our visual imagination. In the next sestiad we see her tricked out again in her priestly garments and working with her needle. We are told little about what she felt during this period of false hope, but we are made to feel it for ourselves because every picture her needle makes is truer than her conscious mind will confess—

> These omenous fancies did her soule expresse,
> And euery finger made a Prophetesse.
>
> (IV, 108)

After that comes the ill-omened sacrifice, the resolve to act a part, and the apparition of Venus. Out of Hero's torn robe and torn hair there rises up in the altar fire a new creation, a 'mayd most faire',[3] girdled with snakes and ending in a scorpion's tail. It is Eronusis, Dissimulation. The thing that Hero's mind has conceived now stands before her, like Athene sprung from Jove's head or Sin from Satan's. We are in the world of nightmare. Yet still

> Betwixt all this and *Hero*, *Hero* held
> *Leanders* picture as a Persian shield.
>
> (IV, 345)

The truth and unexpectedness of this conclusion are surely admirable.

It will be seen that Chapman has his own, highly personal, technique for narrative poetry. It stands about midway between the continuous allegory of Spenser and the phantasmagoric poetry of the moderns. He can mingle at will direct psychological description, full-blown allegory, and emblematic picture. Once we accept it, we do not find

---

[1] *Hero and Leander*, III, 293.
[2] *Ibid.*, III, 298.   [3] *Ibid.*, IV, 289.

ourselves confused. For me at least it has great potency. I do not know that I can find exactly the same sort of power anywhere else.

I must, of course, be careful not to claim too much. Neither Marlowe's nor Chapman's part of *Hero and Leander* is anything like a faultless poem. Here, as always (most inexcusably in his Homer), Chapman is too digressive: he is often obscure, always mannered, sometimes ridiculous. He clogs his lines with consonants. He indulges in that curious sort of false rhyme to which Mr Simpson[1] devoted an article. As for Marlowe's part, it is, after all, a beautiful monstrosity: a thing which, even if no moral objections are felt, can win admission to the mind only in a particular mood. Even in that mood we shall admit, if we are quite honest, that it lasts just a little too long. But heaven forbid that we should never read—and praise—any poems less than perfect. Marlowe's part, with all its limitations, is a very splendid and wonderful expression of accepted sensuality: Chapman's a very grave and moving reply—an antithesis, yet arising naturally, almost inevitably, out of the thesis. My main concern is not to assess the absolute merit of either but to suggest the propriety of reading the composite poem as a whole. I first made that experiment twenty, or it may be nearer thirty, years ago: repeating it the other day, I found my old delight renewed and even deepened. Hence this lecture. I ask you to admire the lucky accident, if it was no more, which, at that particular moment in the history of poetry, brought together upon that particular story two poets so necessary to one another for enabling us to live through the process which that story embodies. I recommend all who have not done so to read the old book, for once, in the spirit of children to whom a book is an ultimate and who, never thinking even of one author, would not care whether two or twenty-two had written it.

---

[1] Percy Simpson, 'The Rhyming of Stressed with Unstressed Syllables in Elizabethan Verse', *The Modern Language Review*, vol. XXXVIII (April 1943), pp. 127–9.

6

Variation in Shakespeare and Others

Sententia cum sit
Unica, non uno veniat contenta paratu,
Sed variet vestes et mutatoria sumat;
Sub verbis aliis praesumpta resume; repone
Pluribus in clausis unum; multiplice forma
Dissimuletur idem; varius sis et tamen idem.

GEOFFROI DE VINSAUF, *Poetria Nova*, 220 *et seq.*

One day* in March, 1781, Mrs Thrale and Boswell presented the Doctor with a problem. Had Shakespeare or Milton drawn the more admirable picture of a man? The passages produced on either side were Hamlet's description of his father, and Milton's description of Adam. They run as follows:

See, what a grace was seated on this brow;
Hyperion's curls, the front of Jove himself,
An eye like Mars, to threaten and command,
A station like the herald Mercury
New-lighted on a heaven-kissing hill,
A combination and a form indeed,
Where every god did seem to set his seal,
To give the world assurance of a man.[1]

His fair large front and eye sublime declar'd
Absolute rule; and hyacinthine locks
Round from his parted forelock manly hung
Clustering, but not beneath his shoulders broad.[2]

It may have seemed a little remarkable that the 'wild genius' should so abound in classical allusions while the scholar poet was so free from them. But this would surprise no one who was familiar with the works of both; nor is it the most important difference. It is, in the logical sense, an accident that the figures which fill Shakespeare's description should come from classical mythology. It is their presence and their function, not their source, that matters. The two passages illustrate two radically different methods of poetical description. Milton keeps

---

* It was between the 21st and the 30th.

[1] *Hamlet*, III, iv, 55. [2] *Paradise Lost*, IV, 300.

74

his eye on the object, and builds up his picture in what seems a natural order. It is distinguished from a prose catalogue largely by the verse, and by the exquisite choice not of the rarest words but of the words which will seem the most nobly obvious when once they have been chosen. 'Fair large front'—any one, you would say, could think of that. And yet how well it does its work. Those three monosyllables, heavy yet easily uttered, with the glorious vowel of *large*, have already smuggled into our minds the sense of massive, leisurely dignity: it is Michelangelo's Adam 'in that majestic indolence so dear to native man'; we are prepared for the words 'absolute rule' in the next line. Shakespeare's method is wholly different. Where Milton marches steadily forward, Shakespeare behaves rather like a swallow. He darts at the subject and glances away; and then he is back again before your eyes can follow him. It is as if he kept on having tries at it, and being dissatisfied. He darts image after image at you and still seems to think that he has not done enough. He brings up a whole light artillery of mythology, and gets tired of each piece almost before he has fired it. He wants to see the object from a dozen different angles; if the undignified word is pardonable, he *nibbles*, like a man trying a tough biscuit now from this side and now from that. You can find the same sort of contrast almost anywhere between these two poets. When Milton wishes to convey to us the greatness of Beelzebub he says:

> and in his rising seemed
> A pillar of state; deep on his front engraven
> Deliberation sat, and public care;
> And princely counsel in his face yet shone,
> Majestic, though in ruin: sage he stood,
> With Atlantean shoulders, fit to bear
> The weight of mightiest monarchies; his look
> Drew audience and attention still as night
> Or summer's noontide air.[1]

But when Cleopatra wants to tell of Antony's greatness, she talks like this:

> His legs bestrid the ocean; his rear'd arm
> Crested the world; his voice was propertied
> As all the tuned spheres, and that to friends;
> But when he meant to quail and shake the orb,
> He was as rattling thunder. For his bounty,
> There was no winter in't, an autumn 'twas
> That grew the more by reaping; his delights

[1] *P.L.*, II, 301.

Were dolphin-like, they show'd his back above
The element they liv'd in, &c.[1]

You see again how simple, how all of one piece, like the clean growth of a tulip, the Milton is: how diversified—more like a chrysanthemum—is the Shakespeare. In Milton you have first the visual impression; then the moral showing through it; the allusion to Atlas, so obvious that any one (we feel) could have guessed it was coming: finally the stillness, compared, so obviously, so un-cleverly, to night or noon, and yet doing to perfection the work it was meant to do. In Shakespeare, as before, you have the ends of the earth all brought together. You begin with the gigantic hyperbole of a man bestriding the ocean, or an arm cresting the world; you go on to the music of the spheres, to thunder, to the seasons, to dolphins. Nor does one image grow out of another. The arm cresting the world is not a development of the legs bestriding the ocean; it is *idem in alio*, a second attempt at the very same idea, an alternative. The dolphin idea is not a continuation of the autumn idea. It is a fresh start. He begins over again in every second line. If you extract the bare logical skeleton, the prose 'meaning' of each image, you will find that it is precisely the same in most of them. That is not so with the Milton: the prose abstract would take nearly as many words as the poetical expression. 'Beelzebub was very big; he looked wise; he looked wise though broken; his shoulders were broad; the people were hushed when they saw him.' If you do the same to Cleopatra's speech you get something like this: 'He was great. He was great. He was great enough to help his friends. He was great enough to hurt his enemies. He was generous. He was generous. He was great.' In short, Milton gives you a theme developing: Shakespeare plays variations on a theme that remains the same. In the one, touch after touch is added to the picture until the whole stands completed; in the other you get rather a series of lightning sketches, each of the same subject, and each tossed aside before the sketcher has really finished. We might distinguish these as the method of *construction* and the method of *variation*. The first does one thing as well as it can and then proceeds to the next; the second cannot do even one thing except by doing it several times, as if even one thing were inexhaustible, and the poet could only go on having shots at it until mere necessity forced him to give it up.

It would be a mistake to suppose that what we have here stumbled

[1] *Antony and Cleopatra*, v, ii, 82.

on is simply the difference between epic and dramatic poetry. If I could presume on endless patience I could show you the opposite. I could take Shakespeare where he is himself handling epic matter and show that the very same difference holds between him and Homer as between him and Milton. I would put the Prologue to the third Act of *Henry V*, where Phoebus is fanning the silken streamers and a city is dancing on the billows beside Homer's picture of the Greeks advancing 'in silence with their eyes upon their captains'.[1] I would put a dozen speeches from ancient tragedy beside a dozen speeches from Shakespeare. Everywhere almost, though not everywhere to the same degree, we should find the same distinction.

Nor is the difference that between classical and romantic art. Milton's Beelzebub with his dim vastness and his ruined splendour is ten times more romantic than Cleopatra's Antony, whose greatness, under all its metaphorical deck hamper, remains greatness of a very mundane and lucrative type. The point can easily be settled by another example. Mr Yeats says, of the fairies,

> How shall I name you, immortal, mild, proud shadows?
> I only know that all we know comes from you.[2]

Prospero tackles them more like this:

> you demi-puppets, that
> By moonshine do the green sour ringlets make
> Whereof the ewe not bites; and you, whose pastime
> Is to make midnight mushrooms; that rejoice
> To hear the solemn curfew.[3]

Here both passages are utterly romantic; but they are as different as any other two that I have cited. Yeats gets his effect by packing as much mystery and longing as he can into a single phrase, without figures: Shakespeare, as always, flits from point to point, and will have five or six attempts to make you see the fairies, by catching them in different places. The method of variation is not a characteristic either of dramatic, or of romantic poetry. Still less is it peculiar to Shakespeare. It is shared by all the Elizabethan dramatists. It was there before Shakespeare.

> I will be Paris, and for love of thee
> Instead of Troy shall Wertenberg be sacked,

[1] *Iliad*, IV, 429–31.   [2] 'I walked among the Seven Woods of Coole', 27.
[3] *The Tempest*, V, i, 36.

> And I will combat with weak Menelaus
> And wear thy colours on my plumed crest;
> Yea, I will wound Achilles in the heel
> And then return to Helen for a kiss.[1]

If we reduce the prose content of this to 'I love you well enough to fight for you, as Paris for Helen,' we have still not done enough. For the Paris and Helen idea is itself merely illustration, and the whole of the rest of the passage is a ringing of the changes on Paris and Helen, who themselves but ring the changes on the original theme. The method is used equally by a poet who piques himself on being different from the general, like Ben Jonson. Thus in *Every Man in his Humour* I read

> Who will not judge him worthy to be robbed
> That sets his doors wide open to a thief
> And shews the felon where his treasure lies?
> Again what earthy spirit but will attempt
> To taste the fruit of beauty's golden tree
> When leaden sleep seals up the dragon's eyes?
> Oh beauty is a *project* of some power
> Chiefly when opportunity attends her.
> She will infuse true motion in a stone,
> Put glowing fire in an icy soul,
> Stuff peasants' bosoms with proud *Caesar's* spleen,
> Pour rich device into an empty brain, &c.*

The whole passage may very profitably be compared with Milton's imitation of it in *Comus*. The six lines beginning 'Oh beauty is a project', which contain four distinct metaphorical expressions of precisely the same idea, he throws out altogether. He keeps the dragon idea, and the stores spread out in the sight of a thief, but reverses the order. The dragon comes first and is used for a different purpose. The marvellous line 'Of dragon watch with unenchanted eye'[2] is the central phrase, and the metaphor as a whole becomes less a rhetorical illustration of the theme than an escape into pure imagination.[3] The hoard-and-thief idea is separated from it by the words 'You may as well', and has the effect of summing up the previous argument. It is not simply one more point that has occurred to the speaker; it is a return to the person addressed, as if he had rounded on him.

* Q. 1601, III, i.

[1] Marlowe, *Doctor Faustus*, 1335.   [2] *Comus*, 394.
[3] See Lewis's 'The Dragon Speaks' in *Poems*, ed. Walter Hooper (London, 1964), pp. 92–3.

It is the same with the later dramatists. If we ever fail to notice it, it is because we are so used to it that it comes to us merged in the general atmosphere of 'Elizabethan play'. 'Gentle father, To you I have unclasped my burdened soul, Emptied the storehouse of my thoughts and heart, Made myself poor of secrets: have not left Another word untold which hath not spoke All that I ever durst or think or know.'* Here are four variations on the theme 'I have confided in you.' There is no movement. Unclasping the burdened soul and emptying the storehouse of one's thoughts are simply alternative metaphors for the same idea. The one does not grow out of the other, nor improve on it. Or again: 'You dreamt of kingdoms, did ye? how to bosom The delicacies of a youngling princess, How with this nod to grace that subtle courtyer, How with that frown to make this noble tremble.'† Here the variation is not by metaphors, but, as we might say, by particularization. You announce the theme of Kingship first and then go on to ring the changes on particular aspects of Kingship. It is one of the simplest ways of turning an abstract conception into poetry, and is perhaps the commonest of all forms of variation in these dramatists. It does not differ essentially from the metaphorical type. The same choice is before the poet. Some abstraction is to be presented, say, luxury, servility, folly. Are you to do it by finding the single most suggestive phrase that you can and then have done with it? Or are you to try to catch a glimpse of it manifested in as many different modes as you can and fling them all together, varying as many aspects of the theme as possible? The Elizabethans nearly always chose the latter; often with beautiful result.

> So shall the spirits of every element
> Be always serviceable to us three;
> Like lions shall they guard us when we please,
> Like Almain rutters with their horseman's staves
> Or Lapland giants trotting by our sides,
> Sometimes like women or unwedded maids
> Shadowing more beauty in their airy brows
> Than have the white breasts of the queen of love.
> From Venice shall they drag huge argosies
> And from America the golden fleece.[1]

That is Marlowe's way. The abstraction 'magical power' is turned into poetry by the process of variation—by offering you a handful of

---

* *'Tis Pity She's a Whore*, I, i.   † *The Broken Heart*, IV, iv.
[1] *Doctor Faustus*, 151.

specimens. One is not enough for him; he tries it from this angle and from that. But there are other ways. Wordsworth has to express a much more abstract conception than that of magical power—the conception, namely, of restraints exercised upon the wiser sort of young men by the wrong sort of old men. He writes simply

> And blind Authority beating with his staff
> The child that might have led him,[1]

and the thing is done. We can all guess how the Elizabethans would have dealt with it. We should have begun, perhaps, with a flourish about authority in the abstract, old and sour as Saturn, but blind as Cupid; and then we should certainly have passed into a series of dissolving views in which we caught glimpses of authority at work—a man being 'progged' in one line, and a conversation with a dean in the next.

It will be understood, of course, that variation occurs to some extent in all poetry whatsoever. What is the Hebrew parallelism but a kind of variation? The synonyms in Anglo-Saxon are the same. But I think it is not likely to be disputed that the Elizabethan dramatists used it more extensively than any other family of poets. All poets use metaphors; all poets turn the abstract into the concrete; but if we want to see multiplication of metaphors about the same idea, and if we want to see concreteness given not by a single imaginative phrase but by multiplication of instances, then we naturally turn to Shakespeare and his neighbours. The faculty which enabled a man to practise such variation, which stocked his mind with images and which brought a riot of images tumbling over one another to greet every single idea was for the Elizabethans the essential faculty of the poet. They called it Wit. Middleton in his *Changeling* writes:

> Love has an intellect that runs through all
> The scrutinous sciences, and, like a cunning poet,
> Catches a quantity of every knowledge,
> Yet brings all home into one mystery.*

This may be taken simply as a description of that esemplastic power which is involved in all poetry. But it has a special meaning for the seventeenth century. Never were the scrutinous sciences and the quantities of every knowledge expected to lie quite so ready to the

---

* III, iii, 131.

[1] *The Prelude*, III, 608.

poet's hand; never were poets so eager to bring them *all* home (if it were possible) on every occasion.

It is no part of my purpose to compare this kind of writing with others. Whether you prefer the poetry which deals chiefly in construction or that which deals chiefly in variation is largely a matter of temperament. Any sane man will want both. In Shirley you may see this style in the last stages of its decay; all its peculiar vices—for every method has its vices—are then painfully visible. But it is more interesting to consider what this practice of variation could do at its best. What were the kingdoms of poetry which it alone could conquer, and whose conquest made it so dangerously attractive to the weaker poets? To ask this is, of course, equivalent to asking what Shakespeare did with it.

If we lay aside all the bardolatrous nonsense of those who would have us believe that Shakespeare was God or Nature, and ask what, in a few words, was his distinctive contribution to poetry, I really do not know why we should be afraid of answering the question. The largest things ought to be the most easily seen. The law of gravity is perhaps simpler than the Law of Tort. It is the minor poets whose quality is really indefinable, because it is nearly nothing. Thus fortified I venture to submit that the mark of Shakespeare (and it is quite enough for one mortal man) is simply this: to have combined two species of excellence which are not, in a remarkable degree, combined by any other artist, namely the imaginative splendour of the highest type of lyric and the realistic presentation of human life and character. Pindar and Aeschylus and Keats are quite as good as he on one side; and Jane Austen, Meredith, and George Eliot can meet him on the other. But Jane Austen could not write stuff like the choruses in the *Agamemnon*, and Keats (judging by 'Cap and Bells') would have made a poor show among the Bennets and the Bingleys—(not such a very poor show, when you remember some of the passages in the letters). Now the possibility of combining two such diverse qualities depends precisely on the use of variation. The problem which Shakespeare solved, perhaps unconsciously, is a very difficult one. If the character speaks as living men speak, how are we to have in his language the revealing splendours of imagination? for real passion is not articulate. He must give his poetic metaphors the air of being thrown off accidentally as he gropes for expression in the very heat of dialogue. He must have a slight stammer in his thought, and his best things must not come at the first attempt. For on those rare occasions when real life finds the inevitable phrase, that is how it arises. The man fumbles and returns again and again to his theme, and hardly knows which of his words has really hit the mark. Listen to Hamlet:

> O! that this too too solid flesh would melt,
> Thaw and resolve itself into a dew;
> Or that the Everlasting had not fix'd
> His canon 'gainst self-slaughter! O God! O God!
> How weary, stale, flat, and unprofitable
> Seem to me all the uses of this world.
> Fie on't! O fie! 'tis an unweeded garden,
> That grows to seed; things rank and gross in nature
> Possess it merely.[1]

The flesh resolving itself into a dew, and the unweeded garden are poetical metaphors that, taken alone, might seem to come from the heights of fully wrought lyric, expressing real experience but not as life expresses it. If Hamlet used either of them he would speak only as a poet. We should not believe that a man spoke thus. We shall believe them only if he seems to stumble upon them by accident, if they come, as it were, spat out amid a chaos of other grumbles as he chews over and over again the cud of the same bitter experience. That is how Shakespeare claims for naturalistic poetry—the poetry of the close up—all the rights of that other poetry which sees its figures at a mythical distance. See how he ballasts his imaginative phrases with mere exclamations—'O God! O God!' and 'Fie on't! O fie!' A magnificent example of the same thing occurs in *Macbeth*:

> Methought I heard a voice cry 'Sleep no more!
> Macbeth does murder sleep', the innocent sleep,
> Sleep that knits up the ravell'd sleave of care,
> The death of each day's life, sore labour's bath,
> Balm of hurt minds, great nature's second course,
> Chief nourisher in life's feast.[2]

Here the metaphors are perhaps even more highly wrought than Hamlet's. If Macbeth had said only 'sleep that knits up the ravell'd sleave of care', he would have said one of the best things that have been said of sleep. But we should not have believed. It is art, not life, that selects from the mind's chaos the one 'predestined and elected phrase That had lain bound long nights and days Until it wore when

[1] *Hamlet*, I, ii, 129.   [2] II, ii, 36.

once set free Immortal pellucidity'. It is the very fact that Macbeth will not leave it at that which carries conviction. Because he is not writing a poem but blurting out the agony of his mind he has no leisure to notice that he has said a good thing. The words come tumbling one after the other, and it is only we the spectators, who gather them up and see that almost every sentence has been a poem in itself. We conclude—and this goes to the root of the matter—that Macbeth was a great poet. It is only in Shakespeare's plays that we call the characters, as well as the author, poets. No one describes Clytemnestra as a poet. The poetry belongs to Aeschylus. We know that a real Clytemnestra would not talk like that. It is the poet, quite legitimately, who puts into her mouth the language she would not, in real life, have used, and thereby enables us to see her character more luminously than real life would have allowed us to see it. But Shakespeare makes you believe that Othello and Macbeth really spoke as we hear them speak. Without sacrificing the splendour, he has kept the lower and more factual reality as well; it is the very marriage of the mimetic and the creative, and it can hardly be done except by variation.

It would be untrue, however, to say that Shakespeare always used variation to such good purpose. Very often, and specially in his earlier work, he uses it as a poetical ornament—to decorate, and not to render more real, the dramatic situation.

> His rash fierce blaze of riot cannot last,
> For violent fires soon burn out themselves;
> Small showers last long, but sudden storms are short;
> He tires betimes that spurs too fast betimes;
> With eager feeding food doth choke the feeder:
> Light vanity, insatiate cormorant,
> Consuming means, soon preys upon itself.[1]

Here, the not very profound idea hardly requires such a wealth of illustration, and we hardly believe that it would have received it. The passage comes trippingly off the tongue: it is written, I think, for the mere fun of the thing. Such examples are frequent in the earlier plays, and it is in these passages that Shakespeare reminds us most strongly of Marlowe; Marlowe who of all others used variation with the minimum of dramatic purpose, and the maximum of musical and rhetorical effect.

[1] *Richard II*, II, i, 33.

Cut is the branch that might have grown full straight,
And burned is Apollo's laurel bough.[1]

In Shakespeare the variations are either ornament, or else, as we have seen, a method of combining poetry and realism. In Shirley they are a recipe for poetry. I do not mean that he uses the figure more constantly than his predecessors; I mean that when he is not using it he has commonly no pretence of poetry. To mark a heightened moment, or to translate an abstract conception into something that looks like poetry, variation is his unfailing resource. When Shirley had jotted down what was to be covered in a given scene, the process of converting it into actual drama consisted either of those purely dramatic articulations in which he does not differ from the prose dramatist or in variation. Where there is poetry there is variation; where there is no variation there is no poetry. Consider the opening scene between Bornwell and his wife in *The Lady of Pleasure*. The theme can be stated in a few words. A husband rebukes his wife for extravagance and is obstinately answered. A real dramatist would have found in this matter as many pages as Shirley; but those pages would have been occupied by the development in dialogue of the emotional situation between the two characters. Every speech would have left them related to each other in a slightly new way. On the other hand, a pure poet, of the constructive type, would have given us in some few unforgettable words an image clearer than life of the essential quality of luxury and extravagance. We should have seen once and for all what prodigality in all its wasteful beauty means to the imagination. A single line might do it, such as Clytemnestra's

Ἔστιν θάλασσα, τίς δέ νιν κατασβέσει;

Who shall quench all the purple of the sea?[2]

A writer who was both a poet and a dramatist would have given us both together. Every speech would have added a new quality to the relation of the speakers and at the same time would have done what Aeschylus does. Shirley's method is different from either. On the strictly dramatic side he has nothing to say that could not have been said in six lines. 'Why are you angry?' asks Bornwell. 'Because you stint me', retorts the lady. 'I don't. On the contrary I allow you to spend far too much,' says Bornwell. 'Well, I still think you're mean,'

---

[1] *Doctor Faustus*, 1478.   [2] *Agamemnon*, 958.

says Lady Bornwell. That is the whole scene, as drama. What swells it
to its 130 odd lines is pure *variation* on the theme 'you spend too
much' put into the mouth of Bornwell. During this the dramatic
situation stands still. 'Have you done, Sir?'[1] Lady Bornwell asks at
the end of her husband's first speech; at the end of his third she is
still asking, 'Have you concluded your lecture?'[2] The angry husband
and the scornful wife remain dramatically immobile and the play
ceases to go forward while the waves of variation roll over the audience.
In other words, what Shirley has here to say as a dramatist is extremely
little; and to convert that little into something that should seem
richer he has to call in variation. The variation consists, of course,
simply of an endless string of examples of the lady's extravagance—
'this Italian master and that Dutchman', 'superfluous plate', 'vanities
of tires', 'petticoats and pearls'.[3] There is no reason why any one
image should stand where it does rather than elsewhere. There is no
reason why the thing should stop where it does: you might just as
well turn the tap off twenty lines sooner or twenty lines later. Nor
does the beauty of the separate items recompense us (as it would in
Marlowe) for their lack of definite tendency. The best that such
writing can do is to give us a vague impression of an angry man who
has a great deal to say; but it does this only by making him as tedious
as he would be in real life. No method could be easier for the writer;
any one who can scan a verse and has a memory well stored can
produce such work *ad libitum*. And as if this were not enough the
scene between Bornwell and his wife is followed almost immediately
by the similar scene between Celestina and her steward.[4] Here, once
again, the theme is extravagance opposed to frugality; once again the
dramatic development, such as it is, could be shown in a few lines; all
the rest is variation. In the next act we have the arrival of Master
Frederick and Lady Bornwell's disgust at his scholarly lack of fashion.
Here is a situation very recalcitrant to poetical treatment, but very
tempting to a real comic dramatist. It would go admirably into a prose
dialogue of short questions and replies. Everything ought to be on the
move. We ought to see Lady Bornwell's gradual discovery of her
nephew's character and opinions: the rift ought to widen at every
speech, and at every speech the audience ought to perceive more
exactly just what the rift is and how comically exasperating. Instead

---

[1] *The Lady of Pleasure*, I, i.   [2] *Ibid.*
[3] *Ibid.*   [4] *Ibid.*, I, ii.

of this, Shirley lets Lady Bornwell grasp the whole truth, beyond hope or error, and express her horror, in the very first line, 'Support me, I shall faint.'[1] The suddenness of this is not without its comic effect; but it is dearly purchased at the price of the following scene, in which, dramatically speaking, there is nothing left to do. The chasm is filled up as usual by the handy rubble of variation. Lady Bornwell's long speech is merely a string of variations on the theme 'I wish he were French and fashionable instead of studious and parsonical', which is itself only an unprogressive amplification of the opening words 'I shall faint'. And Frederick replies:

> Madam, with your pardon you have practised
> Another dialect than was taught me when
> I was commended to your care and breeding.
> I understand not this; Latin or Greek
> Are more familiar to my apprehension:
> Logic was not so hard in my first lectures
> As your strange language.[2]

The whole speech is variation; and even the theme which it varies, namely the theme 'My ways are not your ways' has already been given in the opening lines of the scene. Frederick's speech merely restates the opposition between the two characters; it does not show us that opposition alive and growing; it adds new colours to it rhetorically, not dramatically. Shirley's method is the precise opposite of the true comic method. Shirley gives us endless change of language and leaves us exactly where we were; Molière, on the other hand, can take the very same words—as he takes the misanthrope's 'Je ne dis pas cela'[3] in his scene with the poet—and use them over and over again and yet, at each repetition, give them a new force. The repetition is part of the progression; it is not the same thing for the poet to be relentlessly shut up by the words 'Je ne dis pas cela' the first time as it is the second time. The funniness consists in his bobbing up irresistibly after each suppression, only to be suppressed again.* The identical phrase develops a new *vis comica* in each new context. If Shirley had been writing *George Dandin* he would have taken the theme 'vous l'avez voulu', variated it into thirty lines of creaking blank verse, put it into the mouth of the husband (probably as the opening speech of the play) and then, for the remaining five acts,

---

* *Cf.*, of course, Bergson's analysis of this scene in *Le Rire*.
[1] *The Lady of Pleasure*, II, i.   [2] *Ibid.*   [3] *Le Misanthrope*, I, ii.

would have turned round and round on the same spot like a dog that cannot make up its mind to lie down.

The dangers of variation have, perhaps, as much to do with the decay of the 'Elizabethan' theatre as any other internal cause, and its capabilities, as I have suggested, may be one of the principal conditions of Shakespeare's peculiar greatness. I do not, however, believe that Shakespeare consciously selected the method as a means to that combination of the dramatic and the poetic in which its greatest potential virtue lies. His own early use of it is purely ornamental, and this suggests that he began by accepting it from tradition without much reflection. Its origins, so far as I know, have not been fully examined. I suppose them to lie in Medieval Latin literature of the rhetorical type. A new study of that literature with special reference to its influence on the vernacular poets of what is called the 'Renaissance', and a determined inquiry into the channels by which that influence reached them, would be a very useful work.

7

Hamlet: The Prince or The Poem?

A critic who makes no claim to be a true Shakespearian scholar and who has been honoured by an invitation to speak about Shakespeare to such an audience as this, feels rather like a child brought in at dessert to recite his piece before the grown-ups. I have a temptation to furbish up all my meagre Shakespearian scholarship and to plunge into some textual or chronological problem in the hope of seeming, for this one hour, more of an expert than I am. But it really wouldn't do. I should not deceive you: I should not even deceive myself. I have therefore decided to bestow all my childishness upon you.

And first, a reassurance. I am not going to advance a new interpretation of the character of Hamlet. Where great critics have failed I could not hope to succeed; it is rather my ambition (a more moderate one, I trust) to understand their failure. The problem I want to consider today arises in fact not directly out of the Prince's character nor even directly out of the play, but out of the state of criticism about the play.

To give anything like a full history of this criticism would be beyond my powers and beyond the scope of a lecture; but, for my present purpose, I think we can very roughly divide it into three main schools or tendencies. The first is that which maintains simply that the actions of Hamlet have not been given adequate motives and that the play is so far bad. Hanmer is perhaps the earliest exponent of this view. According to him Hamlet is made to procrastinate because 'had [he] gone naturally to work ... there would have been an End to our Play'.[1] But then, as Hanmer points out, Shakespeare ought to have 'contrived some good reason'[2] for the procrastination. Johnson, while praising the tragedy for its 'variety', substantially agrees with Hanmer: 'of the feigned madness of Hamlet there appears no adequate cause'.[3] Rümelin thinks that the 'wisdom' which Shakespeare has chosen to hide under 'the wild utterances of insanity'[4] is a 'foreign and dis-

---

[1] Thomas Hanmer, *Some Remarks on the Tragedy of Hamlet, Prince of Denmark* (London, 1736), p. 34.
[2] *Ibid.*
[3] Samuel Johnson, *The Plays of Shakespeare*, vol. VIII (London, 1765), p. 311.
[4] Gustav Rümelin, *Shakespearestudien* (Stuttgart, 1866), p. 75.

turbing element' as a result of which the piece 'presents the greatest discrepancies'.[1] In our own time Mr Eliot has taken the same view: *Hamlet* is rather like a film on which two photographs have been taken—an unhappy superposition of Shakespeare's work 'upon much cruder material'.[2] The play 'is most certainly an artistic failure'.[3] If this school of critics is right, we shall be wasting our time in attempting to understand why Hamlet delayed. The second school, on the other hand, thinks that he did not delay at all but went to work as quickly as the circumstances permitted. This was Ritson's view. The word of a ghost, at second hand, 'would scarcely, in the eye of the people, have justifyed his killing their king'. That is why he 'counterfeits madness, and ... puts ... the usurpers guilt to the test of a play'.[4] Klein, after a very fierce attack on critics who want to make the Prince of Denmark 'a German half-professor, all tongue and no hand', comes to the same conclusion.[5] So does Werder,[6] and so does MacDonald;[7] and the position has been brilliantly defended in modern times. In the third school or group I include all those critics who admit that Hamlet procrastinates and who explain the procrastination by his psychology. Within this general agreement there are, no doubt, very great diversities. Some critics, such as Hallam,[8] Sievers,[9] Raleigh,[10] and Clutton-Brock,[11] trace the weakness to the shock inflicted upon Hamlet by the events which precede, and immediately follow, the opening of the play; others regard it as a more permanent condition; some extend it to actual insanity, others reduce it to an almost amiable flaw in a noble nature. This third group, which boasts the names of Richardson,[12]

---

[1] *Ibid.*, p. 81.   [2] T. S. Eliot, 'Hamlet', *Selected Essays* (London, 1951), p. 142.
[3] *Ibid.*, p. 143.
[4] Joseph Ritson, *Remarks Critical and Illustrative, on the Text and Notes of the Last Edition of Shakespeare* (London, 1783), p. 218.
[5] L. Klein, *Berliner Modenspiegel*, no. 24 (1846). This quotation is found in *A New Variorum Edition of Shakespeare*, vol. II, ed. H. H. Furness (Philadelphia, 1877), p. 296.
[6] Carl Werder, *The Heart of Hamlet's Mystery*, trans. from the German by Elizabeth Wilder (London, 1907).
[7] George MacDonald, *The Tragedie of Hamlet, Prince of Denmarke. A study, with the text of the folio of 1623* (London, 1885).
[8] Henry Hallam, *Introduction to the Literature of Europe in the Fifteenth, Sixteenth, and Seventeenth Centuries*, 4 vols. (London, 1837–9).
[9] Eduard W. Sievers, *William Shakespeare, Sein Leben und Dichten* (Gotha, 1866).
[10] Sir Walter Raleigh, *Shakespeare* (London, 1907).
[11] A. Clutton-Brock, *Shakespeare's 'Hamlet'* (London, 1922).
[12] William Richardson, *A Philosophical Analysis and Illustration of Some of Shakespeare's Remarkable Characters* (London, 1780).

Goethe,[1] Coleridge,[2] Schlegel,[3] and Hazlitt,[4] can still, I take it, claim to represent the central and, as it were, orthodox line of *Hamlet* criticism.

Such is the state of affairs; and we are all so accustomed to it that we are inclined to ignore its oddity. In order to remove the veil of familiarity I am going to ask you to make the imaginative effort of looking at this mass of criticism as if you had no independent knowledge of the thing criticized. Let us suppose that a picture which you have not seen is being talked about. The first thing you gather from the vast majority of the speakers—and a majority which includes the best art critics—is that this picture is undoubtedly a very great work. The next thing you discover is that hardly any two people in the room agree as to what it is a picture of. Most of them find something curious about the pose, and perhaps even the anatomy, of the central figure. One explains it by saying that it is a picture of the raising of Lazarus, and that the painter has cleverly managed to represent the uncertain gait of a body just recovering from the stiffness of death. Another, taking the central figure to be Bacchus returning from the conquest of India, says that it reels because it is drunk. A third, to whom it is self-evident that he has seen a picture of the death of Nelson, asks with some temper whether you expect a man to look quite normal just after he has been mortally wounded. A fourth maintains that such crudely representational canons of criticism will never penetrate so profound a work, and that the peculiarities of the central figure really reflect the content of the painter's subconsciousness. Hardly have you had time to digest these opinions when you run into another group of critics who denounce as a pseudo-problem what the first group has been discussing. According to this second group there is nothing odd about the central figure. A more natural and self-explanatory pose they never saw and they cannot imagine what all the pother is about. At long last you discover—isolated in a corner of the room, somewhat frowned upon by the rest of the company, and including few reputable *connoisseurs* in its ranks—a little knot of men who are whispering that the picture is a villainous daub and that the mystery of the central figure merely results from the fact that it is out of drawing.

[1] Johann Wolfgang von Goethe, *Wilhelm Meister*, Book v, trans. Thomas Carlyle (Boston, 1851).

[2] Samuel Coleridge, *Seven Lectures on Shakespeare and Milton* (London, 1856).

[3] A. W. Schlegel, *Lectures on Art and Dramatic Literature*, trans. John Black (London, 1815).

[4] William Hazlitt, *Characters of Shakespeare's Plays* (London, 1817).

Now if all this had really happened to any one of us, I believe that our first reaction would be to accept, at least provisionally, the third view. Certainly I think we should consider it much more seriously than we usually consider those critics who solve the whole *Hamlet* problem by calling *Hamlet* a bad play. At the very least we should at once perceive that they have a very strong case against the critics who admire. 'Here is a picture', they might say, 'on whose meaning no two of you are in agreement. Communication between the artist and the spectator has almost completely broken down, for each of you admits that it has broken down as regards every spectator except himself. There are only two possible explanations. Either the artist was a very bad artist, or you are very bad critics. In deference to your number and your reputation, we choose the first alternative; though, as you will observe, it would work out to the same result if we chose the second.' As to the next group—those who denied that there was anything odd about the central figure—I believe that in the circumstances I have imagined we should hardly attend to them. A natural and self-explanatory pose in the central figure would be rejected as wholly inconsistent with its observed effect on all the other critics, both those who thought the picture good and those who thought it bad.

If we now return to the real situation, the same reactions appear reasonable. There is, indeed, this difference, that the critics who admit no delay and no indecision in Hamlet, have an opponent with whom the corresponding critics of the picture were not embarrassed. The picture did not answer back. But Hamlet does. He pronounces himself a procrastinator, an undecided man, even a coward: and the ghost in part agrees with him. This, coupled with the more general difficulties of their position, appears to me to be fatal to their view. If so, we are left with those who think the play bad and those who agree in thinking it good and in placing its goodness almost wholly in the character of the hero, while disagreeing as to what that character is. Surely the devil's advocates are in a very strong position. Here is a play so dominated by one character that '*Hamlet* without the Prince' is a byword. Here are critics justly famed, all of them for their sensibility, many of them for their skill in catching the finest shades of human passion and pursuing motives to their last hiding-places. Is it really credible that the greatest of dramatists, the most powerful painter of men, offering to such an audience his consummate portrait of a man should produce something which, if any one of them is right, all the rest have in some degree failed to recognize? Is this the sort of thing that happens? Does the meeting of supremely creative with supremely receptive imagination usually produce such results? Or is it not far easier to say that Homer nods, and Alexander's shoulder drooped, and Achilles' heel was vulnerable, and that Shakespeare, for once, either in haste, or over-reaching himself in unhappy ingenuity, has brought forth an abortion?

Yes. Of course it is far easier. 'Most certainly', says Mr Eliot, 'an artistic failure'. But is it 'most certain'? Let me return for a moment to my analogy of the picture. In that dream there was one experiment we did not make. We didn't walk into the next room and look at it for ourselves. Supposing we had done so. Suppose that at the first glance all the cogent arguments of the unfavourable critics had died on our lips, or echoed in our ears as idle babble. Suppose that looking on the picture we had found ourselves caught up into an unforgettable intensity of life and had come back from the room where it hung haunted for ever with the sense of vast dignities and strange sorrows and teased 'with thoughts beyond the reaches of our souls'—would not this have reversed our judgement and compelled us, in the teeth of *a priori* probability, to maintain that on one point at least the orthodox critics were in the right? 'Most certainly an artistic failure.' All argument is for that conclusion—until you read or see *Hamlet* again. And when you do, you are left saying that if this is failure, then failure is better than success. We want more of these 'bad' plays. From our first childish reading of the ghost scenes down to those golden minutes which we stole from marking examination papers on *Hamlet* to read a few pages of *Hamlet* itself, have we ever known the day or the hour when its enchantment failed? That castle is part of our own world. The affection we feel for the Prince, and, through him, for Horatio, is like a friendship in real life. The very turns of expression—half-lines and odd connecting links—of this play are worked into the language. It appears, said Shaftesbury in 1711, 'to have most affected *English* Hearts, and has perhaps been oftnest acted'.[1] It has a taste of its own, an all-pervading relish which we recognize even in its smallest fragments, and which, once tasted, we recur to. When we want that taste, no other book will do instead. It

[1] Anthony Ashley Cooper, 3rd Earl of Shaftesbury, *Characteristics of Men, Manners, Opinions, Times. Treatise III. vis. Soliloquy, or Advice to an Author*, vol. 1 (London, 1711), pp. 275–6.

may turn out in the end that the thing is not a complete success. This compelling quality in it may coexist with some radical defect. But I doubt if we shall ever be able to say, sad brow and true maid, that it is 'most certainly' a failure. Even if the proposition that it has failed were at last admitted for true, I can think of few critical truths which most of us would utter with less certainty, and with a more divided mind.

It seems, then, that we cannot escape from our problem by pronouncing the play bad. On the other hand, the critics, mostly agreeing to place the excellence of it in the delineation of the hero's character, describe that character in a dozen different ways. If they differ so much as to the kind of man whom Shakespeare meant to portray, how can we explain their unanimous praise of the portrayal? I can imagine a sketch so bad that one man thought it was an attempt at a horse and another thought it was an attempt at a donkey. But what kind of sketch would it have to be which looked like a *very good* horse to some, and like a *very good* donkey to others? The only solution which occurs to me is that the critics' delight in the play is not in fact due to the delineation of Hamlet's character but to something else. If the picture which you take for a horse and I for a donkey, delights us both, it is probable that what we are both enjoying is the pure line, or the colouring, not the delineation of an animal. If two men who have both been talking to the same woman agree in proclaiming her conversation delightful, though one praises it for its ingenuous innocence and the other for its clever sophistication, I should be inclined to conclude that her conversation had played very little part in the pleasure of either. I should suspect that the lady was nice to look at.

I am quite aware that such a suggestion about what has always been thought a 'one man play' will sound rather like a paradox. But I am not aiming at singularity. In so far as my own ideas about Shakespeare are worth classifying at all, I confess myself a member of that school which has lately been withdrawing our attention from the characters to fix it on the plays. Dr Stoll[1] and Professor Wilson Knight,[2] though in very different fashions, have led me in this direction;

[1] E. E. Stoll, *Shakespeare Studies* (New York, 1927); *Art and Artifice in Shakespeare* (New York, 1933); *Hamlet the Man*, The English Association, pamphlet no. 91 (March 1935).
[2] G. Wilson Knight, *The Wheel of Fire* (Oxford, 1930); *The Imperial Theme* (Oxford, 1931).

and Aristotle has long seemed to me simply right when he says that tragedy is an imitation not of men but of action and life and happiness and misery. By action he means, no doubt, not what a modern producer would call action but rather 'situation'.

What has attached me to this way of thinking is the fact that it explains my own experience. When I tried to read Shakespeare in my teens the character criticism of the nineteenth century stood between me and my enjoyment. There were all sorts of things in the plays which I could have enjoyed; but I had got it into my head that the only proper and grown-up way of appreciating Shakespeare was to be very interested in the truth and subtlety of his character drawing. A play opened with thunder and lightning and witches on a heath. This was very much in my line: but oh the disenchantment when I was told—or thought I was told—that what really ought to concern me was the effect of these witches on Macbeth's character! An Illyrian Duke spoke, in an air which had just ceased vibrating to the sound of music, words that seemed to come out of the very heart of some golden world of dreamlike passion: but all this was spoiled because the meddlers had told me it was the portrait of a self-deceiving or unrealistic man and given me the impression that it was my business to diagnose like a straightener from Erewhon or Vienna instead of submitting to the charm. Shakespeare offered me a King who could not even sentence a man to banishment without saying:

> The sly slow hours shall not determinate
> The dateless limit of thy dear exile.[1]

Left to myself I would simply have drunk it in and been thankful. That is just how beautiful, wilful, passionate, unfortunate kings killed long ago ought to talk. But then again the critic was at my elbow instilling the pestilential notion that I ought to prize such words chiefly as illustrations of what he called Richard's weakness, and (worse still) inviting me to admire the vulgar, bustling efficiency of Bolingbroke. I am probably being very unjust to the critics in this account. I am not even sure who they were. But somehow or other this was the sort of idea they gave me. I believe they have given it to thousands. As far as I am concerned it meant that Shakespeare became to me for many years a closed book. Read him in *that* way I could not; and it was some time before I had the courage to read him in any

[1] *Richard II*, I, iii, 150.

other. Only much later, reinforced with a wider knowledge of literature, and able now to rate at its true value the humble little outfit of prudential maxims which really underlay much of the talk about Shakespeare's characters, did I return and read him with enjoyment. To one in my position the opposite movement in criticism came as a kind of Magna Carta. With that help I have come to one very definite conclusion. I do not say that the characters—especially the comic characters—count for nothing. But the first thing is to surrender oneself to the poetry and the situation. It is only through them that you can reach the characters, and it is for their sake that the characters exist. All conceptions of the characters arrived at, so to speak, in cold blood, by working out what sort of man it would have to be who in real life would act or speak as they do, are in my opinion chimerical. The wiseacres who proceed in that way only substitute our own ideas of character and life, which are not often either profound or delectable, for the bright shapes which the poet is actually using. Orsino and Richard II are test cases. Interpretations which compel you to read their speeches with a certain superiority, to lend them a note of 'insincerity', to strive in any way against their beauty, are self-condemned. Poets do not make beautiful verse in order to have it 'guyed'. Both these characters speak golden syllables, wearing rich clothes, and standing in the centre of the stage. After that, they may be wicked, but it can only be with a passionate and poetic wickedness; they may be foolish, but only with follies noble and heroical. For the poetry, the clothes, and the stance are the substance; the character 'as it would have to be in real life' is only a shadow. It is often a very distorted shadow. Some of my pupils talk to me about Shakespeare as if the object of his life had been to render into verse the philosophy of Samuel Smiles or Henry Ford.

A good example of the kind of play which can be twisted out of recognition by character criticism is the *Merchant of Venice*. Nothing is easier than to disengage and condemn the mercenary element in Bassanio's original suit to Portia, to point out that Jessica was a bad daughter, and by dwelling on Shylock's wrongs to turn him into a tragic figure. The hero thus becomes a scamp, the heroine's love for him a disaster, the villain a hero, the last act an irrelevance, and the casket story a monstrosity. What is not explained is why anyone should enjoy such a depressing and confused piece of work. It seems to me that what we actually enjoy is something quite different. The real play is not so much about men as about metals. The horror of usury lay in the fact that it treated metal in a way contrary to nature. If you have cattle they will breed. To make money—the mere medium of exchange—breed as if it were alive is a sort of black magic. The speech about Laban and Jacob is put into Shylock's mouth to show that he cannot grasp this distinction;[1] and the Christians point out that friendship does not take 'A breed for barren metal'.[2] The important thing about Bassanio is that he can say, 'Only my blood speaks to you in my veins',[3] and again, 'all the wealth I had Ran in my veins'.[4] Sir Walter Raleigh most unhappily, to my mind, speaks of Bassanio as a 'pale shadow'.[5] *Pale* is precisely the wrong word. The whole contrast is between the crimson and organic wealth in his veins, the medium of nobility and fecundity, and the cold, mineral wealth in Shylock's counting-house. The charge that he is a mercenary wooer is a product of prosaic analysis. The play is much nearer the *Märchen* level than that. When the hero marries the princess we are not expected to ask whether her wealth, her beauty, or her rank was the determining factor. They are all blended together in the simple man's conception of Princess. Of course great ladies are beautiful: of course they are rich. Bassanio compares Portia to the Golden Fleece. That strikes the proper note. And when once we approach the play with our senses and imaginations it becomes obvious that the presence of the casket story is no accident. For it also is a story about metals, and the rejection of the commercial metals by Bassanio is a kind of counter-point to the conquest of Shylock's metallic power by the lady of the beautiful mountain. The very terms in which they are rejected proclaim it. Silver is the 'pale and common drudge 'Tween man and man'.[6] Gold is 'Hard food for Midas'[7]—Midas who, like Shylock, tried to use as the fuel of life what is in its own nature dead. And the last act, so far from being an irrelevant *coda*, is almost the thing for which the play exists. The 'naughty world' of finance exists in the play chiefly that we may perceive the light of the 'good deed',[8] or rather of the good state, which is called Belmont. I know that some will call this 'far-fetched'; but I must ask them to take my word for it that even if I

---

[1] *Merchant of Venice*, I, iii, 72. (The reference in Shylock's speech is to Genesis xxx. 31–43.)

[2] *Ibid.*, I, iii, 135.

[3] *Ibid.*, III, ii, 177.

[4] *Ibid.*, III, ii, 255–6.

[5] Raleigh, *op. cit.*, p. 150.

[6] *Merchant of Venice*, III, ii, 103–4.

[7] *Ibid.*, III, ii, 102.

[8] *Ibid.*, V, i, 91.

am wrong, 'far-fetched' is the last epithet that should be applied to my error. I have not fetched it from far. This, or something like it, is my immediate and spontaneous reaction. A wicked ogre of a Jew is ten thousand miles nearer to that reaction than any of the sad, subtle, realistic figures produced by critics. If I err, I err in childishness, not in sophistication.

Now *Hamlet* is a play as nearly opposite to the *Merchant* as possible. A good way of introducing you to my experience of it will be to tell you the exact point at which anyone else's criticism of it begins to lose my allegiance. It is a fairly definite point. As soon as I find anyone treating the ghost merely as the means whereby Hamlet learns of his father's murder—as soon as a critic leaves us with the impression that some other method of disclosure (the finding of a letter or a conversation with a servant) would have done very nearly as well—I part company with that critic. After that, he may be as learned and sensitive as you please; but his outlook on literature is so remote from mine that he can teach me nothing. Hamlet for me is no more separable from his ghost than Macbeth from his witches, Una from her lion, or Dick Whittington from his cat. The Hamlet formula, so to speak, is not 'a man who has to avenge his father' but 'a man who has been given a task by a ghost'. Everything else about him is less important than that. If the play did not begin with the cold and darkness and sickening suspense of the ghost scenes it would be a radically different play. If, on the other hand, only the first act had survived, we should have a very tolerable notion of the play's peculiar quality. I put it to you that everyone's imagination here confirms mine. What is against me is the abstract pattern of motives and characters which we build up as critics when the actual flavour or tint of the poetry is already fading from our minds.

This ghost is different from any other ghost in Elizabethan drama—for, to tell the truth, the Elizabethans in general do their ghosts very vilely. It is permanently ambiguous. Indeed the very word 'ghost', by putting it into the same class with the 'ghosts' of Kyd and Chapman, nay by classifying it at all, puts us on the wrong track. It is 'this thing',[1] 'this dreaded sight',[2] an 'illusion',[3] a 'spirit of health or goblin damn'd',[4] liable at any moment to assume 'some other horrible form'[5] which reason could not survive the vision of. Critics have

---

[1] *Hamlet*, I, i, 21.   [2] *Ibid.*, I, i, 25.   [3] *Ibid.*, I, i, 127.
[4] *Ibid.*, I, iv, 40.   [5] *Ibid.*, I, iv, 72.

disputed whether Hamlet is sincere when he doubts whether the apparition is his father's ghost or not. I take him to be perfectly sincere. He believes while the thing is present: he doubts when it is away. Doubt, uncertainty, bewilderment to almost any degree, is what the ghost creates not only in Hamlet's mind but in the minds of the other characters. Shakespeare does not take the concept of 'ghost' for granted, as other dramatists had done. In his play the appearance of the spectre means a breaking down of the walls of the world and the germination of thoughts that cannot really be thought: chaos is come again.

This does not mean that I am going to make the ghost the hero, or the play a ghost story—though I might add that a very good ghost story would be, to me, a more interesting thing than a maze of motives. I have started with the ghost because the ghost appears at the beginning of the play not only to give Hamlet necessary information but also, and even more, to strike the note. From the platform we pass to the court scene and so to Hamlet's first long speech. There are ten lines of it before we reach what is necessary to the plot: lines about the melting of flesh into a dew and the divine prohibition of self-slaughter. We have a second ghost scene after which the play itself, rather than the hero, goes mad for some minutes. We have a second soliloquy on the theme 'To die ... to sleep',[1] and a third on the 'witching time of night, When churchyards yawn'.[2] We have the King's effort to pray and Hamlet's comment on it. We have the ghost's third appearance. Ophelia goes mad and is drowned. Then comes the comic relief, surely the strangest comic relief ever written—comic relief beside an open grave, with a further discussion of suicide, a detailed inquiry into the rate of decomposition, a few clutches of skulls, and then 'Alas! poor Yorick.'[3] On top of this, the hideous fighting in the grave; and then, soon, the catastrophe.

I said just now that the subject of the *Merchant* was metals. In the same sense, the subject of *Hamlet* is death. I do not mean by this that most of the characters die, nor even that life and death are the stakes they play for; that is true of all tragedies. I do not mean that we rise from the reading of the play with the feeling that we have been in cold, empty places, places 'outside', *nocte tacentia late*, though that is true. Before I go on to explain myself let me say that here, and

[1] *Hamlet*, III, i, 60 *et seq.*   [2] *Ibid.*, III, ii, 413–14.
[3] *Ibid.*, V, i, 201–2.

throughout my lecture, I am most deeply indebted to my friend Mr Owen Barfield.[1] I have to make these acknowledgements both to him and to other of my friends so often that I am afraid of their being taken for an affectation. But they are not. The next best thing to being wise oneself is to live in a circle of those who are: that good fortune I have enjoyed for nearly twenty years.

The sense in which death is the subject of *Hamlet* will become apparent if we compare it with other plays. Macbeth has commerce with Hell, but at the very outset of his career dismisses all thought of the life to come. For Brutus and Othello, suicide in the high tragic manner is escape and climax. For Lear death is deliverance. For Romeo and Antony, poignant loss. For all these, as for their author while he writes and the audience while they watch, death is the end: it is almost the frame of the picture. They think of dying: no one thinks, in these plays, of *being dead*. In *Hamlet* we are kept thinking about it all the time, whether in terms of the soul's destiny or of the body's. Purgatory, Hell, Heaven, the wounded name, the rights—or wrongs—of Ophelia's burial, and the staying-power of a tanner's corpse: and beyond this, beyond all Christian and all Pagan maps of the hereafter, comes a curious groping and tapping of thoughts, about 'what dreams may come'.[2] It is this that gives to the whole play its quality of darkness and of misgiving. Of course there is much else in the play: but nearly always, the some groping. The characters are all watching one another, forming theories about one another, listening, contriving, full of anxiety. The world of *Hamlet* is a world where one has lost one's way. The Prince also has no doubt lost his, and we can tell the precise moment at which he finds it again. 'Not a whit, we defy augury; there's a special providence in the fall of a sparrow. If it be now, 'tis not to come; if it be not to come, it will be now; if it be not now, yet it will come: the readiness is all. Since no man has aught of what he leaves, what is't to leave betimes?'*

If I wanted to make one more addition to the gallery of Hamlet's portraits I should trace his hesitation to the fear of death; not to a physical fear of dying, but a fear of being dead. And I think I should

---

* *Ibid.*, v, ii, 232–8. I think the last clause is best explained by the assumption that Shakespeare had come across Seneca's *Nihil perdis ex tuo tempore, nam quod relinquis alienum est* (Epist. lxix).

[1] See the chapter on 'The Form of *Hamlet*', in Owen Barfield's *Romanticism Comes of Age* (London, 1944), pp. 85–103. (New and augmented edition, London, 1966.)

[2] *Hamlet*, III, i, 66.

get on quite comfortably. Any serious attention to the state of being dead, unless it is limited by some definite religious or anti-religious doctrine, must, I suppose, paralyse the will by introducing infinite uncertainties and rendering all motives inadequate. Being dead is the unknown x in our sum. Unless you ignore it or else give it a value, you can get no answer. But this is not what I am going to do. Shakespeare has not left in the text clear lines of causation which would enable us to connect Hamlet's hesitation with this source. I do not believe he has given us data for any portrait of the kind critics have tried to draw. To that extent I agree with Hanmer, Rümelin, and Mr Eliot. But I differ from them in thinking that it is a fault.

For what, after all, is happening to us when we read any of Hamlet's great speeches? We see visions of the flesh dissolving into a dew, of the world like an unweeded garden. We think of memory reeling in its 'distracted globe'.[1] We watch him scampering hither and thither like a maniac to avoid the voices wherewith he is haunted. Someone says 'walk out of the air',[2] and we hear the words 'Into my grave'[3] spontaneously respond to it. We think of being bounded in a nut-shell and king of infinite space: but for bad dreams. There's the trouble, for 'I am most dreadfully attended'.[4] We see the picture of a dull and muddy-mettled rascal, a John-a-dreams, somehow unable to move while ultimate dishonour is done him. We listen to his fear lest the whole thing may be an illusion due to melancholy. We get the sense of sweet relief at the words 'shuffled off this mortal coil'[5] but mixed with the bottomless doubt about what may follow then. We think of bones and skulls, of women breeding sinners, and of how some, to whom all this experience is a sealed book, can yet dare death and danger 'for an egg-shell'.[6] But do we really enjoy these things, do we go back to them, because they show us Hamlet's character? Are they, from *that* point of view, so very interesting? Does the mere fact that a young man, literally haunted, dispossessed, and lacking friends, should feel thus, tell us anything remarkable? Let me put my question in another way. If instead of the speeches he actually utters about the firmament and man in his scene with Rosencrantz and Guildenstern Hamlet had merely said, 'I don't seem to enjoy things the way I used to,' and talked in that fashion throughout, should we find him interesting? I think the answer is 'Not very.' It may be

[1] *Hamlet*, I, v, 97. [2] *Ibid.*, II, ii, 212. [3] *Ibid.*, II, ii, 214.
[4] *Ibid.*, II, ii, 281. [5] *Ibid.*, III, i, 67. [6] *Ibid.*, IV, iv, 53.

replied that if he talked commonplace prose he would reveal his character less vividly. I am not so sure. He would certainly have revealed *something* less vividly; but would that something be himself? It seems to me that 'this majestical roof'[1] and 'What a piece of work is a man!'[2] give me primarily an impression not of the sort of person he must be to lose the estimation of things but of the things themselves and their great value; and that I should be able to discern, though with very faint interest, the same condition of loss in a personage who was quite unable so to put before me what he was losing. And I do not think it true to reply that he would be a different character if he spoke less poetically. This point is often misunderstood. We sometimes speak as if the characters in whose mouths Shakespeare puts great poetry were poets: in the sense that Shakespeare was depicting men of poetical genius. But surely this is like thinking that Wagner's Wotan is the dramatic portrait of a baritone? In opera song is the medium by which the representation is made and not part of the thing represented. The actors sing; the dramatic personages are feigned to be speaking. The only character who sings dramatically in *Figaro* is Cherubino. Similarly in poetical drama poetry is the medium, not part of the delineated characters. While the actors speak poetry written for them by the poet, the dramatic personages are supposed to be merely talking. If ever there is occasion to *represent* poetry (as in the play scene from *Hamlet*), it is put into a different metre and strongly stylised so as to prevent confusion.

I trust that my conception is now becoming clear. I believe that we read Hamlet's speeches with interest chiefly because they describe so well a certain spiritual region through which most of us have passed and anyone in his circumstances might be expected to pass, rather than because of our concern to understand how and why this particular man entered it. I foresee an objection on the ground that I am thus really admitting his 'character' in the only sense that matters and that all characters whatever could be equally well talked away by the method I have adopted. But I do really find a distinction. When I read about Mrs Proudie I am not in the least interested in seeing the world from her point of view, for her point of view is not interesting; what does interest me is precisely the sort of person she was. In *Middlemarch* no reader wants to see Casaubon through Dorothea's eyes; the pathos, the comedy, the value of the whole thing is to

<hr/>

[1] *Ibid.*, ii, ii, 313. [2] *Ibid.*, ii, ii, 323.

understand Dorothea and see how such an illusion was inevitable for her. In Shakespeare himself I find Beatrice to be a character who could not be thus dissolved. We are interested not in some vision seen through her eyes, but precisely in the wonder of her being the girl she is. A comparison of the sayings we remember from her part with those we remember from Hamlet's brings out the contrast. On the one hand, 'I wonder that you will still be talking, Signior Benedick',[1] 'There was a star danced, and under that was I born',[2] 'Kill Claudio';[3] on the other, 'The undiscover'd country from whose bourne No traveller returns',[4] 'Use every man after his desert, and who should 'scape whipping?',[5] 'The rest is silence'.[6] Particularly noticeable is the passage where Hamlet professes to be describing his own character. 'I am myself indifferent honest; but yet I could accuse me of such things that it were better my mother had not borne me. I am very proud, revengeful, ambitious.'[7] It is, of course, possible to devise some theory which explains these self-accusations in terms of character. But long before we have done so the real significance of the lines has taken possession of our imagination for ever. 'Such fellows as I'[8] does not mean 'such fellows as Goethe's Hamlet, or Coleridge's Hamlet, or any Hamlet': it means *men*—creatures shapen in sin and conceived in iniquity—and the vast, empty vision of them 'crawling between earth and heaven'[9] is what really counts and really carries the burden of the play.

It is often cast in the teeth of the great critics that each in painting Hamlet has drawn a portrait of himself. How if they were right? I would go a long way to meet Beatrice or Falstaff or Mr Jonathan Oldbuck or Disraeli's Lord Monmouth. I would not cross the room to meet Hamlet. It would never be necessary. He is always where I am. The method of the whole play is much nearer to Mr Eliot's own method in poetry than Mr Eliot suspects. Its true hero is man— haunted man—man with his mind on the frontier of two worlds, man unable either quite to reject or quite to admit the supernatural, man struggling to get something done as man has struggled from the beginning, yet incapable of achievement because of his inability to understand either himself or his fellows or the real quality of the

[1] *Much Ado about Nothing*, I, i, 121–2.
[2] *Ibid.*, II, i, 351–2.
[3] *Ibid.*, IV, i, 294.
[4] *Hamlet*, III, i, 79–80.
[5] *Ibid.*, II, ii, 561–3.
[6] *Ibid.*, V, ii, 372.
[7] *Ibid.*, III, i, 125–9.
[8] *Ibid.*, III, i, 132.
[9] *Ibid.*, III, i, 132–3.

universe which has produced him. To be sure, some hints of more particular motives for Hamlet's delay are every now and then fadged up to silence our questions, just as some show of motives is offered for the Duke's temporary abdication in *Measure for Measure*. In both cases it is only scaffolding or machinery. To mistake these mere *succedanea* for the real play and to try to work them up into a coherent psychology is the great error. I once had a whole batch of School Certificate answers on the Nun's Priest's Tale by boys whose form-master was apparently a breeder of poultry. Everything that Chaucer had said in describing Chauntecleer and Pertelote was treated by them simply and solely as evidence about the precise breed of these two birds. And, I must admit, the result was very interesting. They proved beyond doubt that Chauntecleer was very different from our modern specialised strains and much closer to the Old English 'barn-door fowl'. But I couldn't help feeling that they had missed something. I believe our attention to Hamlet's 'character' in the usual sense misses almost as much.

Perhaps I should rather say that it *would* miss as much if our be-haviour when we are actually reading were not wiser than our criticism in cold blood. The critics, or most of them, have at any rate kept constantly before us the knowledge that in this play there is greatness and mystery. They were never entirely wrong. Their error, on my view, was to put the mystery in the wrong place—in Hamlet's motives rather than in that darkness which enwraps Hamlet and the whole tragedy and all who read or watch it. It is a mysterious play in the sense of being a play about mystery. Mr Eliot suggests that 'more people have thought *Hamlet* a work of art because they found it interesting, than have found it interesting because it is a work of art'.[1] When he wrote that sentence he must have been very near to what I believe to be the truth. This play is, above all else, *interesting*. But artistic failure is not in itself interesting, nor often interesting in any way; artistic success always is. To interest is the first duty of art; no other excellences will even begin to compensate for failure in this, and very serious faults will be covered by this, as by charity. The hypothesis that this play interests by being good and not by being bad has therefore the first claim on our consideration. The burden of proof rests on the other side. Is not the fascinated interest of the critics most naturally explained by supposing that this is the precise

[1] Eliot, *op. cit.*, p. 144.

effect the play was written to produce? They may be finding the mystery in the wrong place; but the fact that they can never leave *Hamlet* alone, the continual groping, the sense, unextinguished by over a century of failures, that we have here something of inestimable importance, is surely the best evidence that the real and lasting mystery of our human situation has been greatly depicted.

The kind of criticism which I have attempted is always at a disadvantage against either historical criticism or character criticism. Their vocabulary has been perfected by long practice, and the truths with which they are concerned are those which we are accustomed to handle in the everyday business of life. But the things I want to talk about have no vocabulary and criticism has for centuries kept almost complete silence on them. I make no claim to be a pioneer. Professor Wilson Knight (though I disagree with nearly everything he says in detail), Miss Spurgeon,[1] Miss Bodkin,[2] and Mr Barfield are my leaders. But those who do not enjoy the honours of a pioneer may yet share his discomforts. One of them I feel acutely at the moment. I feel certain that to many of you the things I have been saying about *Hamlet* will appear intolerably sophisticated, abstract, and modern. And so they sound when we have to put them into words. But I shall have failed completely if I cannot persuade you that my view, for good or ill, has just the opposite characteristics—is naïve and concrete and archaic. I am trying to recall attention from the things an intellectual adult notices to the things a child or a peasant notices—night, ghosts, a castle, a lobby where a man can walk four hours together, a willow-fringed brook and a sad lady drowned, a graveyard and a terrible cliff above the sea, and amidst all these a pale man in black clothes (would that our producers would ever let him appear!) with his stockings coming down, a dishevelled man whose words make us at once think of loneliness and doubt and dread, of waste and dust and emptiness, and from whose hands, or from our own, we feel the richness of heaven and earth and the comfort of human affection slipping away. In a sense I have kept my promise of bestowing all my childishness upon you. A child is always thinking about those details in a story which a grown-up regards as indifferent. If when you first

---

[1] Caroline F. E. Spurgeon, *Shakespeare's Imagery and What It Tells Us* (Cambridge, 1935).

[2] Maud Bodkin, *Archetypal Patterns in Poetry. Psychological Studies of Imagination* (London: Oxford University Press, 1934).

told the tale your hero was warned by three little men appearing on the left of the road, and when you tell it again you introduce one little man on the right of the road, the child protests. And the child is right. You think it makes no difference because you are not living the story at all. If you were, you would know better. *Motifs*, machines, and the like are abstractions of literary history and therefore inter-changeable: but concrete imagination knows nothing of them.

You must not think I am setting up as a sort of literary Peter Pan who does not grow up. On the contrary, I claim that only those adults who have retained, with whatever additions and enrichments, their first childish response to poetry unimpaired, can be said to have grown up at all. Mere change is not growth. Growth is the synthesis of change and continuity, and where there is no continuity there is no growth. To hear some critics, one would suppose that a man had to lose his nursery appreciation of *Gulliver* before he acquired his mature appreciation of it. It is not so. If it were, the whole concept of maturity, of ripening, would be out of place: and also, I believe we should very seldom read more than three pages of *Gulliver* at a sitting.[1]

[1] After reading Professor Dover Wilson's *The Manuscript of Shakespeare's 'Hamlet' and the Problems of Its Transmission* (Cambridge, 1934), Lewis raised the question as to what is the genuine text of *Hamlet*: the manuscript that Shakespeare wrote or the play as acted in the theatre? For Lewis's initial question and the discussion that followed under the same title, see: C. S. Lewis, 'The Genuine Text', *The Times Literary Supplement* (2 May 1935), p. 288; F. W. Bateson, *ibid.* (9 May 1935), p. 301; J. Dover Wilson, *ibid.* (16 May 1935), p. 313; C. S. Lewis, *ibid.* (23 May 1935), p. 331; W. J. Lawrence, *ibid.*; J. Dover Wilson, *ibid.* (30 May 1935), p. 348; M. R. Ridley, *ibid.*; W. W. Greg, *ibid.* (6 June 1935), p. 364; W. J. Lawrence, *ibid.*; J. Dover Wilson, *ibid.* (13 June 1935), p. 380.

8

Donne and Love Poetry in the Seventeenth Century

I have seen an old history of literature in which the respective claims of Shelley and Mrs Hemans to be the greatest lyrist of the nineteenth century were seriously weighed; and Donne, who was so inconsiderable fifty years ago, seems at the moment to rank among our greatest poets.

If there were no middle state between absolute certainty and what Mr Kellett calls the whirligig of taste,[1] these fluctuations would make us throw up criticism in despair. But where it is impossible to go quite straight we may yet resolve to reel as little as we can. Such phenomena as the present popularity of Donne or the growing unpopularity of Milton are not to be deplored; they are rather to be explained. It is not impossible to see why Donne's poetry should be overrated in the twentieth and underrated in the eighteenth century; and in so far as we detect these temporary disturbing factors and explain the varying appearances of the object by the varying positions of the observers, we shall come appreciably nearer to a glimpse of Donne *simpliciter*. I shall concern myself in what follows chiefly with his love poetry.

In style this poetry is primarily a development of one of the two styles which we find in the work of Donne's immediate predecessors. One of these is the mellifluous, luxurious, 'builded rhyme', as in Spenser's *Amoretti*: the other is the abrupt, familiar, and consciously 'manly' style in which nearly all Wyatt's lyrics are written. Most of the better poets make use of both, and in *Astrophil and Stella* much of Sidney's success depends on deliberate contrast between such poetry as

> Nor of that golden sea, whose waves in curles are brok'n[2]

[1] E. E. Kellett, *The Whirligig of Taste*, Hogarth Lectures on Literature, no. 8 (London, 1929).

[2] *Astrophil and Stella*, in *The Poems of Sir Philip Sidney*, ed. William A. Ringler, Jnr (Oxford, 1962), no. 86, Fifth Song, line 39, p. 213.

and such poetry as

He cannot love: no, no, let him alone.[1]

But Wyatt remains, if not the finest, yet much the purest example of the plainer manner, and in reading his songs, with their conversational openings, their surly (not to say sulky) defiances, and their lack of obviously poetic ornament, I find myself again and again reminded of Donne. But of course he is a Donne with most of the genius left out. Indeed, the first and most obvious achievement of the younger poet is to have raised this kind of thing to a much higher power; to have kept the vividness of conversation where Wyatt too often had only the flatness; to sting like a lash where Wyatt merely grumbled. The difference in degree between the two poets thus obscures the similarity in kind. Donne has so far surpassed not only Wyatt but all the Elizabethans in what may be called their Wyatt moments, and has so generally abstained from attempting to rival them in their other vein, that we hardly think of him as continuing one side of their complex tradition; he appears rather as the innovator who substituted a realistic for a decorated kind of love poetry.

Now this error is not in itself important. In an age which was at all well placed for judging the comparative merits of the two styles, it would not matter though we thought that Donne had invented what in fact he only brought to perfection. But our own age is not so placed. The mellifluous style, which we may agree to call Petrarchan though no English poet is very like Petrarch, has really no chance of a fair hearing. It is based on a conception of poetry wholly different from that of the twentieth century. It descends from old Provençal and Italian sources and presupposes a poetic like that of Dante. Dante, we may remember, thinks of poetry as something to be made, to be 'adorned as much as possible', to have its 'true sense' hidden beneath a rich vesture of 'rhetorical colouring'. The 'Petrarchan' sonneteers are not trying to make their work sound like the speaking voice. They are not trying to communicate faithfully the raw, the merely natural, impact of actual passion. The passion for them is not a specimen of 'nature' to be followed so much as a lump of ore to be refined: they ask themselves not 'How can I record it with the least sophistication?' but 'Of its bones what coral can I make?', and to accuse them of insincerity is like calling an oyster insincere because

[1] *Ibid.*, no. 54, line 8, p. 191.

it makes its disease into a pearl. The aim of the other style is quite different. It wishes to be convincing, intimate, naturalistic. It would be very foolish to set up these two kinds of poetry as rivals, for obviously they are different and both are good. It is a fine thing to hear the living voice, the voice of a man like ourselves, whispering or shouting to us from the printed page with all the heat of life; and it is a fine thing, too, to see such life—so pitiably like our own, I doubt not, in the living—caught up and transfigured, sung by the voice of a god into an ecstasy no less real though in another dimension.* There is no necessary quarrel between the two. But there are many reasons why one of them should start with overwhelming odds in its favour at the present moment. For many years our poetics have been becoming more and more expressionistic. First came Wordsworth with his theory, and we have never quite worked it out of our system; even in the crude form that 'you should write as you talk', it works at the back of much contemporary criticism. Then came the final break-up of aristocracy and the consequent, and still increasing, distaste for arduous disciplines of sentiment—the wholesale acceptance of the merely and unredeemedly natural. Finally, the psychological school of criticism overthrew what was left of the old conception of a poem as a construction and set up instead the poem as 'document'. In so far as we admire Donne for being our first great practitioner in one of the many possible kinds of lyric, we are on firm ground; but the conception of him as liberator, as one who substituted 'real' or 'live' or 'sincere' for 'artificial' or 'conventional' love lyric, begs all the questions and is simply a prejudice de siècle.

But of course when we have identified the Wyatt element in Donne, we have still a very imperfect notion of his manner. We have described 'Busie old foole'[1] and 'I wonder by my troth'[2] and 'For Godsake hold your tongue, and let me love';[3] but we have left out the cleaving remora, the triple soul, the stiff twin compasses, and a hundred other things that were not in Wyatt. There were indeed a great many things not in Wyatt, and his manly plainness can easily

---

* Those who object to 'emotive terms' in criticism may prefer to read '. . . used by an accomplished poet to produce an attitude relevant not directly to outer experience but to the central nucleus of the total attitude-and-belief-feeling system'. It must not be supposed, however, that the present writer's theory of either knowledge or value would permit him, in the long run, to accept the restatement.

[1] 'The Sunne Rising', 1.   [2] 'The Good-morrow', 1.
[3] 'The Canonization', 1.

be over-praised—*pauper videri Cinna vult et est pauper*. If Donne had not reinforced the style with new attractions it would soon have died of very simplicity. An account of these reinforcements will give us a rough notion of the unhappily named 'metaphysical' manner.

The first of them is the multiplication of conceits—not conceits of any special 'metaphysical' type but conceits such as we find in all the Elizabethans. When Donne speaks of the morning coming from his mistress's eyes, or tells how they wake him like the light of a taper, these fanciful hyperboles are not, in themselves, a novelty. But, side by side with these, we find, as his second characteristic, what may be called the difficult conceit. This is clearly a class which no two readers will fill up in quite the same way. An example of what I mean comes at the end of 'The Sunne Rising' where the sun is congratulated on the fact that the two lovers have shortened his task for him. Even the quickest reader will be checked, if only for an infinitesimal time, before he sees how and why the lovers have done this, and will experience a kind of astonished relief at the unexpected answer. The pleasure of the thing, which can be paralleled in other artistic devices, perhaps in rhyme itself, would seem to depend on recurrent tension and relaxation. In the third place, we have Donne's characteristic choice of imagery. The Petrarchans (I will call them so for convenience) had relied for their images mainly on mythology and on natural objects. Donne uses both of these sparingly—though his sea that 'Leaves embroider'd works upon the sand'[1] is as fine an image from nature as I know—and taps new sources such as law, science, philosophy, and the commonplaces of urban life. It is this that has given the Metaphysicals their name and been much misunderstood. When Johnson said that they were resolved to show their learning he said truth in fact, for there is an element of pedantry, of dandyism, an *odi profanos* air, about Donne—the old printer's address not to the *readers* but to the *understanders* is illuminating. But Johnson was none the less misleading. He encouraged the idea that the abstruse nature of some of Donne's similes was poetically relevant for good or ill. In fact, of course, when we have once found out what Donne is talking about —that is, when Sir Herbert Grierson has told us—the learning of the poet becomes unimportant. The image will stand or fall like any other by its intrinsic merit—its power of conveying a meaning 'more

---

[1] 'An Elegie uppon the Death of the Ladie Marckham', 19.

luminously and with a sensation of delight'. The matter is worth mentioning only because Donne's reputation in this respect repels some humble readers and attracts some prigs. What is important for criticism is his avoidance of the obviously poetical image; whether the intractable which he is determined to poetize is fetched from Thomas Aquinas or from the London underworld, the method is essentially the same. Indeed it would be easy to exaggerate the amount of learned imagery in his poems and even the amount of his learning. He knows much, but he seems to know even more because his knowledge so seldom overlaps with our own; and some scraps of his learning, such as that of angelic consciousness or of the three souls in man, come rather too often—like the soldiers in a stage army, and with the same result. This choice of imagery is closely connected with the surprising and ingenious nature of the connexions which Donne makes between the image and the matter in hand, thus getting a double surprise. No one, in the first place, expects lovers to be compared to compasses; and no one, even granted the comparison, would guess in what respect they are going to be compared.

But all these characteristics, in their mere enumeration, are what Donne would have called a 'ruinous anatomie'. They might all be used—indeed they all are used by Herbert—to produce a result very unlike Donne's. What gives their peculiar character to most of the *Songs and Sonets* is that they are dramatic in the sense of being addresses to an imagined hearer in the heat of an imagined conversation, and usually addresses of a violently argumentative character. The majority of lyrics, even where nominally addressed to a god, a woman, or a friend, are meditations or introspective narratives. Thus Herbert's 'Throw away thy rod'[1] is formally an apostrophe; in fact, it is a picture of Herbert's own state of mind. But the majority of the *Songs and Sonets*, including some that are addressed to abstractions like Love, present the poet's state of mind only indirectly and are ostensibly concerned with badgering, wheedling, convincing, or upbraiding an imagined hearer. No poet, not even Browning, buttonholes us or, as we say, 'goes for' us like Donne. There are, of course, exceptions. 'Goe, and catch a falling starre', though it is in the form of an address, has not this effect; and 'Twicknam Garden' or the 'Nocturnall' are in fact, as well as in pretension, soliloquies. These exceptions include some of Donne's best work; and indeed, one of the errors of con-

---

[1] 'Discipline', 1 and 29.

temporary criticism, to my mind, is an insufficient distinction between Donne's best and Donne's most characteristic. But I do not at present wish to emphasize this. For the moment it is enough to notice that the majority of his love lyrics, and of the *Elegies*, are of the type I have described. And since they are, nearly always, in the form of arguments, since they attempt to extort something from us, they are poetry of an extremely exacting kind. This exacting quality, this urgency and pressure of the poet upon the reader in every line, seems to me to be the root both of Donne's weakness and his strength. When the thing fails it exercises the same dreadful fascination that we feel in the grip of the worst kind of bore—the hot-eyed, unescapable kind. When it succeeds it produces a rare intensity in our enjoyment—which is what a modern critic meant (I fancy) when he claimed that Donne made all other poetry sound less 'serious'. The point is worth investigation.

For, of course, in one sense these poems are not serious at all. Poem after poem consists of extravagant conceits woven into the preposterous semblance of an argument. The preposterousness is the point. Donne intends to take your breath away by the combined subtlety and impudence of the steps that lead to his conclusion. Any attempt to overlook Donne's 'wit' in this sense, or to pretend that his rare excursions into the direct expression of passion are typical, is false criticism. The paradox, the surprise, are essential; if you are not enjoying these you are not enjoying what Donne intended. Thus 'Womans Constancy' is of no interest as a document of Donne's 'cynicism'—any fool can be promiscuously unchaste and any fool can say so. The merit of the poem consists in the skill with which it leads us to expect a certain conclusion and then gives us precisely the opposite conclusion, and that, too, with an appearance of reasonableness. Thus, again, the art of 'The Will' consists in keeping us guessing through each stanza what universal in the concluding triplet will bind together the odd particulars in the preceding six lines. The test case is 'The Flea'. If you think this very different from Donne's other poems you may be sure that you have no taste for the real Donne. But for the accident that modern cleanliness by rendering this insect disgusting has also rendered it comic, the conceit is exactly on the same level as that of the tears in 'A Valediction: of Weeping'.

And yet the modern critic was right. The effect of all these poems is somehow serious. 'Serious' indeed is the only word. Seldom profound in thought, not always passionate in feeling, they are none the less the very opposite of gay. It is as though Donne performed in deepest depression those gymnastics which are usually a sign of intellectual high spirits. He himself speaks of his '*concupiscence of witt*'.[1] The hot, dark word is well chosen. We are all familiar—at least if we have lived in Ireland—with the type of mind which combines furious anger with a revelling delight in eloquence, nay grows more rhetorical as anger increases. In the same way, wit and the delight in wit are, for Donne, not only compatible with, but actually provoked by, the most uneasy passions—by contempt and self-contempt and unconvinced sensuality. His wit is not so much the play as the irritability of intellect. But none the less, like the angry Irishman's *clausulae*, it is still enjoyed and still intends to produce admiration; and if we do not hold our breaths as we read, wondering in the middle of each complication how he will resolve it, and exclaiming at the end 'How ever did you think of *that*?' (Carew speaks of his 'fresh invention'), we are not enjoying Donne.

Now this kind of thing can produce a very strong and a very peculiar pleasure. Our age has nothing to repent of in having learned to relish it. If the Augustans, in their love for the obviously poetical and harmonious, were blind to its merits, so much the worse for them. At the same time it is desirable not to overlook the special congeniality of such poetry to the twentieth century, and to beware of giving to this highly specialized and, in truth, very limited kind of excellence, a place in our scheme of literary values which it does not deserve. Donne's rejection of the obviously poetical image was a good method —for Donne; but if we think that there is some intrinsic superiority in this method, so that all poetry about pylons and *non obstantes* must needs be of a higher order than poetry about lawns and lips and breasts and orient skies, we are deceived—deceived by the fact that we, like Donne, happen to live at the end of a great period of rich and nobly obvious poetry. It is natural to want your savoury after your sweets; but you must not base a philosophy of cookery on that momentary preference. Again, Donne's obscurity and occasional abstruseness have sometimes (not always) produced magnificent results, and we do well to praise them. But, as I have hinted, an element of dandyism was present in Donne himself—he 'would have no such readers as he could teach'—and we must be very cautious here lest shallow call

[1] 'The Crosse', 58.

to shallow. There is a great deal of dandyism (largely of Franco-American importation) in the modern literary world. And finally, what shall we say of Donne's 'seriousness', of that persistency, that nimiety, that astringent quality (as Boehme would have said) which makes him, if not the saddest, at least the most uncomfortable, of our poets? Here, surely, we find the clearest and most disturbing congeniality of all. It would be foolish not to recognize the growth in our criticism of something that I can only describe as literary Manichaeism —a dislike of peace and pleasure and heartsease simply as such. To be bilious is, in some circles, almost the first qualification for a place in the Temple of Fame.* We distrust the pleasures of imagination, however hotly and unmerrily we preach the pleasures of the body. This seriousness must not be confused with profundity. We do not like poetry that essays to be wise, and Chaucer would think we had rejected 'doctryne' and 'solas' about equally. We want, in fact, just what Donne can give us—something stern and tough, though not necessarily virtuous, something that does not conciliate. Born under Saturn, we do well to confess the liking complexionally forced upon us; but not to attempt that wisdom which dominates the stars is pusillanimous, and to set up our limitation as a norm—to believe, against all experience, in a Saturnocentric universe—is folly.

Before leaving the discussion of Donne's manner I must touch, however reluctantly, on a charge that has been brought against him from the time of Ben Jonson till now. Should he, or should he not, be hanged for not keeping the accent? There is more than one reason why I do not wish to treat this subject. In the first place, the whole nature of Donne's stanza, and of what he does within the stanza, cannot be profitably discussed except by one who knows much more than I do about the musical history of the time. 'Confined Love', for example, is metrically meaningless without the tune. But I could make shift with that difficulty: my real trouble is of quite a different kind. In discussing Donne's present popularity, the question of metre forces me to a statement which I do not make without embarrassment. Some one must say it, but I do not care for the office, for what I have to say will hardly be believed among scholars and hardly listened to by any one else. It is simply this—that the opinions of the modern world

---

* In this we have been anticipated. See *Emma*, ch. 25: 'I know what worthy people they are. Perry tells me that Mr Cole never touches malt liquor. You would not think it to look at him, but he is bilious—Mr Cole is very bilious.'

on the metre of any poet are, in general, of no value at all, because most modern readers of poetry do not know how to scan. My evidence for this amazing charge is twofold. In the first place I find that very many of my own pupils—some of them from excellent schools, most of them great readers of poetry, not a few of them talented and (for their years) well-informed persons—are quite unable, when they first come to me, to find out from the verse how Marlowe pronounced Barabas or Mahomet. To be sure, if challenged, they will say that they do not believe in syllable-counting or that the old methods of scansion have been exploded, but this is only a smoke screen. It is easy to find out that they have not got beyond the traditional legal fiction of longs and shorts and have never even got so far: they are in virgin ignorance. And my experience as an examiner shows me that this is not peculiar to my own pupils. My second piece of evidence is more remarkable. I have heard a celebrated belle-lettrist—a printed critic and poet—repeatedly, in the same lecture, so mispronounce the name of a familiar English poem as to show that he did not know a decasyllabic line when he met it. The conclusion is unavoidable. Donne may be metrically good or bad, in fact; but it is obvious that he might be bad to any degree without offending the great body of his modern admirers. On that side, his present vogue is worth precisely nothing. No doubt this widespread metrical ignorance is itself a symptom of some deeper change; and I am far from suggesting that the appearance of *vers libre* is simply a result of the ignorance. More probably the ignorance, and the deliberate abandonment, of accentual metres are correlative phenomena, and both the results of some revolution in our whole sense of rhythm—a revolution of great importance reaching deep down into the unconscious and even perhaps into the blood. But that is not our business at the moment.

The sentiment of Donne's love poems is easier to describe than their manner, and its charm for modern readers easier to explain. No one will deny that the twentieth century, so far, has shown an extraordinary interest in the sexual appetite and has been generally marked by a reaction from the romantic idealization of that appetite. We have agreed with the romantics in regarding sexual love as a subject of overwhelming importance, but hardly in anything else. On the purely literary side we are wearied with the floods of uxorious bathos which the romantic conception undoubtedly liberated. As psychologists we are interested in the new discovery of the secreter and less reputable operations of the instinct. As practical philosophers we are living in an age of sexual experiment. The whole subject offers us an admirable field for the kind of seriousness I have just described. It seems odd, at first sight, that a sixteenth-century poet should give us so exactly what we want; but it can be explained.

The great central movement of love poetry, and of fiction about love, in Donne's time is that represented by Shakespeare and Spenser. This movement consisted in the final transmutation of the medieval courtly love or romance of adultery into an equally romantic love that looked to marriage as its natural conclusion. The process, of course, had begun far earlier—as early, indeed, as the *Kingis Quair* —but its triumph belongs to the sixteenth century. It is most powerfully expressed by Spenser, but more clearly and philosophically by Chapman in that under-estimated poem, his *Hero and Leander*. These poets were engaged, as Professor Vinaver would say, in reconciling Carbonek and Camelot, virtue and courtesy, divine and human love; and incidentally in laying down the lines which love poetry was to follow till the nineteenth century. We who live at the end of the dispensation which they inaugurated and in reaction against it are not well placed for evaluating their work. Precisely what is revolutionary and creative in it seems to us platitudinous, orthodox, and stale. If there were a poet, and a strong poet, alive in their time who was failing to move with them, he would inevitably appear to us more 'modern' than they.

But was Donne such a poet? A great critic has assigned him an almost opposite rôle, and it behoves us to proceed with caution. It may be admitted at once that Donne's work is not, in this respect, all of a piece; no poet fits perfectly into such a scheme as I have outlined—it can be true only by round and by large. There are poems in which Donne attempts to sing a love perfectly in harmony with the moral law, but they are not very numerous and I do not think they are usually his best pieces. Donne never for long gets rid of a medieval sense of the sinfulness of sexuality; indeed, just because the old conventional division between Carbonek and Camelot is breaking up, he feels this more continuously and restively than any poet of the Middle Ages.

Donne was bred a Roman Catholic. The significance of this in relation to his learned and scholastic imagery can be exaggerated;

scraps of Calvin, or, for that matter, of Euclid or Bacon, might have much the same poetical effect as his scraps of Aquinas. But it is all-important for his treatment of love. This is not easily understood by the modern reader, for later-day conceptions of the Puritan and the Roman Catholic stand in the way. We have come to use the word 'Puritan' to mean what should rather be called 'rigorist' or 'ascetic', and we tend to assume that the sixteenth-century Puritans were 'puritanical' in this sense. Calvin's rigorist theocracy at Geneva lends colour to the error. But there is no understanding the period of the Reformation in England until we have grasped the fact that the quarrel between the Puritans and the Papists was not primarily a quarrel between rigorism and indulgence, and that, in so far as it was, the rigorism was on the Roman side. On many questions, and specially in their view of the marriage bed, the Puritans were the indulgent party; if we may without disrespect so use the name of a great Roman Catholic, a great writer, and a great man, they were much more Chestertonian than their adversaries. The idea that a Puritan was a repressed and repressive person would have astonished Sir Thomas More and Luther about equally. On the contrary, More thought of a Puritan as one who 'loued no lenton fast, nor lightlye no faste elles, sauing brekefast, and eate fast, and drinke fast, and slepe fast, and luske fast in their lechery'[1]—a person only too likely to end up in the 'abominable heresies' of the Anabaptists about communism of goods and wives. And Puritan theology, so far from being grim and gloomy, seemed to More to err in the direction of fantastic optimism. 'I covld for my parte', he writes, 'be very wel content, that sinne and payn and all wer as shortly gone as Tindall telleth vs. But I wer loth that he deceued vs if it be not so.'[2] More would not have understood the idea, sometimes found in the modern writers, that he and his friends were defending a 'merry' Catholic England against sour precisions; they were rather defending necessary severity and sternly realistic theology against wanton labefaction—penance and 'works' and vows of celibacy and mortification and Purgatory against the easy doctrine, the mere wish-fulfilment dream, of salvation by faith. Hence when we turn from the religious works of More to Luther's *Table Talk* we are at once struck by the geniality of the latter. If Luther is

[1] *The Confvtacion of Tyndales Avnswere*, in *The Workes of Sir Thomas More*, ed. William Rastell (London, 1557), p. 651.
[2] *The Confvtacion of Tyndales Avnswere: The defence of the first argument agaynst Tyndall*, *ibid.*, p. 440.

right, we have waked from nightmare into sunshine: if he is wrong, we have entered a fools' paradise. The burden of his charge against the Catholics is that they have needlessly tormented us with scruples; and, in particular, that 'antichrist will regard neither God nor the love of women'.[1] 'On what pretence have they forbidden us marriage? 'Tis as though we were forbidden to eat, to drink, to sleep.'[2] 'Where women are not honoured, temporal and domestic government are despised.'[3] He praises women repeatedly: More, it will be remembered, though apparently an excellent husband and father, hardly ever mentions a woman save to ridicule her. It is easy to see why Luther's marriage (as he called it) or Luther's 'abominable bichery'[4] (if you prefer) became almost a symbol. More can never keep off the subject for more than a few pages.

This antithesis, if once understood, explains many things in the history of sentiment, and many differences, noticeable to the present day, between the Protestant and the Catholic parts of Europe. It explains why the conversion of courtly love into romantic mono-gamous love was so largely the work of English, and even of Puritan, poets; and it goes far to explain why Donne contributes so little to that movement.

I trace in his poetry three levels of sentiment. On the lowest level (lowest, that is, in order of complexity), we have the celebration of simple appetite, as in 'Elegy XIX'. If I call this a pornographic poem, I must be understood to use that ugly word as a descriptive, not a dyslogistic, term. I mean by it that this poem, in my opinion, is intended to arouse the appetite it describes, to affect not only the imagination but the nervous system of the reader.* And I may as well say at once—but who would willingly claim to be a judge in such matters?—that it seems to me to be very nearly perfect in its kind. Nor would I call it an immoral poem. Under what conditions the reading of it could be an innocent act is a real moral question; but the poem itself contains nothing intrinsically evil.

---

* The restatement of this in terms acceptable to the Richardian school (for whom all poetry equally is addressed to the nervous system) should present no difficulty. For them it will be a distinction between parts, or functions, of the system.

[1] *The Table Talk of Martin Luther*, trans. and ed. William Hazlitt, Bohn's Standard Library (London, 1857), 'Of Antichrist', ccccxxx, p. 193.
[2] *Ibid.*, 'Of Marriage and Celibacy', dccxxviii, p. 300.
[3] *Ibid.*, 'Of Antichrist', ccccxxx, p. 194 (with slight alteration in wording).
[4] Sir Thomas More, *The Confvtacion of Tyndales Avnswere: The defence of the first argument agaynst Tyndall*, *op. cit.*, p. 648.

On the highest, or what Donne supposed to be the highest, level we have the poems of ostentatiously virtuous love, 'The Undertaking', 'A Valediction: forbidding Mourning', and 'The Extasie'. It is here that the contrast between Donne and his happier contemporaries is most marked. He is trying to follow them into the new age, to be at once passionate and innocent; and if any reader will make the experiment of imagining Beatrice or Juliet or Perdita, or again, Amoret or Britomart, or even Philoclea or Pamela, as the auditress throughout these poems, he will quickly feel that something is wrong. You may deny, as perhaps some do, that the romantic conception of 'pure' passion has any meaning; but certainly, if there is such a thing, it is not like this. It does not prove itself pure by talking about purity. It does not keep on drawing distinctions between spirit and flesh to the detriment of the latter and then explaining why the flesh is, after all, to be used. This is what Donne does, and the result is singularly unpleasant. The more he labours the deeper 'Dun is in the mire', and it is quite arguable that 'The Extasie' is a much nastier poem than the nineteenth 'Elegy'. What any sensible woman would make of such a wooing it is difficult to imagine—or would be difficult if we forgot the amazing protective faculty which each sex possesses of not listening to the other.

Between these two extremes falls the great body of Donne's love poetry. In certain obvious, but superficial, respects, it continues the medieval tradition. Love is still a god and lovers his 'clergie';[1] oaths may be made in 'reverentiall feare' of his 'wrath';[2] and the man who resists him is 'rebell and atheist'.[3] Donne can even doubt, like Soredamors, whether those who admit Love after a struggle have not forfeited his grace by their resistance, like

> Small townes which stand stiffe, till great shot
> Enforce them.[4]

He can personify the attributes of his mistress, the 'enormous Gyant' her Disdain and the 'enchantresse Honor',[5] quite in the manner of *The Romance of the Rose*. He writes *albas* for both sexes, and in the *Holy Sonets* repents of his love poetry, writing his palinode, in true medieval fashion. A reader may wonder, at first, why the total effect

[1] 'A Valediction: of the Booke', 22.
[2] 'Womans Constancy', 6, 7.   [3] 'Loves Deitie', 22.
[4] 'Loves Exchange', 24.   [5] 'The Dampe', 11, 12.

is so foreign to the Middle Ages: but Donne himself has explained this when he says, speaking of the god of Love,

> If he wroung from mee'a teare, I brin'd it so
> With scorne or shame, that him it nourish'd not.[1]

This admirable couplet not only tells us, in brief, what Donne has effected but shows us that he knew what he was doing. It does not, of course, cover every single poem. A few pieces admittedly express delighted love and they are among Donne's most popular works; such are 'The Good-morrow' and 'The Anniversarie'—poems that again remind us of the difference between his best and his typical. But the majority of the poems ring the changes on five themes, all of them grim ones—on the sorrow of parting (including death), the miseries of secrecy, the falseness of the mistress, the fickleness of Donne, and finally on contempt for love itself. The poems of parting stand next to the poems of happy love in general popularity and are often extremely affecting. We may hear little of the delights of Donne's loves, and dislike what we hear of their 'purity'; the pains ring true. The song 'Sweetest love, I do not goe' is remarkable for its broken, but haunting, melody, and nowhere else has Donne fused argument, conceit, and classical imitation into a more perfect unity. 'A Feaver' is equally remarkable, and that for a merit very rare in Donne—its inevitability. It is a single jet of music and feeling, a straight flight without appearance of effort. The remaining four of our five themes are all various articulations of the 'scorne or shame' with which Donne 'brines' his reluctantly extorted tributes to the god of Love; monuments, unparalleled outside Catullus, to the close kinship between certain kinds of love and certain kinds of hate. The faithlessness of women is sometimes treated, in a sense, playfully; but there is always something—the clever surprise in 'Womans Constancy' or the grotesque in 'Goe, and catche a falling starre'—which stops these poems short of a true anacreontic gaiety. The theme of faithlessness rouses Donne to a more characteristic, and also a better, poetry in such a hymn of hate as 'The Apparition', or in the sad mingling of fear, contempt, and self-contempt in 'A Lecture upon the Shadow'. The pains of secrecy give opportunity for equally fierce and turbulent writing. I may be deceived when I find in the sixteenth Elegy, along with many other nauseas and indignations, a sickened male contempt

---

[1] 'Loves Diet', 13.

for the whole female world of nurses and 'midnights startings'[1] and hysterics; but 'The Curse' is unambiguous. The ending here is particularly delicious just because the main theme—an attack on *Jealosie* or the 'lozengiers'—is so medieval and so associated with the 'honour of love'. Of the poet's own fickleness one might expect, at last, a merry treatment; and perhaps in 'The Indifferent' we get it. But I am not sure. Even this seems to have a sting in it. And of 'Loves Usury' what shall I say? The struggle between lust and reason, the struggle between love and reason, these we know; but Donne is perhaps the first poet who has ever painted lust holding love at arm's length, in the hope 'that there's no need to trouble himself with any such thoughts yet'—and all this only as an introduction to the crowning paradox that in old age even a reciprocated love must be endured. The poem is, in its way, a masterpiece, and a powerful indirect expression of Donne's habitual 'shame and scorne'. For, in the long run, it must be admitted that 'the love of hatred and the hate of love' is the main, though not the only, theme of the *Songs and Sonets*. A man is a fool for loving and a double fool for saying so in 'whining poetry'; the only excuse is that the sheer difficulty of drawing one's pains through rhyme's vexation 'allays' them. A woman's love at best will be only the 'spheare' of a man's—inferior to it as the heavenly spheres are to their intelligences or air to angels. Love is a spider that can transubstantiate all sweets into bitter: a devil who differs from his fellow devils at court by taking the soul and giving nothing in exchange. The mystery which the Petrarchans or their medieval predecessors made of it is 'imposture all', like the claims of alchemists. It is a very simple matter (*foeda et brevis voluptas*), and all it comes to in the end is

> that my man,
> Can be as happy'as I can.[2]

Unsuccessful love is a plague and tyranny; but there is a plague even worse—Love might try

> A deeper plague, to make her love mee too![3]

Love enjoyed is like gingerbread with the gilt off. What pleased the whole man now pleases one sense only—

[1] 'On his Mistris', 51.   [2] 'Loves Alchymie', 15.
[3] 'Loves Deitie', 25.

And that so lamely, as it leaves behinde
A kinde of sorrowing dulnesse to the minde.[1]

The doctors say it shortens life.

It may be urged that this is an unfair selection of quotations, or even that I have arrived at my picture of Donne by leaving out all his best poems, for one reason or another, as 'exceptions', and then describing what remains. There is one sense in which I admit this. Any account of Donne which concentrates on his love poetry must be unfair to the poet, for it leaves out much of his best work. By hypothesis, it must neglect the dazzling sublimity of his best religious poems, the grotesque charm of *The Progresse of the Soule*, and those scattered, but exquisite, patches of poetry that appear from time to time amidst the insanity of *The First and Second Anniversaries*. Even in the Epistles there are good passages. But as far as concerns his love poetry, I believe I am just. I have no wish to rule out the exceptions, provided that they are admitted to be exceptions. I am attempting to describe the prevailing tone of his work, and in my description no judgement is yet implied.

To Judgement let us now proceed. Here is a collection of verse describing with unusual and disturbing energy the torments of a mind which has been baffled in its relation to sexual love by certain temporary and highly special conditions. What is its value? To admit the 'unusual and disturbing energy' is, of course, to admit that Donne is a poet; he has, in the modern phrase, 'put his stuff across'. Those who believe that criticism can separate inquiry into the success of communication from that into the value of the thing communicated will demand that we should now proceed to evaluate the 'stuff'; and if we do so, it would not be hard to point out how transitory and limited and, as it were, accidental the appeal of such 'stuff' must be. But something of the real problem escapes under this treatment. It would not be impossible to imagine a poet dealing with this same stuff, marginal and precarious as it is, in a way that would permanently engage our attention. Donne's real limitation is not that he writes *about*, but that he writes *in*, a chaos of violent and transitory passions. He is perpetually excited and therefore perpetually cut off from the deeper and more permanent springs of his own excitement. But how is this to be separated from his technique—the nagging, nudging, quibbling stridency of his manner? If a man writes thus, what can he

---

[1] 'Farewell to Love', 19.

communicate but excitement? Or again, if he finds nothing but excitement to communicate, how else should he write? It is impossible here to distinguish cause from effect. Our concern, in the long run, must be with the actual poetry (the 'stuff' *thus* communicated, this communication of *such* 'stuff') and with the question how far that total phenomenon is calculated to interest human imagination. And to this question I can see only one answer: that its interest, save for a mind specially predisposed in its favour, must be short-lived and superficial, though intense. Paradoxical as it may seem, Donne's poetry is too simple to satisfy. Its complexity is all on the surface—an intellectual and fully conscious complexity that we soon come to the end of. Beneath this we find nothing but a limited series of 'passions'— explicit, mutually exclusive passions which can be instantly and adequately labelled as such—things which can be readily talked about, and indeed, must be talked about because, in silence, they begin to lose their hard outlines and overlap, to betray themselves as partly fictitious. That is why Donne is always arguing. There are puzzles in his work, but we can solve them all if we are clever enough; there is none of the depth and ambiguity of real experience in him, such as underlies the apparent simplicity of *How sleep the brave* or *Songs of Innocence*, or even Αἰαῖ Λειψύδριον.* The same is true, for the most part, of the specifically 'metaphysical' comparisons. One idea has been put into each and nothing more can come out of it. Hence they tend to die on our hands, where some seemingly banal comparison of a woman to a flower or God's anger to flame can touch us at innumerable levels and renew its virginity at every reading. Of all literary virtues 'originality', in the vulgar sense, has, for this reason, the shortest life. When we have once mastered a poem by Donne there is nothing more to do with it. To use his own simile, he deals in earthquakes, not in that 'trepidation of the spheares' which is so much less violent but 'greater far'.[1]

Some, of course, will contend that his love poems should interest me permanently because of their 'truth'. They will say that he has shown me passion with the mask off, and catch at my word 'uncomfortable' to prove that I am running away from him because he tells me more truth than I can bear. But this is the mere frenzy of anti-

---

* The superficial simplicity here is obvious; the deeper ambiguity becomes evident if we ask whether Lipsydrion is an object of detestation or of nostalgic affection.

[1] 'A Valediction: forbidding Mourning', 11, 12.

romanticism. Of course, Donne is true in the sense that passions such as he presents do occur in human experience. So do a great many other things. He makes his own selection, like Dickens, or Gower, or Herrick, and his world is neither more nor less 'real' than theirs; while it is obviously less real than the world of Homer, or Virgil, or Tolstoy. In one way, indeed, Donne's love poetry is less true than that of the Petrarchans, in so far as it largely omits the very thing that all the pother is about. Donne shows us a variety of sorrows, scorns, angers, disgusts, and the like which arise out of love. But if any one asked 'What is all this *about*? What is the attraction which makes these partings so sorrowful? What is the peculiarity about this physical pleasure which he speaks of so contemptuously, and how has it got tangled up with such a storm of emotions?', I do not know how we could reply except by pointing to some ordinary love poetry. The feeblest sonnet, almost, of the other school would give us an answer with coral lips and Cupid's golden wings and the opening rose, with perfumes and instruments of music, with some attempt, however trite, to paint that iridescence which explains why people write poems about love at all. In this sense Donne's love poetry is parasitic. I do not use this word as a term of reproach; there are so many good poets, by now, in the world that one particular poet is entitled to take for granted the depth of a passion and deal with its froth. But as a purely descriptive term, 'parasitic' seems to me true. Donne's love poems could not exist unless love poems of a more genial character existed first. He shows us amazing shadows cast by love upon the intellect, the passions, and the appetite; to learn of the substance which casts them we must go to other poets, more balanced, more magnanimous, and more humane. There are, I well remember, poems (some two or three) in which Donne himself presents the substance; and the fact that he does so without much luxury of language and symbol endears them to our temporarily austere taste. But in the main, his love poetry is *Hamlet* without the prince.

Donne's influence on the poets of the seventeenth century is a commonplace of criticism. Of that influence at its best, as it is seen in the great devotional poetry of the period, I have not now to speak. In love poetry he was not, perhaps, so dominant. His *nequitiae* probably encouraged the cynical and licentious songs of his successors, but, if so, the imitation is very different from the model. Suckling's impudence, at its best, is light-hearted and very unlike the ferocity of

Donne; and Suckling's chief fault in this vein—a stolid fleshliness which sometimes leads him to speak of his mistress's body more like a butcher than a lecher—is entirely his own. The more strictly metaphysical elements in Donne are, of course, lavishly reproduced; but I doubt if the reproduction succeeds best when it is most faithful. Thus Carew's stanzas 'When thou, poor Excommunicate' or Lovelace's 'To Lucasta, Going beyond the Seas' are built up on Donne's favourite plan, but both, as it seems to me, fail in that startling and energetic quality which this kind of thing demands. They have no edge. When these poets succeed it is by adding something else to what they have learned from Donne—in fact by reuniting Donne's manner with something much more like ordinary poetry. Beauty (like cheerfulness) is always breaking in. Thus the conceit of asking where various evanescent, beautiful phenomena go when they vanish and replying that they are all to be found in one's mistress is the sort of conceit that Donne might have used; and, starting from that end, we could easily work it up into something tolerably like bad Donne. As thus:

> Oh fooles that aske whether of odours burn'd
> The seminall forme live, and from that death
> Conjure the same with chymique arte—'tis turn'd
> To that quintessence call'd her Breath!

But if we use the same idea as Carew uses it we get a wholly different effect:

> Aske me no more where Jove bestowes,
> When June is past, the fading rose:
> For in your beauties orient deepe,
> These flowers as in their causes, sleepe.[1]

The idea is the same. But the choice of the obvious and obviously beautiful rose, instead of the recondite seminal form of vegetables, the great regal name of Jove, the alliteration, the stately voluptuousness of a quatrain where all the accented syllables are also long in quantity (a secret little known)—all this smothers the sharpness of thought in sweetness. Compared with Donne, it is almost soporific; compared with it, Donne is shrill. But the conceit is there; and 'as in their causes, sleepe' which looks at first like a blunder, is in fact a paradox that Donne might have envied. So again, the conceit that the lady's hair outshines the sun, though not much more than an Elizabethan conceit, might well have appeared in the *Songs and Sonets*; but

[1] 'A Song', 1.

Donne would neither have wished, nor been able, to attain the radiance of Lovelace's

> But shake your head and scatter day![1]

This process of enchanting, or, in Shakespeare's sense, 'translating' Donne was carried to its furthest point by Marvell. Almost every element of Donne—except his metrical roughness—appears in the 'Coy Mistress'. Nothing could be more like Donne, both in the grimness of its content and in its impudently argumentative function, than the conceit that

> worms shall try
> That long preserv'd virginity.[2]

All the more admirable is the art by which this, and everything else in that poem, however abstruse, dismaying, or sophistical, is sub-ordinated to a sort of golden tranquillity. What was death to Donne is mere play to Marvell. 'Out of the strong', we are tempted to say, 'has come sweetness', but in reality the strength is all on Marvell's side. He is an Olympian, ruling at ease for his own good purposes, all that intellectual and passionate mobility of which Donne was the slave, and leading Donne himself, bound, behind his chariot.

From all this we may conclude that Donne was a 'good influence' —a better influence than many greater poets. It would hardly be too much to say that the final cause of Donne's poetry is the poetry of Herbert, Crashaw, and Marvell; for the very qualities which make Donne's kind of poetry unsatisfying poetic food make it a valuable ingredient.[3]

[1] 'To Amarantha, That she would dishevell her haire', IV, 4.
[2] 'To his Coy Mistress', 27.
[3] This essay was originally followed by Joan Bennett's 'The Love Poetry of John Donne: A Reply to Mr C. S. Lewis', *Seventeenth Century Studies Presented to Sir Herbert Grierson* (Oxford, 1938), pp. 85–104.

9

The Literary Impact of the
Authorised Version

No translation can preserve the qualities of its original unchanged. On the other hand, except where lyrical poetry is in question, the literary effect of any good translation must be more indebted to the original than to anything else. This is especially true of narrative and of moral instruction. Where the originals are Hebrew it holds in an unusual degree even for lyrical poetry because the parallelism of the form is a translatable quality. There is therefore no possibility of considering the literary impact of the Authorised Version apart from that of the Bible in general. Except in a few passages where the translation is bad, the Authorised Version owes to the original its matter, its images, and its figures. Our aesthetic experience in reading any of the great Old Testament stories or, say, the liberation of St Peter and the shipwreck of St Paul,[1] depends only to a small extent on the translator. That is why I hope I may be excused for prefacing what I have to say about the literary fortunes of our English Bible by some remarks on the literary fortunes of the Bible before it became English. What is common, even from the literary point of view, to the originals and all the versions is after all far more important than what is peculiar. And by carrying the story a little farther back we have more chance to be cured of our dangerous though natural assumption that a book which has always been praised has always been read in the same way or valued for the same reasons. Virgil's Homer was very different from Chapman's, Chapman's from Pope's, Pope's from Andrew Lang's, and Andrew Lang's from Mr Rieu's.

There is a certain sense in which 'the Bible as literature' does not exist. It is a collection of books so widely different in period, kind, language, and aesthetic value, that no common criticism can be passed on them. In uniting these heterogeneous texts the Church was not guided by literary principles, and the literary critic might regard their inclusion between the same boards as a theological and historical

---

[1] Acts xii. 1–11; Acts xxvii.

accident irrelevant to his own branch of study. But when we turn from the originals to any version made by one man, or at least bearing the stamp of one age, a certain appearance of unity creeps in. The Septuagint, the Vulgate, Luther's Bible, or the Authorised Version, can each perhaps be regarded as a book. And in the minds of those who used these translations the impression, if you will the illusion, of unity was increased by the unity of the liturgical context in which they were heard, and also by the doctrine of Inspiration. A belief in strictly verbal inspiration will indeed make all Scripture a book by a single Author. Hence Donne in his Seventy-Ninth Sermon rather comically passes favourable judgement on the style of the Omnipotent, assuring us that 'the Holy Ghost is an eloquent author, a vehement and an abundant author, but yet not luxuriant'.

The Bible thus considered, for good or ill, as a single book, has been read for almost every purpose more diligently than for literary pleasure. Yet certain *testimonia* to it even on that score can be collected from earlier ages.

The oldest literary appreciation that I know is also the most modern in tone. When Longinus* praises the author of Genesis—in his language, 'the lawgiver of the Jews'—for sublimity of conception, he seems to express a literary experience very like our own. Genesis is placed beside Homer and in some respects preferred to him. The Bible is being ranked among the classics on purely secular grounds. But it would be difficult to cite strict parallels from the ages that follow.

The learned M. de Bruyne in his *Études d'esthétique médiévale* (1946) has collected a mass of evidence about the literary appreciation of Scripture in the Middle Ages. Praise is not lacking; but we certainly find ourselves in an alien world. On the threshold of that period we meet St Augustine's curious statement that the Bible uses *humillimum genus loquendi*.† If this referred to style in the narrower sense, if the Psalms and Prophets seemed to him to use 'the lowest language' it would be almost inexplicable. Almost, but not quite; the great, roaring machine of Latin rhetoric can, at times, deafen the human ear to all other literature. But from the context I suppose that St Augustine is referring to something rather different—to that apparent naïvety or simplicity of the literal sense which offended him until he had been taught that it was merely the outer shell, concealing the *sacramen-*

---

* *De Sublimitate*, IX. † *Confessions*, VI, v.

torum altitudo.* This distinction between the literal or historical sense and the allegorical senses—however these are classified by different doctors—is a fundamental factor in all medieval reading of the Bible. It is no doubt true, and must be insisted on, that no superstructure of allegories was allowed to abrogate the truth of the literal sense. Hugo of St Victor urges upon his pupils the necessity of mastering the literal sense first. 'I think', he writes, 'you will never be perfectly subtle in the Allegory unless you are first grounded in the History.'† Yet this very passage reveals how inevitably the medieval exegesis belittled what we should regard as the actual literary quality of the text. It is clear that Hugo expects his pupils to hurry through the historical sense too quickly and perfunctorily. *Noli contemnere minima haec*‡ he adds, 'Despise not these small things.' If you had despised the alphabet you would not now be able to read. An appreciation for which the story of Joseph and his brethren or David and Goliath was merely the alphabet, a necessary preliminary to higher and more delightful studies, may have been keen, but it was very unlike our own. Hence we are not surprised to find him saying that the Scriptures are like a honeycomb. They appear dry on the outside *per simplicitatem sermonis* but are *dulcedine plena* within.§ Notice how the *simplicitas sermonis* echoes St Augustine's *humillimum genus loquendi*. Again, the Scripture may be compared to a lyre. The spiritual senses are like the strings: the historical sense is like the wood which does not sound itself but keeps the strings together.‖

I do not wish in any way to deride the doctrine of multiple senses. Our own age, steeped in the symbolism of dreams and in the allegorical or semi-allegorical work of writers like Kafka and Mr Rex Warner, will not look down on that doctrine with superiority. We may anticipate a revival of the allegorical sense in Biblical criticism. But it will probably be dangerous, and in the Middle Ages I think it was dangerous, to appreciation of the Historical Books as plain heroic narrative.

St Thomas Aquinas throws a little more light on the references which we have already met to the 'lowness' or 'simplicity' of the Bible. He explains why Scripture expresses divine truths not merely through corporeal images but even through images of vile bodies rather than noble.¶ This is done, he says, to liberate the mind from error, to

* *Conf.*, VI, v. † *Eruditionis Didascalicae*, VI, iii.
‡ *Ibid.* § *Ibid.*, IV, i.
‖ *Ibid.*, V, ii. ¶ *Summa Theologica*, Quaest. I, Art. IX.

reduce the danger of any confusion between the symbol and the reality. It is an answer worthy of a profound theologian. At the same time, the passage in which it occurs reveals attitudes most hostile to aesthetic appreciation of the sacred text. It would seem, he says, that Scripture ought not to use metaphors. For what is proper to the lowest kind of learning (*infimae doctrinae*) does not seem suitable to the queen of the sciences. But metaphor is proper to poetry, and poetry is the lowest of all forms of learning—*est infima inter omnes doctrinas*. The answer, so far as it concerns us here, is that poetry and Scripture use metaphor for quite different reasons; poetry for delight, and Scripture *propter necessitatem et utilitatem*.* Where a nineteenth-century critic might have said that Scripture was itself the highest poetry, St Thomas says rather that the highest and the lowest *doctrinae* have, paradoxically, one point in common, but of course for different reasons.

From other medieval writers, notably Ulric of Strasbourg, de Bruyne has collected passages which seem, but perhaps not without illusion, to come nearer to the modern point of view. In general, however, I do not think we shall go too far if we say that medieval appreciation of the Bible is divided from modern by a very wide gulf.

If the medieval approach is alien, that of the Renaissance seems to me sometimes repellent. We reach the age of Ciceronianism, of Humanism, of that deadly classical dignity which so obscured and distorted (along with many other things) the classics themselves. It was an age in which Scaliger could tax Homer with vulgarity and complain that Andromache's lament over Hector smacked of an ill-bred woman—*plebeiam mulierculam*.† Where an aesthetic like this prevailed the simple grandeur of *Kings* and *Judges* and the Gospels had little chance of being valued at its true worth. Hence Vida thought that the story of the Passion could be improved by the tinsel of his *Christiad*. In a sense, of course, it is only a literary counterpart to the religious paintings of the time: there, too, vast Vitruvian halls rise as the background to 'deep, abstracted, holy scenes'. I leave to others a problem I have failed to solve—why this offends in words so much more than it does in paint—and pursue our immediate subject, by tracing the effect of this movement even on so great a man as Sir Thomas More. In his late treatise 'On the Passion' he ventures to put words into the mouth of Our Lord. The thing had been done before. In the *Imitation* it had been so done as to satisfy not only

---

* *Ibid.*   † *Poetics*, v, iii.

piety but our sense of the Dominical style. But More takes the words in Gethsemane, 'This is your hour and the power of darkness',[1] and seems to think they can be strengthened by expansion into the following:

Thys is the shorte whyle that is graunted yee, and the libertie geuen unto darknesse, that nowe ye maye in the night, which till this howre ye coulde neuer be suffered to bryng to passe in the daye, like monstruous rauenynge fowles, lyke skryche owles and hegges, lyke backes, howlettes, nighte crowes, and byrdes of the hellye lake, goe aboute with your billes, your tallentes, your teeth, and your shyrle shryching outerageouslye, but all in vayne thus in the darke to flee uppon me.*

I ought to warn you that I am quoting a translation, that of More's granddaughter. But if anyone looks at the Latin and likes it much better than the English, I shall be surprised. I am not, of course, suggesting for one moment any spiritual flaw. The question is about More's taste. Indeed, the more we reverence him as a man, the more striking the example becomes. Even a man so steeped as he in the spirit of the Dominical utterances could be, by Humanistic rhetoric, so deafened to the majesty of their style.

With the first Protestant translators we get some signs of a changed approach. I would wish to take every precaution against exaggerating it. The history of the English Bible from Tyndale to the Authorised Version should never for long be separated from that European, and by no means exclusively Protestant, movement of which it made part. No one can write that history without skipping to and fro across national and religious boundaries at every moment. He will have to go from the Soncino Hebrew Bible (1488) to Reuchlin's Hebrew Grammar (1506), then to Alcala for Cardinal Ximenes' great Polyglot (1514) and north for Erasmus' New Testament in the same year, and then to Luther for the German New Testament in 1522, and pick up Hebrew again with Munster's Grammar in 1525, and see Luther worked over by Zwinglius and others for the Zürich Bible of 1529, and glance at the two French versions of '34 and '35, and by no means neglect the new Latin translations of Pagninus ('28) and Munster ('34–'35). That is the sort of background against which Tyndale, Coverdale, Geneva, and Rheims must be set. For when we come to compare the versions we shall find that only a very small percentage of variants are

---

* *A treatice upon the passion*, in *The Workes* (London, 1557), p. 1397, D–E.
[1] Luke xxii. 53.

made for stylistic or even doctrinal reasons. When men depart from their predecessors it is usually because they claim to be better Hebraists or better Grecians. The international advance of philology carries them on, and those who are divided by the bitterest theological hatreds gladly learn from one another. Tyndale accepts corrections from More: Rheims learns from Geneva: phrases travel through Rheims on their way from Geneva to Authorised. Willy-nilly all Christendom collaborates. The English Bible is the English branch of a European tree.

Yet in spite of this there is something new about Tyndale; for good or ill a great simplification of approach. 'Scripture', he writes, 'speaketh after the most grossest manner. Be diligent therefore that thou be not deceived with curiousness.'* In the words 'grossest manner' we recognize an echo of Augustine's *humillimum genus* and Hugo of St Victor's *simplicitas sermonis.*† That rusticity or meanness which we find it so hard to discern in the Bible is still apparent to Tyndale. The novelty is the rejection of the allegorical senses. That rejection he shares with most of the Reformers and even, as regards parts of the Bible, with a Humanistic Papist like Colet; and it is no part of my business to decide whether it marked an advance or a retrogression in theology. What is interesting is not Tyndale's negation of the allegories but his positive attitude towards the literal sense. He loves it for its 'grossness'. 'God is a Spirit', he writes, 'and all his words are spiritual. His literal sense is spiritual.'‡ That is very characteristic of Tyndale's outlook. For him, just as God's literal sense is spiritual, so all life is religion: cleaning shoes, washing dishes, our humblest natural functions, are all 'good works'.§ The life of *religion*, technically so called, wins no 'higher room in heaven ... than a whore of the stews (if she repent)'.‖ This would certainly seem to be an attitude more favourable to the literary appreciation of much Scripture than any we have yet encountered. On the other hand Mr Gavin Bone, whose loss we still deplore at Oxford, has said

---

* 'The Parable of the Wicked Mammon', in *Doctrinal Treatises and Introductions to Different Portions of the Holy Scriptures*, ed. H. Walter (Cambridge, 1848), p. 59.
† *Conf.*, VI, v; *Eruditionis Didascalicae*, IV, i. See also Robert Burton, *The Anatomy of Melancholy*, Pt. 3, Sect. 4, Mem. 2, Subs. 6 (London, 1907, pp. 728–729), 'Blasphemous thoughts ... the Scripture [fosters], rude, harsh, immethodical.'
‡ 'The Obedience of a Christian Man', *op. cit.*, ed. Walter, p. 309.
§ 'The Parable of the Wicked Mammon', *op. cit.*, ed. Walter, pp. 100, 102.
‖ 'A Pathway into the Holy Scripture', *op. cit.*, ed. Walter, p. 21.

roundly that Tyndale 'hated literature'. This is based on his fierce condemnation of medieval romance;* a trait which is Humanistic as well as Puritanical. But I do not think he did hate literature. When he speaks of his own work as a translator he sounds like a man with a sense of style; as when he says that Hebrew and Greek go well into English whereas 'thou must seek a compass in the Latin, and yet shall have much work to translate it well-favouredly, so that it hath the same grace and sweetness'.† More important still is the evidence of his own original works.

I wish I had time to digress on those works. Tyndale's fame as an English writer has been most unjustly overshadowed both by the greater fame of More and by his own reputation as a translator. He seems to me the best prose writer of his age. He is inferior to More in what may be called the elbow-room of the mind and (of course) in humour. In every other respect he surpasses him; in economy, in lucidity, and above all in rhythmical vitality. He reaches at times a piercing quality which is quite outside More's range: 'as a man feeleth God in himself, so is he to his neighbour'‡—'I am thou thyself, and thou art I myself, and can be no nearer of kin'§—'be glad, and laugh from the low bottom of his heart'‖—'that he might see love, and love again'¶—'Who taught the eagles to spy out their prey? Even so the children of God spy out their Father.'** Though it is not strictly relevant, may I be excused, since the fact seems to be insufficiently known, for saying that Tyndale's social ethics are almost identical with those of More?—quite equally medieval and equally opposed to what some call the New Economics. The points on which these two brave and holy men agreed may have been few; but perhaps they were sufficient, if they had been accepted, to have altered the course of our history for the better.

It is not, of course, to be supposed that aesthetic considerations were uppermost in Tyndale's mind when he translated Scripture. The matter was much too serious for that; souls were at stake. The same holds for all the translators. Coverdale was probably the one whose

* 'The Obedience of a Christian Man', p. 161.
† *Ibid.*, pp. 148, 149.
‡ 'The Parable of the Wicked Mammon', p. 58.
§ 'The Obedience of a Christian Man', p. 296.
‖ 'A Pathway into the Holy Scripture', p. 9.
¶ 'The Obedience of a Christian Man', p. 136.
** *An Answer to Sir Thomas More's Dialogue*, ed. H. Walter (Cambridge, 1850), p. 49.

choice of a rendering came nearest to being determined by taste. His defects as well as his qualities led to this. Of all the translators he was the least scholarly. Among men like Erasmus, Tyndale, Munster, or the Jesuits at Rheims he shows like a rowing boat among battleships. This gave him a kind of freedom. Unable to judge between rival interpretations, he may often have been guided, half consciously, to select and combine by taste. Fortunately his taste was admirable.

The history of the Authorised Version has been told so often that I will not attempt to re-tell it, and its beauties praised so lavishly that I will not praise them. Instead, I will proceed at once to its influence as an English book. I shall attempt to define that influence, for I think there has been misunderstanding about it and even a little exaggeration.

Let us begin by distinguishing the various senses in which one book can be said to influence the author of another book.

1. A book may be, in the familiar language of research, a *source*. Lydgate mentions the loves of Mars and Venus. The immediate source might be some book like Boccaccio's *De Genealogia*, the ultimate source is Homer. It would, I think, be quite good English to say that Lydgate was here influenced by Homer. But that is not the most useful way of employing the word in literary history, nor is it generally so employed. If anyone wishes to call a Source an Influence, let him do so; but let him recognize a Source as a very special kind of Influence. Most of us, I expect, would prefer to distinguish Source from Influence altogether. A Source gives us things to write about; an Influence prompts us to write in a certain way. Homer is a Source to Lydgate, but Homer was an Influence on Arnold when he wrote *Sohrab and Rustum*. Firdausi's *Shahnameh* was Arnold's Source, but not an Influence on that poem. Malory was both a Source and an Influence in Tennyson's *Morte d'Arthur*; elsewhere in the *Idylls* a Source but perhaps hardly an Influence.

If these terms are accepted, we can distinguish the Bible as a Source for English literature from the Bible as a literary Influence. That it is a Source of immense importance is obvious. For several centuries its persons, scenes, and doctrines were familiar to every Englishman. They are constantly used for illustration and allusion. But, of course, when the Bible is a Source, there is usually nothing to show whether the Authorised Version is being used or not. The Bible is one Source for Dryden's *Absalom and Achitophel*, but his spelling of Achitophel's name is not derived from the Authorised.[1] We may indeed assume that most authors, and all unlearned authors, after the sixteenth century derived their Biblical knowledge from that version. But this does not seem to be a fact of any importance. The persons and stories would be the same in whatever text they were known. In my view the huge mass of Biblical material in our literature has no place in an account of the Influence of the Authorised Version considered as an English book.

2. It would, I suppose, be possible to say that we are influenced by a book whenever we quote it; but probably no literary historian would wish to use the word *influence* in that way. It would seem to me reasonable to say, for example, that my own habit of immoderate quotation showed the Influence of Hazlitt, but not the Influence of the authors I quote; or that Burton's habit of immoderate quotation might be influenced by Montaigne, not by the authors he quotes. Frequent quotation is itself a literary characteristic; if the authors whom we rifle were not themselves fond of quotation, then, in the very act of quoting, we proclaim our freedom from their influence. It is almost the difference between borrowing a man's clothes for a particular occasion and imitating his style of dress. If English literature is full of Biblical quotation, I would not describe this as the influence of the Authorised Version, any more than I would call Virgilians all those who quote Virgil. I am not saying that to do otherwise would be necessarily an improper use of language: I only think mine useful for the purpose in hand.

3. So far I have been speaking of what may be called flagrant quotation—quotation isolated and proclaimed by typographical devices. But besides this, there is of course the embedded quotation—sentences or phrases from the Authorised Version artfully worked into an author's own language so that an ignorant reader might not recognize them. Our literature is full of this, especially in the nineteenth and early twentieth centuries; in Trollope, Swinburne, and Kipling it becomes a positive nuisance; one contemporary American professor is very seriously infected. To this process the word Influence might much more naturally be applied. Yet even this does not seem to me to be Influence in the deepest sense, and I would prefer not to call it Influence at all. I will try to explain why.

Let us begin by laying side by side with it two other phenomena

---

[1] Authorised Version: *Ahithophel* (e.g. 2 Samuel xv. 12).

of the same sort: the ubiquitous embedded quotations from Homer in Plato's prose, or from Shakespeare in English prose. The scraps of Homer slip very artfully in and out of the orchestration of a Platonic period. But of course they are all marked out from their surroundings by their metre and their dialect. No one would maintain that Plato's own style grows out of, or was learned from, Homer's. And indeed the Homeric bits would not be doing their work unless they were felt to be different from the Attic prose that surrounds them. They are used either for solemnity or facetiously—and the facetious is only the solemn stood on its head. The very response they demand depends on our feeling them as aliens. There would be no point in them unless we did. Far from showing that Plato's style has assimilated Homer's, they show the irreducible difference between them. And are not the embedded Shaksperian quotations in English the same? Of course, not every hack who speaks of a man more sinned against than sinning, or a consummation devoutly to be wished, knows that he is quoting Shakespeare. He may think (significantly) that he is quoting the Bible. He may even think he is using a proverb. But he knows quite well, and he expects his readers to know, that he is borrowing from somewhere. He counts on recognition. He is decorating his style. He wants the phrase to stand out from his own composition as gold lace stands out from a coat. The whole pleasure, such as it is, depends on the fact that the embedded quotation is different—in other words that his own style is not influenced by Shakespeare.

I believe that our embedded quotations from the Authorised Version are nearly always in exactly this position. They are nearly always either solemn or facetious. Only because the surrounding prose is different—in other words, only in so far as our English is not influenced by the Authorised Version—do they achieve the effect the authors intended.

4. Here at last we reach what I would describe as Influence in the full and strict sense—the influence of the Authorised Version on vocabulary. I do not think we are being (in this sense) influenced by Shakespeare when we speak of a consummation devoutly to be wished. But I do think we are influenced by him (though the phonetic history is complicated) whenever we use *weird* as an adjective. We do so with no sense of quotation: the word has been really assimilated, has gone into the blood-stream of our language. In the same way we are being influenced by Van Helmont (and perhaps by Paracelsus) whenever we use the word *gas*. In the same way we are being influenced by the

Authorised Version and its predecessors whenever we use the words *beautiful*, *long-suffering*, *peacemaker* or *scapegoat*. Tyndale is our ultimate creditor for all these. But even here I must plead for a distinction. Henry Bradley rightly mentioned *damsel*, *raiment*, *travail*, and *quick* in the sense 'alive', as words saved by the Authorised Version for archaic and poetical use.[1] But only for such use. They are not in the blood-stream. As for *loving-kindness* and *tender mercies*, they are so generally confined either to religious contexts or to mockery (which for our special purpose tells the same tale) that I almost classify them as very short embedded quotations.

5. Finally, we come to literary influence in the fullest sense, the sense it bears when we say that *Paradise Lost* is influenced by Homer and Virgil, or nineteenth-century journalism by Macaulay, or modern English poetry by Mr Eliot. You will perhaps remember that I have defined Influence, in this sense, as that which prompts a man to write in a certain way. But even within this definition further distinctions break out. The influence may show itself in architectonics. That is the most obvious, though by no means the only, manner in which Virgil influences Milton. The whole plan of his epic is Virgilian. Very few English writers have undergone an influence of that sort from any book of the Bible. Tupper's *Proverbial Philosophy* and the *Book of Mormon* are perhaps instances. Some would add Blake's *Prophetic Books*. Again, Influence may show itself in the use of language—in the rhythm, the imagery, or (using that word in its narrowest sense) the style.

The influence of the rhythms of the Authorised Version seems to me to be very hard to detect. Its rhythms are in fact extremely various, and some of them are unavoidable in the English language. I am not at all sure that a resemblance in rhythm, unless supported by some other resemblance, is usually recognisable. If I say 'At the regatta Madge avoided the river and the crowd' would this, without warning, remind you of 'In the beginning God created the heaven and the earth'? Even if it did, is the common rhythm, thus separated from community of thought and temper, a matter of any importance? I believe that wherever an English writer seems to us to recall the scriptural rhythms, he is always recalling other associations as well. The influence of rhythm, isolated from imagery and style, is perhaps an abstraction.

[1] Henry Bradley, *The Making of English* (London, 1904), p. 223.

In imagery I suppose the influence to be very great, though I must frankly confess that I have not been able to invent a method of checking it. If English writers in elevated contexts tend to speak of corn and wine rather than of beef and beer and butter, of chariots rather than chargers, of rain rather than sunshine as a characteristic blessing, of sheep more often than cows and of the sword more often than either the pike or the gun, if bread rather than mutton or potatoes is their lofty synonym for food, if stone is more poetical than brick, trumpets than bugles and purple and fine linen loftier than satin and velvet, I suspect that this is due to the Bible, but I have no rigorous proof. Nor, in this sphere, would it be easy to distinguish the Biblical influence from that generally Mediterranean and ancient influence which comes from the classics as well as the Bible. But I believe the Biblical influence is here very great.

But in our style, in the actual build of our sentences, I think the influence has possibly been less than we suppose. The perfect example of an influence in this field is that exercised on our prose by Dryden and his contemporaries (Tillotson and the like). You remember that he went all through the *Essay of Dramatick Poesie* and altered every sentence that ended with a preposition. This is, I say, a perfect example of Influence. No one can pretend that this curious taboo was inherent in the genius of the language and would have developed even without the action of Dryden and his fellow Gallicists. On the contrary, it is so alien from the language that it has never penetrated into the conversation of even the worst prigs, and serves no purpose but to increase those little bunches of unemphatic monosyllables that English was already prone to. On the other hand, it has so established itself in our formal style that thousands obey it unconsciously. It is, very precisely, a thing that prompts us to write in a certain way: even I, who detest it for a frenchified schoolroom superstition, often feel it plucking at my elbow. I doubt whether the Authorised Version has achieved any comparable dominance over our style. Indeed, what astonishes me here is the failure of some of its most familiar terms to get into our language at all. *It came to pass, answered and said, lo—* have these ever been used by any English writer without full consciousness that he was quoting? If we look into those authors who are usually said to be influenced by the style of the Authorised Version, we shall find that such influence is indeed present but that it is hardly dominant. I will consider Ruskin and Bunyan.

In Ruskin embedded quotation and imagery from the Bible are made great use of, but Homer and Spenser are used not very much less. Dante not infrequently. And all these are used consciously. What Ruskin tells us in *Praeterita*[1] about the formation of his own style is relevant:

> Had it not been for constant reading of the Bible, I might probably have taken Johnson for my model of English. To a useful extent I have always done so; in these first essays, partly because I could not help it, partly of set, and well set, purpose... The turns and returns of reiterated *Rambler* and iterated *Idler* fastened themselves in my ears and mind; nor was it possible for me, till long afterwards, to quit myself of Johnsonian symmetry ... in sentences intended, either with swordsman's or paviour's blow, to cleave an enemy's crest, or drive down the oaken pile of a principle.

In his mature style—in this very passage—I think we can recognize the Johnsonian element: I cannot recognize the Biblical. Elsewhere, though I do not deny its presence—and especially in the images—it is one of many resources. I think *resources* is the best word. It is, so to speak, one of the colours in his paint box, used at his own discretion. He has many others. And what makes the total effect, for me, so very unlike the Authorised Version, is the periodic structure of Ruskin's prose. Already in the passage quoted, which is familiar and epistolary compared with the high passages in *Modern Painters* or *The Stones of Venice*, you will have noticed the transition *nor was it possible*. That is learned from classical Latin. And so, in the long run, is the Ruskinian period as a whole. A structure descending from Cicero through the prose of Hooker, Milton, and Taylor, and then enriched with romantic colouring for which Homer and the Bible are laid under contribution—that seems to me the formula for Ruskin's style. If you could take away what comes from the Bible it would be impaired. It would hardly, I think, be crippled. It would certainly not be annihilated. This is real influence, but limited influence. The influence of Italian epic on Spenser would be a good contrast. If you took away from the *Faerie Queene* everything that is learned from Ariosto and Boiardo, what would be left would be either nothing or a radically different poem. This is quite consistent with the view that Spenser has added something of his own and even transmuted his originals. The alchemist may turn silver into gold: but he has to have the silver.

[1] Vol. i, ch. xii.

Bunyan, at first sight, will strike most of us as far more Biblical than Ruskin. But this impression is partly due to the fact that both are to us rather archaic and rather simple in syntax. To that extent any unlearned author of Bunyan's time would be bound to remind us of the Bible whether he had ever read it or not. We must discount that accidental similarity and look deeper. I take an example at random:

So *Mistrust* and *Timorous* ran down the Hill; and *Christian* went on his way. But thinking again of what he heard from the men, he felt in his bosom for his Roll: that he might read therein and be comforted; but he felt, and found it not. Then was *Christian* in great distress, and knew not what to do, for he wanted that which used to relieve him, and that which should have been his Pass into the Coelestial City. Here therefore he began to be much perplexed, and knew not what to do; at last he bethought himself that he had slept in the *Arbour*.[1]

The question is not how much of this might occur in the Authorised Version, but how much might be expected to occur in Bunyan if he had not read it. Much of it, of course, is quite unlike the Bible: phrases like *Then was* Christian *in great distress, he wanted that which used to relieve him, Here therefore he began to be much perplexed.* There remain *he went on his way, he felt and found it not,* and the use of *so* to introduce a new step in a narrative. These are in the manner of the Authorised Version—though this use of *so* is not very common there and is far commoner in Malory. But I do not feel at all certain that Bunyan is deriving them from his Bible. And if we look through his work we shall find that his best and most characteristic sentences often have a very unscriptural ring:

But the Man, not at all discouraged, fell to cutting and hacking most fiercely.[2]

So I looked up in my Dream, and saw the Clouds rack at an unusual rate, upon which I heard a great sound of a Trumpet . . .[3]

Why he objected against Religion it self; he said it was a pitiful, low, sneaking business for a man to mind Religion.[4]

Some also have wished that the next way to their Fathers House were here, that they might be troubled no more with either Hills or Mountains to go over; but the way is the way, and there's an end.[5]

At last he came in, and I will say that for my Lord, he carried it wonderful lovingly to him. There were but a few good bits at the Table, but some of it was laid upon his Trencher.[6]

[1] *The Pilgrim's Progress*, ed. James Blanton Wharey, second edition revised by Roger Sharrock, Oxford English Texts (Oxford, 1960), Pt. I, p. 43.
[2] *Ibid.*, Pt. I, p. 33.   [3] *Ibid.*, Pt. I, p. 36.   [4] *Ibid.*, Pt. I, p. 72.
[5] *Ibid.*, Pt. II, p. 237.   [6] *Ibid.*, Pt. II, p. 251.

Such passages seem to me the essential Bunyan. His prose comes to him not from the Authorised Version but from the fireside, the shop, and the lane. He is as native as Malory or Defoe. The Scriptural images themselves take on a new homeliness in these surroundings: 'She said, she was sent for to go to her Husband, and then she up and told us, how she had seen him in a Dream, dwelling in a curious place among *Immortals* wearing a Crown, playing upon a Harp.'[1] The Crown and Harp come no doubt, from the Apocalypse, but the rest of the sentence comes from Bedfordshire and in their village setting they are somehow transformed. Just so his Delectable Mountains are Bedfordshire hills magnified, green to the top. Without the Bible he would not have written the *Pilgrim's Progress* at all, for his mind would have been utterly different; but its style might have been much the same without the Authorised Version.

If I am right in thinking that the Authorised Version as a strictly literary influence has mattered less than we have often supposed, it may be asked how I account for the fact. I think there are two explanations.

In the first place, we must not assume that it always gave so much literary pleasure as it did in the nineteenth century. Thanks to Professor Sutherland,[2] most of us now know about the egregious Edward Harwood who in 1768 published his *Liberal Translation of the New Testament: Being an Attempt to translate the Sacred Writings with the same Freedom, Spirit, and Elegance, With which other English Translations from the Greek Classics have lately been executed.* Harwood wrote to substitute 'the elegance of modern English' for 'the bald and barbarous language of the old vulgar version'.[3] And no doubt Harwood was, by our standards, an ass. But can he have been the only one of his kind? Or does he voice a widely spread feeling which only reverence concealed? 'Bald and barbarous', lacking in elegance ... we have heard something not quite unlike this before: 'the most grossest manner', *simplicitas sermonis*, *humillimum genus loquendi*. It is not a charge anyone would be likely to bring against the Authorised Version or its originals today. Those who dislike Scripture are now more likely to call its style florid or inflated; those who like it would praise it for sublimity. When and how did this change occur?

---

[1] *The Pilgrim's Progress*, Pt. II, p. 206.

[2] James Sutherland, 'Some Aspects of Eighteenth-Century Prose', *Essays on the Eighteenth Century Presented to David Nichol Smith in honour of his seventieth birthday* (Oxford, 1945), pp. 109–10.

[3] From the Preface to Harwood's translation, p. v.

The answer, I suggest, is that the modern approach, or what was till lately the modern approach, to the Bible is deeply influenced by the Romantic Movement; by which I here mean not the Lake Poets but that taste for the primitive and the passionate which can be seen growing through nearly the whole of the eighteenth century. The men who were engaged in exhuming the ballads, the Elder Edda, the Sagas, the *Nibelungenlied* and the *Kalevala*, the forgers of *Otranto* and *Ossian*, those who dreamed of bards and druids, must have heard the Bible with new ears. The primitive simplicity of a world in which kings could be shepherds, the abrupt and mysterious manner of the prophets, the violent passions of bronze-age fighting men, the background of tents and flocks and desert and mountain, the village homeliness of Our Lord's parables and metaphors, now first, I suspect, became a positive literary asset. The 'vile bodies' which St Thomas had to explain were no longer felt to be vile. Something of the same sort was happening to Homer. Scaliger had found him low. Chapman had reverenced him for his hidden widsom. With Pope's preface we reach a different attitude. 'I would not be so delicate', he says, 'as those modern Criticks, who are shock'd at the *servile Offices* and *mean Employments* in which we sometimes see the Heroes of *Homer* engag'd. There is a Pleasure in taking a view of that Simplicity in Opposition to the Luxury of succeeding Ages; in beholding Monarchs without their Guards, Princes tending their Flocks, and Princesses drawing Water from the Springs.'* He significantly adds that he has admitted into his version 'several of those general Phrases and Manners of Expression, which have attain'd a Veneration even in our Language from their use in the *Old Testament*'.†

I suggest, then, that until the Romantic taste existed the Authorised Version was not such an attractive model as we might suppose. That would be one cause limiting its influence. The second cause was, I believe, its familiarity.

This may sound paradoxical, but it is seriously meant. For three centuries the Bible was so well known that hardly any word or phrase, except those which it shared with all English books whatever, could be borrowed without recognition. If you echoed the Bible everyone knew that you were echoing the Bible. And certain associations were called up in every reader's mind; sacred associations. All your readers

---

* *The Iliad of Homer, Translated by Mr. Pope* (London, 1715), p. [xxxviii].
† *Ibid.*, p. [xlvi].

had heard it read, as a ritual or almost ritual act, at home, at school, and in church. This did not mean that reverence prevented all Biblical echoes. It did mean that they would only be used either with conscious reverence or with conscious irreverence, either religiously or facetiously. There could be a pious use and a profane use: but there could be no ordinary use. Nearly all that was Biblical was recognizably Biblical, and all that was recognized was *sacer*, numinous; whether on that account to be respected or on that account to be flouted makes very little difference. Mark what Boswell says under Sat. April 3rd. 1773:

He [*sc.* Dr Johnson] disapproved of introducing scripture phrases into secular discourse. This seemed to me a question of some difficulty. A scripture expression may be used, like a highly classical phrase, to produce an instantaneous strong impression.

'Like a highly classical phrase'—that is the point; and producing a strong impression. It is difficult to conceive conditions less favourable to that unobtrusive process of infiltration by which a profound literary influence usually operates. An influence which cannot evade our consciousness will not go very deep.

It may be asked whether now, when only a minority of Englishmen regard the Bible as a sacred book, we may anticipate an increase of its literary influence. I think we might if it continued to be widely read. But this is not very likely. Our age has, indeed, coined the expression 'the Bible as literature'. It is very generally implied that those who have rejected its theological pretensions nevertheless continue to enjoy it as a treasure house of English prose. It may be so. There may be people who, not having been forced upon familiarity with it by believing parents, have yet been drawn to it by its literary charms and remained as constant readers. But I never happen to meet them. Perhaps it is because I live in the provinces. But I cannot help suspecting, if I may make an Irish bull, that those who read the Bible as literature do not read the Bible.

It would be strange if they did. If I am right in thinking that the Bible, apart from its sacred character, appeals most easily to a Romantic taste, we must expect to find it neglected and even disliked in our own age. The Counter-Romantic movement is indeed so violent that those of us who do not share it almost wonder if there is not something pathological in the violence. The hatred of Romanticism has reached that stage at which it can see no differences of kind between the things hated. I read the other day an essay in which the author dismissed Chesterton's *Ballad of the White Horse* on the ground that 'Morris manages these things better than Chesterton ever did; and nobody wants to preserve William Morris.' I can understand, even if I deplore, the taste that does not want to preserve William Morris. What staggers me is the implication that Chesterton and Morris wrote the same sort of poetry. It is as if a man said 'Holbein does all these things better than Titian.' I can only conclude that the author's revulsion from Romantic poetry has reached a degree of violence at which the difference between the cool water-colour effects of Morris, his northern bareness, and his monotonous plashing melody cannot be distinguished from all the gold and scarlet and all the orgiastic drum-beats of Chesterton. Phobias make strange bedfellows. Perhaps to those who cannot endure the presence of a cat, the huge, square-headed tabby Tom and the little smoke-faced goblin from Siam are all one. But clearly in an age so anti-Romantic as this, all those qualities which once helped the Bible as literature will work against it. David weeping over Absalom,[1] Moses at the Burning Bush,[2] Elijah on Carmel,[3] the Horror of Great Darkness,[4] the Maniac among the Tombs[5]—what have these passages to say to an unbeliever unless he is a Romantic or to a Counter-Romantic unless he is a believer?

What I am saying involves the view that an approach to the Bible which seemed to many of us in our youth to be simply human, was in reality the product of a particular period in the history of taste. I hope you will find this the more credible because of our brief glances at the Bible's earlier history. The Medieval taste for which the literal sense was merely the dry crust of the honeycomb concealing the golden sweetness of the allegory, and the Humanistic taste which felt that the simplicity of Scripture would be improved by rhetoric, may each have seemed, in its own day, natural and eternal. Against that background we can see in proper perspective the eighteenth- and nineteenth-century taste. No doubt we may conclude that the Counter-Romantic taste of the twentieth will also prove ephemeral; indeed, whatever the hidden fuel may be, it can hardly blaze in its present fury for very long. It will be succeeded by other attitudes which we cannot predict.

[1] 2 Samuel xviii. 33.
[2] Exodus iii.
[3] 1 Kings xviii. 42.
[4] Genesis xv. 12.
[5] Mark v. 2; Luke viii. 27.

Inevitably we ask whether any of these is likely to be favourable to a literary appreciation of the Bible. Stripped (for most readers) of its divine authority, stripped of its allegorical senses, denied a romantic welcome for its historical sense, will it none the less return on the wave of some new fashion to literary pre-eminence and be read? And of course we do not know. I offer my guess. I think it very unlikely that the Bible will return as a book unless it returns as a sacred book. Longinus came as near to being a Romantic as a Greek could, and his view of the world and man was in its own way a religious one.[1] It would be rash to expect many more of his kind. Unless the religious claims of the Bible are again acknowledged, its literary claims will, I think, be given only 'mouth honour' and that decreasingly. For it is, through and through, a sacred book. Most of its component parts were written, and all of them were brought together, for a purely religious purpose. It contains good literature and bad literature. But even the good literature is so written that we can seldom disregard its sacred character. It is easy enough to read Homer while suspending our disbelief in the Greek pantheon; but then the *Iliad* was not composed chiefly, if at all, to enforce obedience to Zeus and Athene and Poseidon. The Greek tragedians are more religious than Homer, but even there we have only religious speculation or at least the poet's personal religious ideas; not dogma. That is why we can join in. Neither Aeschylus nor even Virgil tacitly prefaces his poetry with the formula 'Thus say the gods'. But in most parts of the Bible everything is implicitly or explicitly introduced with 'Thus saith the Lord'. It is, if you like to put it that way, not merely a sacred book but a book so remorselessly and continuously sacred that it does not invite, it excludes or repels, the merely aesthetic approach. You can read it as literature only by a *tour de force*. You are cutting the wood against the grain, using the tool for a purpose it was not intended to serve. It demands incessantly to be taken on its own terms: it will not continue to give literary delight very long except to those who go to it for something quite different. I predict that it will in the future be read as it always has been read, almost exclusively by Christians.

If many critics, especially older critics, speak of it differently today, I suggest that they may be influenced by amiable but unliterary motives. A sacred book rejected is like a king dethroned. Towards either of them there arises in well-disposed minds a chivalrous com-

[1] *De Sublimitate*, v, xxxiv.

punction. One would like to concede everything except the thing really at issue. Having supported the deposition, one would wish to make it clear that one had no personal malice. Just because you cannot countenance a restoration, you are anxious to speak kindly of the old gentleman in his personal capacity—to praise his fund of anecdote or his collection of butterflies. I cannot help thinking that when a critic old enough to remember the Bible in its power prophesies for it a great future as literature, he is often unconsciously swayed by similar motives. But such courtesies will not preserve it. Neither the Bible nor those who still read it as believers invite them; and the generation which is now growing up will disregard them. For the Bible, whether in the Authorised or in any other version, I foresee only two possibilities; either to return as a sacred book or to follow the classics, if not quite into oblivion yet into the ghost-life of the museum and the specialist's study. Except, of course, among the believing minority who read it to be instructed and get literary enjoyment as a by-product.

The Vision of John Bunyan

There are books which, while didactic in intention, are read with delight by people who do not want their teaching and may not believe that they have anything to teach—works like Lucretius' *De Rerum Natura* or Burton's *Anatomy*. This is the class to which *The Pilgrim's Progress* belongs. Most of it has been read and re-read by those who were indifferent or hostile to its theology, and even by children who perhaps were hardly aware of it. I say, most of it, for there are some long dialogues where we get bogged down in sheer doctrine, and doctrine, too, of a sort that I find somewhat repellent. The long conversation, near the end of Part 1, which Christian and Hopeful conduct '*to prevent drowsiness in this place*'[1]—they are entering the Enchanted Ground—will not prevent drowsiness on the part of many readers. Worse still is the dialogue with Mr Talkative.

Bunyan—and, from his own point of view, rightly—would not care twopence for the criticism that he here loses the interest of irreligious readers. But such passages are faulty in another way too. In them, the speakers step out of the allegorical story altogether. They talk literally and directly about the spiritual life. The great image of the Road disappears. They are in the pulpit. If this is going to happen, why have a story at all? Allegory frustrates itself the moment the author starts doing what could equally well be done in a straight sermon or treatise. It is a valid form only so long as it is doing what could not be done at all, or done so well, in any other way.

But this fault is rare in Bunyan—far rarer than in *Piers Plowman*. If such dead wood were removed from *The Pilgrim's Progress* the book would not be very much shorter than it is. The greater part of it is enthralling narrative or genuinely dramatic dialogue. Bunyan stands with Malory and Trollope as a master of perfect naturalness in the mimesis of ordinary conversation.

To ask how a great book came into existence is, I believe, often futile. But in this case Bunyan has told us the answer, so far as such things

[1] *The Pilgrim's Progress*, ed. James Blanton Wharey, second edition revised by Roger Sharrock, Oxford English Texts (Oxford, 1960), Part 1, p. 136.

can be told. It comes in the very pedestrian verses prefixed to Part I.
He says that while he was at work on quite a different book he '*Fell
suddenly into an Allegory*'.[1] He means, I take it, a little allegory, an
extended metaphor that would have filled a single paragraph. He set
down '*more than twenty things*'.[2] And, this done, '*I twenty more had
in my Crown*'.[3] The '*things*' began '*to multiply*'[4] like sparks flying
out of a fire. They threatened, he says, to '*eat out*'[5] the book he was
working on. They insisted on splitting off from it and becoming a
separate organism. He let them have their head. Then come the
words which describe, better than any others I know, the golden
moments of unimpeded composition:

> For having now my Method by the end;
> Still as I pull'd, it came.[6]

It came. I doubt if we shall ever know more of the process called
'inspiration' than those two monosyllables tell us.

Perhaps we may hazard a guess as to why it came at just that
moment. My own guess is that the scheme of a journey with adventures suddenly reunited two things in Bunyan's mind which had
hitherto lain far apart. One was his present and lifelong preoccupation
with the spiritual life. The other, far further away and longer ago, left
behind (he had supposed) in childhood, was his delight in old wives'
tales and such last remnants of chivalric romance as he had found in
chap-books. The one fitted the other like a glove. Now, as never
before, the whole man was engaged.

The vehicle he had chosen—or, more accurately, the vehicle that
had chosen him—involved a sort of descent. His high theme had to
be brought down and incarnated on the level of an adventure story
of the most unsophisticated type—a quest story, with lions, goblins,
giants, dungeons and enchantments. But then there is a further
descent. This adventure story itself is not left in the world of high
romance. Whether by choice or by the fortunate limits of Bunyan's
imagination—probably a bit of both—it is all visualized in terms of
the contemporary life that Bunyan knew. The garrulous neighbours;
Mr Worldly-Wiseman who was so clearly (as Christian said) 'a
Gentleman';[7] the bullying, foul-mouthed Justice; the field-path,
seductive to footsore walkers; the sound of a dog barking as you

---

[1] *Ibid.*, p. 1.   [2] *Ibid.*   [3] *Ibid.*   [4] *Ibid.*
[5] *Ibid.*   [6] *Ibid.*, p. 2.   [7] *Ibid.*, Pt. I, p. 21.

stand knocking at a door; the fruit hanging over a wall which the children insist on eating though their mother admonishes them 'that Fruit is none of ours'[1]—these are all characteristic. No one lives further from Wardour Street than Bunyan. The light is sharp: it never comes through stained glass.

And this homely immediacy is not confined to externals. The very motives and thoughts of the pilgrims are similarly brought down to earth. Christian undertakes his journey because he believes his hometown is going to be destroyed by fire. When Mathew sickens after eating the forbidden fruit, his mother's anxiety is entirely medical; they send for the doctor. When Mr Brisk's suit to Mercy grows cold, Mercy is allowed to speak and feel as a good many young women would in her situation:

I might a had Husbands afore now, tho' I spake not of it to any; but they were such as did not like my Conditions, though never did any of them find fault with my Person.[2]

When Christian keeps on his way and faces Apollyon, he is not inspired by any martial ardour. He goes on because he remembers that he has armour for his chest but not for his back, so that turning tail would be the most dangerous thing he could do.

A page later comes the supreme example. You remember how the text 'the wages of sin is death'[3] is transformed? Asked by Apollyon why he is deserting him, Christian replies: 'Your wages [were] such as a man could not live on.'[4] You would hardly believe it, but I have read a critic who objected to that. He thought the motive attributed to Christian was too low. But that is to misunderstand the very nature of all allegory or parable or even metaphor. The lowness is the whole point. Allegory gives you one thing in terms of another. All depends on respecting the rights of the vehicle, in refusing to allow the least confusion between the vehicle and its freight. The Foolish Virgins, within the parable, do not miss beatitude; they miss a wedding party.[5] The Prodigal Son, when he comes home, is not given spiritual consolations; he is given new clothes and the best dinner his father can put up.[6] It is extraordinary how often this principle is disregarded. The imbecile, wisely anonymous, who

---

[1] *The Pilgrim's Progress*, Pt. II, p. 194.   [2] *Ibid.*, Pt. II, p. 227–8.

[3] Romans vi. 23.

[4] *The Pilgrim's Progress*, Pt. I, p. 57.

[5] *Matthew* xxv. 1–13.   [6] Luke xv. 11–32.

illustrated my old nursery copy of *The Pilgrim's Progress* makes a similar blunder at the end of Part II. Bunyan has been telling how a post came for Christiana to say that she was to cross the river and appear in the City within ten days. She made her farewells to all her friends and 'entered the *River* with a *Beck'n*' (that is a wave) 'of Fare well, to those that followed her to the River side'.[1] The artist has seen fit to illustrate this with a picture of an old lady on her death-bed, surrounded by weeping relatives in the approved Victorian manner. But if Bunyan had wanted a literal death-bed scene he would have written one.

This stupidity perhaps comes from the pernicious habit of reading allegory as if it were a cryptogram to be translated; as if, having grasped what an image (as we say) 'means', we threw the image away and thought of the ingredient in real life which it represents. But that method leads you continually out of the book back into the conception you started from and would have had without reading it. The right process is the exact reverse. We ought not to be thinking 'This green valley, where the shepherd boy is singing, represents humility'; we ought to be discovering, as we read, that humility is like that green valley. That way, moving always into the book, not out of it, from the concept to the image, enriches the concept. And that is what allegory is for.

There are two things we must not say about the style of *Pilgrim's Progress*. In the first place we must not say that it is derived from the Authorised Version. That is based on confusion. Because his whole outlook is biblical, and because direct or embedded quotations from Scripture are so frequent, readers carry away the impression that his own sentences are like those of the English Bible. But you need only look at them to see that they are not:

Come *Wet*, come *Dry*, I long to be gone; for however the Weather is in my Journey, I shall have time enough when I come there to sit down and rest me, and dry me.[2]

Who in the Old or New Testament ever talked like that?

Mr. *Great-heart* was delighted in him (for he loved one greatly that he found to be a man of his Hands).[3]

Is that like Scripture?

[1] *The Pilgrim's Progress*, Pt. II, p. 306.
[2] *Ibid.*, Pt. II, p. 305.   [3] *Ibid.*, Pt. II, p. 291.

The other thing we must not say is that Bunyan wrote well because he was a sincere, forthright man who had no literary affectations and simply said what he meant. I do not doubt that is the account of the matter that Bunyan would have given himself. But it will not do. If it were the real explanation, then every sincere, forthright, unaffected man could write as well. But most people of my age learned from censoring the letters of the troops, when we were subalterns in the first war, that unliterary people, however sincere and forthright in their talk, no sooner take a pen in hand than cliché and platitude flow from it. The shocking truth is that, while insincerity may be fatal to good writing, sincerity, of itself, never taught anyone to write well. It is a moral virtue, not a literary talent. We may hope it is rewarded in a better world: it is not rewarded on Parnassus.

We must attribute Bunyan's style to a perfect natural ear, a great sensibility for the idiom and cadence of popular speech, a long experience in addressing unlettered audiences, and a freedom from bad models. I do not add 'to an intense imagination', for that also can shipwreck if a man does not find the right words. Here it is in a descriptive passage:

They are, said she, our Countrey Birds: They sing these Notes but seldom, except it be at the Spring, when the Flowers appear, and the Sun shines warm, and then you may hear them all day long. I often, said she, go out to hear them, we also oft times keep them tame in our House. They are very fine Company for us when we are *Melancholy*.[1]

And here it is rendering the exact voice of the rustic wiseacre—Mrs Timorous is speaking:

Well, I see you have a mind to go a fooling too; but take heed in time, and be wise: while we are out of danger we are out; but when we are in, we are in.[2]

Here you see it turning a point in the narrative, very economical but full of suggestion:

Thus they went on till they came to about the middle of the Valley, and then *Christiana* said, Methinks I see something yonder upon the Road before us, a thing of a shape such as I have not seen. Then said *Joseph*, Mother, what is it? An ugly thing, Child; an ugly thing, said she. But Mother, what is it like, said he? 'Tis like I cannot tell what, said she. And now it was but a little way off.[3]

[1] *The Pilgrim's Progress*, Pt. II, p. 235.   [2] *Ibid.*, Pt. II, pp. 183–4.
[3] *Ibid.*, Pt. II, p. 241.

Can anyone read that without hearing both the voices? Here it attempts, successfully, a higher strain:

Then *Apollyon* strodled quite over the whole breadth of the way, and said, I am void of fear in this matter, prepare thy self to dye, for I swear by my Infernal Den, that thou shalt go no further, here will I spill thy soul.[1]

Or here with a more daring image than is usual:

I fought till my Sword did cleave to my Hand, and when they were joyned together, as if a Sword grew out of my Arm, and when the Blood run thorow my Fingers, then I fought with most Courage.[2]

Any of the epic poets would be glad to have thought of that.

In dialogue Bunyan catches not only the cadence of the speech but the tiny twists of thought. Mr Talkative is not allowed to talk much. But note how, when Faithful has tried to correct him, he replies: 'That is it that I said.'[3]

It is perfect for the unteachable man; whatever you put to him will be taken as an endorsement of the last opinion he has expressed. Or consider this, from Mr Great-heart's long story of Mr Fearing:

And I will say that for my Lord, he carried it wonderful lovingly to him.[4]

Great-heart is devoted to his Master. He delights to eulogize him. Yet the form of words in which the praise here comes out—'I will say this for him'—is exactly that with which an honest man would reluctantly concede one, and only one, redeeming feature in an opponent. One could understand this if it were artfully done in the witness box; an apparently reluctant witness impresses the jury. But there is no question of that here. There is some kink in the mind of the English rustic, some innate rhetoric, that makes him talk that way. You may hear it in country pubs any day.

But it is always dangerous to talk too long about style. It may lead one to forget that every single sentence depends for its total effect on the place it has in the whole. There is nothing remarkable about the sentence '*I will pay you when I take my Mony*' and '*I will fight so long as I can hold my Sword in my Hand.*'[5] But in their context they are devastating. For they are uttered by two men lying fast asleep on the Enchanted Ground, talking in their sleep, and not to be waked by any endeavour. The final stroke of the grim irony comes with the

---

[1] *Ibid.*, Pt. I, p. 59.   [2] *Ibid.*, Pt. II, p. 291.   [3] *Ibid.*, Pt. I, p. 76.
[4] *Ibid.*, Pt. II, p. 251.   [5] *Ibid.*, Pt. II, p. 298.

words: 'At that, one of the Children laughed.'[1] How horrifying the joke and the laughter are is perhaps immediately apparent only to those who share Bunyan's premises. Yet perhaps not. Even those who think that the stakes we play for in life are not, as Bunyan believed, strictly infinite, may yet feel in some degree the uneasiness he meant us to feel; may wonder whether what we regard as our firm resolutions, our long industry, and our creditable achievements, are not all talking in our sleep and dreaming, sleep from which, though we may talk louder and louder, we shall not wake. For stakes less than infinite may yet be fairly high.

Part of the unpleasant side of *The Pilgrim's Progress* lies in the extreme narrowness and exclusiveness of Bunyan's religious outlook. The faith is limited 'to one small sect and all are damned beside'. But I suppose that all who read old books have learned somehow or other to make historical allowances for that sort of thing. Our ancestors all wrote and thought like that. The insolence and self-righteousness which now flourish most noticeably in literary circles then found their chief expression in theology, and this is no doubt a change for the better. And one must remember that Bunyan was a persecuted and slandered man.

For some readers the 'unpleasant side' of *The Pilgrim's Progress* will lie not so much in its sectarianism as in the intolerable terror which is never far away. Indeed *unpleasant* is here a ludicrous understatement. The dark doctrine has never been more horrifyingly stated than in the words that conclude Part I:

Then I saw that there was a way to Hell, even from the Gates of Heaven, as well as from the City of *Destruction*.[2]

In my opinion the book would be immeasurably weakened as a work of art if the flames of Hell were not always flickering on the horizon. I do not mean merely that if they were not it would cease to be true to Bunyan's own vision and would therefore suffer all the effects which a voluntary distortion or expurgation of experience might be expected to produce. I mean also that the image of this is necessary to us while we read. The urgency, the harsh woodcut energy, the continual sense of momentousness, depend on it.

We might even say that, just as Bunyan's religious theme demanded for its vehicle this kind of story, so the telling of such a story would

---

[1] *The Pilgrim's Progress*, Pt. II, p. 298.   [2] *Ibid.*, Pt. I, p. 163.

have required on merely artistic grounds to be thus loaded with a further significance, a significance which is believed by only some, but can be felt (while they read) by all, to be of immeasurable importance. These adventures, these ogres, monsters, shining helpers, false friends, delectable mountains, and green or ghastly valleys, are not thereby twisted from their nature. They are restored to the weight they had for the savage or dreaming mind which produced them. They come to us, if we are sensitive to them at all, clothed in its ecstasies and terrors. Bunyan is not lending them an alien gravity. He is supplying, in terms of his own fundamental beliefs, grounds for taking them as seriously as we are, by the nature of our imagination, disposed to do. Unless we are very hidebound we can re-interpret these grounds in terms of our own, perhaps very different, outlook. Many do not believe that either the trumpets 'with melodious noise'[1] or the infernal den await us where the road ends. But most, I fancy, have discovered that to be born is to be exposed to delights and miseries greater than imagination could have anticipated; that the choice of ways at any cross-road may be more important than we think; and that short cuts may lead to very nasty places.

[1] *Ibid.*, Pt. I, p. 160.

II

Addison

'I have always', said Addison, 'preferred Chearfulness to Mirth. The latter I consider as an Act, the former as an Habit of the Mind';[1] or again, 'Though I am always serious, I do not know what it is to be melancholy.'[2] These sentences pretty well give us the measure, if not of the man, yet of the work; just as the limpidity of their style, conveying a distinction of almost a scholastic precision in such manner that even a 'tea-table' could not fail to understand it, gives us the measure of his talent. They serve also to mark the most profound difference between the Whig essayist and his two great Tory contemporaries.

Swift and Pope were by no means always serious and they knew very well what it was to be melancholy. One would have found more mirth in their conversation than in Addison's: not only epigram and repartee, but frolic and extravaganza—even buffoonery. It is true that they regarded satire as a 'sacred weapon', but we must not so concentrate on that idea as to forget the sheer *vis comica* which brightens so much of their work. Swift's 'favourite maxim was *vive la bagatelle*'.[3] *Gulliver* and the *Dunciad* and the whole myth of Scriblerus have missed their point if they do not sometimes make us 'laugh and shake in Rabelais' easy chair'. Even their love of filth is, in my opinion, much better understood by schoolboys than by psychoanalysts: if there is something sinister in it, there is also an element of high-spirited rowdiness. Addison has a sense of humour; the Tories have, in addition, a sense of fun. But they have no 'habit' of cheerfulness. Rage, exasperation, and something like despair are never far away. It is to this that they owe their sublimity—for Pope, no less than Swift, can be sublime. We suspect that the picture he paints of himself is historically false—

---

[1] *Spectator* 381, vol. v, p. 233. All text-references are to *The Spectator: The Text Edited and Annotated*, in eight volumes, ed. G. Gregory Smith, with an introductory essay by Austin Dobson (London, 1897–8).

[2] *Ibid.*, 26, vol. I, p. 98.

[3] Samuel Johnson, 'Life of Swift', in *Lives of the English Poets*, vol. III, ed. George Birkbeck Hill (Oxford, 1905), pp. 45–6.

Yes, I am proud; I must be proud to see
Men not afraid of God, afraid of me.[1]

But it is a sublime poetical image. The picture of surly, contemptuous
virtue had often been attempted before—in Chapman's Bussy and
Clermont, in Dryden's Almanzor, in Wycherley's Manly, even in the
Christ of *Paradise Regained*; but I would give Pope the palm, for in
Milton the discrepancy between the known historical character of his
Hero and the 'Senecal man' he has painted is more shocking than that
between the real and the imagined Pope. There is nothing of so high
a reach in Addison. The grandeur of 'cynical asperity' is a flower
that grows only in a tropical climate, and in passing to Addison's
world we pass to a world where such things are impossible. Surly
virtue is not cheerful nor equable: in the long run it is not, perhaps,
perfectly consistent with good sense.

This contrast between Addison and the Tories comes out with
special clarity in their treatment of enemies. For the Tories, every
enemy—whether it be the Duchess of Marlborough or only a
Shakespearian editor found guilty of some real English scholarship—
becomes a grotesque. All who have, in whatever fashion, incurred
their ill will are knaves, scarecrows, whores, bugs, toads, bedlamites,
yahoos; Addison himself a smooth Mephistopheles. It is good fun,
but it is certainly not good sense; we laugh, and disbelieve. Now
mark Addison's procedure. The strength of the Tory party is the
smaller country gentry with their Jacobite leanings and their opposition
to the moneyed interest. All the material for savage satire is there.
Addison might have anticipated Squire Western (as he did later in
the *Freeholder*) and painted merely the block-headed, fox-hunting sot,
the tyrant of his family and his village. Instead, with the help of Steele,
he invents Sir Roger de Coverley. The measure of his success is that
we can now think of Sir Roger for a long time without remembering
his Toryism; when we do remember it, it is only as a lovable whimsy.

In all our Journey from *London* to his House we did not so much as bait at a
Whig Inn ... This often betrayed us into hard Beds and bad Cheer; for we
were not so inquisitive about the Inn as the Inn-keeper; and provided our
Landlord's Principles were sound, did not take any Notice of the Staleness of
his Provisions.[2]

[1] Pope, *Epilogue to the Satires*, Dial. II, 208.
[2] *Spectator* 126, vol. II, p. 163.

As a natural consequence, Mr Spectator soon 'dreaded entering into an House of any one that Sir Roger had applauded for an honest Man'.[1] It is so beautifully done that we do not notice it. The enemy, far from being vilified, is being turned into a dear old man. The thought that he could ever be dangerous has been erased from our minds; but so also the thought that anything he said could ever be taken seriously. We all love Sir Roger; but of course we do not really attend to him as we do—well, to Sir Andrew Freeport. All through the century which Addison ushered in, England was going to attend more and more seriously to the Freeports, and the de Coverleys were to be more and more effectually silenced. The figure of the dear old squire dominates—possibly, on some views, corrupts—the national imagination to the present day. This is indeed to 'make a man die sweetly'. That element in English society which stood against all that Addison's party was bringing in is henceforth seen through a mist of smiling tenderness—as an archaism, a lovely absurdity. What we might have been urged to attack as a fortress we are tricked into admiring as a ruin.

When I say 'tricked' I am not implying that Steele and Addison calculated the whole effect of their creation just as I have set it down. The actual upshot of their work is obvious; their conscious intentions are another matter. I am inclined to think that Addison really loved Sir Roger—with that 'superior love' which, in England, the victorious party so easily accords to the remnants of a vanishing order. Addison is not a simple man; he is, in the older sense of the word, 'sly'. I do not believe for one moment that he was the fiendlike Atticus; but one sees how inevitably he must have appeared so to the losers. He is so cool, so infuriatingly sensible, and yet he effects more than they. A satiric portrait by Pope or Swift is like a thunderclap; the Addisonian method is more like the slow operations of ordinary nature, loosening stones, blunting outlines, modifying a whole landscape with 'silent overgrowings' so that the change can never quite be reversed again. Whatever his intentions, his reasonableness and amiability (both cheerful 'habits' of the mind) are stronger in the end than the Tory spleen. To rail is the sad privilege of the loser.

I have used the word 'amiability'. Should we go further and say 'charity'? I feel that this Christian word, with its doctrinal implications, would be a little out of place when we are speaking of Addison's

---

[1] *Spectator* 126, vol. II, p. 163.

essays. About the man, as distinct from the work, I will not speculate. Let us hope that he practised this theological virtue. The story that he summoned Lord Warwick to his deathbed *to see how a Christian can die* is ambiguous;[1] it can be taken either as evidence of his Christianity or as a very brimstone proof of the reverse. I give no vote: my concern is with books. And the essays do not invite criticism in terms of any very definite theology. They are everywhere 'pious'. Rational Piety, together with Polite Letters and Simplicity, is one of the hall-marks of the age which Addison was partly interpreting but partly also bringing into existence. And Rational Piety is by its very nature not very doctrinal. This is one of the many ways in which Addison is historically momentous. He ushers in that period—it is just now drawing to a close—in which it is possible to talk of 'piety' or (later) 'religion' almost in the abstract; in which the contrast is no longer between Christian and Pagan, the elect and the world, orthodox and heretic, but between 'religious' and 'irreligious'. The transition cannot be quite defined: absence of doctrine would have to become itself doctrinal for that to be possible. It is a change of atmosphere, which every reader of sensibility will feel if he passes suddenly from the literature of any earlier period to that of the eighteenth century. Hard rocks of Calvinism show up amidst the seemingly innocuous surface of an *Arcadia* or a *Faerie Queene*; Shakespearian comedy reckons on an audience who will at once see the point of jokes about the controversy on Works and Faith. Here also, no doubt, it is difficult to bring Addison to a point. Perhaps the most illuminating passage is the essay on 'Sir Roger at Church', and specially the quotation from Pythagoras prefixed to it—'Honour first the immortal gods according to the established mode.'[2] That is the very note of Rational Piety. A sensible man goes with his society, according to local and ancestral usage. And he does so with complete sincerity. Clean clothes and the sound of bells on Sunday morning do really

---

[1] Edward Young, describing Addison's death in his *Conjectures on Original Composition* (London, 1759), wrote: 'After a long ... struggle with his distemper, he dismissed his physicians, and ... sent for a youth nearly related, and finely accomplished, but not above being the better for good impressions from a dying friend: He came; but life now glimmering in the socket, the dying friend was silent: After a decent, and proper pause, the youth said, "Dear Sir! you sent for me: I believe, and I hope, that you have some commands; I shall hold them most sacred:" ... Forcibly grasping the youth's hand, he softly said, "See in what peace a Christian can die." He spoke with difficulty, and soon expired' (pp. 101–2).

[2] Ἀθανάτους μὲν πρῶτα θεούς, νόμῳ ὡς διάκειται, τιμα, *Spectator* 112, vol. II, p. 109.

throw him into a mood of sober benevolence, not 'clouded by enthusiasm' but inviting his thoughts to approach the mystery of things.

In this matter of Rational Piety one must not draw too sharp a contrast between Addison and the Tories. They are infected with it themselves, and Swift quotes with equal approval the Pagan maxim about worshipping *according to the laws of the Country*.[1] But I think there is *some* contrast. The Tories are a little nearer than Addison to the old period with its uncompromising creeds. Pope's Romanism is not nearly so superficial as some have supposed, and the 'Pantheism' of the *Essay on Man* owes a good deal of its notoriety to critics who would make a very poor shape at defining pantheism. He made an edifying end, and he perhaps understands the conflict in Eloise's mind —it is not simply a conflict of virtue and vice—better than Addison would have done. Swift is harder to classify. There is, to be sure, no doubt of his churchmanship, only of his Christianity, and this, of itself, is significant. If Swift were (as I do not think he is) primarily a Church of England man, only secondly a Christian, and not 'pious' or 'religious' at all, we might say that in Addison's writings the proportions are reversed. And some things would lend colour to such an interpretation of Swift. In the 'Sentiments' his religion seems to be purely political. 'I leave it among the divines to dilate upon the danger of schism, as a spiritual evil, but I would consider it only as a temporal one.'[2] Separation from the established worship, 'although to a new one that is more pure and perfect', is dangerous.[3] More disquieting still are the tormented aphorisms of 'Thoughts on Religion'. To change fundamental opinions is ordinarily wicked 'whether those opinions be true or false',[4] and 'The want of belief is a defect that ought to be concealed when it cannot be overcome.'[5] Some parts of *Gulliver* seem inconsistent with any religion—except perhaps Buddhism. The 'Further Thoughts on Religion' open with the assertion that the Mosaic account of creation is 'most agreeable of all others to probability' and immediately cite—the making of Eve out of Adam's rib![6] Is it possible that this should not be irony? And

---

[1] Swift, 'Sentiments of a Church-of-England Man', in *Writings on Religion and the Church*, vol. I, ed. Temple Scott (London, 1898), p. 62. (This volume is itself vol. III of the complete *Prose Works of Jonathan Swift, D.D.*, ed. Temple Scott, with a biographical introduction by the Rt. Hon. W. E. H. Lecky (London, 1898).)

[2] *Ibid.*, pp. 61–2.   [3] *Ibid.*, p. 62.

[4] 'Thoughts on Religion', *op. cit.*, ed. Scott, p. 307.   [5] *Ibid.*, p. 308.

[6] 'Further Thoughts on Religion', *op. cit.*, ed. Scott, p. 310.

yet there is much to set on the other side. His priestly duties were discharged with a fidelity rare in that age. The ferocity of the later *Gulliver* all works up to that devastating attack on Pride which is more specifically Christian than any other piece of ethical writing in the century, if we except William Law. The prayers offered at Stella's deathbed have a scholastic firmness in their implied moral theology. ('Keep her from both the sad extremes of presumption and despair.'[1] 'Forgive the sorrow and weakness of those among us, who sink under the grief and terror of losing so dear and useful a friend.'[2]) The sermon 'On the Trinity', taken at its face value, preaches a submission of the reason to dogma which ought to satisfy the sternest super-naturalist. And I think it should be taken at its face value. If we ever think otherwise, I believe the explanation to lie in that peculiar ungraciousness which Swift exercised upwards as well as downwards. He gave alms 'without tenderness or civility', so that 'those who were fed by him could hardly love him'.[3] As below, so above. He practises obedience without humility or meekness, takes his medicine with a wry face. But the alms, however given, were hard cash, and I think his acceptance of Christian doctrine is equally real, though offered (as it were) under protest, as if he were resentful of Heaven for putting him in such a ridiculous position. There is a tension and discomfort about all this, but that very tension suggests depths that Addison never knew. It is from those depths that Swift is writing when he says there can be no question in England of any but a nominal Christianity—'the other having been for some time wholly laid aside by general consent, as utterly inconsistent with our present schemes of wealth and power'.[4] This is a far cry from Mr Spectator's pleasing reflections on the Royal Exchange.

As I am a great Lover of Mankind, my Heart naturally overflows with Pleasure at the sight of a prosperous and happy Multitude, insomuch that at many publick Solemnities I cannot forbear expressing my Joy with Tears that have stolen down my Cheeks. For this reason I am wonderfully delighted to see such a Body of Men thriving in their own private Fortunes, and at the same time promoting the Publick Stock; or in other Words, raising Estates for their own Families, by bringing into their Country whatever is wanting, and carrying out of it whatever is superfluous.[5]

[1] 'Three Prayers used by the Dean for Mrs Johnson, in her Last Sickness. 1727', *op. cit.*, ed. Scott, p. 311.

[2] *Ibid.*, p. 314. [3] Johnson, *op. cit.*, pp. 57–8.

[4] 'Argument against abolishing Christianity', *op. cit.*, ed. Scott, p. 7.

[5] *Spectator* 69, vol. I, p. 261.

Compared with this, Swift's remark is like a scorching wind from the hermitages of the Thebaid.

Addison is never blasphemous or irreverent; Swift can be both. That, I think, helps to confirm the kind of distinction I am drawing between them. Swift still belongs, at any rate in part, to the older world. He would have understood Rochester in both Rochester's phases better than he could understand Addison. Rochester unconverted was a Bad Man of the old, thoroughgoing kind,

> he drunk, he fought, he whored,
> He did despite unto the Lord.[1]

Rochester converted was a deathbed penitent. One cannot imagine Mr Spectator or Sir Andrew emulating him in either achievement.

The mention of Rochester suggests yet another gulf between Addison and the preceding age. We may be sure that Rochester's manners lacked that 'simplicity' which the Whig essayists recommended. It is, of course, a commonplace that they addressed themselves to the reform of manners; but I sometimes wonder whether the very degree of their success does not conceal from us the greatness of the undertaking. I sometimes catch myself taking it for granted that the marks of good breeding were in all ages the same as they are today—that swagger was always vulgar, that a low voice, an unpretentious manner, a show (however superficial) of self-effacement, were always demanded. But it is almost certainly false. We catch a glimpse of the truth in Johnson's remark: 'Lord Southwell was the highest-bred man without insolence that I ever was in company with ... Lord Orrery was not dignified: Lord Chesterfield was, but he was insolent.'* Insolence, for us, is a characteristic of the 'beggar on horseback', a mark of ill breeding; we have little idea of the genuine 'high' manners that bordered on it. We catch another glimpse in Polonius's advice, 'Costly thy habit as thy purse can buy',[2] and again in Hotspur's

---

* Boswell, 23 March 1783.

[1] This couplet is, I expect, a paraphrase of some lines in John Masefield's *The Everlasting Mercy* (London, 1911), a narrative in the first-person about the conversion to Christianity of a rural ruffian who says (p. 2):

> From '61 to '67
> I lived in disbelief of heaven.
> I drunk, I fought, I poached, I whored,
> I did despite unto the Lord.

[2] *Hamlet*, I, iii, 70.

humorous indignation at the 'sarcenet' insipidity of his wife's oaths.[1]
We perceive from many scenes of Elizabethan comedy and from the
stir among the servants at Gawain's arrival in the *Green Knight* that
the old courtesy was not a 'pass school' (as it is with us where a man
either knows the right thing to do or not) but an 'honours school'
where competing extravagances of decorum and compliment could
go to any height. I am inclined to think that if we saw it now we
should mistake that high breeding for no breeding at all. The walk of
the courtier would seem to us a Janissary's strut, his readiness to find
quarrel in a straw would seem a yokel touchiness, his clothes an
intolerable ostentation. Even to this day, when we meet foreigners
(only think of some *young* Frenchmen) who have not been subjected
to the Addisonian 'reform', we have to 'make allowances' for them.
I do not suggest that Addison and Steele, simply by writing essays,
abolished the old flamboyancy. Doubtless they gave expression to a
tendency which would have existed even without them. But to
express is partly to mould. That sober code of manners under which
we still live today, in so far as we have any code at all, and which
foreigners call hypocrisy, is in some important degree a legacy from
the *Tatler* and the *Spectator*. It is certainly not to be explained as a
mere imposition of the code of the citizens upon the gentry. No one
denies that a *rapprochement* between the 'cit' and the courtier was an
essential part of the Addisonian synthesis. Sir Andrew Freeport mixes
with those whose grandfather would have regarded his grandfather
simply as a 'cuckoldand'. But the shop and the counting-house are
not of themselves schools of modest and obliging deportment: least
of all when they are prosperous. There was real novelty in the new
manners.

These new manners were a little restrictive; in adopting them we
lost, along with some cruelties and absurdities, a good deal of 'the
unbought grace of life'. But in other respects Addison is a liberator.
His famous defence of 'Chevy Chase' is sometimes taken to show a
'romantic' side in him, but that, I think, is not the best way of
considering it. The word 'romantic' is always ambiguous.[2] The paper
on 'Chevy Chase' is to be taken in its context.[3] It follows a discussion

---

[1] *Henry IV, Pt. I*, III, i, 251.
[2] See Lewis's sevenfold classification of what may be meant by 'romantic' in the Preface
to the revised edition of his book, *The Pilgrim's Regress* (London, 1943), pp. 5–6.
[3] 'Chevy Chase' is discussed in *Spectator* 70 and 74.

on False Wit. False Wit is taken up by poets who lack the 'Strength of Genius' which gives 'majestick Simplicity to Nature' and who are therefore forced 'to hunt after foreign Ornaments'.[1] These writers are to poetry what the Goths were to architecture. Ovid is the type of such 'Gothick' poets, and 'the Taste of most of our *English* Poets, as well as Readers, is extremely *Gothick*'.[2] One mark of true poetry is that it 'pleases all Kinds of Palates', whereas the Gothic manner pleases 'only such as have formed to themselves a wrong artificial Taste upon little fanciful Authors'.[3] It is, therefore, to be expected that common songs or ballads which are 'the Delight of the common People' should be 'Paintings of Nature'.[4] It is after this preamble that Addison proceeds to examine 'Chevy Chase'—according to the rules of Le Bossu—and pronounces in its favour.

No more classical piece of criticism exists. In it Addison touches hands with Scaliger on the one side and Matthew Arnold on the other. What complicates it is, of course, his peculiar use of the word 'Gothick'. Addison must have known perfectly well that the ballad is just the sort of thing to which his contemporaries would spontaneously have applied that word, and that Ovid and Cowley are not. Very well, then; he will prove that it is the ballad which really follows Nature and that the true Goths are the authors whom the Town in fact prefers. In other words he is calling the neo-classical bluff. It is as if he said, 'You all profess to like a great subject, a good moral, unity of action, and truth to Nature. Well, here they all are in the ballad which you despise; and yonder, in the Cowley which you really enjoy, they are not.' One cannot be certain here, as one could not be certain about the invention of Sir Roger, whether Addison is being 'sly' or really innocent. One sees again what is behind the image of Atticus. The man who writes thus will certainly appear 'sly' to his opponents. But is he consciously setting a trap, or is he merely following the truth as he sees it in all simplicity? Perhaps it does not much matter, for the trap is inherent in the facts, and works whether Addison meant to set it or no; in the sense that if the *nominal* standards of Augustan criticism are ever taken seriously they must work out in favour of the ballads (and much medieval literature) and against most of the poetry the Augustans themselves produced. In other words, if we insist on calling an appreciation of ballads 'romantic', then we

[1] *Spectator* 62, vol. I, p. 235.
[2] *Ibid.*, p. 236.
[3] *Ibid.*, 70, p. 264.
[4] *Ibid.*

must say that Addison becomes a romantic precisely because he is a *real* classic, and that every real classic must infallibly do the same. It is inconceivable that Aristotle and Horace, had they known them, should not have put the *Chanson de Roland* above the *Davideis*. Antiquity and the Middle Ages are not divided from each other by any such chasm as divides both from the Renaissance.

But it is better not to use the word 'romantic' in this context at all. What Addison really shows by his appreciation of the Ballad is his open-mindedness, his readiness to recognize excellence wherever he finds it, whether in those periods which Renaissance Humanism had elected to call 'classical' or in those far longer extents of time which it ignored. The obscurantism of the Humanists is still not fully recognised. Learning to them meant the knowledge and imitation of a few rather arbitrarily selected Latin authors and some even fewer Greek authors. They despised metaphysics and natural science; and they despised all the past outside the favoured periods. They were dominated by a narrowly ethical purpose. *Referenda ad mores omnia*, said Vives;* and he thought it fortunate that the Attic dialect contained nearly all the Greek worth reading—*reliquis utuntur auctores carminum quos non tanti est intelligi.*† Their philistine attitude to metaphysics is prettily carried off in modern histories by phrases about 'brushing away scholastic cobwebs', but the Humanist attack is really on metaphysics itself. In Erasmus, in Rabelais, in the *Utopia* one recognizes the very accent of the angry *belle-lettrist* railing, as he rails in all ages, at 'jargon' and 'straw-splitting'. On this side Pope and Swift are true inheritors of the Humanist tradition. It is easy, of course, to say that Laputa is an attack not on science but on the aberrations of science. I am not convinced. The learning of the Brobdingnagians and the Horses is ruthlessly limited. Nothing that cannot plead the clearest immediate utility—nothing that cannot make two blades of grass grow where one grew before—wins any approval from Swift. Bentley is not forgiven for knowing more Greek than Temple, nor Theobald for knowing more English than Pope. Most of the history of Europe is a mere wilderness, not worth visiting, in which 'the *Monks* finish'd what the *Goths* begun'.‡ The terror expressed at the end of the *Dunciad* is not wholly terror at the approach of ignorance: it is also terror lest the compact little fortress of Humanism

---

* *De Tradendis Disciplinis*, IV. † *Ibid.*, III.
‡ Pope, *Essay on Criticism*, 692.

should be destroyed, and new knowledge is one of the enemies. Whatever is not immediately intelligible to a man versed in the Latin and French classics appears to them to be charlatanism or barbarity. The number of things they do not want to hear about is enormous.

But Addison wants to hear about everything. He is quite as good a classical scholar as the Tories but he does not live in the Humanist prison. He notes with satisfaction 'that curiosity is one of the strongest and most lasting Appetites implanted in us, and that Admiration is one of our most pleasing Passions'.[1] He delights to introduce his readers to the new philosophy of Mr Locke and to explain by it, with aid from Malebranche, 'a famous Passage in the *Alcoran*'.[2] He remembers with pleasure how '*Mr. Boyle*, speaking of a certain Mineral, tells us, That a Man may consume his whole Life in the Study of it, without arriving at the Knowledge of all its Qualities'.[3] He gazes on the sea ('the Heavings of this prodigious Bulk of Waters') with 'a very pleasing Astonishment'.[4] Astronomy, revealing the immensities of space, entertains him with sublime meditations,[5] and his reading, he tells us, 'has very much lain among Books of natural History'.[6] Mysteries attract him. He loves to lose himself in an *o altitudo* whether on the marvels of animal instinct[7] or on those of the powers enjoyed by the soul in dreams—on which he quotes Browne himself.[8] He lives habitually in a world of horizons and possibilities which Pope touched, I think, only in the *Essay on Man*, and Swift hardly touches at all. It is a cool, quiet world after that of the Tories—say, a watercolour world, but there is more room in it. On those things which it illuminates at all, the wit of Swift and Pope casts a sharper and (in a sense) more beautiful light; but what huge regions of reality appear to them, as Addison says that life itself appears to ignorance and folly, a 'Prospect of naked Hills and Plains which produce nothing either profitable or ornamental'![9]

This open-mindedness is not particularly 'romantic', though without it we should have had no Wartons, no Ritson, no Percy, and perhaps no Scott; for the medievalism of the eighteenth century, whatever else it may be, is a mighty defeat of sheer ignorance. But Addison is much more closely connected with the Romantic Move-

---

[1] *Spectator* 237, vol. III, p. 254. [2] *Ibid.*, 94, vol. II, p. 51.
[3] *Ibid.*, p. 49. [4] *Ibid.*, 489, vol. VII, p. 58.
[5] *Ibid.*, 565, vol. VIII, pp. 34 ff. [6] *Ibid.*, 120, vol. II, p. 138.
[7] *Ibid.*, p. 139. [8] *Ibid.*, 487, vol. VII, pp. 52–3.
[9] *Ibid.*, 94, vol. II, p. 53.

ment in quite a different way. He stands at the very turning-point in the history of a certain mode of feeling.

I think that perhaps the best piece of criticism Raleigh ever wrote is in the fourth chapter of his *Wordsworth*, where he sets Claudio's shuddering speech ('To be imprisoned in the viewless winds') beside Wordsworth's longing to retain a body 'endued with all the nice regards of flesh and blood' and yet surrender it to the elements 'As if it were a spirit'.[1] He points out, quite justly, that what is Hell to Claudio is almost Heaven to Wordsworth. Between the two passages a profound change in human sentiment has taken place. Briefly put— for the story has often been told before—it is the change from an age when men frankly hated and feared all those things in Nature which are neither sensuously pleasing, useful, safe, symmetrical, or gaily coloured, to an age when men love and actually seek out mountains, waste places, dark forests, cataracts, and storm-beaten coasts. What was once the ugly has become a department (even the major department) of the beautiful. The first conflict between the old and the new taste received striking expression when Addison was already nine years old, in Thomas Burnet's *Telluris Theoria Sacra*. Burnet cannot quite conceal a certain joy in the awfulness of the Alps, but his very argument depends on the conception that they are deformities— *longaeva illa, tristia et squalentia corpora.** Not that they are the only offence. In the face of this Earth as a whole we find *multa sunt superflua, multa inelegantia*: such beauty (*ornamentum*) as it possesses comes chiefly *cultu et habitatione hominum.*†

The position of Addison in this story is very interesting. He divides the sources of imaginative pleasure into three classes—the Great, the Uncommon, and the Beautiful. As specimens of the Great he mentions 'an open Champian Country, a vast uncultivated Desart, of huge Heaps of Mountains, high Rocks and Precipices, or a wide Expanse of Waters'—all of which produce 'a delightful Stilness and Amazement in the Soul'.[2] To a later writer many of these things would have seemed beautiful; to an earlier one they would have seemed simply unpleasant. Addison does not find beauty in them, but he includes them among the sources of pleasure. His category of the Great, clearly distinguished from the Beautiful, exists precisely to make room for

---

* *Telluris Theoria Sacra*, I, ix.　　　　　　　　† *Ibid.*, x.

[1] Sir Walter Raleigh, 'Nature', *Wordsworth* (London, 1903), p. 152.

[2] *Spectator* 412, vol. VI. p. 59.

them. A similar distinction was, of course, the basis of Burke's treatise on 'The Sublime and Beautiful', and dominated the aesthetic thought of the century. Whether it was not much more sensible than the modern practice of bundling Alps and roses together into the single category of Beauty, I do not here inquire. The interesting thing is that Addison stands exactly at the turn of the tide.

Equally important for the historian of taste is *Spectator*, No. 160, where he contrasts the original 'genius' (which tends to be 'nobly wild and extravagant') and the *Bel Esprit* 'refined by Conversation, Reflection, and the Reading of the most polite Authors'.[1] The taste for 'noble extravagance' is not itself a novelty, for audacities in art and graces that overleap the rules are praised by Dryden, Boileau, and Pope. What is interesting is Addison's belief that even the greatest genius is 'broken' by the rules and in becoming learned 'falls unavoidably into Imitation'.[2] This pessimistic view of culture as something naturally opposed to genius received, no doubt, its extreme expression in Macaulay's essay on Milton; but I think it had also a great deal to do with that crop of forgeries which the eighteenth century produced. If sublime genius lies all in the past, before civilization began, we naturally look for it in the past. We long to recover the work of those sublime prehistoric bards and druids who *must* have existed. But their work is not to be found; and the surviving medieval literature conspicuously lacks the sublimity and mysteriousness we desire. In the end one begins *inventing* what the 'bards', 'druids', and 'minstrels' ought to have written. Ossian, Rowley, and *Otranto* are wish-fulfilments. It is always to be remembered that Macpherson had written original epics about prehistoric Scotland before he invented Ossian. By a tragic chance he and Chatterton discovered that their work was marketable, and so make-believe turned into fraud. But there was a sincere impulse behind it: they were seeking in the past that great romantic poetry which really lay in the future, and from intense imagination of what it must be like if only they could find it they slipped into making it themselves.

So far I have been trying to obey Arnold's precept—to get myself out of the way and let humanity decide. I have not attempted to assess the value of Addison's work, having wished rather to bring out its immense potency. He appears to be (as far as any individual can be) the source of a quite astonishing number of mental habits which were

---

[1] *Spectator* 160, vol. II, p. 283.   [2] *Ibid.*

still prevalent when men now living were born. Almost everything which my own generation ignorantly called Victorian seems to have been expressed by Addison. It is all there in the *Spectator*—the vague religious sensibility, the insistence on what came later to be called Good Form, the playful condescension towards women, the untroubled belief in the beneficence of commerce, the comfortable sense of security which, far from excluding, perhaps renders possible the romantic relish for wildness and solitude. If he is not at present the most hated of our writers, that can only be because he is so little read. Everything the moderns detest, all that they call *smugness*, *complacency*, and *bourgeois ideology*, is brought together in his work and given its most perfect expression.

And certainly, if it were at all times true that the Good is the enemy of the Best, it would be hard to defend Addison. His Rational Piety, his smiling indulgence to 'the fair sex', his small idealisms about trade, certainly fall short of actual Christianity, and plain justice to women, and true political wisdom. They may even be obstacles to them; palliatives and anodynes that prolong the disease. In some moods I cannot help seeing Addison as one who, at every point, 'sings charms to ills that ask the knife'. I believe he could defend himself. He is not attempting to write sermons or philosophy, only essays; and he certainly could not foresee what the search for markets would finally make of international trade. These hostile criticisms, made on the basis of our modern experience when all issues have become sharper, cannot really be maintained. All we can justly say is that his essays are rather small beer; there is no iron in them as in Johnson; they do not stir the depths.

And yet, if I were to live in a man's house for a whole twelvemonth, I think I should be more curious about the quality of his small beer than about that of his wine; more curious about his bread and butter and beef than about either. Writers like Addison who stand on the common ground of daily life and deal only with middle things are unduly depreciated today. Pascal says somewhere that the cardinal error of Stoicism was to suppose that we can do always what we do sometimes. No one lives always on the stretch. Hence one of the most pertinent questions to be asked about any man is what he falls back on. The important thing about Malory's world, for example, is that when you fall back from the quest of the Grail you fall back into the middle world of Arthur's court: not plumb down into the level of

King Mark. The important thing about many fierce idealists in our own day is that when the political meeting or the literary movement can be endured no longer they fall plumb down to the cinema and the dance band. I fully admit that when Pope and Swift are on the heights they have a strength and splendour which makes everything in Addison look pale; but what an abyss of hatred and bigotry and even silliness receives them when they slip from the heights! The Addisonian world is not one to live in at all times, but it is a good one to fall back into when the day's work is over and a man's feet on the fender and his pipe in his mouth. Good sense is no substitute for Reason; but as a rest from Reason it has distinct advantages over Jargon. I do not think Addison's popularity is likely to return; but something to fill the same place in life will always be needed—some tranquil middle ground of quiet sentiments and pleasing melancholies and gentle humour to come in between our restless idealisms and our equally restless dissipations. Do we not after all detect in the charge of *smugness* and *complacency* the note of envy? Addison is, above all else, comfortable. He is not on that account to be condemned. He is an admirable cure for the fidgets.

•

12

Four-Letter Words

Ce n'est point ainsi que parle la nature
MOLIÈRE

Literary historians sometimes use the word *Eliʒabethan* qualitatively rather than chronologically and apply it to poems written after the accession of James I. I am going to take a similar liberty with the expression 'four-letter words', and make it mean what are called 'obscene words' in general. Some of my specimens contain more than four letters.

I believe—for I have not found the passage—that Lawrence somewhere says it is hard to know how four-letter words affected the mind of the Middle Ages.[1] Whether he did or not, I think it worth a moment's inquiry. We cannot arrive at an absolutely certain answer, but there are grounds for a good guess. If we want a clue to the way medieval people felt about any word we naturally look to see how they used it. We open, in fact, the glossary of Skeat's Chaucer.

The following four-letter words (in my extended sense) are in alphabetical order.

Bele chose. Comic and roguish euphemism for *muliebria pudenda*. Skeat lists it twice. On both occasions it is used by the Wife of Bath (D 447, 510).

Coillons (testes). Used abusively by the Host to the Pardoner in bitter anger (C 952).

Ers (nates vel anus). This occurs twice in the Miller's Tale (A 3734, 3755). The context is slapstick farce. It occurs also in the Summoner's Tale (D 1690, 1694). There the context is farcical fantasy with a satirical implication; the teller is insulting friars as deeply as he knows how. It is just conceivable, though *ars*

---

[1] Lewis may have had in mind the following passage from 'A Propos of *Lady Chatterley's Lover*', reprinted in *Phoenix II: Uncollected, Unpublished and Other Prose Works by D. H. Lawrence*, ed. Warren Roberts and Harry T. Moore (London, 1968), p. 489: 'We are to-day, as human beings, evolved and cultured far beyond the taboos which are inherent in our culture. This is a very important fact to realize. Probably, to the Crusaders, mere words were potent and evocative to a degree we can't realize. The evocative power of the so-called obscene words must have been very dangerous to the dim-minded, obscure, violent natures of the Middle Ages, and perhaps is still too strong for slow-minded, half-evoked lower natures to-day.'

metrike is good Middle English for 'arithmetic', that the choice of this word in D 2222 contains a *double entendre*.

Fart. Always in slapstick farce. Miller's Tale (A 3338, 3806); Summoner's (D 2149).

Pisse (*n*). Either in slapstick (Miller's Tale, A 3798) or in a pseudo-scientific context (Canon's Yeoman, G 807).

Queynte (*bele chose*). In farce (Miller's Tale, A 3276) and in the mouth of the Wife of Bath (D 332, 444).

Quoniam. Comic synonym for the preceding. Used once (but one MS here reads *queynte*) by the same speaker (D 608).

Swiven. Used in slapstick (Reeve's Tale, A 4178, 4266, 4317; Cook's Tale, A 4422). In Miller's Tale, A 3850, there is a tone of malevolent triumph. There is malice also when it is used by the crow in the Manciple's (H 256). In the Merchant's (E 2378) it is said in furious anger.

I am anxious not to try to prove too much. Skeat's entries are probably not exhaustive. Still, we may note for what it is worth that farce and abuse are the normal contexts of all these words. Any reader who finds the passages in which they occur inflammatory and in that sense 'corrupting' must be, in Johnson's phrase, 'more combustible than most'.

Set against these a passage that, I think, might possibly inflame: the consummation of the love between Troilus and Criseyde (III, 1142–1421). Here every word (though not, to be sure, the whole passage) could have been read aloud in a Victorian girls' school.

None of the eight words I have extracted from Chaucer, so far as I can discover, occurs in Gower.

Having got thus far, and seeing at least the hint of principle, I decided to see whether it went further back. I turned to Latin.* Here are the five words which seem to me to have best claim to the four-letter character.

Cunnus. Martial appears to have worked this word hardest. It occurs in I, 90, a jeering lampoon on a woman suspected of Lesbianism; in III, 72, another abusive piece; and in III, 81, which taunts a man with (perhaps) the most unsavoury of all perversions. It occurs also in the *Priapeia* attached to some editions of Catullus. Horace uses it in contempt—*cunnus taeterrima belli causa* (*Sat.*, I, iii, 107). Some take *cunnus* to be here used, as elsewhere it certainly is, by metonymy for 'whore'. But we can make good sense, taking it literally. Either way the tone is the same.

* On Roman feeling about these matters, see Cicero's *Ad Fam.* IX, 22, and Quintilian, VIII, 3.

Such are the contexts in which it is used. Notice where it is not. In a genuinely pornographic passage, by which I mean one clearly intended to act as an aphrodisiac on the reader, Ovid has occasion to mention the thing; but he knows his trade far too well to use the word. He prefers two very incendiary periphrases: *partibus illis In quibus occulte spicula figit Amor* and *loca ... quae tangi femina gaudet* (*Ars Am.*, II, 707, 719). Apuleius in his bedroom scene (*Met.*, II, 16, 17) uses *feminal*. I am not sure of its status, but I should be surprised if it were as coarse as *cunnus*. The fact that the only two examples of it quoted by Lewis and Short both come from Apuleius, so far as it goes, confirms this. He never used a common word if he could find a rare one.

Penis. This can be used in tranquil and respectable writing if it means lust in general; as when we say a man has spent a fortune on his belly (by being a gourmet) or on his back (by overdressing). But when it is concrete and anatomical it appears chiefly, perhaps solely, in harsh satire: e.g. in Horace's very malodorous twelfth epode, or the stomach-turning speech of the professional joy-boy in Juvenal (IX, 43). Ovid, the real pornographer, has again occasion to mention the thing. He will not use a four-letter word; it becomes *inguinis pars* (*Amores*, III, vii, 6), *membra* (13), *latus* (36), and once more *pars* (69).

For *verpa* the dictionary quotes only Catullus, Martial and (of course) the *Priapeia*. Try looking up the Catullus (XXVIII, *Pisonis comites*).

Vulva (or *volva*). This has two meanings. In its strict, anatomical sense (*uterus*), it turns up in scientific writers. In its vulgar sense, when it becomes a synonym for *cunnus*, it too comes chiefly in satire. Martial uses it in an attack on a male *fellator* (XI, 61); Juvenal, in his savage passage on Messalina—*adhuc ardens rigidae tentigine volvae* (VI, 129).

As for *glubo*, that grossest verb of all, few forget the one place where they have met it. *Glubit magnanimi Remi nepotes* is screamed at us by Catullus in the rage of a man so miserable that his only wish is to wound (LVIII).

The clue, however slender, still seemed to be leading me in the same direction. Encouraged by this I ventured further back into a literature where I am even less at home. I got out my Liddell and Scott and my Aristophanes.

It was surely significant that the great comedian gave one a four-letter word about once in every twenty lines, and even in those passages where my weak scholarship saw no indecency the commentators could usually unearth one. But I must confine myself to single words:

7　　　　　　　　　　171　　　　　　　　　HLL

βδέω (*Pax*, 151; *Acharn.*, 256) means to stink, in scientific texts. In Aristophanes it means to break wind. All the Lexicon's examples of this sense are Aristophanic.

βινεω, to *swive* (*Lys.*, 934; *Thesm.*, 50; *Acharn.*, 1052). All the examples are from Aristophanes and the comic poet Eupolis.

πέος, *penis* (*Lys.*, 124, 928). Only Aristophanes is quoted.

πρωκτός, (*nates vel anus*). Only Aristophanes mentioned.

στύομαι, *penem erigere.* (*Pax*, 728; *Lys.*, 869; *Acharn.*, 1220). Quoted only from Aristophanes and the Anthology.

τιτθίον, *papilla*, but, I think, a much more roguish word (*Pax*, 863). Quoted only from Aristophanes and Cantharus (a comic poet).

χέξω, to excrete. The examples are nearly all from comic writers.

Let me once more confess and even insist that such a tiny research as I have so far made does not warrant anything like a certain conclusion. The strength of my case, if it has any, lies not in the wealth of my evidence but in the fact that all the evidence, such as it is, points in one direction. And the way to refute it is not to expatiate on the scantiness of the evidence but to produce an *instantia contraria*. You must find passages—I have not yet found one myself—where four-letter words are used seriously, neither with belly-laughter nor snarls of hatred, in seriously erotic elegy or lyric; where they are used seductively or at least sympathetically. The nearest thing to such an instance within my own reading comes in Old French, and I believe that it makes for me rather than against me. In the *Roman de la Rose* (5537) Jean de Meung uses the word *coilles*. He puts it into the mouth of Reason herself. The Lover reproves Reason for her bad manners—

> M'avez coilles nomees,
> Que ne sunt pas bien renomees,
> En bouche a cortaise pucele.
> (6929)

Reason, quite unabashed, says that her Father made these things *de ses propres mains* in Paradise and she is determined to speak of them *senz mettre gloses* (6957–60). Here we admittedly have a four-letter word used seriously and with approval. But we notice two facts. First, such usage was not normal; that is why the Lover is shocked. And secondly, Jean de Meung in this passage is not writing love-poetry but philosophical poetry about love. He is indeed putting forward, or making Reason put forward, exactly the case so often argued by the defenders of Lawrence. He is saying that these things ought not to be a subject either of shame or of ridicule. Reason defies (and thus gives evidence for) traditional linguistic behaviour. When Jean de Meung ceases to be a doctrinaire and becomes once more an erotic poet we shall hear no more about *coilles*. The poem ends with the deflowering of the heroine (21583 *et seq.*). But it is all told allegorically and even a fairly intelligent reader might not know what was happening. We should have an exact parallel if a modern wrote a novel which used four-letter words in a reflective passage and omitted them from his descriptions of the *concubitus*.

The value which four-letter words have usually had in actual usage is well attested by two bits of evidence from a much later period. Our ancestors were sometimes shamelessly frank about the kind of pleasure they demanded from certain kinds of literature. As a result we find four-letter words condemned not on the ground that they are aphrodisiacs but precisely on the ground that they are not. Thus Sheffield complains of

> Such nauseous Songs as the late Convert made,
> Which justly call this censure on his Shade;
> Not that warm thoughts of the transporting joy
> Can shock the Chastest or the Nicest cloy,
> But obscene words, too gross to move desire,
> Like heaps of Fuel do but choak the Fire.
> That Author's Name has undeserved praise
> Who pall'd the appetite he meant to raise.*

We see exactly how Sheffield read and how he took it for granted that poets wrote. When I first read this passage I hastily put it down as 'Restoration nastiness'. But I have had to withdraw the chronological epithet. How of this from Montaigne?

Il y a certaines autres choses qu'on cache pour les montrer. Oyez cettuy-là plus ouvert: *et nudam pressi corpus adusque meum*. Il me semble qu'il me chapone. Que Martial retrousse Venus à sa poste, il n'arrive pas à la faire paroistre si entiere. Celuy qui dict tout, il nous saoule et nous desgouste; celuy qui craint à s'exprimer nous achemine à en penser plus qu'il n'en y a. Il y a de la trahison en cette sorte de modestie, et notamment nous entr'ouvrant, comme font ceux cy, une si belle route à l'imagination. Et l'action et la peinture doivent sentir le larrecin.†

---

* 'An Essay upon Poetry', 24 *et seq.* Quoted in *Critical Essays of the Seventeenth Century*, ed. J. E. Spingarn (Oxford, 1957), vol. II, p. 288. The 'late convert' is no doubt Rochester.
† *Essais*, III, v.

There are, indeed, no four-letter words in the line Montaigne is discussing. But the point of view is the same. Immodesty is deprecated not as provoking but as impeding Sheffield's 'warm thoughts' and Montaigne's *belle route à l'imagination*.

Our knowledge will never cover all individual varieties of speech; but the evidence before me, though it cannot establish, suggests a probable generalisation. It looks as if no nation, age, or class has commonly used four-letter words to 'move desire'. If that is so, those who thought Lawrence's vocabulary—we are not discussing his over-all tendency—a grave moral danger were presumably mistaken. But still less does it appear that such words have been used for a reverential and (in the old sense) 'enthusiastick' treatment of sex. They are the vocabulary either of farce or of vituperation; either innocent, or loaded with the very opposite evil to that which prudes suspect—with a gnostic or Swiftian contempt for the body. Lawrence's usage is not to be reckoned a return to nature from some local or recent inhibition. It is, for good or ill, as artificial, as remote from the linguistic soil, as Euphuism or, a closer comparison, the most desperate parts of *Lyrical Ballads*. Here, as in them, the words may be earthy; this use of them is not. It is a rebellion against language. *Lady Chatterley* has made short work of a prosecution by the Crown. It still has to face more formidable judges. Nine of them, and all goddesses.[1]

[1] In an extremely interesting essay, 'Prudery and Philology', *The Spectator*, vol. CXCIV (21 January 1955), pp. 63–4, Lewis discusses the specifically literary problem of attempting to describe parts of the human body. He suggests the following experiment: 'Sit down and *draw* your nude. When you have finished it, take your pen and attempt the *written* description. Before you have finished you will be faced with a problem which simply did not exist while you were working at the picture. When you come to those parts of the body which are not usually mentioned, you will have to make a choice of vocabulary. And you will find that you have only four alternatives: a nursery word, an archaism, a word from the gutter, or a scientific word. You will not find any ordinary neutral word, comparable to "hand" or "nose" ... There never was a falser maxim than *ut pictura poesis*. We are sometimes told that everything in the world can come into literature. This is perhaps true in some sense. But it is a dangerous truth unless we balance it with the statement that nothing can go into literature except words, or (if you prefer) that nothing can go in except by becoming words. And words, like every other medium, have their own proper powers and limitations' (p. 63). See also Lewis's essay, 'Sex in Literature: Is the Law out of Step?', *Sunday Telegraph*, no. 87 (30 September 1962), p. 8

13

A Note on Jane Austen

I begin by laying together four passages from the novels of Jane Austen.

1. Catherine was completely awakened . . . Most grievously was she humbled. Most bitterly did she cry. It was not only with herself that she was sunk—but with Henry. Her folly, which now seemed even criminal, was all exposed to him, and he must despise her for ever. The liberty which her imagination had dared to take with the character of his father, could he ever forgive it? The absurdity of her curiosity and her fears, could they ever be forgotten? She hated herself more than she could express[1] . . . Nothing . . . could be clearer, than that it had been all a voluntary, self-created delusion, each trifling circumstance receiving importance from an imagination resolved on alarm, and every thing forced to bend to one purpose by a mind which, before she entered the Abbey, had been craving to be frightened . . . She saw that the infatuation had been created, the mischief settled long before her quitting Bath[2] . . . Her mind made up on these several points, and her resolution formed, of always judging and acting in future with the greatest good sense, she had nothing to do but forgive herself and be happier than ever.[3]   *Northanger Abbey*, ch. 25.

2. 'Oh! Elinor, . . . you have made me hate myself forever.—How barbarous have I been to you!—you, who have been my only comfort, who have borne with me in all my misery, who have seemed to be suffering only for me!'[4] . . . Marianne's courage soon failed her, in trying to converse upon a topic which always left her more dissatisfied with herself than ever, by the comparison it necessarily produced between Elinor's conduct and her own. She felt all the force of that comparison; but not as her sister had hoped, to urge her to exertion now; she felt it with all the pain of continual self-reproach, regretted most bitterly that she had never exerted herself before;

---

[1] *Northanger Abbey*, in *The Novels of Jane Austen. The Text based on Collation of the Early Editions*, in five volumes, ed. R. W. Chapman, second edition (Oxford, 1926), vol. II, ch. x, p. 199.

Note: References to 'vols.' in the footnotes are not to Chapman's arrangement of the novels into five volumes, but to the sub-division of the novels into volumes by Jane Austen. As *Northanger Abbey* and *Persuasion* were originally published together (i.e. *Northanger* in two volumes, and *Persuasion* in three), this explains why the first chapter of *Persuasion* begins in volume III. Lewis was quoting from modern editions and I have retained his chapter numbering, as well as given those in the Chapman edition.

[2] *Ibid.*, pp. 199–200.   [3] *Ibid.*, p. 201.

[4] *Sense and Sensibility*, ed. Chapman, vol. III, ch. i, p. 264.

but it brought only the torture of penitence, without the hope of amendment[1] ... [Elinor later saw in Marianne] an apparent composure of mind, which, in being the result as she trusted of serious reflection, must eventually lead her to contentment and cheerfulness[2] ... 'My illness has made me think ... I considered the past; I saw in my own behaviour ... nothing but a series of imprudence towards myself, and want of kindness to others. I saw that my own feelings had prepared my sufferings, and that my want of fortitude under them had almost led me to the grave. My illness, I well knew, had been entirely brought on by myself, by such negligence of my own health, as I had felt even at the time to be wrong. Had I died,—it would have been self-destruction ... I wonder ... that the very eagerness of my desire to live, to have time for atonement to my God, and to you all, did not kill me at once ... I cannot express my own abhorrence of myself.'[3]

Sense and Sensibility, chs. 37, 38, 46.

3. As to his real character, had information been in her power, she had never felt a wish of inquiring. His countenance, voice, and manner, had established him at once in the possession of every virtue[4] ... She perfectly remembered everything that had passed in conversation between Wickham and herself, in their first evening at Mr. Philip's[5] ... She was *now* struck with the impropriety of such communications to a stranger, and wondered it had escaped her before. She saw the indelicacy of putting himself forward as he had done, and the inconsistency of his professions with his conduct[6] ... She grew absolutely ashamed of herself ... 'How despicably have I acted!' she cried.—'I, who have prided myself on my discernment! ... who have often disdained the generous candour of my sister, and gratified my vanity, in useless or blameable distrust.—How humiliating is this discovery!—Yet, how just a humiliation!—Had I been in love, I could not have been more wretchedly blind. But vanity, not love, has been my folly ... I have courted prepossession and ignorance, and driven reason away ... Till this moment I never knew myself.'[7]

Pride and Prejudice, ch. 36.

4. Her own conduct, as well as her own heart, was before her in the same few minutes ... How improperly had she been acting by Harriet! How inconsiderate, how indelicate, how irrational, how unfeeling had been her conduct! What blindness, what madness, had led her on! It struck her with dreadful force, and she was ready to give it every bad name in the world[8] ... Every moment had brought a fresh surprise; and every surprise must be matter of humiliation to her.—How to understand it all! How to understand the deceptions she had been thus practising on herself, and living under!—The blunders, the blindness of her own head and heart! ... She perceived that she had acted most weakly; that she had been imposed on by others in a most mortifying degree.[9]

Emma, ch. 47.

---

[1] *Sense and Sensibility*, ch. ii, p. 270.   [2] *Ibid.*, ch. x, p. 342.
[3] *Ibid.*, pp. 345–6.   [4] *Pride and Prejudice*, ed. Chapman, vol. ii, ch. xiii, p. 206.
[5] *Ibid.*   [6] *Ibid.*, p. 207.
[7] *Ibid.*, p. 208.   [8] *Emma*, ed. Chapman, vol. iii, ch. xi, p. 408.
[9] *Ibid.*, pp. 411–12.

Between these four passages there are, no doubt, important distinctions. The first is on a level of comedy which approximates to
burlesque. The delusion from which Catherine Morland has been
awakened was an innocent one, which owed at least as much to
girlish ignorance of the world as to folly. And, being imaginative, it
was a delusion from which an entirely commonplace or self-centred
mind would hardly have suffered. Accordingly, the expiation, though
painful while it lasts, is brief, and Catherine's recovery and good
resolutions are treated with affectionate irony. The awakening of
Marianne Dashwood is at the opposite pole. The situation has come
near to tragedy; moral, as well as, or more than, intellectual deficiency
has been involved in Marianne's errors. Hence the very vocabulary of
the passage strikes a note unfamiliar in Jane Austen's style. It makes
explicit, for once, the religious background of the author's ethical
position. Hence such theological or nearly-theological words as
penitence, even the *torture of penitence*, *amendment*, *self-destruction*, *my
God*. And though not all younger readers may at once recognize it,
the words *serious reflection* belong to the same region. In times which
men now in their fifties can remember, the adjective *serious* ('Serious
reading', 'Does he ever think about serious matters?') had indisputably religious overtones. The title of Law's *Serious Call* is characteristic. Between these two extracts, those from *Pride and Prejudice*
and *Emma* occupy a middle position. Both occur in a context of high
comedy, but neither is merely laughable.

Despite these important differences, however, no one will dispute
that all four passages present the same kind of process. 'Disillusion-
ment', which might by etymology be the correct name for it, has
acquired cynical overtones which put it out of court. We shall have
to call it 'undeception' or 'awakening'. All four heroines painfully,
though with varying degrees of pain, discover that they have been
making mistakes both about themselves and about the world in which
they live. All their *data* have to be reinterpreted. Indeed, considering
the differences of their situations and characters, the similarity of the
process in all four is strongly marked. All realize that the cause of the
deception lay within; Catherine, that she had brought to the Abbey a
mind 'craving to be frightened', Marianne, that 'her own feelings had
prepared her sufferings', Elizabeth, that she has 'courted ignorance'
and 'driven reason away', Emma, that she has been practising deceptions on herself. Self-hatred or self-contempt, though (once more) in

different degrees, are common to all. Catherine 'hated herself'; Elinor abhors herself; Elizabeth finds her conduct 'despicable'; Emma gives hers 'every bad name in the world'. Tardy and surprising self-knowledge is presented in all four, and mentioned by name in the last two. 'I never knew myself', says Elizabeth; Emma's conduct and 'her own heart' appear to her, unwelcome strangers both, 'in the same few minutes'.

If Jane Austen were an author as copious as Tolstoy, and if these passages played different parts in the novels from which they are taken, the common element would not, perhaps, be very important. After all, undeception is a common enough event in real life, and therefore, in a vast tract of fiction, might be expected to occur more than once. But that is not the position. We are dealing with only four books, none of them long; and in all four the undeception, structually considered, is the very pivot or watershed of the story. In *Northanger Abbey*, and *Emma*, it precipitates the happy ending. In *Sense and Sensibility* it renders it possible. In *Pride and Prejudice* it initiates that revaluation of Darcy, both in Elizabeth's mind and in our minds, which is completed by the visit to Pemberley. We are thus entitled to speak of a common pattern in Jane Austen's four most characteristic novels. They have 'one plot' in a more important sense than Professor Garrod suspected.[1] This is not so clearly true of *Sense and Sensibility*, but then it has really two plots or two 'actions' in the Aristotelian sense; it is true about one of them.

It is perhaps worth emphasizing what may be called the hardness—at least the firmness—of Jane Austen's thought exhibited in all these undeceptions. The great abstract nouns of the classical English moralists are unblushingly and uncompromisingly used: *good sense, courage, contentment, fortitude*, 'some duty neglected, some failing indulged', *impropriety, indelicacy, generous candour, blameable distrust, just humiliation, vanity, folly, ignorance, reason*. These are the concepts by which Jane Austen grasps the world. In her we still breathe the air of the *Rambler* and *Idler*. All is hard, clear, definable; by some modern standards, even naïvely so. The hardness is, of course, for oneself, not for one's neighbours. It reveals to Marianne her want 'of

---

[1] Professor H. W. Garrod complained that Jane Austen 'invents no new plots, she repeats her characters, she employs again and again the same setting. The plot is always a husband-hunt ... indeed Miss Austen has but one plot.' 'Jane Austen: A Depreciation', *Essays by Divers Hands, Transactions of the Royal Society of Literature*, new series, vol. VIII (1928), pp. 32–4.

kindness' and shows Emma that her behaviour has been 'unfeeling'. Contrasted with the world of modern fiction, Jane Austen's is at once less soft and less cruel.

It may be added, though this is far less important, that in these four novels, self-deception and awakening are not confined to the heroines. General Tilney makes as big a mistake about Catherine as she has made about him. Mrs Ferrars misjudges her son. Mr Bennet is forced at last to see his errors as a father. But perhaps all this does not go beyond what might be expected from the general nature of human life and the general exigencies of a novelistic plot.

The central pattern of these four has much in common with that of a comedy by Molière.

Two novels remain. In *Mansfield Park* and *Persuasion* the heroine falls into no such self-deception and passes through no such awakening. We are, it is true, given to understand that Anne Elliot regards the breaking off of her early engagement to Wentworth as a mistake. If any young person now applied to her for advice in such circumstances, 'they would never receive any of such certain immediate wretchedness, such uncertain future good'.[1] For Anne in her maturity did not hold the view which Lord David Cecil attributes to Jane Austen, that 'it was wrong to marry for money, but it was silly to marry without it'.* She was now fully 'on the side of early warm attachment, and a cheerful confidence in futurity, against that over-anxious caution which seems to insult exertion and distrust Providence'.[2] (Notice, in passing, the Johnsonian cadence of a sentence which expresses a view that Johnson in one of his countless moods might have supported.) But though Anne thinks a mistake has been made, she does not think it was she that made it. She declares that she was perfectly right in being guided by Lady Russell who was to her 'in the place of a parent'. It was Lady Russell who had erred. There is no true parallel here between Anne and the heroines we have been considering. Anne, like Fanny Price, commits no errors.

Having placed these two novels apart from the rest because they do not use the pattern of 'undeception', we can hardly fail to notice that they share another common distinction. They are the novels of the solitary heroines.

* *Jane Austen* (Cambridge, 1936), p. 33.
[1] *Persuasion*, ed. Chapman, vol. III, ch. iv, p. 29.
[2] *Ibid.*, vol. III, ch. iv, p. 30.

Catherine Morland is hardly ever alone except on her journey from Northanger Abbey, and she is soon back among her affectionate, if placid, family. Elinor Dashwood bears her own painful secret without a confidant for a time; but her isolation, besides being temporary, is incomplete; she is surrounded by affection and respect. Elizabeth always has Jane, the Gardiners, or (to some extent) her father. Emma is positively spoiled; the acknowledged centre of her own social world. Of all these heroines we may say, as Jane Austen says of some other young women, 'they were of consequence at home and favourites abroad'.

But Fanny Price and Anne are of no 'consequence'. The consciousness of 'mattering' which is so necessary even to the humblest women, is denied them. Anne has no place in the family councils at Kellynch Hall; 'she was only Anne'. She is exploited by her married sister, but not valued; just as Fanny is exploited, but not valued, by Mrs Norris. Neither has a confidant; or if Edmund had once been a confidant as well as a hero to Fanny, he progressively ceases to be so. Some confidence, flawed by one vast forbidden topic, we may presume between Anne and Lady Russell; but this is almost entirely off stage and within the novel we rarely see them together. Both heroines come within easy reach of one of the great archetypes—Cinderella, Electra. Fanny, no doubt, more so. She is almost a Jane Austen heroine condemned to a Charlotte Brontë situation. We do not even believe in what Jane Austen tells us of her good looks; whenever we are looking at the action through Fanny's eyes, we feel ourselves sharing the consciousness of a plain woman.

Even physically, we see them alone; Fanny perpetually in the East Room with its fireless grate and its touching, ridiculous array of petty treasures (what Cinderella, what Electra, is without them?) or Anne, alone beside the hedge, an unwilling eavesdropper, Anne alone with her sick nephew, Anne alone in the empty house waiting for the sound of Lady Russell's carriage. And in their solitude both heroines suffer; far more deeply than Catherine, Elizabeth, and Emma, far more innocently than Marianne. Even Elinor suffers less. These two novels, we might almost say, stand to the others as Shakespeare's 'dark' comedies to his comedies in general. The difference in the lot of the heroines goes with a difference in the 'character parts'. Mrs Norris is almost alone among Jane Austen's vulgar old women in being genuinely evil, nor are her greed and cruelty painted with the high spirits which make us not so much hate as rejoice in Lady Catherine de Bourgh.

These solitary heroines who make no mistakes have, I believe—or had while she was writing—the author's complete approbation. This is connected with the unusual pattern of *Mansfield Park* and *Persuasion*. The heroines stand almost outside, certainly a little apart from, the world which the action of the novel depicts. It is in it, not in them, that self-deception occurs. They see it, but its victims do not. They do not of course stand voluntarily apart, nor do they willingly accept the rôle of observers and critics. They are shut out and are compelled to observe: for what they observe, they disapprove.

It is this disapproval which, though shared both by Fanny and Anne, has perhaps drawn on Fanny, from some readers, the charge of being a prig. I am far from suggesting that Fanny is a successful heroine, still less that she is the equal of Anne. But I hardly know the definition of *Prig* which would make her one. If it means a self-righteous person, a Pharisee, she is clearly no prig. If it means a 'precisian', one who adopts or demands a moral standard more exacting than is current in his own time and place, then I can see no evidence that Fanny's standard differs at all from that by which Marianne condemns herself or Anne Elliot corrects Captain Benwick. Indeed, since Anne preaches while Fanny feels in silence, I am a little surprised that the charge is not levelled against Anne rather than Fanny. For Anne's *chastoiement* of poor Benwick is pretty robust: 'She ventured to recommend a larger allowance of prose in his daily study; and ... mentioned such works of our best moralists, such collections of the finest letters, such memoirs of characters of worth and suffering, as occurred to her at the moment as calculated to rouse and fortify the mind by the highest precepts, and the strongest examples of moral and religious endurances' (ch. 11).[1] Notice, too, the standards which Anne was using when she first began to suspect her cousin, Mr Elliot: 'She saw that there had been bad habits; that Sunday-travelling had been a common thing; that there had been a period of his life (and probably not a short one) when he had been, at least, careless on all serious matters.'[2] Whatever we may think of these standards ourselves, I have not the least doubt that they are those of all the heroines, when they are most rational, and of Jane Austen herself.

[1] *Persuasion*, vol. III, ch. xi, p. 101.
[2] *Ibid.*, vol. IV, ch. v, p. 161.

This is the hard core of her mind, the Johnsonian element, the iron in the tonic.

How, then, does Fanny Price fail? I suggest, by insipidity. *Pauper videri Cinna vult et est pauper.* One of the most dangerous of literary ventures is the little, shy, unimportant heroine whom none of the other characters value. The danger is that your readers may agree with the other characters. Something must be put into the heroine to make us feel that the other characters are wrong, that she contains depths they never dreamed of. That is why Charlotte Brontë would have succeeded better with Fanny Price. To be sure, she would have ruined everything else in the book; Sir Thomas and Lady Bertram and Mrs Norris would have been distorted from credible types of pompous dullness, lazy vapidity and vulgar egoism into fiends complete with horns, tails and rhetoric. But through Fanny there would have blown a storm of passion which made sure that we at least would never think her insignificant. In Anne, Jane Austen did succeed. Her passion (for it is not less), her insight, her maturity, her prolonged fortitude, all attract us. But into Fanny, Jane Austen, to counterbalance her apparent insignificance, has put really nothing except rectitude of mind; neither passion, nor physical courage, nor wit, nor resource. Her very love is only calf-love—a schoolgirl's hero-worship for a man who has been kind to her when they were both children, and who, incidentally, is the least attractive of all Jane Austen's heroes. Anne gains immensely by having for her lover almost the best. In real life, no doubt, we continue to respect interesting women despite the preposterous men they sometimes marry. But in fiction it is usually fatal. Who can forgive Dorothea for marrying such a sugarstick as Ladislaw, or Nellie Harding for becoming Mrs Bold? Or, of course, David Copperfield for his first marriage.

Fanny also suffers from the general faults of *Mansfield Park*, which I take to be, if in places almost the best, yet as a whole the least satisfactory, of Jane Austen's works. I can accept Henry Crawford's elopement with Mrs Rushworth: I cannot accept his intention of marrying Fanny. Such men never make such marriages.

But though Fanny is insipid (yet not a prig) she is always 'right' in the sense that to her, and to her alone, the world of *Mansfield Park* always appears as, in Jane Austen's view, it really is. Undeceived, she is the spectator of deceptions. These are made very clear. In chapter 2 we learn that the Bertram girls were 'entirely deficient' in 'self-knowledge'.[1] In chapter 3 Sir Thomas departs for Antigua without much anxiety about his family because, though not perfectly confident of his daughters' discretion, he had ample trust 'in Mrs. Norris's watchful attention, and in Edmund's judgment'.[2] Both, of course, failed to justify it. In chapter 12 when Crawford was absent for a fortnight it proved 'a fortnight of such dulness to the Miss Bertrams, as ought to have put them both on their guard'.[3] Of course it did not. In chapter 16 when Edmund at last consents to act, Fanny is forced to raise the question, 'Was he not deceiving himself?'[4] In 34 when Crawford (whose manners are insufferable) by sheer persistence pesters Fanny into speech when she has made her desire for silence obvious, she says, 'Perhaps, Sir, I thought it was a pity you did not always know yourself as well as you seemed to do at that moment.'[5] But deception is most fully studied in the person of Mary Crawford, 'a mind led astray and bewildered, and without any suspicion of being so: darkened, yet fancying itself light'. The New Testament echo in the language underlines the gravity of the theme. It may be that Jane Austen has not treated it successfully. Some think that she hated Mary and falsely darkened a character whom she had in places depicted as charming. It might be the other way round; that the author, designing to show deception at its height, was anxious to play fair, to show how the victim could be likeable at times, and to render her final state the more impressive by raising in us false hopes that she might have been cured. Either way, the gap between Mary at her best and Mary in her last interview with Edmund is probably too wide; too wide for fiction, I mean, not for possibility. (We may have met greater inconsistency in real life; but real life does not need to be probable.) That last interview, taken by itself, is an alarming study of human blindness. We may—most of us do—disagree with the standards by which Edmund condemns Mary. The dateless and universal possibility in the scene is Mary's invincible ignorance of what those standards are. All through their conversation she is cutting her own throat. Every word she speaks outrages Edmund's feelings 'in total ignorance, unsuspiciousness of there being such feelings' (ch. 47).[6] At last, when we feel that her ghastly innocence (so to call it) could go no further, comes the master stroke. She tries to call him back by

---

[1] *Mansfield Park*, ed. Chapman, vol. I, ch. ii, p. 19.
[2] *Ibid.*, ch. iii, p. 32.
[3] *Ibid.*, ch. xii, p. 114.
[4] *Ibid.*, ch. xvi, p. 156.
[5] *Ibid.*, vol. III, ch. iii, p. 343.
[6] *Ibid.*, ch. xvi, p. 456.

'a saucy, playful smile'.[1] She still thought that possible. The misunderstanding is incurable. She will never know Edmund.

In *Persuasion* the theme of deception is much less important. Sir Walter is, no doubt, deceived both in his nephew and in Mrs Clay, but that is little more than the mechanism of the plot. What we get more of is the pains of the heroine in her rôle of compelled observer. Something of this had appeared in Elinor Dashwood, and more in Fanny Price, constantly forced to witness the courtship of Edmund and Mary Crawford. But Fanny had also, at times, derived amusement from her function of spectator. At the rehearsals of *Lovers' Vows* she was 'not unamused to observe the selfishness which, more or less disguised, seemed to govern them all' (ch. 14).[2] It is a kind of pleasure which we feel sure that Jane Austen herself had often enjoyed. But whether it were that something in her own life now began to show her less of the spectator's joys and more of his pains, forcing her on from 'as if we were God's spies' to 'break my heart for I must hold my tongue', or that she is simply exploring a new literary vein, it certainly seems that Anne's unshared knowledge of the significance of things she hears and sees is nearly always in some degree painful. At Kellynch she has 'a knowledge, which she often wished less, of her father's character'.[3] At the Musgroves 'One of the least agreeable circumstances of her residence ... was her being treated with too much confidence by all parties, and being too much in the secret of the complaints of each house' (ch. 6).[4] One passage perhaps gives the real answer to any charge of priggery that might lie against her or Fanny for the judgements they pass as spectators. Speaking of Henrietta's behaviour to Charles Hayter, Jane Austen says that Anne 'had delicacy which must be pained' by it (ch. 9).[5] This is not so much like the Pharisee's eagerness to condemn as the musician's involuntary shudder at a false note. Nor is it easily avoided by those who have standards of any sort. Do not our modern critics love to use the term 'embarrassing' of literature which violently offends the standards of their own group? and does not this mean, pretty nearly, a 'delicacy' on their part which 'must be pained'? But of course all these spectator's pains sink into insignificance beside that very special, almost unendurable, pain which Anne derives from her understanding

[1] *Mansfield Park*, vol. III, ch. xvi, p. 459. [2] *Ibid.*, vol. I, ch. xiv, p. 131.
[3] *Persuasion*, vol. III, ch. v, p. 34. [4] *Ibid.*, ch. vi, p. 44.
[5] *Ibid.*, ch. ix, p. 77.

of Wentworth's every look and word. For *Persuasion*, from first to last, is, in a sense in which the other novels are not, a love story.

It remains to defend what I have been saying against a possible charge. Have I been treating the novels as though I had forgotten that they are, after all, comedies? I trust not. The hard core of morality and even of religion seems to me to be just what makes good comedy possible. *'Principles'* or *'seriousness'* are essential to Jane Austen's art. Where there is no norm, nothing can be ridiculous, except for a brief moment of unbalanced provincialism in which we may laugh at the merely unfamiliar. Unless there is something about which the author is never ironical, there can be no true irony in the work. 'Total irony'—irony about everything—frustrates itself and becomes insipid.

But though the world of the novels has this serious, unyielding core, it is not a tragic world. This, no doubt, is due to the author's choice; but there are also two characteristics of her mind which are, I think, essentially untragic. The first is the nature of the core itself. It is in one way exacting, in another not. It is unexacting in so far as the duties commanded are not quixotic or heroic, and obedience to them will not be very difficult to properly brought up people in ordinary circumstances. It is exacting in so far as such obedience is rigidly demanded; neither excuses nor experiments are allowed. If charity is the poetry of conduct and honour the rhetoric of conduct, Jane Austen's 'principles' might be described as the grammar of conduct. Now grammar is something that anyone can learn; it is also something that everyone must learn. Compulsion waits. I think Jane Austen does not envisage those standards which she so rigidly holds as often demanding human sacrifice. Elinor felt sure that if Marianne's new composure were based on 'serious reflection' it 'must eventually lead her to contentment and cheerfulness'. That it might lead instead to a hair-shirt or a hermitage or a pillar in the Thebaid is not in Jane Austen's mind. Or not there. There is just a hint in *Persuasion* that total sacrifice may be demanded of sailors on active service; as there is also a hint of women who must love when life or when hope is gone. But we are then at the frontier of Jane Austen's world.

The other untragic element in her mind is its cheerful moderation. She could almost have said with Johnson, 'Nothing is too little for so little a creature as man.' If she envisages few great sacrifices, she also envisages no grandiose schemes of joy. She has, or at least all her favourite characters have, a hearty relish for what would now be regarded as very modest pleasures. A ball, a dinner party, books, conversation, a drive to see a great house ten miles away, a holiday as far as Derbyshire—these, with affection (that is essential) and good manners, are happiness. She is no Utopian.

She is described by someone in Kipling's worst story as the mother of Henry James.[1] I feel much more sure that she is the daughter of Dr Johnson: she inherits his commonsense, his morality, even much of his style. I am not a good enough Jamesian to decide the other claim. But if she bequeathed anything to him it must be wholly on the structural side. Her style, her system of values, her temper, seem to me the very opposite of his. I feel sure that Isabel Archer, if she had met Elizabeth Bennet, would have pronounced her 'not very cultivated'; and Elizabeth, I fear, would have found Isabel deficient both in 'seriousness' and in mirth.

[1] Lewis is referring to 'The Janeites' in *Debits and Credits* (London, 1926), pp. 153–4. Humberstall, repeating the officer Macklin's comment about Jane Austen, says: 'She *did* leave lawful issue in the shape o' one son; an' 'is name was 'Enery James.' Lewis disliked the story because, as he said in an early version of his essay on 'Kipling's World': 'Something so simple and ordinary as an enjoyment of Jane Austen's novels is turned into a pretext for one more secret society, and we have the hardly forgivable *Janeites.' Literature and Life*, vol. 1 (London, 1948), pp. 72–3. Still, as Roger Lancelyn Green helped Lewis and me to see, the *point* of the story is how Jane Austen helped to save the sanity of men serving in the worst horrors of the trenches during the 1914–18 war.

14

Shelley, Dryden, and Mr Eliot

To heanlic me þinceð
þaet ge mid urum sceattum to scype gangon
unbefohtene, nu ge þus feor hider
on urne eard in becomon.   *Maldon*, 55–8

Few poets have suffered more than Shelley from the modern dislike
of the Romantics. It is natural that this should be so. His poetry is,
to an unusual degree, entangled in political thought, and in a kind of
political thought now generally unpopular. His belief in the natural
perfectibility of man justly strikes the Christian reader as foolishness;
while, on the other hand, the sort of perfection he has in view is too
ideal for dialectical materialists. His writings are too generous for our
cynics; his life is too loose for our 'humanist' censors. Almost every
recent movement of thought in one way or another serves to discredit
him. From some points of view, this reaction cannot be regarded as
wholly unfortunate. There is much in Shelley's poetry that has been
praised to excess; much even that deserves no praise at all. In his
metre, with all its sweetness, there is much ignoble fluidity, much of
mere jingle. His use of language is such that he seldom attains for
long to the highest qualities of distinction, and often sinks to a facility
and commonplace almost Byronic. He is not a *safe* poet; you cannot
open his works to refute one of his enemies with any sense of confidence. But reaction must not be allowed to carry us too far; and when
Mr Eliot offers up Shelley as a sacrifice to the fame of Dryden it is
time to call a halt. To be sure, Mr Eliot has his own purpose in that
comparison: he is combating the view of the last century that Shelley
must necessarily be a greater poet than Dryden because his subjects
are more obviously poetical—because the one writes lyrics and the
other satire, because one is in the coffee-house and the other in
the clouds.* But we must not fall over, like Luther's drunk man, on the
other side of the horse. Those who prefer Shelley to Dryden need not
do so on the grounds which Mr Eliot has envisaged; and to prove this

* T. S. Eliot, 'John Dryden', *Selected Essays* (London, 1932), p. 295.

187

I will now maintain that Shelley is to be regarded, on grounds which Mr Eliot himself will allow, as a more masterly, a more sufficient, and indeed a more *classical* poet than Dryden.

The days are, or ought to be, long past in which any well-informed critic could take the couplet poets of our 'Augustan' school at their own valuation as 'classical' writers. This would be quite as grave an error as the romantic criticism which denied them to be men of genius. They are neither bad poets nor classical poets. Their merits are great, but neither their merits nor their limitations are those of ancient literature or of that modern literature which is truly classical. It would be hard to find any excellence in writing less classical than wit; yet it is in wit that these poets admittedly excel. The very forms in which the greatest and most characteristic of classical poetry is cast— the epic and the tragedy—are the forms which they attempt with least success. Their favourite form is Satire, a form not invented by the Greeks, and even in Roman hands not very like *MacFleknoe* or the *Dunciad*. But it is needless to labour the point. To any one who still thinks Pope a classical poet we can only say 'Open your Sophocles, your Virgil, your Racine, your Milton'; and if that experiment does not convince him, we may safely dismiss him for a blockhead.

Of the school in general, then, we may say that it is a good, unclassical school. But when we turn to Dryden, we must, I think, say more than this. We must admit that we have here a great, flawed poet, in whom the flaws, besides being characteristically unclassical, are scarcely forgivable even by the most romantic or revolutionary standards.

I have said 'a great, flawed poet'. Of the greatness I wish to make no question; and it is a greatness to which the name of *genius* is peculiarly applicable. The most abiding impression which Dryden makes upon us is that of exuberant power. He is what Middle English critics would have called 'boisteous'. He excels in beginnings. 'A milk white *Hind*, immortal and unchang'd'[1]—'In pious times, e'r Priest-craft did begin'[2]—there is no fumbling at the exordium. He leaps into his first paragraph as an athlete leaps into the hundred yards' track, and before the fascination of his ringing couplets gives us leisure to take breath we have been carried into the heart of his matter. The famous 'magnanimity' of his satire is another aspect of this same

---

[1] *The Hind and the Panther*, Pt. 1, line 1.
[2] *Absalom and Achitophel*, line 1.

quality of power. His strength is so great that he never needs—or never gives us the impression of needing—to use it all. He is justly praised by Mr Eliot for 'what he made of his material', for his 'ability to make the small into the great, the prosaic into the poetic':* not that the value of a literary result is in a direct ratio to its difficulty—a theory with absurd consequences—but that the sheer strength of the poet is more easily judged when it is thus isolated. Of this trans-forming power I know no better example than the résumé of the political situation which opens *Absalom and Achitophel*. Not only is the prosaic made poetical, but the obscure and complicated is made clear and simple. A child can hardly fail to understand the state of Israel as Dryden describes it; and yet surprisingly little of that situation, as Dryden saw it, has been omitted. If anything is mis-represented, the misrepresentation is deliberate.

Mr Eliot himself selects, to illustrate this transforming power, a passage from *Alexander's Feast* and another from *Cymon and Iphigenia*. The first is that in which the tipsy Alexander 'Fought all his *Battails* o'er again; And thrice He routed all his Foes; And thrice He slew the slain'.[1] Certainly, if the thing was to be done at all, this is the way to do it. The sudden irruption of the country-dancing fourteener among the nobler, if never very subtle, rhythms of the ode, most happily expresses the transition from heroics to a tavern scene. Dryden has brought off his effect—and it is an effect which will be dear to all who hate the heroic and cannot see any civil or religious ceremony without wishing that some one may slip. For a critic like Mr Eliot, however, the question must surely be not only whether a given effect has been attained, but also whether, and why, it ought to have been attempted. Certain classicists would resent the intrusion of the comic into the greater ode at all, as an offence against decorum. I am sure that Mr Eliot remembers, and almost sure he approves, the delicious re-proaches levelled against Racine by French critics for venturing within the remotest hailing distance of comedy in certain scenes of *Andromaque*; and the greater ode is as lofty a form as tragedy. But even if we allow the comic note, can we excuse comedy of quite this hackneyed and heavy-handed type? That Alexander in his cups should resemble exactly the first drunken braggart whom you may meet in a railway refreshment room, appears to Mr Eliot to add 'a

---

* Eliot, *op. cit.*, p. 296.
[1] *Alexander's Feast*, 67–8.

delicate flavour'.* But what is there delicate about it? Indelicacy, in the sense of grossness and crudity of apprehension, ἀγροικία, is surely the very essence of it. It does not seem to have crossed Dryden's mind that when Alexander got drunk he may have behaved like a drunk gentleman or a drunk scholar and not like an 'old soldier'. No: this is not a subtle or delicate joke. If it is to be defended at all, it must be defended as a 'good plain joke'. As such, Mr Eliot apparently likes it, and I do not: and this is of very little consequence. What is important is that the passage raises in our minds a rather disturbing doubt about Dryden's poetical purity of intention. The joke may be good or bad in itself. Let us suppose that it is good;—the question remains whether even a good joke, of this tavern type, really contributes to the total effect of the ode. Does Dryden really care whether it contributes or not? Is he, in fine, a man ready, for every ray of accidental beauty that may come in his way, to sacrifice the integrity of his work—a dabbler in 'good passages'—a man who can produce good poetry but not good poems?

As regards *Alexander's Feast* I am content to leave the question open: when once it has been raised we shall have no difficulty in answering it for the rest of Dryden's more considerable works. What do we enjoy in *Absalom and Achitophel*? Undoubtedly, the incidental merits. Of the poem taken as a whole, as a ποίημα, Johnson has said the last word.

There is . . . an unpleasing disproportion between the beginning and the end. We are alarmed by a faction formed out of many sects various in their principles, but agreeing in their purpose of mischief, formidable for their numbers, and strong by their supports, while the king's friends are few and weak. The chiefs on either part are set forth to view; but when expectation is at the height the king makes a speech, and

'Henceforth a series of new times began.'[1]

No doubt, the very nature of the case compelled Dryden to this fault; but that excuses the man without mending the poem. I do not argue *why* the work is botched, but *that* it is. It is even part of my case that the defect in *Absalom* was unavoidable. It is a radical defect, consubstantial with Dryden's original conception. It is no mere accident. The work is not merely maimed, it is diseased at the heart.

* Eliot, *op. cit.*, p. 297.

[1] Johnson, 'Life of Dryden', in *Lives of the English Poets*, vol. I, ed. George Birkbeck Hill (Oxford, 1905), p. 437.

Like many human invalids, it is not lacking in charms and happy moments; but classicists like Mr Eliot (and myself) should not accept any amount of littered poetry as a poem. If we turn to the *Hind and the Panther* we find the same irredeemable defect in an aggravated form. Of course it is full of 'good things'; but of the plan itself, the nerve and structure of the poem, what are we to say if not that the very design of conducting in verse a theological controversy allegorized as a beast fable suggests in the author a state of mind bordering on aesthetic insanity? If the poet had succeeded it would indeed provide a noble example of the transforming power which Mr Eliot claims for him. But he has not. *The Hind and the Panther* does not exist, as *Phèdre* or *Persuasion* or *The Alchemist* exist. It is not a poem: it is simply a name which we give for convenience to a number of pieces of good description, vigorous satire, and 'popular' controversy, which have all been yoked together by external violence.

It may be objected that I am selecting poems merely occasional, specimens at least of 'applied' poetry, which cannot fairly be judged by the highest standards. But this is dangerous argument for the defenders of Dryden. The two poems I have quoted are among his most considerable works: they contain much of his noblest, and much of his most piquant, poetry. If these have to be thrown to the wolves as mere applied poetry for which special indulgence is sued, it will be hard, on what remains, to support the plea that Dryden is a poet comparable to Shelley. But I pass over this difficulty. Let us turn to works more purely 'poetical', and specially to the *Fables* which no one asked him to write. Here, if anywhere, we may hope to find the real 'maker' at last instead of the mere fountain of brilliant 'passages'. Here, perhaps, Dryden will become the master, not the slave, of inspiration.

It falls out very happily that Mr Eliot should have chosen from one of these fables a passage in illustration of the 'transforming power'. It is the satire on the militia in *Cymon and Iphigenia*.

> The Country rings around with loud Alarms,
> And raw in Fields the rude Militia swarms, &c.[1]

Of this, Mr Eliot observes 'the comic is the material, the result is poetry'.[*] Yes, but comic poetry. The passage, if not so lustily comic

---

[*] Eliot, *op. cit.*, p. 297.
[1] *Cymon and Iphigenia*, 399.

as the picture of Alexander's tipsy valour, is a humorous passage; and I do not know why it shows more power to make comic poetry of comic material than to make idyllic poetry of idyllic material. Yet it shows power enough, and I will not press the point; but I cannot help wondering that Mr Eliot should think it worth while to quote this amusing description (a 'beauty' surely not very recondite), and yet not worth while to tell us why it should be in *Cymon and Iphigenia* at all. To what artistic end, precisely, is this satire on militias inserted in a romantic fable? I am afraid it is there only because Dryden wanted to write it. Doubtless, the fault is here much more venial than in *Alexander's Feast*. The joke itself is less hackneyed, and the lower tone of the fable admits a laxer kind of relevance than the ode. Perhaps, justified as an 'episode', the lines are excusable: and if, in this place, Dryden 'will have his joke', have it he shall, for me. But there is worse behind. In *Sigismonda and Guiscardo* Dryden reveals so much of himself that I question whether any one who has read it with attention can fail to see, once and for all, the *alte terminus haerens* which divides Dryden from the class of great poets. Here he sets out to tell a tragic and 'heroic' story. It is not a story of the highest order. It suffers from that overstrain and tendency to falsetto which is the infallible mark of the prosaic mind desperately determined to be 'poetical'. You could not make an *Oedipus* or a *Lear* out of it; you might make a *Cid*. But it is, at least, a story worth telling. And now mark what Dryden does with it. He does not intend to forgo a single thrill of the tragic ending. He intends to purge our emotions. We are to see the heroine 'devoutly glew'[1] her lips to the heart of her murdered husband, and our respect is to be demanded for her 'Mute solemn Sorrow, free from Female Noise'.[2] That is the note on which the poem is to end. And yet, with such an end in view, this old poet goes out of his way to insert at the beginning of his story a ribald picture of his heroine as the lascivious widow of conventional comedy. I will not quote the pitiful lines in which Dryden winks and titters to his readers over these time-honoured salacities. The reader may turn to the passage for himself. And when he has read on to the bitter end of it, to that couplet where even Dryden's skill in language deserts him and we sink to the scribbled meanness of

> On either Side the Kisses flew so thick,
> That neither he nor she had Breath to speak,[3]

[1] *Sigismonda and Guiscardo*, 641.   [2] *Ibid.*, 685.   [3] *Ibid.*, 161.

then let him remind himself that all this is the beginning of a tragic story, and that Dryden will presently try to make sublime this same woman whom he is here turning into a Widow Wadman. For such sin against the essential principles of all poetry whatever, no excuse can be made. It cannot be accident. Dryden is the most conscious of writers: he knows well what he is doing. He destroys, and is content to destroy, the kind of poem he sat down to write, if only he can win in return one guffaw from the youngest and most graceless of his audience. There is in this a poetic blasphemy, an arrogant contempt for his own art, which cannot, I think, be paralleled in any other great writer.

It would show a serious misunderstanding if Dryden's partisans pleaded at this point that I was enslaved to some Victorian canon of solemnity as the essence of poetry and judging Dryden by an alien standard. I have no quarrel with comic or cynical or even ribald poetry. I have no quarrel with Wycherley, I admire Congreve, I delight in Prior and still more in *Don Juan*. I delight in Dryden himself when he is content to talk bawdy in season and consider 'Sylvia the fair, in the bloom of Fifteen' a very pretty piece. But in these fables—as also in the heroic tragedies which are similarly blemished—it is Dryden, not I, who has chosen that the heroic should be trumps, and has lost the game by rules of his own choosing. It was Dryden, not I, who decided to write *Annus Mirabilis* as a serious and lofty historical poem on what he regarded as the 'successes of a most just and necessary War'.[1] If, after that decision, he describes the enemy as

Vast bulks which little souls but ill supply,[2]

then we have every right to tell that a nation of reasonable men, not to say men of courage and honour, are very ill-celebrated by the insinuation that their enemies are lubbers. This kind of thing runs through all Dryden's attempts at the graver and more enthusiastic kinds of poetry, and it must be remembered that such attempts make up a large part of his work. The sin is so flagrant that I cannot understand how so cultivated a critic as Mr Eliot has failed to see the truth; which truth had now better be stated quite frankly. Dryden fails to be a satisfactory poet because being rather a boor, a gross, vulgar, provincial, misunderstanding mind, he yet constantly attempts those

---

[1] *Annus Mirabilis: An account of the ensuing Poem, in a Letter to the Honorable, Sir Robert Howard*, 10–11.   [2] *Annus Mirabilis*, 280.

kinds of poetry which demand the *cuor gentil*. Like so many men of that age he is deeply influenced by the genuinely aristocratic and heroic poetry of France. He admires the world of the French tragedians —that exalted tableland where rhetoric and honour grow naturally out of the life lived and the culture inherited. We in England had had an aristocratic tradition of our own, to be sure; a tradition at once more sober and more tenderly romantic than the French, obeying a code of honour less dissociated from piety. The Duke and Duchess of Newcastle were perhaps its last exponents. But Dryden seems to know nothing of it. He and his audiences look to Versailles, and feel for it that pathetic yet unprofitable yearning which vulgarity so often feels for unattainable graces. But the yearning does not teach them the secret. Where their model was brilliant they are flashy; where the *Cid* was brave, Almanzor swaggers; refinements of amorous casuistry out of the heroic romances are aped by the loves of grooms and chambermaids. One is reminded of a modern oriental, who may have the blood of old paynim knighthoods in him, but who prefers to dress himself up as a cheap imitation of a European gentleman.

The worst thing about such challenging praise as Mr Eliot offers Dryden—praise, I believe, with which Dryden would be seriously embarrassed—is that it forces the rest of us to remember Dryden's faults. I have dealt with them, as I see them, plainly, not maliciously. The man is irremediably ignorant of that world he chooses so often to write about. When he confines himself to satire, he is at home; but even here, the fatal lack of architectonic power seldom allows him to make a satisfactory poem. That is the case against Dryden. It would have been pleasanter to state the case for him—to analyse, in order to praise, the masculine vigour of his English, the fine breezy, sunshiny weather of the man's mind at its best—his poetical health; the sweetness (unsurpassed in its own way) of nearly all his versification. But we cannot allow him to be used, and so used, as a stick to beat Shelley.

I have now to show that Shelley, with all his faults of execution, is a poet who must rank higher than Dryden with any critic who claims to be classical; that he is superior to Dryden by the greatness of his subjects and his moral elevation (which are merits by classical standards), and also by the unity of his actions, his architectonic power, and his general observance of *decorum* in the Renaissance sense of the word; that is, his disciplined production not just of poetry but of the poetry in each case proper to the theme and the species of composition.

But it is hardly possible in the present age to approach these questions without first removing some popular prejudices.

In the first place there is the prejudice which leads many people to mutter the word 'Godwin' as soon as Shelley is mentioned. They are quite sure that Godwin wrote a very silly book; they are quite sure that the philosophic content of much Shelleyan poetry is Godwinian; and they conclude that the poetry must be silly too. Their first premiss I cannot discuss, since a regrettable gap in my education has left me still the only critic in England who has not that familiar knowledge of *Political Justice* which alone can justify confident adverse criticism. But the second I can.* It is quite clear to any reader of general education—it must be clear, for example, to Mr Eliot—that the influence of Dante and Plato is at least as dominant in Shelley's thought as that of Godwin—unless, indeed, Godwin shared the opinions of Dante and Plato, in which case Godwin cannot have been so very silly. Thus, I do not know what Godwin says about free love; but I see that the passage in *Epipsychidion* beginning

True Love in this differs from gold and clay[1]

may well derive from *Purgatorio*, XV, 49, and thus ultimately from Aristotle's *Ethics* 1169 A. I do not myself agree with Shelley's application of the doctrine to sexual promiscuity; but then Plato, and many communists, would, and neither Shelley nor Godwin need be made the scapegoat. Thus again, in *Prometheus Unbound* I see that the main theme—the myth of a universal rebirth, a restoration of all things—is one which may occur in any age and which falls naturally into place beside Isaiah or the Fourth Eclogue, and that to pin it down to Godwin is a provincialism. Something it may owe to Godwin; but its debts to Aeschylus and, as Mr Tillyard has shown, to Plato's *Politicus* are at least equally interesting.[2] If Shelley were an ignoramus who had read no book but *Political Justice*, or a dullard who could invent nothing, we might be driven to suppose that his Asia was merely a personification of Godwinian benevolence; but

* It will be noticed that even if the premises were true, the inference is invalid. A similar paralogism has occurred about Mr Housman (of course, since his death) in the form, 'Kipling is bad. Some lines of Housman are like some lines of Kipling. Therefore Housman is bad.'

[1] *Epipsychidion*, 160.
[2] E. M. W. Tillyard, 'Shelley's *Prometheus Unbound* and Plato's *Statesman*', *The Times Literary Supplement* (29 September 1932), p. 69.

when we know that he had read of divine love and beauty in Plato and remember that he wrote the 'Hymn to Intellectual Beauty', the identification becomes merely perverse. And finally, whatever Godwin may really have said, one of the chief tenets attributed to him is explicitly rejected at the end of Act III. Let us hear no more of Godwin.*

Another prejudice is harder to combat because it is ill-defined. It usually expresses itself by the damning epithet 'adolescent'; it began with Arnold's phrase about the 'ineffectual angel'.[1] Shelley is supposed to be not merely *seely* in the Elizabethan sense, but *silly* in the modern sense; to believe ludicrously well of the human heart in general, and crudely ill of a few tyrants; to be, in a word, insufficiently disillusioned. Before removing this misunderstanding, I must point out that if it were granted it would not place him below Dryden. Dryden is equally ignorant of the world, though in the opposite direction, as his sorry joke about Alexander would be sufficient to show. Whenever he attempts to be lofty he betrays himself. There are senile and vulgar illusions no less than illusions adolescent and heroical; and of the two, I see no reason for preferring the former. If I must, in either event, be blindfold, why should I choose to have my eyes bandaged with stinking clouts rather than with cloth of gold? The fashion indeed is all for the stinking clouts, and it is easy to see why. Men (and, still more, boys) like to call themselves disillusioned because the very form of the word suggests that they have had the illusions and emerged from them—have tried both worlds. The claim, however, is false in nine cases out of ten. The world is full of impostors who claim to be disenchanted and are really unenchanted: mere 'natural' men who have never risen so high as to be in danger of the generous illusions they claim to have escaped from. Mr Mencken is the perfect example. We need to be on our guard against such people. They talk like sages who have passed through the half-truths of humanitarian benevolence, aristocratic honour, or romantic passion, while in fact they are clods who have never yet advanced so far. Ἀπειροκαλία is their disease; and Dryden himself is not free from it. He has not escaped from those enchantments which some find in Shelley; he has

---

* That is, nothing more in the usual strain. For a reprint of *Political Justice* (a book very difficult to find) I am all agog: it is not likely to be so dull as our critical tradition proclaims.

[1] Matthew Arnold, Preface to *Poetry of Byron* (London, 1881), p. xxxi.

tried desperately to taste the like, and failed, and the fustian remains in his poetry like a scar on his face. He indeed deserves pity, since he has struggled against the disease, unlike our modern impostors who glory in it and call it health; but this does not alter the conclusion that he cannot be set against Shelley as one who knows against one who is deluded. If we granted the doctrine of Shelley's amiable ignorance of the one half of life, it would still but balance Dryden's banausic ignorance of the other.

But I do not grant the doctrine, and I do not see how it can be accepted by any one who has read Shelley's poetry with attention. It is simply not true to say that Shelley conceives the human soul as a naturally innocent and divinely beautiful creature, interfered with by external tyrants. On the contrary no other heathen writer comes nearer to stating and driving home the doctrine of original sin. In such an early work as *The Revolt of Islam* those who come 'from pouring human blood'[1] are told to

> Disguise it not—we have one human heart—
> All mortal thoughts confess a common home.
>
> (VIII, xix)

and again,

> Look on your mind—it is the book of fate—
> Ah! it is dark with many a blazoned name
> Of misery—*all are mirrors of the same.*[2]
>
> (VIII, xx)

This is weak, exclamatory poetry, I grant you, but my concern is with the *sentens*. When Shelley looks at and condemns the oppressor he does so with the full consciousness that he also is a man just like that: the evil is within as well as without; all are wicked, and this of course is the significance of the allegorical passage in *Prometheus Unbound*, where the Furies say to Prometheus

> we will live through thee, one by one,
> Like animal life, and though we can obscure not
> The soul which burns within, that we will dwell
> Beside it, like a vain loud multitude
> Vexing the self-content of wisest men:
> That we will be dread thought beneath thy brain,
> And foul desire round thine astonished heart,
> And blood within thy labyrinthine veins
> Crawling like agony.
> *Prom.*   Why ye are thus now.[3]

---

[1] *The Revolt of Islam*, VIII, xviii.   [2] Lewis's italics.   [3] *Prometheus Unbound*, I, 483.

The same doctrine, more briefly and suggestively expressed, occurs in the *Triumph of Life*, where he explains the failure of the wise, the great, and the unforgotten by saying

> their lore
> Taught them not this, to know themselves; their might
> Could not repress *the mystery within*,
> And for the morn of truth they feigned, deep night
> Caught them ere evening.[1]
>
> (211–15)

We mistake Shelley wholly if we do not understand that for him, as certainly as for St Paul, humanity in its merely natural or 'given' condition is a body of death. It is true that the conclusion he draws is very different from that of St Paul. To a Christian, conviction of sin is a good thing because it is the necessary preliminary to repentance; to Shelley it is an extremely dangerous thing. It begets self-contempt, and self-contempt begets misanthropy and cruelty. In the *Revolt of Islam* the passage I have already quoted leads up to the statement that it is this self-contempt which arms Hatred with a 'mortal sting'.[2] The man who has once seen the darkness within himself will soon seek vengeance on others; and in *Prometheus* self-contempt is twice mentioned as an evil. I do not think we can seriously doubt that Shelley is right. If a man will not become a Christian, it is very undesirable that he should become aware of the reptilian inhabitants in his own mind. To know how bad we are, in the condition of mere nature, is an excellent recipe for becoming much worse. The process is very accurately described in some of the most memorable lines Shelley ever wrote:

> 'tis a trick of this same family
> To analyse their own and other minds.
> Such self-anatomy shall teach the will
> Dangerous secrets: for it *tempts our powers*,
> *Knowing what must be thought, and may be done*,
> Into the depth of darkest purposes:
> So Cenci fell into the pit; even I
> Since Beatrice *unveiled me to myself*,
> *And made me shrink from what I cannot shun*,
> *Show a poor figure to my own esteem*,
> *To which I grow half reconciled*. . . .
>
> (*Cenci*, II, ii, 108 *et seq.*)

---

[1] Lewis's italics.
[2] *The Revolt of Islam*, VIII, xxi, 3.

The lines which I have italicized provide an excellent short history of thought and sentiment in the early twentieth century, and the whole passage is a measure of the difference between Byron and Shelley. Byron, speaking through his Byronic heroes, is in the very article of that process which Shelley describes, and rather proud of it. He suffers the predicament; Shelley observes and understands it. He understands it, I think, a good deal better than most of his modern critics.

Shelley's poetry presents a variety of kinds, most of them traditional. The elegy and the greater ode come down to him from the *exemplaria graeca* through eighteenth-century practice; the metrical structure of the latter is indeed rooted in a misunderstanding of Pindar, but a misunderstanding which had become itself a precedent by Shelley's time. *Swellfoot* is almost an attempt to revive the Old Comedy—an attempt which should interest Mr Eliot since Shelley in it faces the cardinal problem of much of Mr Eliot's poetry: namely, whether it is possible to distinguish poetry about squalor and chaos from squalid and chaotic poetry. I do not think it a great success. The lyrical drama is in part Aeschylean; in part, I think, Shelley's redemption of a bad eighteenth-century form. It derives from, and redeems, the drama of Mason, just as *The Prelude* and *Excursion* derive from, and confer new power upon, the eighteenth-century treatise-poem. Shelley's lyric is a greater novelty, but heavily indebted on the metrical side to Dryden himself. The fantastic tale or idyll (as in *Alastor* or the *Witch of Atlas*) probably derives from the mythological epyllion of the Elizabethans. In all these kinds Shelley produces works which, though not perfect, are in one way more satisfactory than any of Dryden's longer pieces: that is to say, they display a harmony between the poet's real and professed intention, they answer the demands of their forms, and they have unity of spirit. Shelley is at home in his best poems, his clothes, so to speak, fit him, as Dryden's do not. The faults are faults of execution, such as over-elaboration, occasional verbosity, and the like: mere stains on the surface. The faults in Dryden are fundamental discrepancies between the real and the assumed poetic character, or radical vices in the design: diseases at the heart. Shelley could almost say with Racine, 'When my plan is made my poem is done'; with Dryden the plan itself usually foredooms the poem's failure.

Thus *Alastor* is a poem perfectly true to itself. The theme is universally interesting—the quest for ideal love. And both the theme and the treatment are fully suited to Shelley's powers. Hence the poem has an apparent ease, a noble obviousness, which deceives some readers. Mr Eliot himself is too experienced a writer to be guilty of the delusion that he could write like Shelley if he chose; but I think many of Mr Eliot's readers may suffer from it. They mistake the inevitability of *Alastor*, which really springs from the poet's harmony with his subject, for the facility of commonplace, and condemn the poem, precisely because it is successful. Of course it has its faults—some of the scenery is over-written, and the form of line which ends with two long monosyllables comes too often. But these are not the sort of defects that kill a poem: the energy of imagination, which supports so lofty, remote, and lonely an emotion almost without a false note for seven hundred lines, remains; and it deserves to be admired, if in no higher way, at least as we admire a great suspension-bridge. I address myself, of course, only to those who are prepared, by toleration of the theme, to let the poem have a fair hearing. For those who are not, we can only say that they may doubtless be very worthy people, but they have no place in the European tradition.

Perhaps this muscular sustaining power is even more noticeable in the *Witch of Atlas*, for there Shelley goes more out of himself. In *Alastor* the congeniality of the theme was fully given in Shelley's temper; in the *Witch* he is going successfully beyond the bounds of his temper—making himself something other than he was. For in this poem we have, indeed, Shelley's ordinary romantic love of the fantastical and ideal, but all keyed down, muted, deftly inhibited from its native solemnity and intensity in order to produce a lighter, more playful effect. The theme, at bottom, is as serious as ever; but the handling 'turns all to favour and to prettiness'. The lightness and liquidity of this piece, the sensation which we feel in reading it of seeing things distinctly, yet at a vast distance, cannot be paralleled in any poem that I know. We must go to another art, namely to music, to find anything at all similar; and there we shall hardly find it outside Mozart. It could not, indeed, have been written if Shelley had not read the Italians; but it is a new modification, and in it all the light-hearted dancing perfection of Ariosto is detached from Ariosto's hardness and flippancy (though not from his irony) and used with a difference—disturbed by overtones, etherialized. The whole poem is a happy reproof to that new Puritanism which has captured so many

critics and taught us to object to pleasure in poetry simply because it
is pleasure. It is natural, though regrettable, that such people should
be exasperated by this mercurial poem; for to them it is miching
mallecho (as Shelley said of *Peter Bell*) and means, as so much of his
poetry means, mischief. They know very well that they are being
laughed at; and they do not like to be told how

> Heaven and Earth conspire to foil
> The over-busy gardener's blundering toil.[1]

If Shelley had written only such poems he would have shown his
genius: his artistry, the discipline and power of obedience which makes
genius universal, are better shown elsewhere. *Adonais* naturally occurs
to the mind, for here we see Shelley fruitfully submitting to the
conventions of a well-established form. It has all the traditional features
of the elegy—the opening dirge, the processional allegory, and the
concluding consolation. There is one bad error of taste. The Muse,
lamenting Adonais, is made to lament her own immortality,

> I would give
> All that I am to be as thou now art!
> But I am chained to Time, and cannot thence depart!
> (xxvi)

This is to make a goddess speak like a new-made human widow,
and to dash the public solemnity of elegy with the violent passions of
a personal lyric. How much more fitting are the words of the Roman
poet:

> Immortales mortales si foret fas flere
> Flerent divae Camenae Naevium poetam.[2]

But it is a slip soon recovered, and not to be compared with the
prolonged indecorum of Dryden's satiric conceits in his elegy for
Mrs Anne Killigrew:

> To the next Realm she stretcht her Sway,
> For *Painture* neer adjoyning lay,
> A plenteous Province, and alluring Prey.
> *A Chamber of Dependences* was fram'd,

[1] *Witch of Atlas*, Dedication, IV, 7.
[2] Naevius's epitaph which he wrote for himself. *Remains of Old Latin*, vol. II, ed. and
trans. E. H. Warmington, Loeb Classical Library (London, 1936), p. 154.

(As conquerors will never want Pretence,
When arm'd, to justifie the Offence)
And the whole Fief, in right of Poetry she claim'd.
The Country open lay without Defence, &c.[1]

There are eighteen lines of it, and I not do know whether any major poet other than Dryden ever played such silly tricks at a funeral. No one demands that every poet should write an elegy: let each man be a master of his own trade. But the fact remains that when Shelley intends to do so, he does so; Dryden, equally intending, does not—*nimium amator ingenii sui*. I do not now speak of the unexampled rapture of Shelley's close. I might do so if I were to argue with Dryden, for he loves this ecstasy and quotes with approval *furentis animi vaticinatio*; being often a romantic in wish, though seldom happily romantic in the event. But I do not know whether Mr Eliot shares Dryden's admiration for 'those enthusiastic parts of poetry'; and I would prefer to argue from positions that are, or ought in logic to be, admitted by Mr Eliot. But I have slipped into that sentence 'If I were to argue with Dryden' unawares. Let no one suppose I am such a coxcomb as to think that my defence of Shelley could stand against Dryden's humane and luminous and Olympian dialectic; or, indeed, that it would be required in the presence of one who would almost certainly shame and anticipate me with such generous praise of Shelley as he has given to Shakespeare, or Milton, or Tasso, and a frank acknowledgement (he made more than one) of his own offences against the laws of poetry. Whoever else is a Drydenian in Mr Eliot's way, I have no fear lest Dryden himself should be one.

Of course Shelley too had his failures. The *Revolt of Islam* does not really exist much more than the *Hind and the Panther* exists, and the ruin is less redeemed by fine passages. The *Letter to Maria Gisborne* is little better than a draft—a thing scrawled as quickly as the pen would cover the paper and really unfit for the printer. *Peter Bell the Third* is a more doubtful case. I am not prepared to endure either its squalors or its obscurity by any such moderate promise of enjoyment as it holds out; but perhaps the creator of Sweeney ought to have more patience both with the one and with the other. I do not greatly admire—but perhaps some of Mr Eliot's weaker disciples should—this little picture.

[1] 'To the Pious Memory of the Accomplisht Young Lady Mrs Anne Killigrew, Excellent in the two Sister-Arts of Poësie, and Painting. An Ode', 92.

As he was speaking came a spasm,
  And wrenched his gnashing teeth asunder;
Like one who sees a strange phantasm
He lay,—there was a silent chasm
  Between his upper jaw and under.[1]

Epipsychidion raises in an acute form a problem with which Mr Eliot has been much occupied: I mean the problem of the relation between our judgement on a poem as critics, and our judgement as men on the ethics, metaphysics, or theology presupposed or expressed in the poem. For my own part, I do not believe that the poetic value of any poem is identical with the philosophic; but I think they can differ only to a limited extent, so that every poem whose prosaic or intellectual basis is silly, shallow, perverse, or illiberal, or even radically erroneous, is in some degree crippled by that fact. I am thus obliged to rate *Epipsychidion* rather low, because I consider the thought implied in it a dangerous delusion. In it Shelley is trying to stand on a particular rung of the Platonic ladder, and I happen to believe firmly that that particular rung does not exist, and that the man who thinks he is standing on it is not standing but falling. But no view that we can adopt will remove *Epipsychidion* from the slate. There is an element of spiritual, and also of carnal, passion in it, each expressed with great energy and sensibility, and the whole is marred, but not completely, by the false mode (as Mr Eliot and I would maintain) in which the poet tries to blend them. It is particularly interesting to notice the internal, perhaps unconscious, control which arises amidst the very intensity of the experience and tightens up the metrical form: the first forty lines are almost 'stopped couplets' and the whole movement is much closer to Dryden's couplet than to that of Keats.

But we are now rapidly approaching that part of our subject where the difference between Mr Eliot and myself ceases. In his essay on Dante, Mr Eliot says that he thinks the last canto of the *Paradiso* 'the highest point that poetry has ever reached'.* I think the same—and since it is so pleasant to agree, let me add irrelevantly that I think as he does about the *Bhagavad-Gita*.† And a few pages later Mr Eliot singles Shelley out as the one English poet of his century (I would have said the one English poet yet recorded) 'who could even have begun to follow' Dante's footsteps;‡ and he generously allows that

---

* Eliot, 'Dante', *op. cit.*, p. 237. † *Ibid.*, p. 244. ‡ *Ibid.*, p. 250.
[1] *Peter Bell the Third*, I, x, 1.

Shelley, at the end of his life, was beginning to profit by his knowledge of Dante. I do not know how much of Shelley's work Mr Eliot would admit by this concession. I suppose he would admit, at the very least, the *Triumph of Life*. If any passage in our poetry has profited by Dante, it is the unforgettable appearance of Rousseau in that poem—though admittedly it is only the Dante of the *Inferno*. But I am not without hope that Mr Eliot might be induced to include more. In this same essay he speaks of a modern 'prejudice against beatitude as material for poetry'.* Now Dante is eminently the poet of beatitude. He has not only no rival, but none second to him. But if we were asked to name the poet who most nearly deserved this inaccessible *proxime accessit*, I should name Shelley. Indeed, my claim for Shelley might be represented by the proposition that Shelley and Milton are, each, the half of Dante. I do not know how we could describe Dante better to one who had not read him, than by some such device as the following:

'You know the massive quality of Milton, the sense that every word is being held in place by a gigantic pressure, so that there is an architectural sublime in every verse whether the matter be sublime at the moment or not. You know also the air and fire of Shelley, the very antithesis of the Miltonic solidity, the untrammelled, reckless speed through pellucid spaces which makes us imagine while we are reading him that we have somehow left our bodies behind. If now you can imagine (but you cannot, for it must seem impossible till you see it done) a poetry which combined these two all-but incompatibles—a poetry as bright and piercing and aereal as the one, yet as weighty, as pregnant and as lapidary as the other, then you will know what Dante is like.'

To be thus half of Dante (Caesar is my authority for such a rarefied critical symbolism)[1] is fame enough for any ordinary poet. And Shelley, I contend, reaches this height in the fourth act of *Prometheus*.

* Eliot, 'Dante', p. 250.

[1] Lewis is referring, I believe, to the few surviving lines which Julius Caesar wrote on Terence (see *Suetonius*, vol. II, ed. J. C. Rolfe, Loeb Classical Library (London, 1914), p. 462). Immediately following an opinion on Terence ascribed to Cicero, Suetonius goes on:

> Item C. Caesar: Tu quoque, tu in summis, o dimidiate Menander,
> Poneris, et merito, puri sermonis amator.
> Lenibus atque utinam scriptis adiuncta foret vis
> Comica, ut aequato virtus polleret honore

Genetically considered, the fourth act, we know, is an afterthought: teleologically it is that for which the poem exists. I do not mean by this that the three preceding acts are mere means; but that their significance and beauty are determined by what follows, and that what came last in the writing (as it comes last in the reading) is 'naturally prior' in the Aristotelian sense. It does not add to, and therefore corrupt, a completed structure; it gives structure to that which, without it, would be imperfect. The resulting whole is the greatest long poem in the nineteenth century, and the only long poem of the highest kind in that century which approaches to perfection.

The theme is one of sane, public, and perennial interest—that of rebirth, regeneration, the new cycle. Like all great myths its primary appeal to the will and the understanding can therefore be diversely interpreted according as the reader is a Christian, a politician, a psycho-analyst, or what not. Myth is thus like manna; it is to each man a different dish and to each the dish he needs. It does not grow old nor stick at frontiers racial, sexual, or philosophic; and even from the same man at the same moment it can elicit different responses at different levels. But great myth is rare in a reflective age; the temptation to allegorize, to thrust into the story the conscious doctrines of the poet, there to fight it out as best they can with the inherent tendency of the fable, is usually too strong. *Faust* and the *Niblung's Ring*—the only other great mythical poems of modern times—have in this way been partially spoiled. The excellence of Shelley is that he has avoided this. He has found what is, for him, the one perfect story and re-made it so well that the ancient version now seems merely embryonic. In his poem there is no strain between the literal sense and the imaginative significance. The events which are needed to produce the λύσις seem to become the symbols of the spiritual process he

---

Cum Graecis neve hac despectus parte iaceres!
Unum hoc maceror ac doleo tibi desse, Terenti.

Which lines have been translated for me by Austin Farrer as:

You too, you half-Menander, fairly reach
The foremost rank, for love of limpid speech.
And would your gentle humour were allied
With comic fire to match the scenic pride
Of Greece, that in that part you might not pine
Nor one lack, Terence, lame your golden line.

Lewis may have thought that in the missing lines Caesar gave the *other* half of Menander (the 'comic fire') to Terence's rival in fame, Plautus, but we do not know anything beyond the fragment we have here.

is presenting without effort or artifice or even consciousness on his part.

The problem was not an easy one. We are to start with the soul chained, aged, suffering; and we are to end with the soul free, rejuvenated, and blessed. The selection of the Prometheus story (a selection which seems obvious only because we did not have to make it) is the first step to the solution. But nearly everything has still to be done. By what steps are we to pass from Prometheus in his chains to Prometheus free? The long years of his agony cannot be dramatically represented, for they are static. The actual moment of liberation by Heracles is a mere piece of 'business'. Dramatic necessity demands that the Titan himself should do or say something before his liberation —and if possible something that will have an effect on the action. Shelley answers this by beginning with Prometheus's revocation of the curse upon Jupiter. Now mark how everything falls into place for the poet who well and truly obeys his imagination. This revocation at once introduces the phantasm of Jupiter, the original curse on the phantasm's lips, and the despair of Earth and Echoes at what seems to be Prometheus's capitulation. We thus get at one stroke a good opening episode and a fine piece of irony, on the dramatic level; but we also have suggested the phantasmal or nightmare nature of the incubus under which the soul (or the world) is groaning, and the prime necessity for a change of heart in the sufferer, who is in some sort his own prisoner. Prometheus, we are made to feel, has really stepped out of prison with the words, 'It doth repent me.'[1] But once again structural and spiritual necessities join hands to postpone his effective liberation. On the structural side, the play must go on; on the other, we know, and Shelley knows, how long a journey separates the first resolve, from the final remaking, of a man, a nation, or a world. The Furies will return, and the act closes with low-toned melodies of sadness and of hopes that are as yet remote and notional.

The whole of the next act, in story, is occupied with the difficult efforts of Asia to apprehend and follow a dream dreamed in the shadow of Prometheus: the difficult journey which it leads her; her difficult descent to the depths of the earth; and her final re-ascension, transformed, to the light. Difficulty is, so to speak, the subject of this act. The dramatic advantage of splitting the sufferer's rôle into two parts, those of Prometheus and Asia, and of giving the latter a task to

[1] *Prometheus Unbound*, I, 303.

perform in the liberation, is sufficiently obvious. But we hardly need to notice this. Most of us, while we read this act, are too absorbed, I fancy, by the new sensation it creates in us. The gradual ineluctable approach of the unknown, where the unknown is sinister, is not an uncommon theme in literature; but where else are we to find this more medicinable theme—these shy approaches, and sudden recessions, and returnings beyond hope, and swellings and strengthenings of a far-off, uncertainly prognosticated good? And again, it is a necessity for Shelley, simply because he has placed his fiend in the sky, to make Asia go down, not up, to fetch this good; but how miraculously it all fits in! Does any reader, whether his prepossessions be psychological or theological, question this descent into hell, this return to the womb, this death, as the proper path for Asia to take? Our imaginations, constrained by deepest necessities, accept all that imagery of interwoven trees and dew and moss whereby the chorus drench the second scene with darkness, and the softness and damp of growing things: by the same necessity they accept the harsher images of the final precipitous descent to Demogorgon's cave, and the seated darkness which we find there. It is out of all this, silver against this blackness, that the piercing song of Asia's reascension comes; and if any one who has read that song in its setting still supposes that the poet is talking about Godwin or the Revolution, or that Shelley is any other than a very great poet, I cannot help him. But for my own part I believe that no poet has felt more keenly, or presented more weightily the necessity for a complete unmaking and remaking of man, to be endured at the dark bases of his being. I do not know the book (in profane literature) to which I should turn for a like expression of what von Hügel would have called the 'costingness' of regeneration.

The third act is the least successful: Shelley's error was not to see that he could shorten it when once he had conceived the fourth. Yet some leisure and some slackened tension are here allowable. We are certainly not ready for the fourth act at once. Between the end of torment and the beginning of ecstasy there must be a pause: peace comes before beatitude. It would be ridiculous, in point of achievement, to compare this weak act in Shelley's play with the triumphant conclusion of the *Purgatorio*; but structurally it corresponds to the position of the earthly paradise between purgatory and heaven. And in one scene at least it is worthy of its theme. The dialogue between Ocean and Apollo (at 'the mouth of a great river in the island

Atlantis') is among his best things: a divine indolence soaks it, and if there are better lines in English poetry there are none that breathe a more heartfelt peace than Ocean's:

> It is the unpastured sea hungering for calm.
> Peace, monster; I come now. Farewell.[1]

The fourth act I shall not attempt to analyse. It is an intoxication, a riot, a complicated and uncontrollable splendour, long, and yet not too long, sustained on the note of ecstasy such as no other English poet, perhaps no other poet, has given us. It can be achieved by more than one artist in music: to do it in words has been, I think, beyond the reach of nearly all. It has not, and cannot have, the solemnity and overwhelming realism of the *Paradiso*, but it has all its fire and light. It has not the 'sober certainty of waking bliss' which makes Milton's paradise so inhabitable—but it sings from regions in our consciousness that Milton never entered.

Some anti-romantic repudiations of such poetry rest, perhaps, on a misunderstanding. It might be true, as the materialists must hold, that there is no possible way by which men can arrive at such felicity; or again, as Mr Eliot and I believe, that there is one Way, and only one, and that Shelley has missed it. But while we discuss these things, the romantic poet has added meaning to the word Felicity itself. Whatever the result of our debate, we had better attend to his discovery lest we remain more ignorant than we need have been of the very thing about which we debated.

[1] *Prometheus Unbound*, III, ii, 49.

15

Sir Walter Scott

Here in Edinburgh, on 7th June 1826, Walter Scott was kept awake nearly all night by a howling dog. He was in poor health. He was working at the highest pressure, convinced that such efforts might still recover his honour and perhaps even his fortune. His wife was barely three weeks dead. But he must not stop to think of that. He chides himself in his *Gurnal* for the 'hysterical passion ... of terrible violence—a sort of throttling sensation' which impelled his solitary tears and was followed by 'a state of dreaming stupidity' (30th May).[1] For all depended on work; and work on health; and health on sleep. In such circumstances we can imagine what most men would have said about that howling dog; especially most literary men. One thinks of Carlyle. What Scott said will be familiar to many members of this society: 'Poor cur! I dare say he had his distresses, as I have mine.'[2] In those dozen words the whole sweetness and light of Scott's mind is revealed. I think I want to stress the light even more than the sweetness. We know from other evidence that few men have loved dogs more judiciously. As Lockhart's Mr Adolphus delightfully says: 'He was a gentleman even to his dogs.'[3] But that is hardly the point here. There is no parade of his love for animals. He flings to the poor cur a word of commiseration, but what is chiefly before his mind is indisputable fact; dogs don't howl at night if they are happy. There is here a clear-eyed recognition that there are in the world all sorts of creatures and that Scott with his distresses is only one of them. It is of a piece with his last recorded words, in answer to Lockhart's question whether he should send for Sophia and Anne: 'No. Don't disturb them ... I know they were up all night.'[4] There is in both the same fidelity to common facts. Scott may be ruined, or bereaved, or dying; but dogs will howl and young women need sleep.

[1] *The Journal of Sir Walter Scott, 1825–26*, ed. J. G. Tait (Edinburgh, 1939), p. 178.
[2] *Ibid.* (8th June), p. 182.
[3] J. G. Lockhart, *Memoirs of the Life of Sir Walter Scott, Bart.*, complete in one volume (Edinburgh, 1850), ch. lxxviii, p. 708.
[4] *Ibid.*, ch. lxxxiii, p. 753.

For the whole of that *Gurnal*, indeed, we might borrow a title from an author whom Scott himself fully appreciated, and call it 'Sense and Sensibility'. The sense, I presume, is obvious enough. We see it, first and foremost, in his cool and moderate estimate of his own literary powers; a modesty almost (one would have thought) impossible in one whose reputation had filled Europe and been blown up until he was put above Goethe and almost equalled with Shakespeare. Yet it is not mere self-depreciation. Though never deceived about his weaknesses, he knows his real strength too; the 'hurried frankness of composition which pleases soldiers[,] sailors[,] and young people of bold and active disposition'.[1] He recognizes, in his own way, the quality of what a more pretentious writer would call 'inspiration':— 'I shall get warm as I work'—the morning, fresh from the labours of subconscious artistry, is *musis amica*. We see it also in his unchanging, cheerfully unemphatic, contempt for 'the imaginary consequence of literary triflers' and the 'affectations of literature'. We see it, this time co-operating with something even more precious than good sense, in his attitude to certain feelings which prey upon most of us at time; as when he notes (6th April 1826):

I had the great pleasure to hear, through a letter from Sir Adam, that Sophia was in health, and John[n]ie gaining strength. It is a fine exchange from deep and aching uncertainty ... to the little spitfire feeling of '*Well, but they might have taken the trouble to write.*'[2]

Of all who have 'little spitfire feelings', few, I believe, name them so honestly or so happily.

But we should do Scott little service with some modern critics by insisting exclusively on his sense; for there is a widespread opinion that genius is never free from neurosis, and unless we can find *Angst* in an author's soul he will hardly be taken seriously. Well, if we demand *Angst*, Scott can supply that, too. He confesses to 'idle fears[,] gloomy thoughts' (11th April 1826);[3] to 'A thick throbbing at my heart ... fancies thronging on me ... a disposition ... to think on things melancholy and horrible' (24th October 1827).[4] He notes repeatedly, and notes as irrational, a horror of 'redding' his papers, so great that the task would leave him with 'nerves shaking like a

---

[1] 16th June 1826, *Journal (1825–26)*, pp. 186–7.
[2] *Ibid.*, p. 149. Lewis's italics.
[3] *Ibid.*, p. 152.
[4] *The Journal of Sir Walter Scott, 1827–28*, ed. J. G. Tait (Edinburgh, 1941), p. 120.

frightened child' (10th May 1829).[1] He has known a day when there was 'a vile sense of want of reality' in all he did and said. He was aware of some connection between these infirmities and the powers which made him an author. These sinkings of the imagination 'come to a gifted, as it is called, but often unhappy, class', who, as he unexpectedly adds, 'but for the dictates of religion, or the natural recoil of the mind from the idea of dissolution', would often have been disposed to commit suicide (28th November 1826).[2] All this, however, must be sought in the *Gurnal* and there alone. That, perhaps, is where Scott differs most from the type of artist dear to the modern psychological critic. The blue devils do not haunt his work; they leave no trail of laudanum, drink, divorce, tantrums, perversions, or paranoia across his life. As he says, 'I generally affect good spirits in company of my family, whether I am enjoying them or not' (24th September 1827).[3]

This is plainly a different thing from that 'sincerity' which is often praised, and which might perhaps better be called incontinence. Yet the *Gurnal* is, I believe, one of the sincerest books in the world, and (which is not exactly the same thing) full of self-knowledge. How severely he exercised this sincerity may be gauged by the entry of 5th March 1826, where, finding something that savours a little of rhodomontade in the entry of the previous evening, he says, 'I have sworn I will not blot out what I have once written here.'[4] I believe few of us would care to keep a diary under a strict rule against erasure. And to Scott such a rule would perhaps be more costly than to most men; Scott who rightly diagnosed pride as his ruling passion (5th February 1826), and who, when the pen dropped finally from his hand and irresistible tears from his eyes, said, 'Friends, don't let me expose myself—get me to bed.'[5]

The absence of the blue devils from his work, its freedom from all petulance, morbidity or shrillness, will not now, I am afraid, be regarded as wholly a virtue. Some will feel that, with the devils, much else, which ought to have come in, was excluded. We should certainly not guess from reading the Waverley Novels that their author had said in his diary, 'Life could not be endured were it seen in reality'

---

[1] *The Journal of Sir Walter Scott, 1829–32*, ed. W. M. Parker (Edinburgh, 1946), pp. 63–4.
[2] *Journal (1825–26)*, p. 284. Scott actually wrote 'belonging to this gifted, etc.'.
[3] *Journal (1827–28)*, p. 105.   [4] *Journal (1825–26)*, p. 124.
[5] Lockhart, *op. cit.*, ch. lxxxiii, p. 752.

(21st December 1925);[1] or again, 'I never have yet found . . . that ill-will dies in debt, or what is called gratitude distresses herself by frequent payments' (2nd March 1826).[2] Many moderns will think his maxim that 'a melancholy catastrophe' or unhappy ending should 'always be avoided' in fiction (28th July 1826),[3] unsound and arbitrary in itself, and veritably disgraceful when we find it in conjunction with such dark estimates of life and men. This will seem to them, for all I have said about the sincerity of the man, to impute a fundamental dishonesty in the work.

But I think much can be said in answer to such a charge. In the first place, these tragic, or disillusioned passages in the *Gurnal* are only occasional, and spring very clearly from Scott's momentary situation. We are not called upon to believe, and I myself do not believe, that they represent Scott's settled criticism of life. And if they did, what then? Need we reject as worthless that gusto, that ease and good temper, that fine masculine cheerfulness, which is diffused over all the best of his novels and is perhaps their greatest permanent attraction? If this could be shown to be indeed inconsistent with Scott's most permanent conscious thoughts, what should we have to say but that something in his less conscious mind, something that brought his stories to him while he slept, had taken over the pen and forced him to utter the life he experienced rather than the life he saw when he reflected. For, of course, something far more is involved than the mere choice between happy and unhappy endings. Both can be contrived, and both with good or bad motives. But the general tone, the thing that makes, as it were, the smell or taste of the whole book, cannot. In modern times we have been advised (and on the whole, I think, rightly) always to trust the tone or impression of a man's work rather than his conscious and articulate reflections, where the two disagree. The maxim is, of course, most often applied by those who are finding concealed scepticism, prurience, or despair in authors professedly pious, edifying, or optimistic. Perhaps we shall have to use it the other way round for Scott, and say that the tapestry in Jonathan Oldbuck's spare room, the language of Ochiltree, or the whole character of Baillie Nicol Jarvie, convey to us a sense of life which is more important, more fully realised, than any mere 'views' to the contrary which Scott may be supposed to have held.

[1] *Journal (1825–26)*, p. 52.   [2] *Ibid.*, p. 120.
[3] *Ibid.*, p. 207.

Secondly—and this is of more importance to literature—I think any such criticism would involve trying Scott by laws which he never acknowledged. It is now very generally demanded that a novel should be 'a comment on life'. Unless the meaning of this phrase is attenuated almost to nonentity, I do not think Scott supposed a novel to be anything of the sort. As Lord David Cecil has pointed out, the English novel descends from the English comedy. Not, of course, from English farce, nor necessarily from the comedy of intrigue; we must include under our definition of comedy things like *The Merchant of Venice* and *Twelfth-Night*. The purpose of the older novel, as of such pieces, was not to comment on life. I do not think that was the primary purpose of the tragedies either, nor of such novels as ended tragically. I do not think tragedy and comedy differed by expressing different views of life. The difference was more that between Forms. Both were deliberate patterns or arrangements of possible (but by no means necessarily probable) events chosen for their harmonious unity in variety, deliberately modified, contrasted, balanced in a fashion which real life never permits. Different degrees of verisimilitude occur in different pieces, but I think the verisimilitude is always a means, not an end. Improbability is avoided, when at all, not because the author wants to tell us what life is like, but because he fears lest too gross an improbability should make the audience incredulous and therefore unreceptive of the mood or passion he is trying to evoke. I think this was Scott's attitude. He usually rejected unhappy endings not because he believed, or wanted his readers to believe, or even for a moment supposed they would believe, that irretrievable disasters never occurred in real life, but because they were inconsistent with the sort of work he was making and would not contribute to its οἰκεία ἡδονή. He was not (save very incidentally) saying something about the world but making an *objet d'art* of a particular kind. If you like you may, no doubt, say that he was an entertainer; if you must, I suppose no one can prevent your saying 'a mere entertainer'. That is, his work belongs with the *Decameron*, *The Canterbury Tales*, the *Furioso* (one of his own great favourites), *The Marriage of Figaro*, *Pickwick*, and *The Moonstone*; not with *The Divine Comedy*, *War and Peace*, or *The Ring*.

The distinction I am making is sometimes expressed by using the word *serious* of the works which fall in my second class. But I think the adjective unhappy because it is ambiguous. In one sense (and this

I think is the most useful sense for critics) *serious* is simply the opposite of *comic*. In that sense, of course, Tupper and Patience Strong are serious artists, and Aristophanes is not. But *serious* may mean 'worthy of serious consideration'. In that sense a gay song by Prior may be more *serious* than some of the most lugubrious items in our hymn-books. What is more, a pure *divertissement* may be more *serious* than a long, well-documented, tendentious, ethical, or sociological novel: *Guy Mannering* more *serious* than *Mr Britling Sees It Through*.

There remains, however, a third sense in which Scott can be accused of insufficient seriousness. This has nothing to do with the *genre* he was writing. The *Furioso* is a light work, but Ariosto did not take it lightly; witness those famous variations in the first line. But Scott often took his work very lightly indeed. There is little sign, even in his best days, of a serious and costly determination to make each novel as good in its own kind as he could make it. And at the end, when he is writing to pay off his debts, his attitude to his own work is, by some standards, scandalous and cynical. Anything will do, provided it will sell. He says of *Castle Dangerous* and *Count Robert of Paris*, 'I think it is the publick that are mad for passing these two volumes. But I will not be the first to cry them down' (26th January 1832).[1]

Here we come to an irreducible opposition between Scott's outlook and that of our more influential modern men of letters. These would blame him for disobeying his artistic conscience; Scott would have said he was obeying his conscience. He knew only one kind of conscience. It told him that a man must pay his debts if he possibly could. The idea that some supposed obligation to write good novels could override this plain, universal demand of honesty, would have seemed to him the most pitiful subterfuge of vanity and idleness, and a prime specimen of that 'literary sensibility' or 'affected singularity' which he most heartily despised.

Two different worlds here clash. And who am I to judge between them? It may be true, as Curtius has said, that 'the modern world immeasurably overvalues art'. Or it may be that the modern world is right and that all previous ages have greatly erred in making art, as they did, subordinate to life, so that artists worked to teach virtue, to adorn the city, to solemnize feasts and marriages, to please a patron, or to amuse the people. Or again, a middle view may be possible; that works of art are in reality serious, and ends in themselves, but that all

---

[1] *Journal (1829–32)*, p. 213.

is lost when the artists discover this, as Eros fled when Psyche turned the lamp upon him. But wherever the truth may lie, there are two things of which I feel certain. One is, that if we do overvalue art, then art itself will be the greatest sufferer; when second things are put first, they are corrupted. The other is that, even if we of all generations have first valued art aright, yet there will certainly be loss as well as gain. We shall lose the fine careless, prodigal artists. For, if not all art, yet some art, flows best from men who treat their work as a kind of play. I at any rate cannot conceive how the exuberance, the elbow-room, the heart-easing quality of Dickens, or Chaucer, or Cervantes, could co-exist with that self-probing literary conscience we find in Pater or Henry James. Lockhart speaks somewhere of Scott 'enjoying rather than exerting his genius'. We may be coming to a period when there will be no room for authors who do that. If so, I admit there may be gain; I am sure there will be losses.

This leads me naturally to the question of Scott's style. One is sometimes tempted to say that the veriest journeyman among us could mend a thousand passages in the novels. Nothing could easily be worse than the sentence in which Mannering looks up and the planets 'rolled' above him, 'each in its orbit of liquid light'.[1] This, perhaps, is exceptional; what is unfortunately constant is the poly-syllabic, uneconomical, even florid, texture of his narrative and descriptive writing. His dialogue, of course, is a wholly different thing. Let but Andrew Fairservice, or the Baillie, or douce Davie Deans, or Jonathan Oldbuck, or even Julia Mannering open their mouths, and at once we have race and piquancy, the living and the concrete. Most interestingly, in the *Gurnal*, we find Scott using in his own person both the style that repels and that which conquers us.

Thus he refers to the news of his wife's death as 'the melancholy intelligence' (15th May 1826).[2] What a choke-pear! And what a use of the word *melancholy*, how calculated to spoil it for contexts where it is really needed! Nor must we plead that Lady Scott was not, after all, the great passion of her husband's life. That, I think, is true; but the phrase is still far too vague and ready-made for the deep affliction which her death was to him. He himself puts that beyond doubt by the words with which, next day, he expresses its precise nature and

---

[1] What Scott actually says in ch. iii of *Guy Mannering* is: 'Above rolled the planets, each, by its own liquid orbit of light, distinguished from the inferior or more distant stars.'

[2] *Journal* (*1825–26*), p. 170.

degree: 'I wonder how I shall do with the large portion of thoughts which were hers for thirty years' (16th May 1826).[1] I think the experience of all bereavements, the daily and hourly setting out of the thoughts upon a familiar road, forgetful of the grim frontier-post that now blocks it, the repeated frustration which renews not only sorrow but the surprise of sorrow, has seldom been more truthfully conveyed.

Here is another example. On 18th December 1825 he is facing the thought that Abbotsford may have to be sold. He writes, 'The recollection of the extensive woods I have planted, and the walks I have formed from which strangers must derive both the pleasure and profit will excite feelings likely to sober my gayest moments ... My dogs will wait for me in vain.'[2] This is, of course, better writing than 'the melancholy intelligence'. But the vocabulary is curiously dead. Then comes a space in the MS; then the unconscious master-stroke— 'I find my dogs' feet on my knees.'[3]

And this happens again and again in the *Gurnal*. We find side by side that style which Scott habitually used for narrative and another style, far more sensitive, which, if he had more often employed it, would have given him a far higher literary place than he actually holds. In the novels this better style hardly appears except in dialogue and (especially) in dialect. As a stylist Wandering Willie can play his creator off the field; he has more music in his sporran than the Sheriff in his whole body; and Julia Mannering, at her best, more wit.

For his public, and inferior, style reasons can be found, one local, the other historical. It was Professor Nichol Smith who first pointed out to me that a love of the polysyllable had been endemic in Scotland ever since the time of Henryson. He said that in this very city he himself had attended, in youth, a debating society where students were always rising 'to homologate the sentiments of the previous speaker'. But in Scott's time this local and national infirmity was only the aggravation of a disease which then held the whole island in its grip. We must not allow a few great and highly idiosyncratic writers like Lamb, Hazlitt, and Landor, to blind us to the fact that the early nineteenth century found English in a bloated condition. The abstract is preferred to the concrete. The word farthest from the soil is liked best; we find *personage* or *individual* for *man*, *female* for *woman*, *monarch* for *king*. Hence Wordsworth, even in poetry, will have his *itinerant vehicle*, *female vagrant*, and *casual refreshment*. Scott, I am

---

[1] *Journal* (1825–26), p. 171.   [2] *Ibid.*, p. 46.   [3] *Ibid.*

afraid, nearly always called food *refreshment*, and is among those who have helped to spoil that potentially beautiful word for ever.

Stylistically, then, Scott lived in an unfortunate period, and his real strength was allowed to come out only in dialogue. This, I think, must be conceded. But let us not concede too much. Even his narrative style has the qualities of its defects. The cheerful rattle of his poly-syllables (often energetic in rhythm even where flaccid in syntax and vocabulary), the very sense that not much care is being taken, and the brisk, virile pace, all help us to feel that we are off on a journey of pleasure. The jingle of the harness creates the holiday mood; and 'with tolerable horses and a civil driver' (as Scott promises in *Waverley*, ch. v) we jog along, on the whole, very contentedly.

But whatever may be said against Scott's style or his contrived (and often ill-contrived) plots it will not touch the essential glory of the Waverley Novels. That glory is in my opinion, twofold.

First, these novels almost created that historical sense which we now all take for granted, and by which we often condemn Scott himself. Of course, he makes historical blunders and even treasures historical illusions. But he, first of men, taught us the feeling for period. Chaucer's Trojans are medieval people. Shakespeare's Romans are Elizabethan people. The characters in *Otranto* are so patently Walpole's contemporaries that no one could now believe in them. Scott everywhere—insufficiently, no doubt, but he was a pioneer—reminds us that our ancestors were different from ourselves. I have high authority for my statement. It was the Master of Trinity, Professor Trevelyan, who first pointed out to me the difference in this respect between the *Decline and Fall* and Macaulay's *History*. Gibbon, he said, writes as if every Roman emperor, every Gothic chieftain, and every hermit in the Thebaid, was an eighteenth-century man. But Macaulay is always pressing upon us the difference between his own age and the age he depicts. 'And I attribute this almost wholly', said the Master, 'to the fact that the Waverley Novels had come in between.' Once it had been said, it seemed to me obvious. And if it is, then to concentrate on Scott's errors in history is like trying to make Columbus unimportant because he failed to produce a full map of America. Scott, like Columbus, is among the great discoverers. If we are now so conscious of period, that we feel more difference between decades than our ancestors felt between centuries, we owe this, for good or ill, to Scott.

Secondly, the novels embody these immensely valuable qualities of mind which I have claimed for the *Gurnal*. They may lack many virtues which the novel has achieved since; but they have those virtues of which no age is in more desperate need than our own. They have their own essential rectitude. They slur some things; they exaggerate nothing. Minor frailties are never worked up into enormous sins, nor petty distresses into factitious tragedies. Everything is in proportion. Consider what either Dickens on the one hand, or George Moore on the other, would have made of Effie Deans. Then turn back to Scott and breathe the air of sense.

But I must come to an end. You may feel that I have spent too much time on this great author's faults and too little on his excellences. But that is because I am speaking among his friends. Where else does one mention the faults of a man one loves? And Scott today has few friends. Our juniors are ill at ease in his presence. One of these has said that Scott wholly misunderstood his own story in *The Heart of Midlothian*, for the tale makes it quite clear that the heroine's real motive for refusing to commit perjury 'must have been' unconscious jealousy of her sister's beauty. It is like reading a review by a jackal on a book written by a lion. But we must not grow bitter. Perhaps we shall some day climb out of this present trough; as Scott delighted to quote, 'Patience, cousin, and shuffle the cards.'[1] And even if no change ever comes, if the barbarism on which we now seem to be entering is to prove the last illness, the death-bed of humanity, we must not rail at those who are its victims. Let us only say, adapting Scott's own words, 'Poor curs. I dare say they have their distresses.' And indeed they have.

---

[1] Spoken by Durandarte in *Don Quixote*, Pt. II, ch. xxiii.

16

William Morris

In ordinary life a thousand considerations prohibit for most of us any complete working out of our responses: . . . but in the 'imaginative experiences' these obstacles are removed.   I. A. RICHARDS, *Principles of Literary Criticism*, ch. xxxi

It has been said that if you tell ten people you are reading Thomas Aquinas, nine will reply with something about angels dancing on the point of a needle. The saw is already out of date and Thomism in the ascendant; but it is worth remembering as a reminder of the misleading labels which great writers bear during the periods of their obscurity, and also of the sudden changes of fashion which strip those labels off. In spite of some excellent critics, William Morris is still commonly among the labelled. A mention of him in many literary circles still produces a torrent of objections which have been learned by heart—he wrote *Wardour Street*, he was a victim to false medievalism, his poetry is the poetry of escape, his stories are mere tapestries. It is true that these charges have never had any effect on his persistent admirers. But these are a company ill fitted to defend their favourite. They are few—though perhaps not so few as each in his solitude supposes—and they read humbly for the sake of pleasure, a pleasure so inexhaustible that after twenty or fifty years of reading they find it worked so deeply into all their emotions as to defy analysis. I knew one who could come no nearer to an explanation of Morris's charm than to repeat 'It's the Northernness—the Northernness'; and though I knew very well what he meant, I felt it was not war. Yet as the lovers of Morris now are, the lovers of Donne once were, and not so very long ago. It is possible that a critical revolution may yet embarrass these scattered and inoffensive readers with the discovery that what they regard as a private, perhaps a shamefaced, indulgence has all along been a gratifying proof of their penetration and 'contemporaneity'. The thing is feasible because even the sternest theories of literature cannot permanently suppress an author who is so obstinately pleasurable. It is certain that the common cries against Morris, where they are not mere ignorance, are based on *a priori* dogmatisms that will go down at a touch; and it is arguable that of all the romantics he lies least open to the usual attacks of what we may now,* perhaps, begin to call Georgian anti-romanticism.

The objection to his language is largely a hangover from the old Wordsworthian theory of diction. It is, of course, perfectly true that Morris invented for his poems and perfected in his prose-romances a language which has never at any period been spoken in England; but I suppose that most instructed people are now aware (as Wordsworth was not aware) that what we call 'ordinary' or 'straight-forward' English prose, as we have all tried to write it since Dryden's time, is almost equally an artificial speech—a literary or 'hypothetical' language based on a French conception of elegance and a highly unphilological ideal of 'correctness'. When we begin to teach boys 'essay-writing' at school we are teaching them to translate into this language, and if they continue to write as they talk we plough them in School Certificate. The question about Morris's style is not whether it is an artificial language—all endurable language in longer works must be that—but whether it is a good one. And it is here that sheer ignorance begins to play its part. I cannot help suspecting that most of the detractors when they talk of Morris's style are really thinking of his printing: they expect the florid and the crowded, and imagine something like Sidney's *Arcadia*. In fact, however, this style consistently departs from that of modern prose in the direction of simplicity. Except for a few archaic words—and since the appearance of the S.O.E.D. it is a pleasure to be sent to the dictionary—it is incomparably easier and clearer than any 'natural' style could possibly be, and the 'dull finish', the careful avoidance of rhetoric, gloss, and decoration, is of its very essence. Those who are really repelled by it after a fair trial are being repelled not by its romanticism but by its classicism, for in one sense Morris is as classical as Johnson. Long ago, Mr Alfred Noyes noticed the self-imposed limitation under which Morris describes nature whether in prose or verse—the birds that are merely 'brown', the sea that is never anything more remarkable than 'blue' or 'green'.[1] Morris, in fact, obeys the doctrine of generality; he does not number the streaks on the tulip but 'exhibits in his portraits of nature such prominent and striking features as recall the original to every mind'. That such 'just representations of

---

* Written in the reign of Edward VIII (1936).

[1] Alfred Noyes, *William Morris* (London, 1908), p. 48.

general nature' can, as Johnson claims, 'please many and please long', his own writing, and that of Morris, will equally prove.

I sat down on a bank, such as a writer of romance might have delighted to feign. I had, indeed, no trees to whisper over my head, but a clear rivulet streamed at my feet. The day was calm, the air was soft, and all was rudeness, silence and solitude.[1]

The road was rough that day, and they went not above a foot-pace the more part of the time; and daylong they were going up and up, and it grew cold as the sun got low, though it was yet summer.[2]

The first sentence is from Johnson and the second from Morris. There are a dozen differences between them, but there are two important similarities; both are content with recording obvious facts in very general language, and both succeed so that we really taste the mountain air. It is, indeed, this matter-of-factness, as Clutton-Brock pointed out, which lends to all Morris's stories their sober air of conviction.[3] Other stories have only scenery: his have geography. He is not concerned with 'painting' landscapes; he tells you the lie of the land, and then you paint the landscapes for yourself. To a reader long fed on the almost botanical and entomological niceties of much modern fiction—where, indeed, we mostly skip if the characters go through a jungle—the effect is at first very pale and cold, but also very fresh and spacious. We begin to relish what my friend called the 'Northernness'. No mountains in literature are as far away as distant mountains in Morris. The world of his imagining is as windy, as tangible, as resonant and three-dimensional, as that of Scott or Homer.

He treats the passions, for the most part, in the same way. A lover's night of anxiety for his mistress who is a captive is thus described. 'He could not choose but make stories of her meeting of the tyrant, and her fear and grief and shame, and the despair of her heart.'[4] Morris does not particularize the imagery that passed through the young man's mind; 'he could not choose but make stories', that is all. Later in the same book Morris has to describe the lover's

---

[1] *Journey to the Hebrides*, in *The Works of Samuel Johnson*, vol. IX, Oxford English Classics (Oxford, 1825), p. 36.

[2] *The Well at the World's End*, bk. II, ch. 20, p. 235. All text-references to Morris's prose and poetry are from *The Collected Works of William Morris* with introductions by his daughter May Morris (24 vols. London: Longmans, Green & Co., 1910–15).

[3] A. Clutton-Brock, *William Morris: His Work and Influence* (London, 1914), pp. 178–99.

[4] *The Well at the World's End*, bk. II, ch. 41, p. 336.

behaviour when alone with his mistress for some weeks in the wilderness. It is a situation about which almost any other author, sentimental, sensual, or cynical, would have made what Locke calls a 'pudder'. Morris gives the fact—'All this while he durst not kiss or caress her, save very measurely'—and the reason 'for he deemed that she would not suffer it'.[1] What could be more sensible? And this brings us to the whole question of Morris's treatment of love; it is in this that he differs most remarkably from the majority of romantics and is most immune from anti-romantic criticism. On the one hand, it is no use invoking modern psychology to reveal the concealed eroticism in his imagination, because the eroticism is not concealed: it is patent, ubiquitous, and unabashed. On the other hand, Morris, except in his first volume and in such an anomalous poem as *Love is Enough*, makes no attempt to paint Passion as understood by the Romantics. Havelock Ellis's definition of love ('lust *plus* friendship'), monstrously inadequate if applied to the love expressed by Dante or Coventry Patmore or Meredith, is a perfectly good definition of love in Morris's stories—unless, indeed, 'lust' is too heavy and breathless a name for anything so bright and youthful and functional as his kind of sensuality. The experience of his lovers is at the opposite extreme from the dizzying or swooning states described in common romantic poetry. The beauty of Keats's Madeline made Porphyro 'faint'.[2] But when the young man in the *Roots of the Mountains* thought of the young woman's body 'it stirred him up to go swiftlier as he strode on, the day brightening behind him'.[3] Morris, in fact, describes the sort of love that is a function of health; it quickens a man's pace. It is not surprising that the hero of the *Roots of the Mountains* should soon after be in love with a different woman. Morris does not deal much in world-without-end fidelities, and his heroes are seldom so enamoured of one damsel that they are quite indifferent to the beauty of others. When infidelities occur they are, of course, regrettable, as any other breach of faith, because they wound the social health and harmony of the tribe; they are not felt as apostasies from any god of love. Morris's Jason is felt to be a treacherous and ungrateful man for deserting Medea; but the poet does not share Chaucer's feeling about the mere change of love considered in itself. Still less does he understand the Christian and

---

[1] *The Well at the World's End*, bk. III, ch. 11, p. 47.   [2] 'Eve of St. Agnes', xxv, 8.
[3] *The Roots of the Mountains*, ch. 4, p. 26.

sacramental view of such things. He is the most irreligious of all our poets—*anima naturaliter pagana.*

To see this is, of course, to see that his medievalism is a kind of accident. The real interests of the Middle Ages—Christian mysticism, Aristotelian philosophy, Courtly Love—mean nothing to him. The world of the sagas, at once homely and heroic, is in some ways more congenial to him than that of the romances, just as their hard-bitten style with its almost excessive use of litotes is of all influences upon his language the most fruitful. That is another aspect of the 'Northern-ness'. But it would be a misunderstanding to inquire into the date and place of the society he depicts: you might as well apply historical criticism to Chaucer's Troy or Sidney's Arcadia or the plays of Lord Dunsany. Morris chose to build up his imaginary world on hints furnished by the Middle and the Dark Ages as these existed in the imagination of his own time and his own circle in particular. With that circle he doubtless shared many historical errors. But his choice was poetically right simply because that misconception of the Middle Ages (for reasons which go far back into the time of Percy and the Wartons) already existed, and existed poetically, in the public imagination. It was, and to some extent still is, part of our mythology.

This is only to repeat that his stories in verse and prose represent an imaginary world. It is a recognition of this fact which has earned them such epithets as 'faint', 'shadowy', 'decorative', and the like. Nineteenth-century criticism was unconsciously dominated by the novel, and could praise only with reservations work which does not present analysed characters ('living men and women' as they called them) in a naturalistic setting. Modern Shakespearian criticism dates from the abandonment of the attempt to treat Shakespeare's plays as if they were novels. The change perhaps began with Raleigh's unemphasized observation that for Shakespeare plot comes first and character has to be fitted into it.[1] Since then such critics as Miss Spurgeon,[2] Stoll,[3] and Wilson Knight[4] have all, in their several

---

[1] Sir Walter Raleigh, *Shakespeare* (London, 1907): 'The story came first with him,—as it came first with his audience, as it comes first with every child', p. 133.

[2] Caroline F. E. Spurgeon, *Shakespeare's Imagery and What It Tells Us* (Cambridge, 1935).

[3] E. E. Stoll, *Shakespeare Studies* (New York, 1927); *Art and Artifice in Shakespeare* (New York, 1933).

[4] G. Wilson Knight, *Myth and Miracle: An Essay on the Mystic Symbolism of Shakespeare* (London, [1929]); *The Shakespearian Tempest* (London: Oxford University Press, 1932).

directions, moved away from the old conception. We are free to recognize that in the *Winter's Tale* the Pygmalion myth or resurrection myth in the last act is the substance and the characters, motives, and half-hearted attempts at explanation which surround it are the shadow. We may even regret that the convention in which Shakespeare worked did not allow him to make Paulina frankly a fairy or an angel and thus be rid of his 'improbable possibilities'. It will soon, we may hope, be impossible to relegate Morris to the shades because his whole world is an invention. All we need demand is that this invented world should have some intellectual or emotional relevance to the world we live in.

And it has. The travels of the Argonauts or of those more ambitious wanderers in the *Earthly Paradise*, the quest for the well at the world's end or the wood beyond the world, the politics of Mirkwood and the sorrow of Odin the Goth—all these are attached in a dozen ways first to Morris's life and then to the lives of us all. They express the author's deepest sense of reality, which is much subtler and more sensitive than we expect—a mass of 'tensions' as von Hügel would have said. It is a pity that so many readers begin with the *Earthly Paradise*, not only because it contains much of his dullest work but also because it can hardly be understood in isolation. The opening stanzas state the theme of mutability and mortality, which seems at first a romantic common-place, and the author seems himself to invite that very estimate of his work which I am rejecting, calling himself an idle singer, whose

> murmuring rhyme
> Beats with light wing against the ivory gate,
> Telling a tale not too importunate.[1]

It is only when we have read the Prologue and all the 'links' that we perceive this complaint of mortality as the recoil from a positive and violent passion for immortality. The Prologue, in fact, is the breaking of a wave: the whole of the rest of the book is the 'melancholy, long, withdrawing roar',[2] and into it Morris has put all that negative and compensatory poetry which has earned him his reputation. The scheme could hardly have escaped monotony and he never tried it again. But even here the first 'tension' becomes visible and redeems the whole thing from mere *fin de siècle* pessimism. On the one hand we have the passion for immortality, which in Morris is as wild, as

---

[1] *The Earthly Paradise*, introductory verses, l. 24, p. 1.
[2] Matthew Arnold, 'Dover Beach', 25.

piercing, as orgiastic and heart-breaking as his presentations of sexual love are simple, sensuous, and unimpassioned; and this in itself is something very different from mere melancholy. But it is balanced by an opposite feeling which no one has expressed quite so forcibly as Morris—the feeling that such desire is not wholly innocent, that the world of mortality is more than enough for our allegiance, and that the traitor and apostate who follows a wilder possibility will look back too late on the

> land that might have been to me
> A kindly giver of wife, child and friend,
> And happy life, or at the worser end
> A quiet grave till doomsday rend the earth.[1]

This poise between two moods must not be mistaken for a debate about two doctrines. Morris, like a true Pagan, does not tell us (because he does not think he knows) the ultimate significance of those moments in which we cannot help reaching out for something beyond the visible world and so discovering 'at what unmeasured price Man sets his life'.[2] He neither seeks to justify them like a Christian nor to repress them like a materialist. He simply presents the tension. And it is one that cannot be resolved: for that same impression of the goodness of mere living which corrects our desire for some Acre of the Undying must also aggravate the sting of mortality. As Byron had said, there is no sterner moralist than pleasure; and so for Morris it is not unhappiness but happiness which is the real fountain of misgiving, making us 'more mindful that the sweet days die'.[3] The idyllic, which admittedly fills so large a place in his work, is not simply an escape; its temporary exclusion of ill luck, disease, and injustice serves to disengage the real and unalterable trouble about temporal existence as such. It is as if Morris said to the ordinary pessimists, 'Yes, yes, I know all about the slums, and Tess, and Jude. Perhaps we can abolish them in a rational society; but it is then that the real problem appears.'

No doubt many will be tempted to reply that this 'is going far to seek disquietude' in a world where scarce one per cent. of the population have ever been so fortunate as to have leisure for those delicate distresses. But Morris has not left himself open to this reply. No one could be less of 'a *cui bono* man'; no one more concerned, both in

---

[1] *The Earthly Paradise*, Prologue, l. 308, p. 12.
[2] *Ibid.*, l. 978, p. 28.   [3] *Ibid.*, introductory verses, l. 12, p. 1.

practice and imagination, with 'the people's praise' and the 'good of the folk'. This second tension, between the fundamental unsatisfactoriness of mortal life and a conviction that the vigorous enjoyment and improvement of such life is infinitely worth while, now begins to appear. Already in *The Life and Death of Jason* the haunting desire for immortality is opposed—and, again, I do not mean *doctrinally* opposed—not so much to ordinary happiness as to heroic exploit. The Argonauts are teased and solicited over and over again by paradises, gardens, and islands, 'not made for men that die', and every pause of the action is but a silence to make audible the

> Formless and wailing thoughts, that press
> About our hour of happiness.[1]

But the answer to these is simply to get on with the job—to mend the sails, or launch the boat, or gather firewood. This admirable solution —at times almost as surprising as that in the *Bhagavad-Gita*, 'Defeat and victory are the same: therefore fight'—becomes more and more characteristic of Morris as he proceeds. In *Sigurd* it amounts almost to a complete trampling underfoot of the whole ideal of happiness in any shape or form. It is contemptible to ask 'a little longer, and a little longer to live'.[2] The gods have not made the world for happiness but to be 'a tale', and it is good, when they ask us for one deed, to give them two. We find even a hint that there may be some ultimate justification of all things which will explain

> Why the brave man's spear is broken, and his war-shield fails
> at need.[3]

But Morris soon withdraws from these supposals. For one so enamoured of 'the Northernness' these doomed Eddaic gods—the very type of Stoical Romanticism—had a strong appeal. But Morris cannot forget that he does not really know whether anything like them exists, and he feels that the whole thing is getting too like a philosophy or a theology. He will not hammer his world into any simplified shape. Hence in the great prose romances, which are the real crown of his work, we come back to something much more actual. The answer to the 'formless and wailing thoughts' is found in the daily life, health, and preservation of the community. The 'kindreds', 'houses', or 'little lands' of the romances are the points

---

[1] *The Life and Death of Jason*, bk. x, l. 539, p. 152.
[2] *The Story of Sigurd the Volsung*, bk. ii, p. 72.   [3] *Ibid.*, bk. i, p. 22.

where Morris's career as a socialist touches his career as a poet. For Morris—let there be no mistake about it—is in one sense as good a 'totalitarian' as ever came out of Moscow or Berlin; his romantic socialism, if it be romantic, is at the opposite pole from the individualism of Shelley or Tom Payne. He immerses the individual completely in the society. 'If thou diest to-day, where then shall our love be?' asks the heroine in the *House of the Wolfings*. 'It shall abide with the soul of the Wolfing[s],'[1] comes the answer. The good tribesman cannot 'see' the 'grave-night', but rather the 'tale of the Wolfings through the coming days' and himself 'amidst it ever reborn and yet reborn'.[2] The opposite state of mind is an enchantment of the dwarfs, when a man becomes separated in soul from the kindred—'I loved them not, and was not of them, and outside myself there was nothing: *within me was the world.*'[3] The last words, which I have ventured to italicize, are Morris's penetrating analysis of the poison inherent in one type of romanticism: its dandyism, and subjectivity, and its pitiful war-cry *au moins je suis autre*. Morris has nothing here to learn from our own century. Rather he has something to teach. Many sociological writers are dull because while they talk of a just distribution of goods they give us no assurance that they know what Good means: we remain in doubt lest the gold they would distribute so equitably may be but fairy gold which will turn by daylight into ballot papers or soup tickets. The great use of the idyllic in literature is to find and illustrate the good—to give a real value to the x about which political algebra can then work. The tribal communities which Morris paints in *The House of the Wolfings* or *The Roots of the Mountains* are such attempts, perhaps the most successful attempts ever made, to give x a value. Morris knows as concretely as Burke or Tolstoy what he wants. A modern poet of the Left, praising that same solidarity with the group which Morris praises, invites a man to be 'one cog in the singing golden hive'. Morris, on the other hand, paints the actual going on of the communal life, the sowing, planting, begetting, building, ditching, eating, and conversation. And for this reason, where the modern poet (squeezing two of the commonest journalistic metaphors together, whether inadvertently or in the vain hope of a lively oxymoron) goes no deeper than the excitement of a political meeting, Morris, from remote Mirkwood and unhistoric Burgstead,

---

[1] *The House of the Wolfings*, ch. 26, p. 166.
[2] *Ibid.*, ch. 17, p. 109.   [3] *Ibid.*, ch. 26, p. 169.

brings back a sentiment that a man could really live by. He may seem, in one way, to be as ideal as Shelley, but in another he is as earthly, as rooted, as Aristotle or Dr Johnson. He is everywhere concrete. Comte's 'subjective immortality' and Godwin's 'benevolence' are mere philosophemes: Morris's life beyond life with the soul of the Wolfings, because we know them and indeed are bone of their bone, is something solid. He tells of what he has tried and found good.

I spoke just now of the enchantment which separated one of Morris's heroes from this unity. Significantly, it came from a 'dwarf-wrought hauberk'[1] which offered him immunity from death. His temptation to use it and his final rejection of it are the main theme of *The House of the Wolfings*: the conflict between the love of the tribe and the fear of death is here explicit. And if Morris were mainly concerned with the fear of death, this romance would have resolved the tension, for on this level life and death with the kindred has only to be seen to be preferred to anything else in the world or out of the world. But the fear of death was never one of Morris's chief concerns: it is only an aspect of something very different, and much harder to extinguish— the positive and passionate thirst for immortality. And so the solution is only momentary: in the romances that follow, the rebel passion breaks out again, never more impressive than when it is thus expressed by an old, unwearied poet. In the later romances the claims of the tribe are not forgotten, and the young hero who goes to the end of the world to drink of the well of life carries thither with him, and carries back, the determination to settle down and be a good king in his own small country. No wanderings are allowed to obliterate our love for 'the little platoon we belong to'. The tension is felt not now between the love of mortal life and the longing for immortality; it is rather discovered within the longing itself. We cannot help wishing that human life and youth should last for ever: yet is it really to be wished? Long ago in *Jason* Morris had hinted that life owes all its sweets to that same death whence rise all its bitters. He had stumbled unawares on the real dialectic of natural desire which cannot help wanting (as philosophers would say) 'the bad infinite', though that infinite is a horror and a torment. In *The Story of the Glittering Plain* the land of the ever-living is reached, but it turns out to be only a gorgeous prison. The hero finds 'the falseness of this unchanging land':[2] among

[1] *The House of The Wolfings*, heading to ch. 16 *et passim*, p. 102.
[2] *The Story of the Glittering Plain or The Land of Living Men*, ch. 15, p. 272.

its 'soft and merry folk' he 'long[s] for the house of his fathers and the men of the spear and the plough'.[1] So in *The Well at the World's End* the Innocent folk, whose name is significant, say that 'the Gods [have] given us the gift of death lest we weary of life'.[2]

If we were dealing with any author but Morris we should say that this is the conclusion of the whole matter. But in Morris there are no conclusions. The opposed desires change into their opposites and are lulled asleep and reawake; balance is attained and immediately lost; everything is always beginning over again: it is a dance, not a diagram. It can no more be seized in an epigram, summed up and docketed, than experience itself. One feeling alone never alters, and attains something of the stability of a doctrine. He is always sure that we must labour for the kindred and 'love ... the earth and the world with all [our] souls'.[3] This is the central altar: the dance moves round it. Love of the world and earth must tempt desire to sail beyond the frontier of that earth and world. Those who sail must look back from shoreless seas to find that they have abandoned their sole happiness. Those who return must find that happiness once more embittered by its mortality, must long again. Even if we found what we wanted it might be the ruin, not the consummation, of desire. But we cannot therefore cease to desire it. This hithering and thithering is too irregular and shot too full of colours to be compared to the sad Buddhist wheel, the circle too beautiful to be called a vicious circle; the conclusion drawn, wherever a mere luxury of pessimism threatens, is always practical, heroic, and commonsensible. And as the world of Morris cannot be summed up, so Morris himself escapes definition. What shall we call him? An imaginative Positivist—an animal man flawed by the longing for a coloured cloud—a potential mystic inhibited by a too-convinced love of the material world—all these err by representing as fixed something which is really always in solution. It is better to say simply that he is a good story-teller who has presented perhaps more faithfully than any other writer the whole scene of life as it must appear on the natural level.

The old indeterminate, half-Christian, half-Pantheistic, piety of the last century is gone. The modern literary world is increasingly divided into two camps, that of the positive and militant Christians

---

[1] *Ibid.*, ch. 14, p. 271.
[2] *The Well at the World's End*, bk. iii, ch. 16, p. 65.
[3] *Ibid.*, bk. iii, ch. 8, p. 36.

and that of the convinced materialists. It is here that Morris may be of incalculable value in saving us from 'dissociation'; for both camps can find in him something that they need. The appeal of this Pagan poet to the Christian reader is obvious. No one else states quite so clearly that dilemma in the natural virtues and the natural desires from which all philosophical religion must start—the question which all theologies claim to answer. And Morris is the more precious because he is content simply to state the question. His work is the fresh fruit of naïve experience, uncontaminated by theorizing. When William Allingham in 1882 talked to him 'among other things, of believing or not believing in a God' he replied, 'It's so unimportant' and 'went on to say that all we can get to, do what we will, is a form of words'.[1] This scepticism—a true scepticism with no unacknowledged bias to the negative—leaves his statement of Pagan experience chemically pure. If he had started from the concept of Eternity we might suspect his exposure of the dialectic of time to be tendentious: as it is, the exposure is forced upon him by mere obedience to desire and he remains quite unaware of the doctrines which he is supporting. He thus becomes one of the greatest Pagan witnesses—a prophet as unconscious, and therefore as far beyond suspicion, as Balaam's ass. As for the readers of the Left, I do not say that they will find him directly useful in politics. His conception of public good is too deeply rooted in agriculture, handicrafts, and the family to be applied to any modern Utopia. What will interest the Left will be those very same qualities that interest the Christians. The Left agrees with Morris that it is an absolute duty to labour for human happiness in this world. But the Left is deceiving itself if it thinks that any zeal for this object can permanently silence the reflection that every moment of this happiness must be lost as soon as gained, that all who enjoy it will die, that the race and the planet themselves must one day follow the individual into a state of being which has no significance—a universe of inorganic homogeneous matter moving at uniform speed in a low temperature. Hitherto the Left has been content, as far as I know, to pretend that this does not matter. It has perhaps been afraid of the 'formless and wailing thoughts' because these seem to lead inevitably into the paralysing kind of pessimism—'There be many that say, Who will shew us any good?'[2] At the same time, modern psychology

---

[1] *William Allingham: A Diary*, ed. H. Allingham and D. Radford (London, 1907), p. 316. [2] Psalm v. 6.

does not encourage us to base a single life, much less a civilization, on so gigantic a repression. It is here, surely, that Morris can come to their assistance. In Morris they will find a political creed which is, in principle, the same as their own, combined with an absolute refusal to paint out 'the great bar of black that runs across the shield of man'. Morris will show them how to acknowledge what they are tempted to camouflage and yet not to draw from it the conclusion they rightly fear. Nay, he will show them how this thirst for immortality, tinglingly alive in the perpetual motion of its dialectic, will but add a more urgent motive to their endeavours, an honourable firmness in defeat, and a keener edge to victory.

For Morris has 'faced the facts'. This is the paradox of him. He seems to retire far from the real world and to build a world out of his wishes; but when he has finished the result stands out as a picture of experience ineluctably true. No full-grown mind wants optimism or pessimism—philosophies of the nursery where they are not philosophies of the clinic; but to have presented in one vision the ravishing sweetness and the heart-breaking melancholy of our experience, to have shown how the one continually passes over into the other, and to have combined all this with a stirring practical creed, this is to have presented the *datum* which all our adventures, worldly and otherworldly alike, must take into account. There are many writers greater than Morris. You can go on from him to all sorts of subtleties, delicacies, and sublimities which he lacks. But you can hardly go behind him.[1]

[1] For further evidence of Lewis's deeply-founded interest in Morris, see his unsigned review of Dorothy M. Hoare's *The Works of Morris and of Yeats in Relation to Early Saga Literature* in *The Times Literary Supplement* (29 May 1937), p. 409.

17

Kipling's World

Kipling is intensely loved and hated. Hardly any reader likes him a little. Those who admire him will defend him tooth and nail, and resent unfavourable criticism of him as if he were a mistress or a country rather than a writer. The other side reject him with something like personal hatred. The reason is not hard to find and will, I hope, become apparent as we go on. For the moment, I will only say that I do not fully belong to either side.

I have been reading him off and on all my life, and I never return to him without renewed admiration. I have never at any time been able to understand how a man of taste could doubt that Kipling is a very great artist. On the other hand, I have never quite taken him to my heart. He is not one of my indispensables; life would go on much the same if the last copy of his works disappeared. I can go even further than this. Not only is my allegiance imperfect, it is also inconstant. After I have been reading Kipling for some days together there comes a sudden check. One moment I am filled with delight at the variety and solidity of his imagination; and then, at the very next moment, I am sick, sick to death, of the whole Kipling world. Of course, one can reach temporary saturation point with any author; there comes an evening when even Boswell or Virgil will do no longer. But one parts from them as a friend: one knows one will want them another day; and in the interval one thinks of them with pleasure. But I mean something quite different from that; I mean a real disenchantment, a recoil which makes the Kipling world for the moment, not dull (it is never that), but unendurable—a heavy, glaring, suffocating monstrosity. It is the difference between feeling that, on the whole, you would not like another slice of bread and butter just now, and wondering, as your gorge rises, how you could ever have imagined that you liked vodka.

I by no means assume that this sudden change of feeling is reasonable. But it must certainly have causes, and I hope that to explore them may cast some light on Kipling. I am going to suggest that they are two in number, one arising from what may be called the formal, the other from what may be called the material, character of his work. I admit that this distinction of form from matter breaks down if you press it too far, or in certain directions, but I think it will do for the purpose I have in hand.

The first cause for my sudden recoil from Kipling, I take to be not the defect but the excess of his art. He himself has told us how he licked every story into its final shape. He dipped a brush in Indian ink and then re-read the manuscript 'in an auspicious hour', considering faithfully 'every paragraph, sentence and word' and 'blacking out where requisite'. After a time he re-read the story and usually found that it would bear 'a second shortening'. Finally there came a third reading at which still more deletion might or might not be found necessary.[1] It is a magnificent example of self-discipline, which Horace would have approved. But I suggest that even an athlete can be over-trained. Superfluous flesh should be sweated off; but a cruel trainer may be too severe in judging what is superfluous. I think Kipling used the Indian ink too much. Sometimes the story has been so compressed that in the completed version it is not quite told—at least, I still do not know exactly what happened in "Mrs Bathurst".[2] But even when this is not so, the art overreaches itself in another way. Every sentence that did not seem to Kipling perfectly and triumphantly good has been removed. As a result the style tends to be too continuously and obtrusively brilliant. The result is a little fatiguing. Our author gives us no rest: we are bombarded with felicities till they deafen us. There is no elbow room, no leisureliness. We need roughage as well as nourishment in a diet; but there is no roughage in a Kipling story—it is all unrelieved vitamins from the first word to the last.

To this criticism I think Kipling could make an almost perfectly satisfactory answer. He might say that he was writing short stories and short poems, each of which was to be the only specimen of Kipling in some number of a periodical. His work was meant to be taken in small doses. The man who gobbles down one story after another at a

---

[1] *Something of Myself* (London, 1937), p. 208. All text-references to Kipling's prose are from the Uniform and Pocket editions (pagination the same in both) published by Macmillan. Text-references to Kipling's verse are to *Rudyard Kipling's Verse: Definitive Edition* (London: Hodder and Stoughton, 1940), referred to throughout this essay as '*Verse*'. In the text and footnotes, titles of books are printed in italic, stories between double and poems between single inverted commas.

[2] In *Traffics and Discoveries* (London, 1904).

sitting has no more right to complain if the result is disastrous than the man who swills liqueurs as if they were beer. This answer, I have said, seems to me almost complete. Almost—because even inside a single story the brilliance of the parts, in my opinion, sometimes damages the effect of the whole. I am thinking of "My Sunday at Home".[1] The fancied situation is excellent; one ought to remember the story with chuckles as one remembers *The Wrong Box*.[2] But I know I am not alone in finding that one actually laughed less than one would have thought possible in the reading of it and that in remembering it one always reverts to the summer drowsiness of the Wiltshire country around the railway station. That superb piece of scene painting has almost blotted out the comic action. Yet I suppose it was originally introduced for no other purpose than to emphasize the solitude of the place.

The fault of which I am here accusing Kipling is one which only a great artist could commit. For most of us the old rule of cutting out every word that can be spared is still a safe one: there is no danger that even after this process the result will be too vivid and too full of sense. And, as far as mere art is concerned, I think this is almost the only fault I can find in Kipling's mature work; I say his mature work for, of course, like all men he made some unsuccessful experiments before he found his true vein. It is when I turn to his matter that my serious discontents begin.

The earliest generation of Kipling's readers regarded him as the mouthpiece of patriotism and imperialism. I think that conception of his work is inadequate. Chesterton did a great service to criticism by contradicting it in a famous chapter of *Heretics*. In that chapter he finds the essential characteristics of Kipling's mind to be two. In the first place he had discovered, or rediscovered, the poetry of common things; had perceived, as Chesterton says, 'the significance and philosophy of steam and of slang'.[3] In the second place, Kipling was the poet of discipline. Not specially, nor exclusively, of military discipline, but of discipline of every shape. 'He has not written so well of soldiers', says Chesterton, 'as he has about railway men or bridge builders, or even journalists.'[4] This particular judgement may be disputed, but I feel no doubt at all that Chesterton has picked up the right scent.

[1] In *The Day's Work* (London, 1898).
[2] By Robert Louis Stevenson and Lloyd Osbourne (London, 1889).
[3] G. K. Chesterton, 'On Mr. Rudyard Kipling and making the World Small', *Heretics* (London, 1905), pp. 42–3.   [4] *Ibid.*, p. 45.

To put the thing in the shortest possible way, Kipling is first and foremost the poet of work. It is really remarkable how poetry and fiction before his time had avoided this subject. They had dealt almost exclusively with men in their 'private hours'—with love-affairs, crimes, sport, illness and changes of fortune. Mr Osbourne may be a merchant, but *Vanity Fair* has no interest in his mercantile life. Darcy was a good landlord and Wentworth a good officer, but their activities in these capacities were all 'offstage'. Most of Scott's characters, except the soldiers, have no profession; and when they are soldiers the emphasis is on battles and adventures, not on the professional routine. Business comes into Dickens only in so far as it is criminal or comic. With a few exceptions* imaginative literature in the eighteenth and nineteenth centuries had quietly omitted, or at least thrust into the background, the sort of thing which in fact occupies most of the waking hours of most men. And this did not merely mean that certain technical aspects of life were unrepresented. A whole range of strong sentiments and emotions—for many men, the strongest of all—went with them. For, as Pepys once noted with surprise, there is a great pleasure in talking of business. It was Kipling who first reclaimed for literature this enormous territory.

His early stories of Anglo-Indian society still conform to the older convention. They are about love-affairs, elopements, intrigues and domestic quarrels. They are indeed connected with his later and more characteristic work by a thread which I shall discuss presently; but on the surface they are a different kind of thing. The 'Departmental Ditties' are much more typical of the author's real interests. The point about Potiphar Gubbins is not simply that he is a cuckold, but that his horns bring him advancement in the Civil Service, and that he builds very bad bridges.[1] The sting of 'The Story of Uriah' lies not merely in the wife's depravity but in the fact that the husband was sent, for her lover's convenience, to die at Quetta, 'Attempting two men's duty In that very healthy post'.[2] Exeter Battleby Tring, who really knows something about railways, has his mouth silenced with rupees in order that 'the Little Tin Gods (long may Their Highnesses thrive!)' may keep 'their Circle intact'.[3] Boanerges Blitzen ruins his official career by exposing 'office scandals' in the papers.[4] The whole

---

* Of these *Middlemarch* is perhaps the finest.

[1] 'Study of an Elevation, in India Ink', *Verse*, pp. 6–7. [2] *Ibid.*, p. 10.
[3] 'Public Waste', *ibid.*, p. 15. [4] 'The Man Who could Write', *ibid.*, p. 17.

bitter little collection presents a corrupt society, not in its leisure, but in its official corruption. In his later work this preference for depicting men at their jobs becomes his most obvious characteristic. Findlayson's hopes and fears about his bridge,[1] McPhee's attitude both to engines and owners,[2] William the Conqueror's work in the famine district, a lighthouse-keeper at his post on a foggy night,[3] Gisborne and his chief in the forest,[4] McAndrew standing his watch[5]—these are the things that come back to us when we remember Kipling; and there had really been nothing like them in literature before. The poems again and again strike the same note. Lord Dufferin (heavily influenced by Bishop Blougram) hands on the *arcana imperii* to Lord Lansdowne; the professional spies set out, 'Each man reporting for duty alone, out of sight, out of reach, of his fellow';[6] the crew of the *Bolivar*, 'Mad with work and weariness', see 'Some damned Liner's lights go by like a grand hotel';[7] H. Mukerji sends with the Boh's head a covering letter in perfect Babu officialese;[8] the fans and beltings in a munition factory roar round a widowed war worker.[9] The rhythms of work—boots slogging along a road,[10] the Harrild and the Hoe devouring 'Their league-long paper-bale',[11] the grunting of a water-wheel[12]—echo through Kipling's verse and prose as through no other man's. Even Mowgli in the end accepts a post in the Civil Service.[13] Even "The Brushwood Boy"[14] turns aside from its main theme to show how much toil its hero suffered and inflicted in the course of his profession. Even when we are taken into the remote past, Kipling is not interested in imagining what it felt like to be an ancient and pagan man; only in what it felt like to be a man doing some ancient job—a galley slave, a Roman officer. How the light came in through the oar-holes in the galley—that little detail which everyone who had served in a galley would remember and which no one else would know[15]—that is Kipling's quarry.

[1] "The Bridge-Builders", *The Day's Work*.
[2] "Bread Upon the Waters", *ibid.*   [3] "William the Conqueror", *ibid.*
[4] "In the Rukh", *Many Inventions* (London, 1893).
[5] 'McAndrew's Hymn', *Verse*, pp. 120–7.
[6] 'The Spies' March', *ibid.*, p. 101.   [7] 'The Ballad of the "Bolivar"', *ibid.*, p. 138.
[8] 'The Ballad of Boh Da Thone', *ibid.*, pp. 255–62.
[9] 'The Song of the Lathes', *ibid.*, pp. 310–11.
[10] 'Boots', *ibid.*, pp. 473–4.   [11] 'The Press', *ibid.*, p. 534.
[12] "Below the Mill Dam", *Traffics and Discoveries*.
[13] "In the Rukh", *Many Inventions*.   [14] In *The Day's Work*.
[15] "The Finest Story in the World", *Many Inventions*.

It would be a mistake, however, to accuse Kipling of swamping the human interest in his mass of material and technical detail. The detail is there for the sake of a human interest, but that human interest is one that no previous writer had done justice to. What Kipling chiefly communicates—and it is, for good and for ill, one of the strongest things in the world—is the peculiar relation which men who do the same work have to that work and to one another; the inescapable bond of shared experiences, and, above all, of shared hardships. It is a commitment for life:

> Oh, was there ever sailor free to choose,
>> That didn't settle somewhere near the sea? ...
> *We've only one virginity to lose,*
>> *And where we lost it, there our hearts will be!*[1]

That is why in "Steam Tactics" Hinchcliffe, who, when starting on his leave, had 'thanked his Maker, ... that he wouldn't see nor smell nor thumb a runnin' bulgine till the nineteenth prox',[2] nevertheless fell immediately to studying the engine of Kipling's steam-car.

For the same reason, Kipling, the old journalist, writes:

> But the Jew shall forget Jerusalem
> Ere we forget the Press![3]

In the next stanza he goes on to explain why. The man who has 'stood through the loaded hour' and 'lit his pipe in the morning calm' —who has, in fact, been through the nocturnal routine of producing a newspaper—'hath sold his heart'.[4] That is the whole point. We who are of one trade (whether journalists, soldiers, galley slaves, Indian Civilians, or what you will) know so many things that the outsiders will never, never understand. Like the two child lovers in *The Light that Failed*, 'we belong'.[5] It is a bond which in real life sometimes proves stronger than any other:

> The men of my own stock,
>> They may do ill or well,
> But they tell the lies I am wonted to,
>> They are used to the lies I tell;
> And we do not need interpreters
>> When we go to buy and sell.[6]

[1] 'The Virginity', *Verse*, pp. 353, 354.   [2] In *Traffics and Discoveries*, p. 181.
[3] 'The Press', *Verse*, p. 534.   [4] *Ibid.*
[5] *The Light that Failed* (London, 1891), p. 13.   [6] 'The Stranger', *Verse*, p. 549.

How true to life is the immediate alliance of the three journalists whom chance has thrown together in the story called "A Matter of Fact".[1]

This spirit of the profession is everywhere shown in Kipling as a ruthless master. That is why Chesterton got in a very large part of the truth when he fixed on discipline as Kipling's main subject. There is nothing Kipling describes with more relish than the process whereby the trade-spirit licks some raw cub into shape. That is the whole theme of one of his few full-length novels, *Captains Courageous*.[2] It is the theme of 'The Centaurs',[3] and of 'Pharaoh and the Sergeant',[4] and of 'The 'Eathen'.[5] It is allegorically expressed in "The Ship that Found Herself".[6] It is implicit in all the army stories and the sea-stories; indeed, it may be thought that the author turns aside from his narrative rather too often to assure us that Mulvaney was invaluable for 'lick[ing] the new batch of recruits into shape'.[7] Even when we escape the jungle and the wolf pack we do not escape the Law. Until he has been disciplined—'put through it', licked into shape —a man is, for Kipling, mere raw material. 'Gad', says Hitchcock to Findlayson in "The Bridge-Builders", 'what a Cooper's Hill cub I was when I came on the works!' And Findlayson muses, 'Cub thou wast; assistant thou art.'[8] The philosophy of the thing is summed up at the end of "A Walking Delegate" where the yellow horse (an agitator) has asked the old working horse, 'Have you no respec' whatever fer the dignity o' our common horsehood?' He gets the reply, 'Horse, sonny, is what you start from. We know all about horse here, an' he ain't any high-toned, pure-souled child o' nature. Horse, plain horse, same ez you, is chock-full o' tricks, an' meannesses, an' cussednesses, ... an' monkeyshines ... Thet's *horse*, an' thet's about his dignity an' the size of his soul 'fore he's been broke an' raw-hided a piece.'[9] Reading 'man' for 'horse', we here have Kipling's doctrine of Man.

This is one of the most important things Kipling has to say and one which he means very seriously, and it is also one of the things which has aroused hatred against him. It amounts to something like a doctrine of original sin, and it is antipathetic to many modern modes

---

[1] In *Many Inventions*.
[2] (London, 1897.)
[3] *Verse*, pp. 752–3.
[4] *Ibid.*, pp. 198–200.
[5] *Ibid.*, pp. 451–3.
[6] In *The Day's Work*.
[7] "The Incarnation of Krishna Mulvaney", *Life's Handicap* (London, 1891), p. 22.
[8] In *The Day's Work*, pp. 3, 4.
[9] *Ibid.*, p. 76.

of thought. Perhaps even more antipathetic is Kipling's presentation of the 'breaking' and 'raw-hiding' process. In "His Private Honour" it turns out to consist of prolonged bullying and incessant abuse; the sort of bullying (as we learn from 'The 'Eathen') which sends grown men off to cry in solitude, followed by the jeers of the old hands. The patient is not allowed to claim any personal rights whatever; there is nothing, according to Kipling, more subversive. To ask for justice is as the sin of witchcraft. The disaster in the poem called 'That Day' began with the fact that 'every little drummer 'ad 'is rights an' wrongs to mind'.[1] In contrast, 'My right!' Ortheris answered with deep scorn, 'My rights! I ain't a recruity to go whinin' about my rights to this an' my rights to that, just as if I couldn't look after myself. My rights! 'Strewth A'mighty! I'm a man.'[2]

Now there is no good whatever in dismissing this part of Kipling's message as if it were not worth powder and shot. There is a truth in it which must be faced before we attempt to find any larger truths which it may exclude. Many who hate Kipling have omitted this preliminary. They feel instinctively that they themselves are just the unlicked or unbroken men whom Kipling condemns; they find the picture intolerable, and the picture of the cure more intolerable still. To escape, they dismiss the whole thing as a mere Fascist or 'public school' brutality. But there is no solution along those lines. It may (or may not) be possible to get beyond Kipling's harsh wisdom; but there is no getting beyond a thing without first getting as far. It is a brutal truth about the world that the whole everlasting business of keeping the human race protected and clothed and fed could not go on for twenty-four hours without the vast legion of hard-bitten, technically efficient, not-over-sympathetic men, and without the harsh processes of discipline by which this legion is made. It is a brutal truth that unless a great many people practised the Kipling *ethos* there would be neither security nor leisure for any people to practise a finer *ethos*. As Chesterton admits, 'We may fling ourselves into a hammock in a fit of divine carelessness—but we are glad that the net-maker did not make the hammock in a fit of divine careless-ness.'[3] In 'The Pro-Consuls', speaking of those who have actually ruled with a strong hand, Kipling says:

[1] *Verse*, p. 438.
[2] "His Private Honour", *Many Inventions*, p. 162.
[3] Chesterton, *op. cit.*, p. 46.

On the stage their act hath framed
For thy sports, O Liberty!
Doubted are they, and defamed
By the tongues their act set free.[1]

It is a true bill, as far as it goes. Unless the Kipling virtues—if you
will, the Kipling vices—had long and widely been practised in the
world we should be in no case to sit here and discuss Kipling. If all
men stood talking of their rights before they went up a mast or down
a sewer or stoked a furnace or joined an army, we should all perish;
nor while they talked of their rights would they learn to do these things.
And I think we must agree with Kipling that the man preoccupied
with his own rights is not only a disastrous, but a very unlovely object;
indeed, one of the worst mischiefs we do by treating a man unjustly
is that we force him to be thus preoccupied.

But if so, then it is all the more important that men should in fact
be treated with justice. If we all need 'licking into shape' and if,
while undergoing the process, we must not guard our rights, then it
is all the more important that someone else should guard them for
us. What has Kipling to say on this subject? For, quite clearly, the
very same methods which he prescribes for licking the cub into
shape, 'making a man of him' in the interests of the community,
would also, if his masters were bad men, be an admirable method of
keeping the cub quiet while he was exploited and enslaved for their
private benefit. It is all very well that the colts (in 'The Centaurs')
should learn to obey Chiron as a means to becoming good cavalry
chargers; but how if Chiron wants their obedience only to bring
them to the knacker's yard? And are the masters never bad men?
From some stories one would almost conclude that Kipling is ignorant
of, or indifferent to, this possibility. In "His Private Honour" the
old soldiers educate the recruits by continued bullying. But Kipling
seems quite unaware that bullying is an activity which human beings
enjoy. We are given to understand that the old soldiers are wholly
immune to this temptation; they threaten, mock, and thrash the
recruits only for the highest possible motives. Is this naïvety in the
author? Can he really be so ignorant? Or does he not care?

He is certainly not ignorant. Most of us begin by regarding Kipling
as the panegyrist of the whole imperial system. But we find when we
look into the matter that his admiration is reserved for those in the

[1] *Verse*, p. 108.

lower positions. These are the 'men on the spot': the bearers of the burden; above them we find folly and ignorance; at the centre of the whole thing we find the terrible society of Simla, a provincial smart set which plays frivolously with men's careers and even their lives. The system is rotten at the head, and official advancement may have a *teterrima causa*. Findlayson had to see 'months of office work destroyed at a blow when the Government of India, at the last moment, added two feet to the width of the bridge, under the impression that bridges were cut out of paper'.[1] The heart-rending death of Orde (one of Kipling's best tragic scenes) is followed by the undoing of his life's work when the ignorant Viceroy sends a Babu to succeed him.[2] In "Tod's Amendment" disaster is averted by a child who knows what all the rulers of India (the 'little Tin Gods') do not know.[3] It is interesting to compare 'The 'Eathen' with 'The Sergeant's Weddin''.[4] In the one, the sergeants are benevolent despots—it is only the softness and selfishness of the recruit that make him think they are cruel tyrants. In the other, we have a sergeant who uses his position to make money by cheating the men. Clearly this sergeant would have just as strong a motive as the good ones for detesting privates who talked about their 'rights and wrongs'.

All this suggests that the disciplinary system is a very two-edged affair; but this does not in the least shake Kipling's devotion to it. That, he says in effect, is what the world has always been like and always will be like. Even in prehistoric times the astute person

> Won a simple Viceroy's praise
> Through the toil of other men.[5]

And no one can rebuke more stunningly than Kipling those who exploit and frustrate the much-enduring 'man on the spot':

> When the last grim joke is entered
> In the big black Book of Jobs,
> And Quetta graveyards give again
> Their victims to the air,
> I shouldn't like to be the man
> Who sent Jack Barret there.[6]

[1] "The Bridge-Builders", *op. cit.*, p. 4.
[2] "The Head of the District", *Life's Handicap*.
[3] In *Plain Tales from the Hills* (London, 1888).
[4] *Verse*, pp. 447–9.   [5] 'A General Summary', *Verse*, p. 4.
[6] 'The Story of Uriah', *ibid.*, p. 10.

But this makes no difference to the duty of the sufferer. Whatever corruptions there may be at the top, the work must go on; frontiers must be protected, epidemics fought, bridges built, marshes drained, famine relief administered. Protest, however well grounded, about injustice, and schemes of reform, will never bring a ship into harbour or a train into the station or sow a field of oats or quell a riot; and 'the unforgiving minute'[1] is upon us fourteen-hundred and forty times a day. This is the truest and finest element in Kipling; his version of Carlyle's gospel of work. It has affinities with Piers Plowman's insistence on ploughing his half-acre. But there are important differences.

The more Kipling convinces us that no plea for justice or happiness must be allowed to interfere with the job, the more anxious we become for a reassurance that the work is really worthy of all the human sacrifices it demands. 'The game', he says, 'is more than the player of the game.' But perhaps some games are and some aren't. 'And the ship is more than the crew'[2]—but one would like to know where the ship was going and why. Was its voyage really useful—or even innocent? We want, in fact, a doctrine of Ends. Langland could supply one. He knows how Do Well is connected with Do Bet and Do Best; the ploughing of the half-acre is placed in a cosmic context and that context would enable Langland, in principle, to tell us whether any given job in the whole universe was true worship or miserable idolatry; it is here that Kipling speaks with an uncertain voice. For many of the things done by his Civil Servants the necessity is perhaps obvious; but that is not a side of the matter he develops. And he writes with equal relish where the ultimate ends of the work described are much less obvious. Sometimes his choice of sides seems to be quite accidental, even frivolous. When William the Conqueror met a schoolmaster who had to teach the natives the beauties of Wordsworth's *Excursion* she told him, rather unnecessarily, 'I like men who do things.'[3] Teaching English Literature to natives is not 'doing things', and we are meant to despise that schoolmaster. One notes that the editor of the local paper, whom we met a few pages before, is visited with no similar ignominy. Yet it is easy enough to imagine the situations reversed. Kipling could have written a perfect Kipling story about two men in the Educational Department

[1] 'If —', *Verse*, p. 577.
[2] 'A Song in Storm: 1914–1918', *ibid.*, p. 148.
[3] "William the Conqueror", *loc. cit.*, p. 187.

working eighteen hours a day to conduct an examination, with punkah flapping and all the usual background. The futility of the curriculum which makes them set Wordsworth to Indian schoolboys would not in the least have detracted from their heroism if he had chosen to write the story from that point of view. It would have been their professional grievance—ironically and stoically endured—one more instance of that irresponsible folly at the top which wastes and breaks the men who really do the work. I have a disquieting feeling that Kipling's actual respect for the journalist and contempt for the schoolmaster has no thought-out doctrine of ends behind it, but results from the accident that he himself worked for a newspaper and not for a school. And now, at last, I begin to suspect that we are finding a clue to that suffocating sensation which overtakes me if I read Kipling too long. Is the Kipling world really monstrous in the sense of being misshaped? How if this doctrine of work and discipline, which is so clear and earnest and dogmatic at the periphery, hides at the centre a terrible vagueness, a frivolity or scepticism?

Sometimes it hides nothing but what the English, whether fairly or unfairly, are inclined to call Americanism. The story called "Below the Mill Dam" is an instance. We are expected to rejoice that the native black rat should be superseded by the alien brown rat; that the mill wheel could be yoked to a dynamo and the countryside electrified. None of the questions which every thinking man must raise about the beneficence of this whole transition have any meaning for Kipling. They are to him mere excuses for idleness. 'We have already learned six refined synonyms for loafing', say the Waters; and, to the Wheel itself, 'while you're at work you'll work'.[1] The black rat is to be stuffed. Here is the creed of Activism—of 'Progress', hustle, and development—all blind, naked, uncritical of itself. Similarly in 'The Explorer', while we admire the man's courage in the earlier stanzas, the end which he has in view gives us pause. His Holy Grail is simply the industrialisation of the country he has discovered. The waterfalls are 'wasting fifty thousand head an hour' and the forests are 'axe-ripe';[2] he will rectify this. The End, here as in the Mill Dam story, may be a good one; it is not for me to decide. But Kipling does not seem to know there is any question. In "Bread Upon the Waters" all the usual hardships are described and with all Kipling's usual relish; but the only end is money and revenge—though I confess, a very

---

[1] *Loc. cit.*, pp. 388, 389.   [2] *Verse*, p. 106.

excusable revenge. In "The Devil and the Deep Sea"[1] the job, which is treated with his usual reverence, the game, which is still more than the player of the game, is merely the triumph of a gang of criminals.

This might be explained by saying that Kipling is not a moralist but a purely objective writer. But that would be false. He is eminently a moralist; in almost every story we are invited, nay forced, to admire and condemn. Many of the poems are versified homilies. This is why this chanciness or uncertainty about the End to which the moralism of his *bushido* is applied in any particular instance makes us uncomfortable. And now we must take a step farther. Even Discipline is not a constant. The very people who would be cubs to be licked into shape in one story may, in another, be the heroes we are asked to admire.

Stalky and his friends are inveterate breakers of discipline. How easily, had his own early memories been different, could Kipling have written the story the other way round. In "Their Lawful Occasions"[2] Moorshed, because he is rich and able to leave the navy next year, can afford to take an independent line. All Kipling's sympathy is with him and against the ship which is significantly named H.M.S. *Pedantic*. Yet Kipling need only have altered the lighting (so to speak) to make Moorshed, and the grounds of his independence, particularly odious and the odium would have been of a characteristically Kiplingese kind. In "Without Benefit of Clergy"[3] Holden's inefficiency as a civil servant is made light of; but had Kipling written in a different mood the very cause of this inefficiency—namely keeping a native mistress—would have been made into a despicable aggravation. In the actual story it is almost an excuse. In "A Germ-Destroyer" we actually find Kipling laughing at a man because he has 'a morbid passion for work'![4] In "The Bisara of Pooree" that whole Anglo-Indian world, whose work for the natives elsewhere seems so necessary and valuable, is contrasted with the natives as 'the shiny, top-scum stuff that people call "civilisation"'.[5] In the "Dream of Duncan Parrenness", the apparition offers the hero success in the Anglo-Indian career in return for his Trust in Man, his Faith in Woman, and his Boy's Conscience. He gives them all and receives in return 'a little piece of dry bread'.[6] Where is now the Kipling we thought we

[1] In *The Day's Work.*
[2] In *Traffics and Discoveries.*
[3] In *Life's Handicap.*
[4] In *Plain Tales from the Hills,* p. 122.
[5] *Ibid.,* p. 262.
[6] In *Life's Handicap,* p. 407.

knew—the prophet of work, the activist, the writer of 'If'? 'Were it not better done as others use . . .?'

You may say that some of these examples are taken from early stories; perhaps Kipling held these sceptical views in his youth and abandoned them in his maturity. Perhaps—as I once half-believed myself—he is a 'lost leader'; a great opposition writer who was somehow caught by government. I think there was a change in his views, but I do not think that goes to the root of the matter. I think that nearly all his work (for there are a few, and very valuable exceptions), at all periods is dominated by one master passion. What he loves better than anything in the world is the intimacy within a closed circle—even if it be only a circle of shared misery as in "In the Same Boat",[1] or of shared crime as in "The Devil and the Deep Sea". In the last resort I do not think he loves professional brotherhood for the sake of the work; I think he loves work for the sake of professional brotherhood. Out of that passion all his apparently contradictory moods arise. But I must attempt to define the passion itself a little more closely and to show how it has such a diversified offspring.

When we forgather with three or four trusted cronies of our own calling, a strong sense of community arises and is enjoyed. But that enjoyment can be prolonged by several different kinds of conversation. We may all be engaged in standing together against the outer world— all those fools outside who write newspaper articles about us which reveal their ghastly ignorance of the real work, and propose schemes which look very fine on paper but which, as we well know, are impracticable. As long as that conversation lasts, the profession appears a very fine one and its achievements very remarkable; if only those yapping outsiders would leave us alone to get on with the job. And that conversation, if we could do it well enough, would make *one* kind of Kipling story. But we might equally spend the evening standing together against our own seniors; those people at the top— Lord knows how they got there while better men rot in provincial lectureships, or small ships, or starving parishes!—who seem to have forgotten what the real work is like and who spoil all our best efforts with their meddling and are quite deceived about our relative merits. And while that conversation lasted, our profession would appear a very rotten and heart-breaking profession. We might even say it was high time the public learned the sort of things that really go on. A

---

[1] In *A Diversity of Creatures* (London, 1917).

rousing scandal might do good. And out of all that, *another* kind of Kipling story might be made. But then, some other evening, or later the same evening, we might all be standing together against our juniors. As if by magic our profession would now once more appear in a favourable light—at least, our profession as it used to be. What may happen with the sort of young cubs we're getting into it nowadays is another question. They need licking into shape. They'll have to learn to pull their socks up. They haven't begun to realize what is expected of them. And heaven knows, things are made easy enough for them now! They haven't been through the sort of mill we were through. God! If they'd worked under old So-and-so ... and thus, yet *another* Kipling story might arise. But we sometimes like talking about our juniors in exactly the opposite way. We have been in the job so long that we have no illusions about it. We know that half the official regulations are dead letters. Nobody will thank you for doing more than you need. Our juniors are laughably full of zeal, pedantic about discipline, devoured with a morbid passion for work. Ah, well, they'll soon get over it!

Now the point is that the similarity between all these conversations is overwhelmingly more important than the differences. It may well be chance which launches the evening on one of them rather than another, for they all give the same sort of pleasure, and this is the kind of pleasure which the great majority of Kipling's works both express and communicate. I am tempted to describe it as the pleasure of freemasonry; but this would be confusing because Kipling became a Mason in the narrower and official sense. But in the wider sense you may say he was born a Mason. One of the stories that pleased his childhood was, significantly, about 'lions who were all Freemasons' and in 'confederacy against some wicked baboons'.[1] The pleasure of confederacy against wicked Baboons, or even of confederacy *simpliciter*, is the cardinal fact about the Kipling world. To belong, to be inside, to be in the know, to be snugly together against the outsiders —that is what really matters; it is almost an accident who are cast for the rôle of outsiders (wicked Baboons) on any given occasion. And no one before Kipling had fully celebrated the potency of that snugness—the esoteric comedies and tragedies, the mutual understanding, the highly specialised smile, or shrug, or nod, or shake of the head,

---

[1] *Something of Myself*, p. 8. Kipling was referring to *King Lion* by James Greenwood (London, 1894).

which passes between fellow-professionals; the exquisite pleasure of being approved, the unassuaged mortification of being despised, within that charmed circle, compared with which public fame and infamy are a mere idle breath. What is the good of the papers hiding it ''andsome' if 'you know the Army knows'?[1] What is the good of excuses accepted by government if 'the men of one's own kind' hold one condemned?

And this is how the Simla stories really fit in. They are not very good—all Kipling's women have baritone voices—and at first sight they are not very mature work. But look again. 'If you do not know about things Up Above', says Kipling, after recording one of Mrs Hauksbee's most improbable exploits, 'you won't undersand how to fill in, and you will say it is impossible.'[2] In other words, at this stage of Kipling's career Simla society (to which, it may be supposed, his *entrée* was rather precarious) is itself a secret society, an inner ring, and the stories about it are for those who are 'in the know'. That the secrets in this case should be very shabby ones and the knowledge offered us very disillusioned knowledge, is an effect of the writer's youth. Young writers, and specially young writers already enchanted by the lure of the Inner Ring, like to exaggerate the cynicism and sophistication of the great world; it makes them feel less young. One sees how he must have enjoyed writing 'Simla is a strange place . . . nor is any man who has not spent at least ten seasons there qualified to pass judgement!'[3] That is the spirit of nearly all Kipling's work, though it was later applied to inner rings more interesting than Simla. There is something delicious about these early flights of esotericism. 'In India', he says, 'where everyone knows everyone else';[4] and again, 'I have lived long enough in this India to know that it is best to know nothing.'[5]

The great merit in Kipling is to have presented the magic of the Inner Ring in all its manifold workings for the first time. Earlier writers had presented it only in the form of snobbery; and snobbery is a very highly specialised form of it. The call of the Inner Ring, the men we know, the old firm, the talking of 'shop', may call a man away from high society into very low society indeed; we desire not to be in a *junto* simply, just to be in that *junto* where we 'belong'.

[1] 'That Day', *Verse*, p. 438.
[2] "Consequences", *Plain Tales from the Hills*, p. 105.
[3] "At the Pit's Mouth", *Wee Willie Winkie* (London, 1895), p. 35.
[4] "Wressley of the Foreign Office", *Plain Tales from the Hills*, p. 315.
[5] "By Word of Mouth", *ibid.*, p. 318.

Nor is Kipling in the least mistaken when he attributes to this esoteric spirit such great powers for good. The professional point of honour (it means as much, said McPhee, as her virginity to a lassie),[1] the *Aidôs* we feel only before our colleagues, the firm brotherhood of those who have 'been through it' together, are things quite indispensable to the running of the world. This masonry or confederacy daily carries commonplace people to heights of diligence or courage which they would not be likely to reach by any private moral ideals. Without it, no good thing is operative widely or for long.

But also—and this Kipling never seems to notice—without it no bad thing is operative either. The nostalgia which sends the old soldier back to the army ('I smelt the smell o' the barricks, I 'eard the bugles go')[2] also sends the recidivist back to his old partner and his old 'fence'. The confidential glance or rebuke from a colleague is indeed the means whereby a weak brother is brought or kept up to the standard of a noble profession; it is also the means whereby a new and hitherto innocent member is initiated into the corruption of a bad one. 'It's always done', they say; and so, without any 'scenes' or excitement, with a nod and a wink, over a couple of whiskies and soda, the Rubicon is crossed. The spirit of the Inner Ring is morally neutral—the obedient servant of valour and public spirit, but equally of cruelty, extortion, oppression, and dishonesty.[3]

Kipling seems unaware of this, or indifferent to it. He is the slave of the Inner Ring; he expresses the passion, but does not stand outside to criticise it. He plays for his side; about the choice of sides, about the limitations of partisanship after the side has been chosen, he has nothing very much to say to us. Mr Eliot has, I think rightly, called him a Pagan.[4] Irreverence is the last thing of which one could accuse him. He has a reverent Pagan agnosticism about all ultimates. 'When man has come to the turnstiles of Night', he says in the preface to *Life's Handicap*, 'all the creeds in the world seem to him wonderfully alike and colourless.'[5] He has the Pagan tolerance too; a tolerance so wide (which is unusual) that it extends even to Christianity, whose phraseology he freely uses for rhetorical effect in

---

[1] "Bread Upon the Waters", *loc. cit.*, p. 291.
[2] 'Back to the Army Again', *Verse*, p. 431.
[3] Cf. C. S. Lewis, 'The Innner Ring', *Transposition, and Other Addresses* (London, 1949), pp. 55–64.
[4] Eliot's essay on Kipling prefixed to *A Choice of Kipling's Verse*, ed. T. S. Eliot (London, 1941), p. 33.   [5] Pp. vii–viii.

his more Swinburnian moments.* But the tolerance is weary and sceptical; the whole energy of the man goes into his worship of the little demigods or daemons in the foreground—the Trades, the Sides, the Inner Rings. Their credentials he hardly examines. These servants he has made masters; these half-gods exclude the gods.

There are, I allow, hints of another Kipling. There are moments of an almost quivering tenderness—he himself had been badly hurt—when he writes of children or for them. And there are the 'queer' or 'rum' stories—"At the End of the Passage",[1] "The Mark of the Beast",[2] "They",[3] "Wireless".[4] These may be his best work, but they are not his most characteristic. If you open him at random, the chances are you will find him enslaved to some Inner Ring. His English countryside with its way of life is partly loved because American millionaires can't understand it, aren't in the know.[5] His comic stories are nearly all about hoaxes: an outsider mystified is his favourite joke. His jungle is not free from it. His very railway engines are either recruits or Mulvaneys dressed up in boilers.[6] His polo-ponies are public school ponies.[7] Even his saints and angels are in a celestial civil service.[8] It is this ubiquitous presence of the Ring, this unwearied knowingness, that renders his work in the long run suffocating and unendurable. And always, ironically, that bleak misgiving—almost that Nothingness—in the background.

But he was a very great writer. This trade-passion, this business of the Inner Ring, fills an immense area of human life. There, though not in the conventional novel, it frequently proves itself stronger than family affection, national loyalty, religion, and even vice. Hence Kipling deserved success with thousands of readers who left older fiction to be read by women and boys. He came home to their bosoms by coming home to their business and showed them life as they had found it to be. This is merit of a high order; it is like the discovery of a new element or a new planet; it is, in its way and as far as it goes, a 'return to nature'. The remedy for what is partial and dangerous in

---

* Some poems could not, on internal evidence alone, be distinguished from Christian work.

[1] In *Life's Handicap*.   [2] *Ibid.*
[3] In *Traffics and Discoveries*.   [4] *Ibid.*
[5] "An Error in the Fourth Dimension", *The Day's Work*.
[6] ".007", *ibid.*   [7] "The Maltese Cat", *ibid.*
[8] "On the Gate: A Tale of '16", *Debits and Credits* (London, 1926), and "Uncovenanted Mercies", *Limits and Renewals* (London, 1932).

his view of life is to go on from Kipling and to add the necessary correctives—not to deny what he has shown. After Kipling there is no excuse for the assumption that all the important things in a man's life happen between the end of one day's work and the beginning of the next. There is no good putting on airs about Kipling. The things he mistook for gods may have been only 'spirits of another sort'; but they are real things and strong.

18

Bluspels and Flalansferes:
A Semantic Nightmare

We are often compelled to set up standards we cannot reach ourselves and to lay down rules we could not ourselves satisfy.

LORD COLERIDGE, C.J. (Law Reports, Queen's Bench Division XIV, p. 288 in *Reg. v. Dudley and Stephen*)

Philologists often tell us that our language is full of dead metaphors. In this sentence, the word 'dead' and the word 'metaphors' may turn out to be ambiguous; but the fact, or group of facts, referred to, is one about which there is no great disagreement. We all know in a rough and ready way, and all admit, these things which are being called 'dead metaphors', and for the moment I do not propose to debate the propriety of the name. But while their existence is not disputed, their nature, and their relation to thought, gives rise to a great deal of controversy. For the benefit of any who happen to have avoided this controversy hitherto, I had better make plain what it is, by a concrete example. Bréal in his *Semantics*[1] often spoke in metaphorical, that is consciously, rhetorically, metaphorical language, of language itself. Messrs Ogden and Richards in *The Meaning of Meaning* took Bréal to task on the ground that 'it is impossible thus to handle a scientific matter in metaphorical terms'.[2] Barfield in his *Poetic Diction* retorted that Ogden and Richards were, as a matter of fact, just as metaphorical as Bréal. They had forgotten, he complained, that all language has a figurative origin and that the 'scientific' terms on which they piqued themselves—words like *organism, stimulus, reference*—were not miraculously exempt. On the contrary, he maintained, 'those who profess to eschew figurative expressions are really confining themselves to one very old kind of figure'—'they are absolutely rigid under the spell of those verbal ghosts of the physical sciences, which today make up practically the whole meaning-system

[1] M. J. A. Bréal, *Semantics: studies in the science of meaning*, trans. Mrs Henry Cust, with a Preface by J. P. Postgate (London, 1900).
[2] C. K. Ogden and I. A. Richards, *The Meaning of Meaning* (London, 1923), pp. 4–5.

of so many European minds'.* Whether Ogden and Richards will see
fit, or have seen fit, to reply to this, I do not know; but the lines on
which any reply would run are already traditional. In fact the whole
debate may be represented by a very simple dialogue.

A. You are being metaphorical.

B. You are just as metaphorical as I am, but you don't know it.

A. No, I'm not. Of course I know all about *attending* once having
meant *stretching*, and the rest of it. But that is not what it
means now. It may have been a metaphor to Adam—but I
am not using it metaphorically. What I *mean* is a pure concept
with no metaphor about it at all. The fact that it *was* a metaphor
is no more relevant than the fact that my pen is made of wood.
You are simply confusing derivation with meaning.

There is clearly a great deal to be said for both sides. On the one
hand it seems odd to suppose that what we *mean* is conditioned by a
dead metaphor of which we may be quite ignorant. On the other
hand, we see from day to day, that when a man uses a current and
admitted metaphor without knowing it, he usually gets led into
nonsense; and when, we are tempted to ask, does a metaphor become
so old that we can ignore it with impunity? It seems harsh to rule that
a man must know the whole semantic history of every word he uses
—a history usually undiscoverable—or else talk without thinking.
And yet, on the other hand, an obstinate suspicion creeps in that we
cannot entirely jump off our own shadows, and that we deceive
ourselves if we suppose that a new and purely conceptual notion of
attention has replaced and superseded the old metaphor of stretching.
Here, then, is the problem which I want to consider. How far, if at
all, is thinking limited by these dead metaphors? Is Anatole France in
any sense right when he reduces 'The soul possesses God' to 'the
breath sits on the bright sky'? Or is the other party right when it
urges 'Derivations are one thing. Meanings are another'? Or is the
truth somewhere between them?

The first and easiest case to study is that in which we ourselves
invent a new metaphor. This may happen in one of two ways. It
may be that when we are trying to express clearly to ourselves or to
others a conception which we have never perfectly understood, a
new metaphor simply starts forth, under the pressure of composition
or argument. When this happens, the result is often as surprising and

* Owen Barfield, *Poetic Diction: A Study in Meaning* (London, 1928), p. 140.

illuminating to us as to our audience; and I am inclined to think that this is what happens with the great, new metaphors of the poets. And when it does happen, it is plain that our new understanding is bound up with the new metaphor. In fact, the situation is for our purpose indistinguishable from that which arises when we hear a new metaphor from others; and for that reason, it need not be separately discussed. One of the ways, then, in which we invent a new metaphor, is by *finding* it, as unexpectedly as we might find it in the pages of a book; and whatever is true of the new metaphors that we find in books will also be true of those which we reach by a kind of lucky chance, or inspiration. But, of course, there is another way in which we invent new metaphors. When we are trying to explain, to some one younger or less instructed than ourselves, a matter which is already perfectly clear in our own minds, we may deliberately, and even painfully, pitch about for the metaphor that is likely to help him. Now when this happens, it is quite plain that our thought, our power of meaning, is not much helped or hindered by the metaphor that we use. On the contrary, we are often acutely aware of the discrepancy between our meaning and our image. We know that our metaphor is in some respects misleading; and probably, if we have acquired the tutorial shuffle, we warn our audience that it is 'not to be pressed'. It is apparently possible, in this case at least, to use metaphor and yet to keep our thinking independent of it. But we must observe that it is possible, only because we have other methods of expressing the same idea. We have already our own way of expressing the thing: we could say it, or we suppose that we could say it, literally instead. This clear conception we owe to other sources—to our previous studies. We can adopt the new metaphor as a temporary tool which we dominate and by which we are not dominated ourselves, only because we have other tools in our box.

Let us now take the opposite situation—that in which it is we ourselves who are being instructed. I am no mathematician; and some one is trying to explain to me the theory that space is finite. Stated thus, the new doctrine is, to me, meaningless. But suppose he proceeds as follows.

'You', he may say, 'can intuit only three dimensions; you therefore cannot conceive how space should be limited. But I think I can show you how that which must appear infinite in three dimensions, might nevertheless be finite in four. Look at it this way. Imagine a race of people who knew only two dimensions—like the Flatlanders.[1] And suppose they were living on a globe. They would have no conception, of course, that the globe was curved—for it is curved round in that third dimension of which they have no inkling. They will therefore imagine that they are living on a plane; but they will soon find out that it is a plane which nowhere comes to an end; there are no edges to it. Nor would they be able even to imagine an edge. For an edge would mean that, after a certain point, there would be nothing to walk on; nothing below their feet. But that *below* and *above* dimension is just what their minds have not got; they have only backwards and forwards, and left and right. They would thus be forced to assert that their globe, which they could not see as a globe, was infinite. You can see perfectly well that it is finite. And now, can you not conceive that as these Flatlanders are to you, so you might be to a creature that intuited four dimensions? Can you not conceive how that which seems necessarily infinite to your three-dimensional consciousness might none the less be really finite?' The result of such a metaphor on my mind would be—in fact, has been—that something which before was sheerly meaningless acquires at least a faint hint of meaning. And if the particular example does not appeal to every one, yet every one has had experiences of the same sort. For all of us there are things which we cannot fully understand at all, but of which we can get a faint inkling by means of metaphor. And in such cases the relation between the thought and the metaphor is precisely the opposite of the relation which arises when it is we ourselves who understand and then invent the metaphors to help others. We are here entirely at the mercy of the metaphor. If our instructor has chosen it badly, we shall be thinking nonsense. If we have not got the imagery clearly before us, we shall be thinking nonsense. If we have it before us without knowing that it is metaphor—if we forget that our Flatlanders on their globe are a copy of the thing and mistake them for the thing itself—then again we shall be thinking nonsense. What truth we can attain in such a situation depends rigidly on three conditions. First, that the imagery should be originally well chosen; secondly, that we should apprehend the exact imagery; and thirdly that we should know that the metaphor is a metaphor. (That metaphors misread as statements of fact are the source of monstrous errors need hardly be pointed out.)

[1] The inhabitants in the book by 'A Square' [Edwin A. Abbott], *Flatland. A romance of many dimensions* (London, 1884).

I have now attempted to show two different kinds of metaphorical situation as they are at their birth. They are the two extremes, and furnish the limits within which our inquiry must work. On the one hand, there is the metaphor which we invent to teach by; on the other, the metaphor from which we learn. They might be called the Master's metaphor, and the Pupil's metaphor. The first is freely chosen; it is one among many possible modes of expression; it does not at all hinder, and only very slightly helps, the thought of its maker. The second is not chosen at all; it is the unique expression of a meaning that we cannot have on any other terms; it dominates completely the thought of the recipient; his truth cannot rise above the truth of the original metaphor. And between the Master's metaphor and the Pupil's there comes, of course, an endless number of types, dotted about in every kind of intermediate position. Indeed, these Pupil-Teachers' metaphors are the ordinary stuff of our conversation. To divide them into a series of classes and sub-classes and to attempt to discuss these separately would be very laborious, and, I trust, unnecessary. If we can find a true doctrine about the two extremes, we shall not be at a loss to give an account of what falls between them. To find the truth about any given metaphorical situation will merely be to plot its position. In so far as it inclines to the 'magistral' extreme, so far our thought will be independent of it; in so far as it has a 'pupillary' element, so far it will be the unique expression, and therefore the iron limit of our thinking. To fill in this framework would be, as Aristotle used to say, 'anybody's business'.

Our problem, it will be remembered, was the problem of 'dead' or 'forgotten' metaphors. We have now gained some light on the relation between thought and metaphor as it is at the outset, when the metaphor is first made; and we have seen that this relation varies greatly according to what I have called the 'metaphorical situation'. There is, in fact, one relation in the case of the Master's metaphor, and an almost opposite relation in that of the Pupil's metaphor. The next step must clearly be to see what becomes of these two relations as the metaphors in question progress to the state of death or fossilization.

The question of the Master's Metaphor need not detain us long. I may attempt to explain the Kantian philosophy to a pupil by the following metaphor. 'Kant answered the question "How do I know that whatever comes round the corner will be blue?" by the supposition "I am wearing blue spectacles."' In time I may come to use 'the blue spectacles' as a kind of shorthand for the whole Kantian machinery of the categories and forms of perception. And let us suppose, for the sake of analogy with the real history of language, that I continue to use this expression long after I have forgotten the metaphor which originally gave rise to it. And perhaps by this time the form of the word will have changed. Instead of the 'blue spectacles' I may now talk of the *bloospel* or even the *bluspel*. If I live long enough to reach my dotage I may even enter on a philological period in which I attempt to find the derivation of this mysterious word. I may suppose that the second element is derived from the word *spell* and look back with interest on the supposed period when Kant appeared to me to be magical; or else, arguing that the whole word is clearly formed on the analogy of *gospel*, may indulge in unhistorical reminiscences of the days when the *Critique*[1] seemed to me irrefragably true. But how far, if at all, will my thinking about Kant be affected by all this linguistic process? In practice, no doubt, there will be some subtle influence; the mere continued use of the word *bluspel* may have led me to attribute to it a unity and substantiality which I should have hesitated to attribute to 'the whole Kantian machinery of the categories and forms of perception'. But that is a result rather of the noun-making than of the death of the metaphor. It is an interesting fact, but hardly relevant to our present inquiry. For the rest, the mere forgetting of the metaphor does not seem to alter my thinking about Kant, just as the original metaphor did not limit my thinking about Kant; provided always—and this is of the last importance—that it was, to begin with, a genuine Master's metaphor. I had my conception of Kant's philosophy before I ever thought of the blue spectacles. If I have continued philosophical studies I have it still. The 'blue spectacles' phrase was from the first a temporary dress assumed by my thought for a special purpose, and ready to be laid aside at my pleasure; it did not penetrate the thinking itself, and its subsequent history is irrelevant. To any one who attempts to refute my later views on Kant by telling me that I don't know the real meaning of *bluspel*, I may confidently retort 'Derivations aren't meanings.' To be sure, if there was any *pupillary* element in its original use, if I received, as well as gave, new understanding when I used it, then the whole situation will be different.

[1] Immanuel Kant, *Critique of Practical Reason, and other works on the Theory of Ethics*, trans. T. K. Abbott (London, 1879).

And it is fair to admit that in practice very few metaphors can be purely magistral; only that which to some degree enlightens ourselves is likely to enlighten others. It is hardly possible that when I first used the metaphor of the blue spectacles I did not gain some new awareness of the Kantian philosophy; and, so far, it was not purely magistral. But I am deliberately idealizing for the sake of clarity. Purely magistral metaphor may never occur. What is important for us is to grasp that *just in so far* as any metaphor began by being magistral, so far I can continue to use it long after I have forgotten its metaphorical nature, and my thinking will be neither helped nor hindered by the fact that it was originally a metaphor, nor yet by my forgetfulness of that fact. It is a mere accident. Here, derivations are irrelevant to meanings.

Let us now turn to the opposite situation, that of the Pupil's Metaphor. And let us continue to use our old example of the unmathematical man who has had the finitude of space suggested to him (we can hardly say 'explained') by the metaphor of the Flatlanders on their sphere. The question here is rather more complicated. In the case of the Master's metaphor, by hypothesis, the master knew, and would continue to know, what he meant, independently of the metaphor. In the present instance, however, the fossilization of the metaphor may take place in two different ways. The pupil may himself become a mathematician, or he may remain as ignorant of mathematics as he was before; and in either case, he may continue to use the metaphor of the Flatlanders while forgetting its real content and its metaphorical nature.

I will take the second possibility first. From the imagery of the Flatlanders' sphere I have got my first inkling of the new meaning. My thought is entirely conditioned by this imagery. I do not apprehend the thing at all, except by seeing 'it could be something like this'. Let us suppose that in my anxiety to docket this new experience, I label the inkling or vague notion 'the Flatlanders' sphere'. When I next hear the fourth dimension spoken of, I shall say, 'Ah yes—the Flatlanders' sphere and all that.' In a few years (to continue our artificial parallel) I may be talking glibly of the *Flalansfere* and may even have forgotten the whole of the imagery which this word once represented. And I am still, according to the hypothesis, profoundly ignorant of mathematics. My situation will then surely be most ridiculous. The meaning of *Flalansfere* I never knew except through the imagery. I could get beyond the imagery, to that whereof the imagery was a copy, only by learning mathematics; but this I have neglected to do. Yet I have lost the imagery. Nothing remains, then, but the conclusion that the word *Flalansfere* is now really meaningless. My thinking, which could never get beyond the imagery, at once its boundary and its support, has now lost that support. I mean strictly nothing when I speak of the *Flalansfere*. I am only talking, not thinking, when I use the word. But this fact will be long concealed from me because *Flalansfere*, being a noun, can be endlessly fitted into various contexts so as to conform to syntactical usage and to give an appearance of meaning. It will even conform to the logical rules; and I can make many judgements about the *Flalansfere*; such as *it is what it is*, and has *attributes* (for otherwise of course it wouldn't be a thing, and if it wasn't a thing, how could I be talking about it?), and is a *substance* (for it can be the subject of a sentence). And what *affective* overtones the word may have taken on by that time it is dangerous to predict. It had an air of mystery from the first: before the end I shall probably be building temples to it, and exhorting my countrymen to fight and die for the *Flalansfere*. But the *Flalansfere*, when once we have forgotten the metaphor, is only a noise.

But how if I proceed, after once having grasped the metaphor of the Flatlanders, to become a mathematician? In this case, too, I may well continue to use the metaphor, and may corrupt it in form till it becomes a single noun, the *Flalansfere*. But I shall have advanced, by other means, from the original symbolism; and I shall be able to study the thing symbolized without reference to the metaphor that first introduced me to it. It will then be no harm though I should forget that *Flalansfere* had ever been metaphorical. As the metaphor, even if it survived, would no longer limit my thoughts, so its fossilization cannot confuse them.

The results which emerge may now be summarized as follows. Our thought is independent of the metaphors we employ in so far as these metaphors are optional: that is, in so far as we are able to have the same idea without them. For that is the real characteristic both of the magistral metaphors and of those which become optional, as the Flatlanders would become, if the pupil learned mathematics. On the other hand, where the metaphor is our only method of reaching a given idea at all, there our thinking is limited by the metaphor so long as we retain the metaphor; and when the metaphor becomes fossilized, our 'thinking' is not thinking at all, but mere sound or mere incipient movements in the larynx. We are now in a position to reply to the statement that 'Derivations are not meanings', and to claim that 'we know what we mean by words without knowing the fossilized metaphors they contain'. We can see that such a statement, as it stands, is neither wholly true nor wholly false. The truth will vary from word to word, and from speaker to speaker. No rule of thumb is possible, we must take every case on its merits. A word can bear a meaning in the mouth of a speaker who has forgotten its hidden metaphor, and a meaning independent of that metaphor, but only on certain conditions. Either the metaphor must have been optional from the beginning, and have remained optional through all the generations of its use, so that the conception has always used and still uses the imagery as a mere tool; or else, at some period subsequent to its creation, we must have gone on to acquire, independently of the metaphor, such new knowledge of the object indicated by it as enables us now, at least, to dispense with it. To put the same thing in another way, meaning is independent of derivation only if the metaphor was originally 'magistral'; or if, in the case of an originally pupillary metaphor, some quite new kind of apprehension has arisen to replace the metaphorical apprehension which has been lost. The two conditions may be best illustrated by a concrete example. Let us take the word for *soul* as it exists in the Romance language. How far is a man entitled to say that what he means by the word *âme* or *anima* is quite independent of the image of *breathing*, and that he means just the same (and just as much) whether he happens to know that 'derivation' or not? We can only answer that it depends on a variety of things. I will enumerate all the formal possibilities for the sake of clearness: one of them, of course, is too grotesque to appear for any other purpose.

1. The metaphor may originally have been magistral. Primitive men, we are to suppose, were clearly aware, on the one hand, of an entity called *soul*; and, on the other, of a process or object called *breath*. And they used the second figuratively to suggest the first— presumably when revealing their wisdom to primitive women and primitive children. And we may suppose, further, that this magistral relation to the metaphor has never been lost: that all generations, from the probably arboreal to the man saying 'Blast your soul' in a pub this evening, have kept clearly before them these two separate entities, and used the one metaphorically to denote the other, while at the same time being well able to conceive the soul unmetaphorically, and

using the metaphor merely as a colour or trope which adorned but did not influence their thought. Now if all this were true, it would unquestionably follow that when a man says *anima* his meaning is not affected by the old image of breath; and also, it does not matter in the least whether he knows that the word once suggested that image or not. But of course all this is not true.

2. The metaphor may originally have been pupillary. So far from being a voluntary ornament or pedagogic device, the ideas of *breath* or *something like breath* may have been the only possible inkling that our parents could gain of the soul. But if this was so, how does the modern user of the word stand? Clearly, if he has ceased to be aware of the metaphorical element in *anima*, without replacing the metaphorical apprehension by some new knowledge of the soul, borrowed from other sources, then he will mean nothing by it; we must not, on that account, suppose that he will cease to use it, or even to use it (as we say) intelligibly—i.e. to use it in sentences constructed according to the laws of grammar, and to insert these sentences into those conversational and literary contexts where usage demands their insertion. If, on the other hand, he has some independent knowledge of the entity which our ancestors indicated by their metaphor of breath, then indeed he may mean something.

I take it that it is this last situation in which we commonly suppose ourselves to be. It doesn't matter, we would claim, what the majestic root GNA really stood for: we have learned a great deal about *knowing* since those days, and it is these more recent acquisitions that we use in our thinking. The first name for a thing may easily be determined by some inconsiderable accident. As we learn more, we mean more; the radical meaning of the old syllables does not bind us; what we have learned since has set us free. Assuredly, the accident which led the Romans to call all Hellenes *Graeci* did not continue to limit their power of apprehending Greece. And as long as we are dealing with sensible objects this view is hardly to be disputed. The difficulty begins with objects of thought. It may be stated as follows.

Our claim to independence of the metaphor is, as we have seen, a claim to know the object otherwise than through that metaphor. If we can throw the Flatlanders overboard and still think the fourth dimension, then, and not otherwise, we can forget what *Flalansfere* once meant and still think coherently. That was what happened, you will remember, to the man who went on and learned mathematics. He came to apprehend that of which the Flatlanders' sphere was only the image, and consequently was free to think beyond the metaphor and to forget the metaphor altogether. In our previous account of him, however, we carefully omitted to draw attention to one very remarkable fact: namely, that when he deserted metaphor for mathematics, he did not really pass from symbol to symbolized, but only from one set of symbols to another. The equations and what-nots are as unreal, as metaphorical, if you like, as the Flatlanders' sphere. The mathematical problem I need not pursue further; we see at once that it casts a disquieting light on our linguistic problem. We have hitherto been speaking as if we had two methods of thought open to us: the metaphorical, and the literal. We talked as if the creator of a magistral metaphor had it always in his power to think the same concept *literally* if he chose. We talked as if the present-day user of the word *anima* could prove his right to neglect that word's buried metaphor by turning round and giving us an account of the soul which was not metaphorical at all. That he has power to dispense with the particular metaphor of *breath*, is of course agreed. But we have not yet inquired what he can substitute for it. If we turn to those who are most anxious to tell us about the soul—I mean the psychologists—we shall find that the word *anima* has simply been replaced by complexes, repressions, censors, engrams, and the like. In other words the *breath* has been exchanged for *tyings-up*, *shovings-back*, *Roman magistrates*, and *scratchings*. If we inquire what has replaced the metaphorical *bright sky* of primitive theology, we shall only get a *perfect substance*, that is, a *completely made lying-under*, or—which is very much better, but equally metaphorical—a universal Father, or perhaps (in English) a *loaf-carver*, in Latin a *householder*, in Romance *a person older than*. The point need not be laboured. It is abundantly clear that the freedom from a given metaphor which we admittedly enjoy in some cases is often only a freedom to choose between that metaphor and others.

Certain reassurances may, indeed, be held out. In the first place, our distinction between the different kinds of metaphorical situation can stand; though it is hardly so important as we had hoped. To have a choice of metaphors (as we have in some cases) is to know more than we know when we are the slaves of a unique metaphor. And, in the second place, all description or identification, all direction of our own thought or another's, is not so metaphorical as definition. If, when challenged on the word *anima*, we proceed to define, we shall only reshuffle the buried metaphors; but if we simply say (or think) 'what I am', or 'what is going on in here', we shall have at least something before us which we do not know by metaphor. We shall at least be no worse off than the arboreal psychologists. At the same time, this method will not really carry us far. 'What's going on here' is really the content of *haec anima*: for *anima* we want '*The sort of thing* that is going on here', and once we are committed to *sorts* and *kinds* we are adrift among metaphors.

We have already said that when a man claims to think independently of the buried metaphor in one of his words, his claim may sometimes be allowed. But it was allowed only in so far as he could really supply the place of that buried metaphor with new and independent apprehension of his own. We now see that this new apprehension will usually turn out to be itself metaphorical; or else, what is very much worse, instead of new apprehension we shall have simply words—each word enshrining one more ignored metaphor. For if he does not know the history of *anima*, how should he know the history of the equally metaphorical words in which he defines it, if challenged? And if he does not know their history and therefore their metaphors, and if he cannot define *them* without yet further metaphors, what can his discourse be but an endless ringing of the changes on such *bluspels* and *Flalansferes* as seem to mean, indeed, but do not mean? In reality, the man has played us a very elementary trick. He claimed that he could think without metaphor, and in ignorance of the metaphors fossilized in his words. He made good the claim by pointing to the knowledge of his object which he possessed independently of the metaphor; and the proof of this knowledge was the definition or description which he could produce. We did not at first observe that where we were promised a freedom from metaphor we were given only a power of changing the metaphors in rapid succession. The things he speaks of he has never apprehended *literally*. Yet only such genuinely literal apprehension could enable him to forget the metaphors which he was actually using and yet to have a meaning. Either literalness, or else metaphor understood: one or other of these we must have; the third alternative is nonsense. But literalness we cannot have. The man who does not consciously use metaphors talks without meaning. We might even formulate a rule: the meaning in any given composition is in inverse ratio to the author's belief in his own literalness.

If a man has seen ships and the sea, he may abandon the metaphor of a *sea-stallion* and call a boat a boat. But suppose a man who has never seen the sea, or ships, yet who knows of them just as much as he can glean, say from the following list of *Kenningar*—sea-stallions, winged-logs, wave-riders, ocean-trains. If he keeps all these together in his mind, and knows them for the metaphors they are, he will be able to think of ships, very imperfectly indeed, and under strict limits, but not wholly in vain. But if instead of this he pins his faith on the particular *kenning, ocean-trains*, because that *kenning*, with its comfortable air of machinery, seems to him somehow more safely prosaic, less flighty and dangerous than its fellows, and if, contracting that to the form *oshtrans*, he proceeds to forget that it was a metaphor, then, while he talks grammatically, he has ceased to think of anything. It will not avail him to stamp his feet and swear that he is literal; to say 'An *oshtran* is an *oshtran*, and there's an end. I mean what I mean. What I mean is what I say.'

The remedy lies, indeed, in the opposite direction. When we pass beyond pointing to individual sensible objects, when we begin to think of causes, relations, of mental states or acts, we become incurably metaphorical. We apprehend none of these things except through metaphor: we know of the ships only what the *Kenningar* will tell us. Our only choice is to use the metaphors and thus to think something, though less than we could wish; or else to be driven by unrecognized metaphors and so think nothing at all. I myself would prefer to embrace the former choice, as far as my ignorance and laziness allow me.

To speak more plainly, he who would increase the meaning and decrease the meaningless verbiage in his own speech and writing, must do two things. He must become conscious of the fossilized metaphors in his words; and he must freely use new metaphors, which he creates for himself. The first depends upon knowledge, and therefore on leisure; the second on a certain degree of imaginative ability. The second is perhaps the more important of the two: we are never less the slaves of metaphor than when we are making metaphor, or hearing it new made. When we are thinking hard of the Flatlanders, and at the same time fully aware that they *are* a metaphor, we are in a situation almost infinitely superior to that of the man who talks of the *Flalansfere* and thinks that he is being literal and straightforward.

If our argument has been sound, it leads us to certain rather remarkable conclusions. In the first place it would seem that we must be content with a very modest quantity of thinking as the core of all our talking. I do not wish to exaggerate our poverty. Not all our words are equally metaphorical, not all our metaphors are equally forgotten. And even where the old metaphor is lost there is often a hope that we may still restore meaning by pointing to some sensible object, some sensation, or some concrete memory. But no man can or will confine his cognitive efforts to this narrow field. At the very humblest we must speak of things in the plural; we must point not only to isolated sensations, but to groups and classes of sensations; and the universal latent in every group and every plural inflection cannot be thought without metaphor. Thus far beyond the security of literal meaning all of us, we may be sure, are going to be driven by our daily needs; indeed, not to go thus far would be to abandon reason itself. In practice we all really intend to go much farther. Why should we not? We have in our hands the key of metaphor, and it would be pusillanimous to abandon its significant use, because we have come to realize that its meaningless use is necessarily prevalent. We must indeed learn to use it more cautiously; and one of the chief benefits to be derived from our inquiry is the new standard of criticism which we must henceforward apply both to our own apparent thought and to that of others. We shall find, too, that real meaning, judged by this standard, does not come always where we have learned to expect. *Flalansfere* and *bluspels* will clearly be most prevalent in certain types of writers. The percentage of mere syntax masquerading as meaning may vary from something like 100 per cent. in political writers, journalists, psychologists, and economists, to something like forty per cent. in the writers of children's stories. Some scientists will fare better than others: the historian, the geographer, and sometimes the biologist will speak significantly more often than their colleagues; the mathematician, who seldom forgets that his symbols are symbolic, may often rise for short stretches to ninety per cent. of meaning and ten of verbiage. The philosophers will differ as widely from one another as any of the other groups differ among themselves: for a good metaphysical library contains at once some of the most verbal, and some of the most significant literature in the world. Those who have prided themselves on being literal, and who have endeavoured to speak plainly, with no mystical tomfoolery, about the highest abstractions, will be found to be among the least significant of writers: I doubt if we shall find more than a beggarly five per cent. of meaning in the pages of some celebrated 'tough-minded' thinkers, and how the account of Kant or Spinoza stands, none knows but heaven. But open your Plato, and you will find yourself among the great creators of metaphor, and therefore among the masters of meaning. If we turn to Theology—or rather to the literature of religion—the result will be more surprising still; for unless our whole argument is wrong, we shall have to admit that a man who says *heaven* and thinks of the visible sky is pretty sure to mean more than a man who tells us that heaven is a state of mind. It may indeed be otherwise; the second man may be a mystic who is remembering and pointing to an actual and concrete experience of his own. But it is long, long odds. Bunyan and Dante stand where they did; the scale of Bishop Butler, and of better men than he, flies up and kicks the beam.

It will have escaped no one that in such a scale of writers the poets will take the highest place; and among the poets those who have at once the tenderest care for old words and the surest instinct for the creation of new metaphors. But it must not be supposed that I am in any sense putting forward the imagination as the organ of truth. We are not talking of truth, but of meaning: meaning which is the ante-cedent condition both of truth and falsehood, whose antithesis is not error but nonsense. I am a rationalist. For me, reason is the natural organ of truth; but imagination is the organ of meaning. Imagination, producing new metaphors or revivifying old, is not the cause of truth, but its condition. It is, I confess, undeniable that such a view indirectly implies a kind of truth or rightness in the imagination itself. I said at the outset that the truth we won by metaphor could not be greater than the truth of the metaphor itself; and we have seen since that all our truth, or all but a few fragments, is won by meta-phor. And thence, I confess, it does follow that if our thinking is ever true, then the metaphors by which we think must have been good metaphors. It does follow that if those original equations, between good and light, or evil and dark, between breath and soul and all the others, were from the beginning arbitrary and fanciful—if there is not, in fact, a kind of psycho-physical parallelism (or more) in the universe—then all our thinking is nonsensical. But we cannot, without contradiction, believe it to be nonsensical. And so, admittedly, the view I have taken has metaphysical implications. But so has every view.

19

High and Low Brows

Quick, quick.—Fling *Peregrine Pickle* under the toilet—throw *Roderick Random* into the closet—put *The Innocent Adultery* into *The Whole Duty of Man*—cram *Ovid* behind the bolster—there—put *The Man of Feeling* into your pocket—so, so—now lay *Mrs Chapone* in sight, and leave Fordyce's *Sermons* open on the table.

SHERIDAN

Aristotle often begins his argument with what he calls an Isagoge, a collection of instances which is not, if I understand the matter, intended (like Mill's induction) to prove a general principle, but merely to open our eyes to it. The following instances are meant to form such an isagoge.

1. Not many years ago a lady whose studies I was attempting to supervise, propounded a literary theory of general application which I found myself unable to accept. Applying the elenchus after my fashion I inquired whether her theory would cover *The Tale of Peter Rabbit*. After a silence of some minutes, she asked me if I thought there was any use in introducing such an example into a serious literary discussion. I replied that *Peter Rabbit* was a book and certainly not so bad a book that it could be left outside the classification 'literature'. The lady, who is as honest as she is learned (and whom I mention here with all respect), was not prepared to call *Peter Rabbit* 'bad'. 'Trivial' was the word she finally fixed on. But she was quite sure that doctrines about 'literature' need not apply to it.

2. I have heard of a preparatory school where the library regulations divide the contents of the library into two classes: Good Books and Books. The boys are allowed to take out two Good Books for every one Book. To read a Good Book is meritorious, to read a Book only tolerable. At the same time, those responsible for the regulations have hesitated to label as 'bad' the books which they thus contrast with the 'good'.

3. I have heard the Head of a great college* praise the novels of Anthony Hope and conclude by declaring with enthusiasm, 'They

---

* I have learned since that I misunderstood him, but as my Isagoge is meant for pure illustration, not proof, I have thought it no dishonesty to let the example stand.

are the best "bad" books I've ever read.' Here, it will be seen, the word 'bad' is actually used but used in a sense which admits, inside the class Bad, distinctions of good, better, and best.

4. I have often heard—and who has not?—a plain man praise even to rapture the delightful merits of some favourite story and end with the humble reservation, 'Of course, I know it's not real literature.'

I trust that these four instances are already making clear to you what it is I want to discuss. In all of them we see a distinction made between two kinds of book, to the one of which a certain honour is attached, and to the other a certain note of ignominy. Yet in spite of this there is a reluctance to identify this distinction with the plain distinctions of good from bad or better from worse. Those who uphold the distinction prefer to call the inferior class popular, common, commercial, cheap, trashy, or the like, and the superior class literary, classical, serious, or artistic. In our own time the two odious adjectives *Lowbrow* and *Highbrow* have been introduced as the names of the two classes and bid fair to oust all their rivals. There will also be noticed in the first, third, and fourth of my instances a suggestion that the lowbrow works are so different in kind from the highbrow that they have a goodness and badness of their own, a servile virtue and servile vice peculiar to themselves, that they are to be judged by peculiar standards, and that what is said of literature *simpliciter* is not said of them.

Now it seems to me that in this popular distinction there is some confusion between degrees and kinds of merit. If the lowbrow books are really a special kind of book I do not see how they can be inferior to the high. You cannot be beaten by a man unless you enter the same competition with him, nor overtaken by a man (as Chesterton observes) unless you both run in the same direction. At present the distinction is certainly used to allow us the satisfaction of despising certain authors and readers without imposing on us the labour of showing that they are bad. It is also used, I find, to allow people to enjoy lowbrow art without gratitude on the one hand or shame on the other, and those who would hesitate to say, 'Let's go and see something bad' will cheerfully say 'Let's go to a lowbrow film.' The whole distinction seems to be made in order to enable us to have it both ways.

In the following paper I propose two questions. (1) Is the class of lowbrow books (or 'books' simply as at the Preparatory School) really the class of bad books? (2) If not, is the distinction useful in some other way?[1]

As soon as we approach the first question we notice that even if all the lowbrow books—which I am going to call Class A—are in fact bad, even so the distinction between lowbrow and highbrow—or between class A and class B—will not coincide with the distinction between bad books and good books, for the very obvious reason that class B contains bad books too. *Gorbuduc* and Glover's *Leonidas* and Dyer's *Fleece*, Gabriel Harvey's hexameters and Johnson's *Irene*, Tennyson's tragedies and Southey's epics—all these are classical enough, serious enough, and literary enough, in all conscience. If they entered the school library it would certainly be as Good Books, not as Books. And it will hardly be denied that some of them are bad. In fact, as soon as we look at the question from this point of view, it becomes apparent that class A is not simply the class of bad books. Mere failure does not infallibly give the right of entry to it. If all the books in it are bad it must be with some special sort of badness—an A badness.

But are they all bad? As I have not read the novels of Anthony Hope, I cannot, though my third instance invites me, select them for analysis; but perhaps Rider Haggard will do as well, for his books are certainly in the A class and, in my opinion, some of them are good—are therefore 'good "bad" books' as the Head of that college would say. And of his books I select *She*. If I ask myself why it is that I have more than once read *She* with enjoyment, I find that there is every reason why I should have done so. In the first place the story makes an excellent approach; the central theme is suffered, in the first chapters, to woo us across great distances of space and time. What we are presently to see at close quarters is seen at first, as it were, through the wrong end of the telescope. This is a fine exercise in the art of alluring—you may see the same thing at work in the opening of the *Utopia*, in the second act of *Prometheus Unbound*, and in the early books of the *Odyssey*. In the second place it is a quest story, which is an attractive thing. And the object of the quest combines two strong appeals—it is the 'fountain of youth' theme and the *princesse lointaine* in one. Finally, the withdrawal or conclusion,

---

[1] Lewis later wrote *An Experiment in Criticism* (Cambridge, 1961) in which the 'experiment' consists in judging literature itself by the way men read it. His purpose is, as he says, 'to discover how far it might be plausible to define a good book as a book which is read in one way, and a bad book as a book which is read in another' (p. 1).

which is always the difficulty in quest stories, is effected by unexpected means which are nevertheless, on the author's suppositions, sufficiently plausible. In the conduct of the story the detail is mostly convincing. The characters who are meant to be amiable are amiable and those who are meant to be sinister are sinister. The goodness of *She* is grounded, as firmly as that of any book whatever, on the fundamental laws of the imagination. But there is badness in it as well as goodness. Two things deter us from regarding it as a quite satisfactory romance. One of them is the continuous poverty of the style, by which, of course, I do not mean any failure to conform to certain *a priori* rules, but rather a sloth or incompetence of writing whereby the author is content always with a vague approximation to the emotion, the reflection, or the image he intends, so that a certain smudging and banality is spread over all. The other fault is the shallowness and folly of the things put into the mouth of She herself and offered us for wisdom. That She, in her secular loneliness, should have become a sage, is very proper, and indeed essential to Haggard's story, but Haggard has not himself the wisdom wherewith to supply her. A poet of Dante's depth could have given her things really wise to say; a poet of Shakespeare's address would have made us believe in her wisdom without committing himself.

If my analysis is correct, *She* is not a 'good "bad" book' in the sense of being a good specimen of a bad kind; it is simply good and bad, like many other books, in the sense that it is good in some respects and bad in others. And those who have read it with enjoyment have been enjoying real literary merits, and merits which it shares with the *Odyssey* or *The Life and Death of Jason*. Certainly, it is not a *very* good book, but since its vices are not sufficient to overwhelm its virtues (as the experience of many wiser readers than I has proved) it is better, say, than *Leonidas* or the *Epic of Hades*. In other words, this book of the A class is better than some books of the B class. It is better by every test; it shows more skill in the author and produces more pleasure in the reader; it is more in touch with the permanent nature of our imagination; it leaves those who have read it richer. And with this, the attempt to identify the classes A and B with the classes bad and good or worse and better has surely collapsed.[1]

[1] For more detailed criticism of Haggard's romances see Lewis's essays, 'On Stories' *Of Other Worlds: Essays and Stories*, ed. Walter Hooper (London, 1966), pp. 5 ff. and 'Haggard Rides Again', *Time and Tide*, vol. XLI (3 September 1960), pp. 1044–5.

We must now cast about for some other possible definition of the two classes; and it comes at once into my mind that the lady in my first instance ruled *Peter Rabbit* out as 'trivial'. Perhaps the A class consists of trivial, and the B class of grave, or weighty, or momentous books. I think that those who use the A–B antithesis very often have something of this sort in their mind, but it is difficult to fix the exact sense of any of the words they use to express it. It is clear that the contrast cannot be simply between comic and serious, for then the stories in our Parish Magazine would be labelled B and *Le Misanthrope*, A. It might be argued, no doubt, that Molière's play, though comic, is momentous as touching life at many points and dealing with the depths of our nature, and this might furnish the ground for a restatement of the distinction—B books being 'momentous' in the sense just suggested, while A books touch us only superficially, or concern only highly specialized areas of our consciousness. But this would make *The Importance of Being Earnest* an A. Nor is it clear that all the books already in the A class are thus superficial. They are often accused of being 'sentimental'; and this charge, on inspection, often conceals an admission that their appeal is to emotions very basic and universal—to the same emotions that are concerned in great tragedies. Even Dr Richards's *Boosey Ballad*,* which is not only A but bad simply, has a theme that Petrarch might not have disdained. Indeed, the more I look into it the more I am convinced that any contrast of weighty and frivolous, solid and slight, deep and shallow, must cut right across the A and B distinction. How many of the most perfect things are, after all, trifles! The weighty and frivolous are kinds of literature, and in each kind we shall find good A's, bad A's, good B's, and bad B's. This is not what we are looking for.

Among the lowbrows themselves I find that the distinction is often based on style. When the plain man confesses that the books he delights in are not 'real Literature' he will often, if pressed, explain this by saying that they 'haven't got style' or 'style and all that'. And when the plain man has been captured and made into a pathetically willing and bewildered university student he will sometimes praise the great works which he has dutifully read and not enjoyed, for the excellence of their style. He has missed the jokes in the comedy, remained unmoved by the tragedy, failed to respond to the suggestions of the lyric, and found the episodes of the romance uninteresting;

* See his *Principles of Literary Criticism*, ch. 24.

utterly at a loss to explain the value traditionally set on what has proved to him so tedious, he hands it over to the thing he knows least about, to a mysterious entity called Style, which is to him merely what occult forces were to the old scientists—an *asylum ignorantiae*. He does so because he has a radically false conception of style. He thinks of it not as the linguistic means by which the writer produces whatever results he desires but as a sort of extra—an uncovenanted pedantry tacked on to the book proper, to gratify some specifically 'literary' or 'critical' taste which has nothing to do with the ordinary pleasures of the imagination. It is for him a meaningless addition which, by a convention, gives access to a higher rank—like the letters Esq. after a man's name on an envelope. Now it must be confessed that the highbrows sometimes talk of style in a way which gives their weaker brethren some excuse for such misconceptions; but I think that most of them, in a cool hour, would admit that 'Style', in the sense in which the lowbrow uses the word, does not exist. When we say that the descriptions of country in *She* are marred by their deficiency of style, we do not mean (as the ignorant suppose) that they are good as descriptions but lacking in some abstractly 'literary' and undescriptive grace which might have been superadded; we mean that they are imperfect descriptions; and we call their imperfection 'stylistic' because it is due not to faults in the author's conception but to his careless or insensitive language. A better choice of epithets, and those distant mountains would have stood out sharper on the horizon; a well chosen metaphor, and the whole picture, now dimly discerned through seas of wasteful words, would have printed itself for ever on the inner eye; a nobler rhythm, and the sense of space and movement would have been given us, not left, as it now is, for us to infer. Turn from *She* to almost any page in *Eōthen*, and you will soon see what style in a descriptive passage means. There is no class of books which can be 'good in their own way' without bothering about style. There are books in which what the author is saying imperfectly, partly failing to say, is sufficiently interesting to keep us reading in spite of his failure. Though he has done only half his work, we are content to do some of it for him. Such books are books defective in style. And they do not come only in class A. Scott, Dickens, Byron, Spenser, Alanus, and Apuleius have detestable faults of style, but they are usually put in class B. St Paul, despite some passages of striking beauty, seems to me to write badly, but he is hardly an A; and I have found in the style of Donne, Chapman, Meredith, Saintsbury, and others, obstacles to the enjoyment of what they have to give me as great as those I find in Rider Haggard. It is not important here that any reader should agree with the instances I am choosing; what matters is the recognition that badness of style (like triviality) will be found in B books. It cannot be made the basis of a dichotomy between two kinds of book.

Another common way of using the distinction tends to fix on 'popular' as the best adjective for class A. 'Popular' art is supposed to aim at mere *entertainment*, while 'real' or 'serious' art aims at some specifically 'artistic' or 'aesthetic' or even 'spiritual' satisfaction. This is an attractive view because it would give those who hold it a ground for maintaining that popular literature has its own good and bad, according to its own rules, distinct from those of Literature proper. The popular novel aiming only at passing the reader's time, the popular comedy content to raise a laugh, and be forgotten, the popular tragedy which only wants to give us 'a good cry', would have their low, separate, legitimate places. And since I observe that many of my highest-browed acquaintances spend much of their time in talking of the vulgarity of popular art, and therefore must know it well, and could not have acquired that knowledge unless they enjoyed it, I must assume that they would welcome a theory which justified them in drinking freely of that fountain without forfeiting their superiority. But there is a troublesome difficulty in this form of the distinction. We know, without going to look, that the Good Books in that preparatory school library would include the novels of Scott and Dickens. But these, in their own day, were popular *entertainment*, best sellers. Some of the contemporary highbrows may retort that they ought never to have been allowed into the B class. I do not agree, but let us concede it. Let us even concede the same about Scott's poems, and about Byron, which were also once A's and are now B's. But what of Fielding, of Malory, of Shakespeare and all his colleagues? Of the metrical romances? Of Ovid, scribbled on the walls at Pompeii? What of Molière, finding the best judge of his work in the old woman who never failed to laugh in the same place as the audience—the audience whom he wrote to please? What, in another art, of Mozart's operas? It is not sufficient to say that a work designed for the popular market may sometimes, by a happy freak, outshoot its mark. The thing has happened too often to be called a freak. What survives from most ages is chiefly either the work that had some religious or national appeal, or else the popular, commercial work produced for entertainment. I say 'chiefly' because the work of the 'pure' artists is not always ephemeral; a little, a very little, of it survives. But the great mass of literature which now fills class B is the work of men who wrote either piously, to edify their fellows, or commercially, to earn their living by 'giving the public what it wanted'.

This leads to the very interesting conclusion that the B's of one age have most often been the A's of another. We are sometimes warned by the supporters of difficult new movements in literature not to imitate our fathers in stoning the prophets; those who dislike Pound or Joyce are told 'so you would have disliked Wordsworth and Shelley if you had lived then'. The warning may be useful, but clearly it should be supplemented by another—'Beware how you scorn the best sellers of today; they may be classics for the intelligentsia of the Twenty-Third Century.'

If our age is known to posterity not as that of Eliot and Auden but as that of Buchan and Wodehouse (and stranger things have come to pass), Buchan and Wodehouse will then be B's and little boys will get good marks for reading them. Shakespeare and Scott, once A's, are now B's. If we could find what it is that the mere passage of time does to a book, we should have found out something about the real nature of the A and B distinction. And surely, it is obvious that what time does to a book is to make it difficult. There are indeed other operations of time. It makes a book more widely known or spreads on it that rich patina we now enjoy in Virgil or Malory; but neither of these would furnish the basis for a B class since this is to include contemporary books as well. We want a quality which some books have at once but which mere time can confer on books that originally lacked it; and difficulty seems to be the quality required. It would be amusing if difficulty turned out to be the real criterion of Literature, Good Books, or classics—if a comedy which was mere commercial art as long as every one could see the jokes became aesthetic and spiritual as soon as you need commentators to explain them. Yet I think this comes much nearer to the ground of the distinction actually made than any of the hypotheses we have yet discussed.

A distinction simply between easy and difficult books is a reasonable one; and it is certainly better to be able to enjoy both kinds than to be limited to the easy. A man who has hitherto relished only the easy and now learns to relish the difficult as well, may properly be said to have improved his taste, for enlargement, other things being equal, is improvement. But there is a great difference between improvement in this sense—the mere enlargement of a taste which may already have been perfectly good within its own limits—and improvement in the sense of correction or of conversion from the bad to the good. There is also a great difference between the easy and the bad. No book can be bad because it is easy or good because it is hard: a book may be bad because it is hard. If ease and difficulty is the real antithesis behind the A and B distinction, then the distinction is being widely misused and from the true premise 'it is better to advance to the difficult books (without leaving the easy ones) if you can' some draw the false conclusions that the difficult books are better and that you can advance to them only by leaving the easy ones behind. We shall see presently the psychological causes of this error.

Closely connected with this form of the distinction is that other which makes 'vulgarity' the criterion of an A book. It might be sufficient in answer to this to inquire what sense can possibly be given to the word Vulgar which will apply to the work of Beatrix Potter, John Buchan, George Birmingham, P. G. Wodehouse, 'Somerville and Ross', and a dozen more writers of the A class. But Vulgar is a word so difficult and, in our days, so ubiquitous that perhaps we should examine it more closely. It seems to me to have two principal meanings. In its first sense it is a purely privative term meaning 'not refined', 'not subtle or delicate or many-sided'. What is vulgar in this sense (cf. 'the vulgar tongue') may be perfectly good: to lack refinement or subtlety when refinement or subtlety are not required is no blemish. Thus the line

Then come kiss me, sweet and twenty[1]

is, in its context, good and yet 'vulgar' because it expresses a conception of love neither elevated nor discriminating, and this is all that the song requires. The very same line would be vulgar in a bad sense if any one were absurd enough to put it into the mouth of Launcelot addressing Guinevere after he has broken the bars or Zeus addressing Danae as he merges from the shower of gold. From this point of view we might admit that all A literature is and ought to be irreproachably 'vulgar'. It ought to deal strongly and simply with strong, simple

[1] *Twelfth-Night*, II, iii, 54.

emotions: the directness, the unelaborate, downright portraiture of easily recognizable realities in their familiar aspects, will not be a fault unless it pretends to be something else. If it essays, without delicacy, that which demands delicacy, it will then become faultily vulgar; but the whole art of good A writers stands upon not doing so. But there is a second sense of Vulgar; it may be used to mean something essentially and, in the long run, morally, bad: the base, the mean, the ignoble. These terms themselves are ambiguous, but perhaps an example will make the matter clear. The best instance I know of Vulgarity in this evil sense occurs in Chapman's *Iliad*. Homer has said of the old men on the wall,

Οἱ δ' ὡς οὖν εἴδονθ' Ἑλένην ἐπὶ πύργον ἰοῦσαν,
ἦκα πρὸς ἀλλήλους ἔπεα πτερόεντ' ἀγόρευον.[1]

Chapman translates

when they sawe the powre
Of beautie, in the Queene ascend; euen those *cold-spirited* Peeres,
Those wise, and almost withered men, found *this heate* in their yeares,
That they were forc't (though whispering) to say, &c.[2]

I do not mean, of course, that the suggestion of senile eroticism which Chapman has foisted on the original is in itself and necessarily vulgar; a man might make good lines, whether comic or tragic, even on this subject. But to have let it creep in here of all places, to be unaware of gulfs of difference between this and anything Homer need be supposed to have meant, argues an ungentle heart and a bestial ignorance of the whole hierarchy of human feelings. It is something more than lack of delicacy where delicacy is required (though of course it is that too); it is a fatal, unconscious welcome held out to the lower when the lower has offered to usurp the place of the higher, 'a downward appetite to mix with mud'. And we cannot here avoid such words as Lower and Higher, for Vulgar, in its deeper sense, is really a term of moral reproof. It has nothing to do with the distinction of popular and classic. It is low hearts and not low brows that are vulgar.*

We have now made a fairly determined effort to find some useful

---

* Another example, more venial, but perhaps even clearer, of such vulgarity, occurs when Dryden renders *Quare agite, o tectis, iuvenes, succedite nostris* (*Aen.* 1, 627), 'Enter, my noble guest, and you shall find, If not a costly welcome, yet a kind.' The descent here is to the 'genteel'. Cf. Gavin Douglas's excellent version of the same line.

[1] *Iliad*, III, 154-5.
[2] *Homer Prince of Poets, Translated according to the Greeke, in twelue Bookes of his Iliads* (London, [1610?]), p. 43.

meaning for the separation of literature into the two classes of classical and popular, Good Books and Books, literary and commercial, highbrow and lowbrow, and we have failed. In fact, the distinction rests upon a confusion between degrees of merit and differences of kind. Our map of literature has been made to look like an examination list—a single column of names with a horizontal line drawn across it, the honour candidates above that line, and the pass candidates below it. But we ought rather to have a whole series of vertical lines representing different kinds of work, and an almost infinite series of horizontal lines crossing these to represent the different degrees of goodness in each kind. Thus 'Simple Adventure Story' is a vertical line with the *Odyssey* at the top and Edgar Wallace at the bottom; Rider Haggard, R. L. Stevenson, Scott, William Morris will be placed on horizontal lines crossing 'Adventure Story' at such heights as we may decide. 'Psychological Story' is a separate column, with its own top (Tolstoy or another) and its own bottom. With such a picture in our minds we should avoid the confusion of those who say to a boy, 'You should not read trash like *King Solomon's Mines*. Try Meredith.' Such an exhortation urges him at once to move horizontally, from one kind to another, and vertically, from the less good to the better. But you are also doing something worse; you are instilling into his mind a notion (often henceforward indelible) that the pleasure he already has in not very good books is of a quite different nature from anything he is to expect in 'real literature'—that the latter is something to be read 'in school', an affair of marks and School Certificates and conceit and self-improvement.

I believe that this misconception is likely to grow and to be one day no longer confined to schoolboys. There are many circumstances which encourage it. Until quite modern times the reading of imaginative literature in a man's own tongue was not regarded as meritorious. The great authors of the past wrote to entertain the leisure of their adult contemporaries, and a man who cared for literature needed no spur and expected no good conduct marks for sitting down to the food provided for him. Boys at school were taught to read Latin and Greek poetry by the birch, and discovered the English poets as accidentally and naturally as they now discover the local cinema. Most of my own generation, and many, I hope, of yours, tumbled into literature in that fashion. Of each of us some great poet made a rape when we still wore Eton collars. Shall we be thought immodest if we claim that most of the books we loved from the first were good books and our earliest loves are still unrepented? If so, that very fact bears witness to the novelty of the modern situation; to us, the claim that we have always liked Keats is no prouder than the claim that we have always liked bacon and eggs.

For there are changes afoot. The growth of English Schools at Universities, the School Certificate, and the Educational Ladder—all excellent things—may yet produce unexpected results. I foresee the growth of a new race of readers and critics to whom, from the very outset, good literature will be an accomplishment rather than a delight,[1] and who will always feel, beneath the acquired taste, the backward tug of something else which they feel merit in resisting. Such people will not be content to say that some books are bad or not very good; they will make a special class of 'lowbrow' art which is to be vilified, mocked, quarantined, and sometimes (when they are sick or tired) enjoyed. They will be sure that what is popular must always be bad, thus assuming that human taste is *naturally* wrong, that it needs not only improvement and development but veritable conversion. For them a good critic will be, as the theologians say, essentially a 'twice-born' critic, one who is regenerate and washed from his Original Taste. They will have no conception, because they have had no experience, of spontaneous delight in excellence. Their 'good' taste will have been acquired by the sweat of their brows, its acquisition will often (and legitimately) have coincided with advancement in the social and economic scale, and they will hold it with uneasy intensity. As they will be contemptuous of popular books, so they will be naïvely tolerant of dullness and difficulty in any quack or sloven who comes before them with lofty pretensions; *all* literature having been as hard to them as that, so much an acquired taste, they will not see the difference. They will be angry with a true lover of literature who does not take pains to unravel the latest poetical puzzle, and call him a *dilettante*. Having obtained the freedom of Parnassus at a great price, they will be unable to endure the nonchalance of those who were free-born.

---

[1] Those who have read Lewis's autobiography will remember how he lost his literary innocence when, at Malvern College (or 'Wyvern', as he calls it), he began to learn about the glories of literature. He met there, he recalls, 'a world in which a taste for such things was almost meritorious. I felt as Siegfried felt when it first dawned on him that he was not Mime's son. What had been "my" taste was apparently "our" taste ... And if "our" taste, then—by a perilous transition—perhaps "good" taste or "the right taste". For that transition involves a kind of Fall. The moment good taste knows itself, some of its goodness is lost.' (*Surprised by Joy: The Shape of My Early Life* (London, 1955), p. 103.)

The cure for this is not to remove the Educational Ladder, the English Schools, nor the Certificate examinations. If the danger is recognized it can be combated by teaching and by criticism at every point. Those in the predicament I have described can combat it in themselves if they will. A very little attention will soon discover in any 'lowbrow' book what is really good and really bad, and will show us the very same kinds of goodness and badness in books that are lowbrow. A little patience, a little humility, and all will be well. It is the vanity of new acquisitions and the lazy desire for over-simplification which threatens to impound a hundred books, some irredeemably bad, some excellently good, in a class which can be dismissed from criticism. A man ought not to be ashamed of reading a good book because it is simple and popular, and he ought not to condone the faults of a bad book because it is simple and popular. He should be able to say (altering the names to suit his own judgement), 'I read Buchan and Eliot for the same reason, because I think them good; I leave Edgar Wallace and Ezra Pound unread for the same reason, because I think them bad.' It is by no means for the protection of bad books that I wish the distinction of high- and lowbrow abolished. That distinction itself protects bad books. As it robs excellent A books of deserved praise, it teaches its victims to tolerate bad A books. Why was Dr Richards reading a bad book when he had influenza?* Was it not that in his illness he needed an easy book, and having lumped all easy books together as contemptible, he made no further distinctions? That is the usual result of having a pariah class. Slavery, while depressing the slave of noble character, allows the vile slave liberties never conceded to the free servant. Those who most despise the class from which prostitutes are recruited are not necessarily those who abstain from fornication. And indeed, I am often shocked at what slips out sometimes about the recreational reading, the off-duty intellectual amusements, of those who are sternest in their contempt for popular art and demand least pleasure of the art they approve.†

---

* See *Practical Criticism* (1929), p. 257. I am sorry to have to mention in this context an admission whose candour deserves so much imitation and a critic whose works are almost the necessary starting-point for all future literary theory. But the point is very important, and *magis amica veritas*.

† A full treatment of the subject broached in this essay would demand consideration of the historical theory that there is some peculiarity in our own age really producing an unprecedented cleavage between the Few and the Many, and imposing on popular

taste the need of veritable conversion. My own view is that such a situation exists, but that the Highbrow-Lowbrow distinction is one of the things that have helped to produce it. If the people have never shown less taste for good books, it is also true that those capable of writing good books have seldom taken less pains to please the people, or, indeed, so freely insulted them. There are members of the *intelligentsia* at present (some of them socialists) who cannot speak of their cultural inferiors except in accents of passionate hatred and contempt. Certainly it is fatal to approach this or any other quarrel with the assumption that all the faults are on one side: and just as certainly, in all quarrels the task of conciliation belongs *jure divino* to the more reasonable of the two disputants.

20

Metre

It seems clear to me that questions like 'How does this line scan?' or 'What is the metre of this poem?' are not questions of the same sort as 'What is bronze?' This is a question about physical fact. But the only physical facts about which a metrical question could be put are presumably phonetic facts. And when we ask how a line scans we cannot be asking simply for the phonetic facts which occur when it is pronounced. For:

(a) If the scansion of a line meant all the phonetic facts, no two lines would scan the same way, for no two different lines are phonetically identical. If, on the other hand, we are asking only for some of the phonetic facts then we must want those which are relevant. But to what? Clearly, not to phonetic fact but to something else.

(b) Individuals differ in their pronunciation of a line. Even a single individual can hardly pronounce it twice in exactly the same way. If scansion meant physically phonetic fact no line would scan twice in the same way.

Are we then asking not how this or that individual reads the line aloud but how he ought to?

Unfortunately, even when we have ruled out gross barbarisms, there remain different and defensible ways of reading poetry aloud and they do not coincide with differences of opinion about metre. The two main schools may be called Minstrels and Actors. They differ about the proper relation between the noises they make and something else; that something else being the thing we are looking for, namely metre. Minstrels, singing or intoning, make their utterance conform to this, leaving you to imagine the rhythm and tempo which the words would have in ordinary speech. Actors give you that rhythm and tempo out loud, leaving you to imagine the metre. Yet both may be fully agreed as to what the metre is. They differ by deliberately making, or refusing to make, an imaginary archetype or paradigm actual. This paradigm is metre. Scansion is the conformity, made audible by Minstrels and concealed by Actors, of the individual line to this paradigm.

When we ask for the metre of a poem we are asking for the paradigm. But again, what sort of question is this? If one man describes our Blank Verse paradigm in terms of 'feet' and another in terms of crotchets and quavers, what sort of difference is the difference between them?

We cannot, or should not, be asking how the poet himself would have described it. As regards the greater part of the world's poetry we do not know the answer to this. And even when poets have told us how they analysed their own metres, it is always open to us to say that their analysis was wrong, that their instinct or genius enabled them to produce what their often limited analytical powers did not enable them to understand.

Our results are so far discouraging. I am therefore going to suggest that metrical questions are profitable only if we regard them, not as questions about fact, but as purely practical. That is, when we ask 'What is the metre of this poem?', we are not, or should not be, asking which analysis of the paradigm is 'true' but which is the most useful. The utility of the analysis would, I submit, be in a direct ratio to the degree in which it gives those who adopt it the following powers:

(1) To say whether, so far as metre goes, a given line could or could not have occurred in a given poem.

(2) To quote any line, if not correctly, yet certainly without any *metricidal* error.

(3) Within any poem to distinguish normal from irregular lines.

(4) To detect textual corruption by the damage it has done to metre.

(5) To teach the metre quickly and easily to others.

That hardly any of our modern students possess these powers every university teacher knows.

Such is my conception of a good—or even 'the right'—analysis. How are we to achieve it?

The first rule is 'Avoid the Inductive Method'. It sounds very plausible to say: 'Let us not be *a priori*. Instead of bringing to the actual lines some arbitrary idea of what is Regular, let us stick to facts—what the poet actually wrote. Let us, without any prejudice, tabulate all the types of line we find in the poem and then, inductively, construct the paradigm to cover them, to *save the appearances*.' This commends itself to a scientific age. But surely it is quite fatal?

For if you proceed thus you will have no irregular lines at all. If your inductive paradigm 'gets them in', they have become regular. That is, they are specimens of alternatives, though rather rare ones, among those which the paradigm prescribes. In fact, they are like Virgil's *procumbit humi bos*, which does not break the hexametrical paradigm at all but fulfils it in an unusual way.

But that is not what irregular lines do in English poetry. A poem in Latin hexameters where every single line ended in a monosyllable would be a very bad poem but it would still be unmistakably in hexameters. Similarly if Shelley's 'The weight of the superincumbent hour'* were really one of the alternatives allowed in Shelley's paradigm, then a whole poem in such lines, though a bad poem, ought to be still a poem in the metre of *Adonais*. If this line fulfils the paradigm, no succession of such lines could break it.

Well, try:
> The weight of the superincumbent hour,
> The blows of a darkly returning power,
> The roll of the breakers and (while we speak)
> The glare of the sun on a faded flower,
> The blight of the moon on a fevered cheek.

This is not the metre of *Adonais* at all. Worse still, it is a metre: a quite different one. So with Milton's 'Burnt after them to the bottomless pit'.† Add 'Hell then received the unfortunate crew' and a few more such lines and you will get a new and perfectly recognisable (though detestable) metre.

Inductively constructed paradigms thus fail because they 'cover the facts' *too well*. A formula which accommodates all the actual lines accommodates lines which, if repeated, would not be in the metre of the poem. We must adopt exactly the opposite procedure. We must not begin with individual lines, nor even with classified types of line. We must begin with the whole poem. That, if it is any good, will teach you the tune, the pattern, the paradigm. It is only in relation to this that the lines are lines at all.

The paradigm is theoretically, or ostensibly, or by legal fiction, or by make-believe, obeyed in every single line. In many lines it is actually obeyed. The continual approximations to and recessions from actual obedience, as of waves on a beach, make much of the excellence of any long poem. If you once start monkeying with the paradigm so as to 'get in' all the lines, this beauty is lost. One does not want the shore as well as the sea to be in motion.

* *Adonais*, 283.   † *Paradise Lost*, VI, 866.

The irregular lines are those in which the make-believe is strained to the utmost point. 'The weight of the superincumbent hour' is feigned to be, or deemed to be, 'The wéight of thé supérincúmbent hóur'; and 'Burnt after them to the bottomless pit', to be 'Burnt áfter thém to thé bottómless pít'. Of course not even the hardiest Minstrel would so read them. But equally the hardiest Actor is not appreciating them as verse at all unless his inner ear still hears the inner metronome ticking away. It has been set ticking by all the thousands of decasyllabic lines he has ever read.

If it ceased to tick, nearly all the merit of such lines would vanish. In Shelley's, the very laboriousness of the suggested pronunciation ('the supérincúmbent') symbolizes the burden of the hour; in Milton's, the denial, in fact, of the accents suggested by the metronome gives the sense of falling into a void.

When it comes to defining the paradigm, say, of decasyllabic verse, I do not see how we can avoid saying that each line contains five units of some sort. We do not of course mean, as some apparently think, that the poet 'built them up' out of such units, as a bricklayer builds a wall out of pre-existing bricks. Nor do we mean that any reader makes pauses between these units in pronunciation. We mean that wherever the paradigm is completely obeyed, analysis cannot help finding that certain phonetic configurations occur five times in the line.

Much metrical controversy is concerned merely with nomenclature; whether we should talk about these units as 'feet' or in some other language. Here again I maintain that we should be guided by utility.

Musical notation I would rule out at once. Book-lovers will not like the look, nor publishers the cost, of a page all spotted over with musical notation. Nor will it be of any use to readers of poetry unless they are also musicians.

The stock argument against calling the units by classical names (*feet*—or, in particular, *iambi*, *trochees*, and the rest) is that they are not really the same as the units of ancient verse. And even if we warn the student that the so-called English iambus is not to be confused with the quantitative iambus, he will in fact be encouraged to read Latin poetry in the wrong way. This has certainly done much harm to schoolboys in the past. They have been allowed to think that Virgil's hexameters ended with the tempo of 'strawberry jam-pot', when they were probably most often like 'All men have idols'—in fact, more like the slow movement of the Seventh Symphony and less like the *Walkürenritt*.

But it will be noticed that the whole danger here is not to the student's English, but to his Latin, reading. This was certainly so in my own experience. Metrics of this type spoiled my appreciation of Latin poetry for years; I have never been able to find that they did my English studies anything but good. But if this is so, then the main objection to the classical nomenclature in English poetics is already out of date. We need not be afraid of encouraging our pupils to read Latin wrongly because we know they are not going to read Latin at all. We need no precaution against corns in a man who has already had both his legs amputated at the hip.

This being so, it is surely time to re-avail ourselves of the enormous advantages which the classical terms offer. They are as follows:

(1) If you talk of feet everyone knows what you mean. Do not be deceived by those purists who will reply, 'I never know what people mean by a foot in connection with English verse.' That's only their fun. They know perfectly well that you mean the things which come seven times in a fourteener, five times in a blank verse line, and four times in an octosyllabic. If, on the other hand, you devise what you take to be a more scientific language, you will never in discussing this or that line (outside your own book) be able to use it without explanation. Even if it won universal acceptance it would be swept away by the next, and even purer, purist. Almost any agreed terminology is better than a perpetual reformation.

(2) If I am allowed to use all the classical names I can describe shortly and clearly all the metrical phenomena in English verse. If I may not speak of Choriambics I must take endless trouble to write, and you to read, any reference to what is happening in 'This, this is he; softly awhile . . . or do my eyes misrepresent?' (*Samson Agonistes*, 115–24).

(3) It enables us to present paradigms hard, jejune, dry, as paradigms ought to be, uninfected by questions of beauty. We need metrics if we are to become fully sensitive to poetry, as we need grammar before we can enjoy Homer and anatomy before we can draw. But the less these studies get mixed up with 'sensibility' the more they will ultimately do for it.

(4) Have you ever had a pupil *not* brought up on this scheme who was aware of metre at all? We are coming to acquiesce in a hair-

raising barbarism on this subject. I have met an undergraduate who, after reading it, thought *The Prelude* was written in Spenserian stanzas. Hardly one out of five Honours candidates can quote three or four lines of blank verse without false lineation. Every day we hear Donne praised for startling metrical audacity in passages where the metre is as regular as anyone else's. It is plain that our present methods do not work. Might we not go back to one that did?

Psycho-Analysis and Literary Criticism

The purpose of this paper is by no means to attack psycho-analysis, but only to contribute to the solution of some frontier problems between psycho-analysis and literary criticism. One of these I consider a pseudo-problem. I am referring to the use which some critics make of psycho-analysis to infer the pathology of a poet from his work. When this is all that is done, and when it is made quite clear that the result is intended as a contribution not to literary criticism but to pathology, or pathological biography, I have, of course, nothing, good or bad, to say to it. Unfortunately, however, we sometimes meet with a real confusion in which the proposition 'This poem is an inevitable outcome, and an illuminating symptom, of the poet's repressions' is somehow treated as an answer to the proposition 'This poem is rubbish.' The critic has allowed himself to be diverted from the genuinely critical question 'Why, and how, should we read this?' to the purely historical question 'Why did he write it?'—and that, too, in a sense which makes the word 'why' mean not 'with what intention?' but 'impelled by what causes?' He is asking not for the Final Cause, which would still have some literary importance, but for the Efficient, which has none. With misunderstandings of this kind we need not concern ourselves.

I am going to deal with two Freudian positions, of which one will be found in the twenty-third of the *Introductory Lectures*. At the end of that lecture all art is traced to the fantasies—that is the day-dreams or waking wish-fulfilments—of the artist. The artist wants 'honour, power, riches, fame and the love of women',* but being unable to get these in the real world, he has to do the best he can by imagining or pretending that he has got them. So far, according to Freud, he does not differ from the rest of us. What makes him an artist is the curious faculty he possesses of 'elaborating his day-dreams, so that they lose that personal note which grates upon strange ears and become enjoyable to others'.† As we others also like a good wish-

---

* Freud, *Introductory Lectures on Psycho-analysis*, trans. Joan Riviere (London, 4th impression, 1933), p. 314.　　　　　　　† *Ibid.*

fulfilment dream, we are now ready to pay for the privilege of sharing his. Thus, for the artist, as Freud says, there is a path through fantasy back to reality: by publishing his mere dreams of 'honour, power, riches, fame, and the love of women', he acquires 'honour, power, riches, fame, and the love of women' in reality.

You will notice that this is a theory about readers as well as about writers. If Freud had been content to say that all works of art could be causally traced to Fantasy in the artist, he would be merely stating an efficient cause which we might find difficult to disprove. But he makes it clear that we enjoy the product as a fantasy—that reading, as well as writing, is wish-fulfilment. Indeed it is obvious that he believes all imagining or day-dreaming to be of a single kind—that kind in which the dreamer pretends that he is a famous man, or a millionaire, or an irresistible lady-killer, while in reality he is no such thing. That is what I disbelieve. I want to introduce an addition or emendation, and it is one for which Freud has given me the example.

In an earlier lecture (the sixth), after telling us that a psycho-analytic explanation can usually be found for the tunes that we whistle when we seem to be thinking about nothing in particular, Freud adds the following: 'I must, however, make this reservation, that I do not maintain this in the case of really musical people, of whom I happen to have had no experience.'* This is both honest and penetrating, and leads me to hope that the professor would not have resisted the suggestion that a similar limiting clause would improve his theory of imagination. At any rate that is what I feel that the theory needs. It is true enough, if we do not apply it to imaginative people.

I am ready to admit that there may be human beings whose day-dreams always run in the channels which Freud describes: but surely, for most of us, there has been a fairly clear distinction between two kinds of day-dreams ever since we can remember. With the sort which he acknowledges—the dreams of success, fame, love, and the like—I confess that I am lamentably familiar. I have had dozens of them. But I cannot recall a period when I did not know another kind. The earliest of these which now comes back to me is what might be called the Snug Town. I can see that little town still, with its river and bridge and shipping, the cheeses and barrels piled on the quays,

* *Ibid.*, p. 89.

the high-pitched roofs and the bright green shutters. I am vaguer about the inhabitants, but I think they were anthropomorphised Mice—'dressed mice' as I would have called them then, with woollen comforters and wide trousers like Dutchmen, and pipes in their mouths. Obviously most of the images came out of books and the whole thing is quite commonplace. But the point is that I myself was not a feature in it. I dare say that after the dream had taken full possession of me I may have wished, and wished intensely, that I might find this town in reality and go to it. But that was because I had first imagined the town and judged it to be simply delightful, almost adorable, in its own right. My only reason for wishing to go to it was its adorableness: there was no idea that I was to become a great man there, or marry a mouse-princess, or make my fortune out of the local trade in cheeses.[1] And all this time, of course, I was having concurrently the sort of dreams that Freud allows—dreams in which I said clever things, scored off my governess, fought battles, and generally forced the world to acknowledge what a remarkable person I was.

You will have divined that this part of my paper is great fun to write. Who could not go on for hours in the same vein? I wish I had time to tell you of all the other constructions—the unknown room in the house which one was always hoping to discover, the chessmen coming alive as in *Alice*, the garden which was partly in the West and partly in the past—but I reflect that these will hardly interest you as much as they interest me. You would rather write your own ones.

I assume, in fact, that most of you have experienced the same sort of thing, and if you have you will understand me when I say that the two kinds of imagining are really distinguished by their mere taste. We can, if we are challenged, show differences in the content by pointing out that the self is absent from the one and present as hero in the other: but for our own guidance we hardly need to do so. Surely the peculiar 'tang' of the merely personal wish-fulfilment is immediately recognisable—its extreme surface realism, its deliberately prosaic temper, and above all its *nagging* character, the stealthy

---

[1] It might be worth recording here that, when Lewis was a boy, he wrote many stories about his invented world of Boxen. I have read all those that survive. Though the earliest characters are chivalrous mice, as Lewis grew older he introduced many other kinds of 'dressed animals' into his juvenilia. The interesting thing is that few of the Boxen characters are human, and not one, as far as I can see, is meant to represent Lewis himself.

insistence with which it recurs again and again like an anxiety? Surely this is utterly different from the unpredictable ecstasy, the apparent 'otherness' and externality of disinterested imagination?

It is worth while, I think, to emphasize the 'realism' of the mere wish-fulfilment dream, and to draw the literary consequence that a liberal use of the marvellous, the mythical, and the fantastical in a story is, as far as it goes, an argument *against* the charge of wish-fulfilment. The Freudian fantasy exists to give us the nearest substitute it can for real gratification; naturally it makes itself as lifelike as possible. It has to be unreal as regards the main issue—for we are not really famous men, millionaires or Don Juans—and to make up for this it will be scrupulously 'real' everywhere else. Does not all experience confirm this? A man who is really hungry does not dream of honey-dew and elfin bread, but of steak and kidney puddings: a man really lustful does not dream of Titania or Helen, but of real, prosaic, flesh and blood. Other things being equal, a story in which the hero meets Titania and is entertained with fairies' food is much less likely to be a fantasy than 'a nice love-story' of which the scene is London, the dialogue idiomatic, and the episodes probable. But this is by the way.

I do not wish to deny that both sorts of day-dream may become the source of literature. I think it probable, for example, that the novels of Charlotte Brontë began as wish-fulfilment dreams, while certain possibly disinterested imaginations about King Julius and the rest, which she shared with her sisters, attempted to express themselves in verse and failed to overcome technical incompetence. Trollope has told us in his *Autobiography* that his novels grew out of what he calls 'castle-building' and makes the character of his early reveries quite clear by adding 'I myself was of course my own hero.' The wish-fulfilling function explains why, as he tells us, 'nothing impossible was ever introduced ... I never became a king, or a duke ... I never was a learned man, nor even a philosopher. But I was a very clever person, and beautiful young women used to be fond of me ... and altogether I was a very much better fellow than I have ever succeeded in being since.' It is, plainly, a text-book case of the self-regarding day-dream. But Trollope significantly adds: 'In after years ... I have *discarded the hero* of my early dreams, and have been able to lay my own identity aside.'[1]

---

[1] *An Autobiography*, ed. H. M. Trollope (2 vols. London, 1883), vol. i, ch. iii, pp. 57–8.

This 'discarding of the hero' is Trollope's account of what Freud calls the 'elaboration' that removes the 'grating personal note', and I do not suppose that I am in disagreement with psycho-analysis if I say that, even where a work of art originated in a self-regarding reverie, it becomes art by ceasing to be what it was. It is hard to imagine a more radical change than the disappearance of the self who was, by hypothesis, the *raison d'être* of the original dream. The very root from which the dream grew is severed and the dream is planted in a new soil; it is killed as fantasy before it is raised as art. Two other things are worth noting. Trollope's work, which admittedly springs from wish-fulfilment, is work of an unusually solid, realistic, and humdrum kind, which is, on my view, just what we should expect. In the second place, the work is now valued by most readers for just those characters whose fortunes and temperament no one would wish to share, like Bishop Proudie and his wife, or Mr Crawley and the Archdeacon: whereas the fortunes of the young hero and heroine, where, if anywhere, the last traces of the original self-flattering motive might be expected to survive, are read with indifference.

On these grounds I wish to emend the Freudian theory of literature into something like this. There are two activities of the imagination, one free, and the other enslaved to the wishes of its owner for whom it has to provide imaginary gratifications. Both may be the starting-point for works of art. The former or 'free' activity continues in the works it produces and passes from the status of dream to that of art by a process which may legitimately be called 'elaboration': incoherences are tidied up, banalities removed, private values and associations replaced, proportion, relief, and temperance are introduced. But the other, or servile kind is not 'elaborated' into a work of art: it is a motive power which starts the activity and is withdrawn when once the engine is running, or a scaffolding which is knocked away when the building is complete. Finally, the characteristic products of free imagination belong to what may be roughly called the fantastic, or mythical, or improbable type of literature: those of fantasy, of the wish-fulfilling imagination, to what may, in a very loose sense, be called the realistic type. I say '*characteristic* products' because the principle doubtless admits of innumerable exceptions.

By this time I imagine that some of you can hardly contain your laughter at what seems to you the spectacle of a man jumping unconsciously out of the frying-pan into the fire. You have been longing for some time to ask me whether I really suppose that in turning from dreams of power and fame and adult love to dreams of secret rooms, and gardens in the past I have much mended matters; whether I can really be ignorant that all I have done is to exchange dreams that fulfil the comparatively rational and respectable wishes of the Ego for those that fulfil the much darker wishes of the Id. For of course the psycho-analyst will know what to make of that secret room. The garden in the West is child's play to him; and though I do not know how he will explain my town of the Mice, I have no doubt he will make of it something that pertains to infantile sexuality. This brings me to the second of the two Freudian doctrines which I have proposed to discuss: the doctrine of Symbolism.

The doctrine, as stated in the tenth lecture,* is this. When we are analysing a dream, that is, when we are trying to find the latent or unconscious thought of which the dream images are a concealed expression, we find some elements with which nothing in the mind of the dreamer is associated. But it fortunately happens that we can find out what such elements are concealing 'by drawing', as Freud says, 'on our own resources'. 'Our own resources' apparently means the psycho-analytic examination of folk-lore and language. The result of 'drawing on them' is the theory that there are certain things in the real world whose images, when they appear in dreams or stories, bear a constant meaning. That is, whether you or I dream of a house, or read of one in a tale, the latent thought behind the house image is always the same. These images with constant meanings he calls symbols—the words, so to speak, of a universal image-language. He gives us a few specimens. A *House* signifies the human body; *Kings and Queens*, fathers and mothers; *Journeys*, death; *small animals* (here come my poor mice, after all, you see) one's brothers and sisters; *Fruit*, *Landscapes*, *Gardens*, *Blossoms*, the female body or various parts of it.

As I have said, I have no intention of disputing with Freud as regards the matter of fact. This is his special subject and as a layman I have no means of finding out whether he is right or wrong; for the purposes of the present argument I am going to assume that he is right as regards fact. But we must be quite clear what it is that I am granting. I am granting three things: (1) That infantile sexual experience of the sort described by Freud does occur in all human

* Freud, *op. cit.*, pp. 125 *et seq.*

beings; (2) That latent thought on such subjects does utilise the images I have mentioned; and (3) which is going very far indeed—that wherever such images occur in dream, imagination, or literature, the latent thought which Freud mentions is really unconsciously present in the mind of the dreamer, the imaginer, and the writer or reader.

I grant all this because if all this were true it would have no literary bearing. All sorts of unconscious thought may be present while we are reading a book—for example, thought aroused by the shape of the letters or by the tactual sensations which the paper affords to our fingers—without making our enjoyment other than it seems to be. If latent thought of an erotic character is present in the same irrelevant way whenever I read about a garden, I have, as a critic, no objection. But we reach something much more formidable when Freud says: 'Does it not begin to dawn upon us that the many fairy tales which begin with the words "once upon a time there were a king and queen" simply mean "once upon a time there were a father and mother"?'* *Simply mean* is the crucial expression. They do not 'mean' this *inter alia*: they 'simply' mean this, this is all that they mean, they mean neither more, nor less, nor other, than this.

But how is the word *mean* to be interpreted? We are certainly not being asked to believe that the teller of the fairy-tale *intends* 'king' to be understood as 'father', or that the hearer consciously so understands it. I suggest—and let me apologize in advance to all psychoanalysts if I am wrong—that Freud is implicitly making at least the following claims: (1) That the whole of the excitement, pleasure, or interest occasioned by the image, wherever it occurs, is due to the latent erotic thought. (2) That the image, as opposed to the latent thought, effects nothing at all except disguise: or, in other words, that if our inhibitions allowed it to become conscious without shock, the latent thought would give us the same kind and degree of satisfaction as the image now does. It will be seen, of course, that the two claims are really identical: for if the image is anything more than a disguise, if it adds any attractiveness to the latent thought on its own account, then it must follow that the latent thought is not the whole source of the reader's pleasure.

If this is not what Freud means, I have nothing to say to him. But I am sure that this is what is meant by many of his self-styled followers;

* *Op. cit.*, p. 134.

and it is certainly this, and this alone, which brings psycho-analytic symbolism into contact with literary values. It is in this that the sting lies. We do not mind being told that when we enjoy Milton's description of Eden some latent sexual interest is, as a matter of fact, and along with a thousand other things, present in our unconscious. Our quarrel is with the man who says 'You know why you're *really* enjoying this?' or 'Of course you realize what's behind this?' or 'It *all* comes from so-and-so.' What we resent, in fact, is not so much the suggestion that we are interested in the female body as the suggestion that we have no interest in gardens: not what the wiseacre would force upon us, but what he threatens to take away. If it is true that all our enjoyment of the images, without remainder, can be explained in terms of infantile sexuality, then, I confess, our literary judgements are in ruins. But I do not believe it is true.

My first argument against it is based on the reaction I have just described—the way in which we find our enjoyments disturbed by the psycho-analyst's suggestion. He may reply that such a reaction of resistance is just what he expected to find and confirms his suspicions. But is this really so? If the image of a garden is only a disguise for the female body, and if all the excitement with which I read *Paradise Lost*, Book IV, is really erotic, then surely, when the psycho-analyst has kindly removed the veil and conducted me to the thought which (on his view) I was wanting to think all along, I ought to feel not an anticlimax but a climax—the affective temperature ought to rise, not fall? A man may go to a dinner under the illusion that he wants conversation when he really wants alcohol; but this does not mean that he suddenly loses interest in the proceedings when the champagne appears. He is more likely to realize, as he raises his glass, that this *is* what he really wanted—or at least to find the conversation very much better. It is one thing to admit unconscious desires; it is another to admit desires so unconscious that their satisfaction is felt as a disappointment and an irrelevance. What is the sense in attributing even unconscious thirst to a man who feels less at ease after you have given him drink? The psycho-analyst will probably reply that our conscious taste rejects his interpretation because of our inhibitions. He would say that the true parallel is not an ordinary man who wants alcohol without knowing it but a fanatical teetotaller who wants alcohol without knowing it; and that such a man might with apparent physical horror reject the champagne when it arrived. In other words, it would be maintained that though, at some level, we 'really' wanted to think of the female body, yet our conscious self is so shocked at the disclosure of our real interest that enjoyment ceases.

I am sometimes tempted to wonder whether Freudianism is not a great school of prudery and hypocrisy. The suggestion that we are 'shocked' by such interpretations, or that a disgusted recoil is the cause of our resistance, sounds to me like nonsense. I can speak, of course, only for my own sex, and class, and I readily admit that the Viennese ladies who came to consult Freud may have had either chaster or sillier minds than our own: but I can confidently assert that neither I nor anyone I have ever met suffers from such shrinking nausea in the presence of sexual phenomena as the theory seems to demand. I am not speaking of ethics. A man may, of course, have good reason for checking his own thoughts in certain directions or disapproving many of his own actions, but this is something very different from horror. Indeed such a man is likely to look forward with trembling hope to the day when he will become capable of being really shocked, when a light at present inaccessible reveals as essential darkness what still seems to the natural man in him merely ordinary and familiar. To be sure, infantile perversions are in a different category from normal and adult instincts: but I am not sure that even infantile perversions are quite so shocking to us as is claimed. Is not the attitude towards them which Freud assumes something of a public gesture? Does not Freud underrate the extent to which nothing, in private, is really shocking so long as it belongs to ourselves? *Suum cuique bene olet.* . . . I have watched with equanimity the decline and fall of one of my own fingernails at which I would have shuddered in someone else. Again, the feeling with which we reject the psycho-analytic theory of poetry is not one of shock. It is not even a vague disquietude or an unspecified reluctance. It is a quite definite feeling of anticlimax, of frustration. It is not as if we had drawn an embroidered curtain and found earwigs behind it: it is as if we had drawn it expecting to find a whole new wing of the house and found merely a door that led back into the old familiar dining-room. Our feelings would be most unsuitably expressed by the exclamation 'Not that!' They demand rather the disappointed grunt 'Oh! so that's all.'

In general, of course, the fact that a supposed discovery is disappointing does not tend to prove that it is false: but in this question

I think it does, for desires and fulfilments and disappointments are what we are discussing. If we are disappointed at finding only sex where we looked for something more, then surely the something more had a value for us? If we are conscious of loss in exchanging the garden for the female body, then clearly the garden added something more than concealment, something positive, to our pleasure. Let us grant that the body was, in fact, concealed behind the garden: yet since the removal of the garden lowers the value of the experience, it follows that the body gained some of its potency by association with the garden. We have not merely removed a veil, we have removed ornaments. Confronted with what is supposed to be the original (the female body) we still prefer the translation—from which any critic must conclude that the translation had merits of its own. Or perhaps 'prefer' is the wrong word. We really want both. Poetry is not a substitute for sexual satisfaction, nor sexual satisfaction for poetry. But if so, poetical pleasure is not sexual pleasure *simply* in disguise. It is, at worst, sexual pleasure *plus* something else, and we really want the something else for its own sake.

I now wish to direct your attention to a part of the evidence which is sometimes overlooked. The *Romance of the Rose* seems at first an ideal illustration of the Freudian symbolism, for in it we have not only the garden but the rosebud, which 'means' in the second half of the poem exactly what Freud would have it mean. But the trouble is that the whole process here seems to be the wrong way round. The author, and his readers, start with a fully conscious attention to the erotic material and then deliberately express it in the symbols. The symbols do not conceal and are not intended to conceal: they exhibit. The *Romance* may furnish evidence that gardens and rosebuds are excellent symbols for the things Freud has mentioned: but why are any symbols adopted? It becomes clear that humanity has some motive other than concealment for comparing erotic experience to gardens and flowers: that the erotic experience, thus compared, becomes somehow more interesting—that it is borrowing attractiveness from the flowers, not they from it. And this situation is very common. Donne, in elegies which express quite frankly the most ravenous and unidealised appetite, yet finds that he can improve his poem by comparing his mistress to the earth or to a landscape. Burns tells us that his love is like a red, red rose. These phenomena which might, in a confused glance, be taken to support the Freudian view, are really its refutation. If in the *Romance of the Rose* the erotic thought owes much of its poetical charm to the garden, why should the garden in *Paradise Lost* owe all its poetical charm to the erotic thought? Eroticism on the conscious level seeks not to conceal, but to decorate itself with images taken from gardens. But that which decorates must be, in itself, and for its own sake, pleasing. A necklace of pearls is put around a woman's neck because we think pearls beautiful. If we thought nothing but women beautiful we could not beautify women—we should have no materials with which to do so.

As far as this I think the Freudians are forced to go, and this is enough to save literature. In order to explain the symbols which they themselves insist on we must admit that humanity is interested in many other things besides sex, and that admission is the thin end of the wedge. Once it is allowed that our enjoyment of *Paradise Lost* Book IV, is a compound of latent erotic interest and real though conscious interest in gardens, then it becomes impossible to say *a priori* in what proportion the two are mixed. And even if it could be shown that the latent erotic interest was as 90 and the interest in gardens as 10, that 10 would still be the subject of literary criticism. For clearly the 10 is what distinguishes one poem from another—the 90 being a monotonous continuum spread under all our reading alike and affording no ground for the distinction we actually draw between banality and freshness, dullness and charm, ugliness and beauty. For we must remember that a story about a golden dragon plucking the apple of immortality in a garden at the world's end, and a dream about one's pen going through the paper while one scribbles a note, are, in Freudian terms, the same story. But they are not the same as literature.

That is my defence against the psycho-analytic theory of literature taken in its most uncompromising form. A much more civil and humane interpretation of myth and imagery is, however, advanced by Jung, and one which in the pages of Miss Bodkin and Dr Tillyard[1] has found some interesting critical expression. Indeed I have slipped into it at times myself. It may be called the doctrine of Primordial Images or Archetypal Patterns.

[1] E. M. W. Tillyard, *Poetry Direct and Oblique* (London, 1934); 'Milton and Primitive Feeling', *The Miltonic Setting* (London, 1938), pp. 43–59. Of particular relevance, though it was published after this essay was written, is Professor Tillyard's *Some Mythical Elements in English Literature* (London, 1961).

According to Jung* there exists, in addition to the individual unconscious, a collective unconscious which is common to the whole human race and even, in some degree, to the whole animal world. Being thus common, it contains the reactions of mind or psyche as such to the most universal situations. Being very primitive, it is pre-logical and its reactions are expressed not in thought but in images. Myths, or at any rate the older and greater myths, are such images recovered from the collective unconscious. Their power of moving us—which Jung himself obviously experiences in a very high degree—is explained as follows:

If this supra-individual mind exists, everything that is translated into its picture speech would be depersonalised and, if it became conscious, would appear to us *sub specie aeternitatis*. Not as my sorrow, but as the sorrow of the world, not a personal isolating pain, but a pain without bitterness that unites all humanity. That this can help us needs no proof.†

You will gather that Jung, when he wrote that sentence, was thinking mainly of collective reactions to painful situations, expressed in tragic myths: to complete his argument we should therefore add a similar explanation about the joyous myths 'Not as my joy, but as the joy of the world, &c.'.

The most interesting thing about this theory is the strength of the emotional reaction it awakes in nearly all those who hear it. Before its scientific merits have been considered, some are instantly repelled; they have a sense of being lured by sirens or got at by mystagogues; they feel something between fright and contempt; and they resolve to remain, at all costs, outside the magic circle, to stick to modern, self-conscious, self-explanatory aesthetics. Others, with equal suddenness, are enchanted: every half-conscious expectation which they have formed in the presence of great art seems to be fulfilled, and their hearts are enlisted on the side of the theory before their heads have had time to examine it. Let me confess at once that I belong, by temperament, to the second group, but have, by my training, acquired a certain sympathy with the first. Thanks to my training I can suspend my judgement about the scientific value of Jung's essay on 'Mind and the Earth': but I perceive at once that even if it turns out to be bad science it is excellent poetry.

* 'Mind and the Earth', *Contributions to Analytical Psychology*, trans. H. G. and C. F. Baynes (London, 1928), pp. 27 *et seq.*
† Jung, *op. cit.*, p. 108.

This brings us to a most important point—to nothing less, if I were qualified to carry it out, than the psycho-analysis of psycho-analysis itself. Such a hyper-analysis ought to be limited as Freud limited his analysis of whistling, no doubt; it would not refer to 'really scientific people', but to the great mass of ordinary people who read psycho-analytic books with avidity and undergo their influence. I do not think we can doubt that for such people psycho-analysis itself satisfied certain very strong emotional needs. I have just stated Jung's theory in the coldest and least evocative language I could find: let us now see it as it actually appears in the essay on 'Mind and the Earth'.

We have to deal with the beginnings and *foundations* of the mind, with *things that from immemorial time have lain buried in the depths* ... the unexpected question *whether the unconscious also has dreams* ... are there resultants of *yet deeper and, if possible, more unconscious* processes? ... altogether *too adventurous* ... this mind of *venerable age* ... a rationalist may laugh, but *something deep* is *stirred* in us ... those *far-away* backgrounds, those *most ancient* forms ... inherited from the *dim ages* of the past ... I have found that an intellectual apprehension of these things in no way detracts from their value; on the contrary, it helps us not only to feel, but to comprehend their *immense significance* ... *not idly* did Faust say '*The Mothers! The Mothers! it sounds so strange*'.

Do not for one moment suppose that I am laughing at Jung: but, quite frankly, my unreflective reaction to all this can only be expressed in some such words as 'Isn't this grand?' *Agnosco veteris vestigia flammae!* Something dim and far removed—buried in the depths from immemorial time—stirring beneath the surface—coming to life—coming up at last—well, I know where I am now. I am with Schliemann digging up what he believed to be the very bones of Agamemnon, king of men: I am with Collingwood discovering behind the Arthurian stories some far-off echo of real happenings in the thick darkness of British history: with Asia in the fourth act of *Prometheus* following her dream down, down into the cave of Demogorgon: with Wordsworth, sinking deep and ascending into regions 'to which the heaven of heavens is but a veil': with Alice, finding beneath the curtain the little door which she could not pass, which led to the delectable garden: with my own past self, hoping, as a child, for that forgotten, that undiscovered, room. I am with British Israelites and Baconians and historians of Atlantis, with Renaissance magicians and seekers for the sources of the Nile. In a word I am enjoying myself immensely;

but the point I wish to make is simply this: that Jung's discussion of 'primordial images' itself awakes a primordial image of the first water: that Miss Bodkin's *Archetypal Patterns** itself exhibits an archetypal pattern of extreme potency.

I trust that you recognize which it is; it might be called the Recovery Pattern, or the Veiled Isis, or the Locked Door, or the Lost-and-Found. The Freudians will explain it in terms of infantile sexual curiosity—indeed I have seen Alice and the curtained door so explained—but that need not bother us. Such curiosity may, in the life of each one of us, have been the earliest embodiment of it, for all I know: but since then we have learned to prefer it in several more exciting and less obvious forms—the thirst which it kindles in us has long outrun 'those perishing waters'. It is, indeed, an image inevitably embodying certain absolutely universal features of our experience, religious, intellectual, aesthetic, and sexual alike.

The presence of such a primordial image in the psycho-analytic process itself is, I think, the explanation of its popularity—for the same image is aroused by Freudian analysis too. In this respect psycho-analysis heals some of the wounds made by materialism. For the general effect of materialism is to give you, where you expected an indefinite depth of reality, a flat wall only a few inches away. Psycho-analysis offers you some kind of depth back again—lots of things hidden behind the wall. Hence those who have once tasted it feel that they are being robbed of something if we try to take it from them.

The emotional power of Jung's essay is, as far as it goes, a proof that he is quite right in claiming that certain images, in whatever material they are embodied, have a strange power to excite the human mind. Every sentence he writes helps to prove this. At the same time we may be cautious about accepting his explanation, since there are some grounds for suspecting that the argument seems plausible not because of its real cogency but because of the powerful emotions it arouses. Has Jung, in fact, worked us into a state of mind in which almost anything, provided it was dim, remote, long buried, and mysterious, would seem (for the moment) an adequate explanation of the 'leap in our blood' which responds to great myth? Let us look at the matter in cold prose. We want to know why

* Maud Bodkin, *Archetypal Patterns in Poetry. Psychological Studies of Imagination* (London: Oxford University Press, 1934).

certain images are exciting. Jung replies, 'because they are ancient, because, in contemplating them, we are doing what our prehistoric ancestors did'. Now the *idea* that we are doing so is certainly exciting, as all ideas of antiquity are. But this idea is not necessarily entertained by the man in the moment of responding to a myth. He may not have read Jung's theory; he may think that what he is contemplating is quite new: he may not raise the question of its age at all. Nevertheless he will respond. If Jung is right, then, it is not the *idea* of following our remote ancestors which produces the response but the mere *fact* of doing so, whether we are conscious of this fact or no. But there is no evidence that the actual reproduction of prehistoric behaviour, apart from the reflection that we are reproducing it, is at all exciting or impressive. We reproduce very ancient modes of behaviour in all our humblest animal operations. We are at one with our pre-Adamite sires when we scratch; and though I have no wish to underrate the pleasures of a good scratch, I think them very unlike those of a good poem. No doubt even scratching may be made poetical if we reflect on the antiquity of the practice: but the pleasure we shall then get will not be the pleasure of scratching (the οἰκεία ἡδονή) but the pleasure of historico-poetical meditation. In the same way, I suggest, Jung has not explained the pleasure of entertaining primordial images but exhibited the pleasure of meditating on them and of entertaining, in the process, one particular primordial image, which itself needs explanation as much as any of the others. The *idea* that our sorrow is part of the world's sorrow is, in certain moods, moving enough: the mere *fact* that lots of other people have had toothache does not make toothache less painful.

I have no answer to the question Jung has raised. I can only say—indulging once more in the same primordial image—that the mystery of primordial images is deeper, their origin more remote, their cave more hid, their fountain less accessible than those suspect who have yet dug deepest, sounded with the longest cord, or journeyed farthest in the wilderness—for why should I not be allowed to write in this vein as well as everyone else?

22

The Anthropological Approach

It is not to be disputed that literary texts can sometimes be of great use to the anthropologist. It does not immediately follow from this that anthropological study can make in return any valuable contribution to literary criticism. The attention now paid by medievalists to the mythical and ritual origins (real or supposed) of the romances suggests a widespread belief that it can. I want to consider how far this is so.

It is clear that an anthropological statement (supposing it to be a true one) can often explain some detail in a text. Thus Gawain's property* of growing stronger as the sun ascends can be explained as the last vestige of a myth about the sun-god. But let us be quite clear in what sense we are using the word 'explain'. We mean 'to account for causally' (as in 'we can easily explain his behaviour by the fact that he was drunk'). The word has a different meaning when we say that someone first 'explained' to us the Deduction of the Categories or the beauties of the Virgilian hexameter. To 'explain' in this second sense is to open our eyes; to give us the power of receiving, or receiving more fully, what Kant or Virgil intended to give us. The causal explanation of Gawain's peculiarity 'explains', in this other sense, nothing whatever. That peculiarity remains, in Malory's book, a complete irrelevance. Nothing leads up to it; nothing of any importance depends on it. Apart from it there is nothing divine and nothing solar about Gawain. All that he does, suffers, or says elsewhere would have exactly the same value if this odd detail had been omitted. The anthropological explanation may be true and it may have an interest of its own; but it cannot increase our understanding or enjoyment of one single sentence in the *Morte*.

I proceed to a more complicated instance. R. S. Loomis stresses the 'astonishing disharmony', the offences against 'common sense and ordinary morality', the 'absurdities', and the 'irrational freakish features', in the literature of the Grail. He concludes that 'no procedure

---

* *The Works of Sir Thomas Malory*, ed. E. Vinaver (Oxford, 1947), i, 161 (Bk. IV, 18), iii, 1216–20 (Bk. XX, 21–2).

could be more reasonable than to seek the cause of the sanctification of the Grail legends in a series of misunderstandings'.* Now since the Grail (as distinct from various analogues to it in pagan stories) is fully sanctified in all the Grail stories we have, the 'cause of the sanctification' means the cause of its character in those stories— Chrétien's, Wolfram's, and the rest. We need not examine the theory that this is due to misunderstandings, for we are here concerned not with its truth or falsehood but with its literary relevance.

There are two ways in which we could interpret Professor Loomis's procedure. One is that he is leaving the literary quality of these romances severely alone and is exclusively interested in the pagan myths from which he believes them to be derived. If that is so, then he is doing something which, however legitimate in its own field, makes no contribution to literary criticism. Alternatively, if we give full force to the charges of absurdity and freakishness which he brings, we could take him to be saying in effect, 'Here is a great deal of shockingly bad fiction. I will explain how Chrétien and his fellows come to be guilty of it. They were led astray by blunders—mistaking *cors* (a horn) for *cors* (a body) or *sang real* for *saint graal*.' I am myself very disinclined to believe that this is the correct account of Professor Loomis's activity. Indeed, if he gave this account of it himself, I should venture to believe that he was misrepresenting his own experience and doing himself a grave injustice. The spectacle of a great scholar spending a lifetime of learning to discover why some bad literature was bad would be a portent that clamoured for explanation no less than the Grail itself.[1] And if this were what he was doing, this also would have hardly any critical interest. It is, though far more complex, essentially the same sort of thing that a textual critic is doing when he explains a meaningless passage by dittography. If the Grail romances are nonsensical this fault is neither lessened nor aggravated by the discovery of its causes. Meanwhile the specifically literary problem remains untouched. What we want to know as critics is how and why these romances, with all their elusiveness and mystery, delighted so many medieval readers and delight so many today. Is it in spite of this character or because of it?

* 'The Origin of the Grail Legends', *Arthurian Literature in the Middle Ages* (Oxford, 1959), pp. 274–94, esp. p. 287.

[1] See Professor Loomis's riposte: 'Literary History and Literary Criticism: A Critique of C. S. Lewis', *The Modern Language Review*, vol. LX (October 1965), pp. 508–11.

We must now make a distinction. The Celtic cornucopia, supposing it to be a source of the Grail, is irrelevant for literature because the inward side of the horn stories, their spirit and quality, is hardly at all present in the romances. How could it be, if the romances so mis-understood their sources that they mistook a horn for a body? Where the parallel between the Grail romance and the Celtic analogue is most striking, the abyss between them in atmosphere and significance may be most emphatic. The question 'To whom shall this cup be given?' in *The Prophetic Ecstasy*** is certainly in one way very like the question 'Whom does one serve with the Grail?' But the first question is answered. Its literary function is to introduce a list of the kings of Tara. It has much the same purpose as the vision of future heroes in *Aeneid* VI or the figures on the shield in *Aeneid* VIII or the phantoms in *Macbeth* (IV, i). The second question is not even asked. Perceval's failure to ask it—which is the ganglion of the whole episode—leads to mysterious and almost illimitable disaster. If the medieval poet knew the Celtic story at all (which I need not deny), it has been to him merely a starting point from which he went on to invent something radically new, indeed incommensurable. That new invention, not its trivial and external similarity to some earlier thing, is the proper object of literary criticism.

But this is only one possible relation between a literary text and an anthropological background. There is another.

In the sagas, or *Hamlet*, the ethos of a society where revenge was not, as with us, a passion, but an obligation, is operative throughout. A certain attitude to the dead is similarly operative throughout the *Antigone*. To appreciate these works we certainly need to grasp these ancient outlooks. But that is because they have more than a merely causal connexion with the works. They are not antecedents but presuppositions, still immanent and alive in the completed product. The authors reckon on our understanding them. Not merely on our knowing them externally as historical curiosities, but on our entering into them with imaginative sympathy. And this fact usually enables us to dispense with anthropological study. The authors themselves, speaking from within the archaic *ethos*, recreate it in our minds. Anthropology might have told us that such and such customs existed. But the authors do not need to tell; they show, they infect, they constrain. It is they who bring the anthropology to life, not *vice versa*.

* Loomis, p. 282.

And surely this must always be so. It has been maintained that Bercilak in *Gawain and the Green Knight* 'is'—that is, was influenced by—an *eniautos daimon*.* Let us suppose, for purposes of argument, that this is so. The question is which of the two, *eniautos daimon* or Bercilak, throws light on the other.

Bercilak is as vivid and concrete as any image I have met in literature. He is a living *coincidentia oppositorum*; half giant, yet wholly a 'lovely knight'; as full of demoniac energy as old Karamazov, yet, in his own house, as jolly as a Dickensian Christmas host; now exhibiting a ferocity so gleeful that it is almost genial, and now a geniality so outrageous that it borders on the ferocious; half boy or buffoon in his shouts and laughter and jumpings; yet at the end judging Gawain with the tranquil superiority of an angelic being. There has been nothing really like him in fiction before or since. No one who has once read the poem forgets him. No one while reading it disbelieves in him.

But what is the *eniautos daimon*? It is a concept; something constructed from the actual practices of the ancient world and the conjectured practices of our own ancestors. I have never seen Jack in the Green. None of us have, as believers, taken part in a pagan ritual. We cannot experience such things from inside. We may sometimes know, and sometimes guess, that certain myths were told and certain rites enacted. We do not know what it felt like. That world-old religion, with its baffling mixture of agriculture, tragedy, obscenity, revelry, and clowning, eludes us in all but its externals.

To expect that the *eniautos daimon* should help us to understand Bercilak is to expect that the unknown should illuminate the known; as if we hoped that a man would learn more about the taste of oranges on being told that it is like the taste of some other fruit which he has never eaten.

The opposite process is the only rational one. Tell me that the unknown fruit is like an orange, and I have learned something. I learn nothing about the quality of Bercilak from being told he is derived from the daimon; I may learn something about the daimon. Perhaps this rumbustious, irresistible figure has preserved for me just what anthropology can never penetrate; has given me knowledge-by-acquaintance (*connaître*) where anthropology could give me at best

* J. Speirs, *Medieval English Poetry. The Non-Chaucerian Tradition* (London, 1957), pp. 218 ff.

knowledge-about (*savoir*). If this is so, then our poetic experience has helped us as anthropologists, but our anthropology has not helped us to read the poetry. When savage beliefs or practices inform a work of art, that work is not a puzzle to which those beliefs and practices are the clue. The savage origins are the puzzle; the surviving work of art is the only clue by which we can hope to penetrate the inwardness of the origins. It is either in art, or nowhere, that the dry bones are made to live again.

Mr Speirs maintains the literary relevance of such origins on two grounds. One is that they affect the poet; the other, that a knowledge of them affects the reader.

After quoting the place about the perilous fountain from *Ywain and Gawain* (352–42),* he connects it conjecturally with a rain-making ritual. He then very properly asks what difference this makes to the poetry; especially since the poets may have known nothing about the ritual origin. Part of his answer is that, whether they knew the origin or not, 'they surely inherited with such episodes something of the traditional attitude of reverence towards them, a sense of their mystery, a sense too of the mystery of all life'.

Now our only evidence for how the poet felt is what he wrote. This passage apparently makes Mr Speirs feel reverence and a sense of mystery; he infers that the poet had felt it too. Mr Speirs, whatever else he may be, is a very honest critic; if he says that the passage makes him feel like that, we may be sure it does. But I am not equally sure that the consequences he wants us to draw will follow. For one thing, as I shall suggest presently, Mr Speirs's sensation may not result from the quality of the poetry in the direct fashion he supposes; I can imagine a somewhat different process. But suppose it is the actual writing that has done the trick. And suppose, further, that the feelings an author arouses in a sensitive reader are always the same as he had himself. We could then say: 'The author of this passage felt reverence and a sense of mystery.' But where is the evidence that ritual origins are the only or commonest source of such feelings or that such feelings always result from (even a forgotten) ritual origin? Might not the poet equally well be awed and mystified by a mere unexplained magic fountain such as this purports to be? Might he not have believed in such things? Is it not more probable he believed in them than that he cared about rain-rituals? Or, even without belief, might not the idea

* *Medieval English Poetry*, p. 117.

of perilous adventures in enchanted forests have moved him deeply? It moved Milton.

This type of criticism which always takes us away from the actual poem and the individual poet to seek the sources of their power in something earlier and less known—which, in fact, finds the secret of poetic pleasure anywhere rather than in talent and art—has lately received a dolorous stroke from Professor Vinaver.* He has cured us, if we can be cured, of the bad habit which regards the finished romances as mere rubble left over from some far statelier, non-existent building. This is the reverse of the truth. The romance is the cathedral; the anthropological material is the rubble that was used by the builders. He has shown as regards one particular story that every step away from the dark origins is an advance in coherence, in suggestion, in imaginative power.

But I must now turn to the second part of Mr Speirs's theory—or rather to his second theory, for the two are independent. Besides doing something to the poets, the ritual origins, or the knowledge of them, or the conjecture of them, does something to the reader.

The mere conjecture that the perilous fountain has something to do with rain-making means for Mr Speirs 'that the episode is more serious than simply a sport of fancy'. It means 'that we might have to correct our way of taking these episodes as if they belonged to something of the order of a boy's adventure story—taking them, that is, too easily'.† Elsewhere he says that 'anthropological facts, or even guesses' may make the reader of medieval literature 'alert to things in the poems which he might not otherwise have noticed'.‡

This is where Mr Speirs's honesty is invaluable. He lets us see what is really going on in the minds of some anthropologizing critics. But for anthropology 'we' should have taken the ferlies in medieval romance like trivial excitements in a boy's blood. 'We' should have taken them 'too easily'. Without anthropological preparation 'we' may leave some things unnoticed altogether.

I have no doubt whatever that this is true to the experience of Mr Speirs and of many of his generation. For them the garden of marvellous romance is—as it was not either for medieval or for nineteenth-century man—a walled and locked-up garden to which anthropology is the only key. They become free of it only if they carry the golden

* 'The Dolorous Stroke', *Medium Ævum*, xxv (1957), 175–80.
† *Medieval English Poetry*, p. 117.　　　　　‡ *Ibid.*, pp. 23–4.

bough. This awakes in them a sensibility they otherwise lack. This being so, one understands for the first time why they value—why in a sense they are right to value—anthropology so highly. For if (to them) the only choice lies between taking the Grail as if it were a mere surprise-packet out of Boiardo or Munchausen and achieving an awed and solemn response with the aid of some Celtic cauldron, it is certainly well that they should embrace the second alternative.

With this, it may be said, I have conceded the whole position. Anthropology increases the sensibility, and even the attention, of certain readers. Therefore it does throw light for them on literature. I admit it. But let us be sure exactly what we mean.

Anything that helps anyone to read more sensitively and attentively is welcome. But there are helps of different kinds. On the one hand they may consist of knowledges or sympathies which enable the reader to enter more fully into the author's intentions. History is often such a help. So is scholarship. So is experience; *ceteris paribus* we read love poetry and religious poetry more perceptively if we have had some experience of love and of religion. But there are other helps that have no intrinsic connection with the art or matter of the book but merely dispose us psychologically to be pleased. They are accidental in the sense that their necessity varies from one reader to another, and for the same reader from time to time, and the best readers need them least. Health, quiet, an easy chair, a full, but not too full, stomach, can all help in this way. Some approach a book receptively because it is recommended, others because it is forbidden. Children are attracted by coloured pictures, adults by fine paper and printing. One is attracted and another repelled by the knowledge that 'everyone is reading this'.

To discover, exhibit, and supply helps of the first kind is critically relevant and useful in the highest degree. But helps of the second kind are more properly mentioned in an autobiography. They are facts about this or that reader rather than about literature. There seem to me grounds for assigning to the second, or merely subjective, class the help which Mr Speirs and his contemporaries derive from anthropology.

In the first place it is not universally necessary. At a great price (in the way of anthropological study) Mr Speirs obtains his freedom to respond deeply and solemnly to the romances; but earlier generations, including my own, were free born. We never thought of responding

—never had power to respond—in any other way. The ferlies, simply for what they are shown to be in the texts, conquered us at once and have never released us. We stand amazed when our juniors think to interest us in the Grail by connecting it with a cauldon of plenty or a prehistoric burning glass,* for the Grail as Chrétien or Malory presents it seems to us twenty times more interesting than the cauldron or the glass. Apparently there has grown up a generation in whom, for reasons I will not discuss here, the direct response has been inhibited. They find that anthropology releases the inhibition. I congratulate them. But it merely restores to them powers which humanity often has without any such preliminary *askesis*. The insight into romance which it gives them is new to them, not to men in general. The fact that they needed such therapy is a fact about them, not about the literary quality of the romances. To regard their anthropological approach as a discovery in literary criticism is like regarding insulin as a discovery in gastronomy. I am very glad diabetics now have insulin. But it is a medical, not a gastronomic, discovery.

In the second place, it is clear that the therapeutic value of the anthropological *askesis* does not depend on the *fact* of ritual origins. The fact, if it is one, and if it produces literary results, must have been doing so before anyone knew about it, just as poison will kill or alcohol intoxicate us whether we know we have taken them or not. If a ritual origin worked that way, readers of the romances would receive its exciting effect without knowing its existence. If that were so, why should we need to learn of it before we can fully enjoy the romances? And indeed Mr Speirs does not think we need exactly 'learn' in the sense of 'coming to know'. The connexion between the perilous fountain and a rain-making ritual is, on his own showing, a 'conjecture'.† In 'Maiden in the mor lay' the reference to a well-spring merely 'suggests the possibility'‡ that the poem is connected with well-worship. Obviously what does the therapeutic work is not the fact but the mere idea of ritual origins; the idea, as an idea, not known to be true, not affirmed, but simply entertained. The case is not like that of a man who gets sick from eating poison or drunk from taking spirits. It is as if a suggestible person felt sick or felt drunk simply at the idea of having done so. If he believes (however

* Lady Flavia Anderson, *The Ancient Secret* (London, 1953).
† *Medieval English Poetry*, p. 117.
‡ *Ibid.*, p. 63.

erroneously) that he has, or even if without belief he dwells on the idea, the vomit or the euphoria will follow. It makes no difference to the utility Mr Speirs finds in his anthropological ideas whether they are true or false.

Thirdly, the anthropological 'softening' is not the only one available. Others find their inhibitions similarly released by the idea that ferlies are Jungian outcroppings from the collective unconscious. Others, though not in academic circles, can enjoy them by thinking they are the hieroglyphs of an ancient, but still living, esoteric wisdom. Since all three exercises serve the same purpose, it is natural to ask what they have in common. The answer does not seem to me to be very difficult.

All are alike in suggesting that the ferly actually presented to us in the old poem or romance is the far-borne echo, the last surviving trace, the tantalizing glimpse, the veiled presence, of something else. And the something else is always located in a remote region, 'dim-discovered', hard of access. On this its value depends, I think, in all three exercises; almost certainly, in the anthropological one. Are ancient rituals in themselves—rituals that lie in broad, historical daylight and need not be groped after—so moving? I should be surprised if all those who are moved by the idea that the Grail story 'is really' a ritual respond with equal excitement to the full-length descriptions of ritual in the *Aeneid* or Leviticus. The whole pleasure comes from feeling, as they read of the ferly, that 'more is meant than meets the ear', that they have surprised a long-kept secret, that there are depths below the surface, that something which the un-initiate might pass over as a triviality is big with meaning. They must have the sense of descending to 'the Mothers'. Who would bother to pluck the golden bough unless it led you to *res alta terra et caligine mersas*?

Now all these sensations are in my opinion pretty like those the authors meant to give you. The romancers create a world where everything may, and most things do, have a deeper meaning and a longer history than the errant knight would have expected; a world of endless forest, quest, hint, prophecy. Almost every male stranger wears armour; not only that there may be jousts but because visors hide faces. Any lady may prove a fay or devil; every castle conceal a holy or unholy mystery. The hero is a sort of intruder or trespasser; always, unawares, stumbling on to forbidden ground. Hermits and voices explain just enough to let us know how completely he is out of his depth, but not enough to dissipate the overall mystery. The hard, gay colours make this world very unlike that of Kafka, but it has some of the same qualities. You might call it inverted (or converted) Kafka; a Kafka who enjoyed the labyrinth.

Until our own age readers accepted this world as the romancers' 'noble and joyous' invention. It was not, to be sure, wholly unrelated to the real world. It was invented by and for men who felt the real world, in its rather different way, to be also cryptic, significant, full of voices and 'the mystery of all life'. There has now arisen a type of reader who cannot thus accept it. The tale in itself does not seem to him to provide adequate grounds for the feelings to which he is dimly aware that he is being prompted. He therefore invents new grounds for them in his own life as a reader. And he does this by building up round himself a second romance which he mistakes for reality. This second romance is a distorted version of the first one. It also is a quest story, but it is he, not Perceval or Gawain, that is on the quest. The forests are not those of Broceliande but those of anthropological theory. It is he himself who quivers at the surmise that everything he meets may be more important, and other, than it seemed. It is to him that such hermits as Frazer and Miss Weston, dwelling in the heart of the forest, explain the *significacio* of the ferlies. Prompted by them, he does not, like Perceval, omit to ask the all-important question.

And he has his reward. He gets in the end an experience qualitatively not unlike the experience the romancers meant to give. The process is very roundabout. He rejects the fiction as it was actually written. He can respond to it only indirectly, only when it is mirrored in a second fiction, which he mistakes for a reality. This is better than nothing. But it might do a good deal of harm to real literary and cultural history and even to anthropology itself if it were taken as a serious contribution to any of these disciplines. And to criticism it has already done some. Already there are students who describe as 'enjoyment of medieval literature' what is really the enjoyment of brooding upon things (mostly hypothetical) in the dark past with which that literature is, often so doubtfully, connected in their minds. Mr Speirs himself would reassure us by the proposition that in a poem 'one cannot find what is not there'.* But the instances of thinking you have found

* *Op. cit.*, p. 24.

what is not there are generally allowed to be pretty numerous. Is Mr Speirs himself quite sure that the allegory Fulgentius found in Virgil, or the philosophy Chapman found in Homer, were really there? Is he absolutely convinced that the *Song of Solomon* was really and truly about 'The mutual love of Christ and his Church'? The forest is after all enchanted: mares have built nests in every tree.

Index

Bentley, Richard, 163
Beowulf, xvii, 4, 6, 44, 47, 55
Bercilak, Sir, 304
Berdan, J. M.: *Early Tudor Poetry*, 1
Bergson, Henri: *Le Rire*, 86 n.*
Berkshire, 18, 21
Bertram, Sir Thomas and Edmund (in Austen's *Mansfield Park*), 180, 182, 183
Beryn, Tale of, 45
Bestiary (Middle English), 56
Bhagavad-Gita, 203, 226
Bialacoil (in *Romance of the Rose*), 43 n.*
Bible, The (*see also* the Authorised Version): aesthetic experience depends only to small extent on translation, 126; sense in which 'Bible as literature' does not exist, 126–7; has been read for almost every purpose more diligently than for literary pleasure, 127–33; distinction between Bible as Source for English literature and as literary Influence, 133–40; modern approach influenced by Romantic Movement, 141; so well known for three centuries that words and phrases could not be borrowed without recognition, 141–2; implication that those who reject theological pretensions yet continue to enjoy it as literature denied, 142; effects of Counter-Romantic movement, 142–3; unlikely to return except as sacred book, 144–5; mentioned, 149
Birmingham, George, 274
Black, John: trans. *Lectures on Art and Dramatic Literature*, 90 n. 3
Blake, William: *Prophetic Books*, 136; *Songs of Innocence*, 122
Boccaccio, Giovanni; Rossetti's collation of *Troilus* and *Filostrato*, 27; aim to paint sentimentality alone, 27; slightly medieval, 29; errors against code of courtly love, 29–30; wrote for audience who were beginning to look at poetry in our own way, 30; gave lyrical instead of rhetorical turn to invocation in *Filostrato*, 31; morning parting between lovers compared with Chaucer's medievalization, 32; his second assignation of Troilus and Criseida compared to *Troilus*, 33; request that lovers will pray for him, 36; example of Latin spirit, 37; use of unconscious and fossilized metaphors, 38; first dialogue between Troilus

and Pandaro compared to Chaucer's, 40–2; cynical Latin gallantries, 44; *Decameron*, 213; *Filostrato*, discussed, 27–44, mentioned and quoted, 27, 28, 29, 30, 31, 33, 36, 37, 38, 40, 41, 42, 43; *De Genealogia*, 133
Bodkin, Maud: *Archetypal Patterns in Poetry*, 104, 299; mentioned, 296
Bodleian Library, viii
Boehme, Jacob, 113
Boethius, 33
Boiardo, Matteomaria, 138, 307
Boileau, Nicolas, 166
Bold, Mrs, *née* Nellie Harding (in Trollope), 182
Bolingbroke (in Shakespeare), 94
Bone, Gavin, 131–2
Book of Mormon, see *Mormon*
Boosey Ballad, 270
Bossu, Le, 162
Boswell, James: *Life of Samuel Johnson*, 74, 142, 160; mentioned, 232
Boyle, John, *see* Orrery, Lord
Bradley, Henry: *The Making of English*, 136
Bréal, M. J. A.: *Semantics*, 251
Bridges, Robert, 46
Brightman, F. E., 18 n. 1
Brisk, Mr (in Bunyan), 148
Britomart (in Spenser), 118
Brobdingnagians, the (in Swift), 163
Broceliande, 310
Broken Heart, The, see Ford, John
Brontë, Charlotte, 180, 182, 289
Brown, Carleton: ed. *Religious Lyrics of the XVth Century*, 50 n. 2
Browne, Sir Thomas, 5, 164
Browning, Robert: *The Ring and the Book*, xvi, 213; mentioned, 110
Brunchild (in Venantius), 39
Brutus (in Shakespeare), 99
Bruyne, Edgar de: *Études d'esthétique médiévale*, 127, 129
Buchan, John, 273, 274, 278
Buddhism, 158
Bunyan, John, on his *Pilgrim's Progress*: any unlearned author of his time would remind us of the Bible, 139; most characteristic sentences have unscriptural ring, 139; prose comes not from Authorised Version but Bedfordshire surroundings, 140; style would have been much

Bunyan (*cont.*)

the same without AV, 140; read with delight even by those who do not believe his doctrine, 146; story spoilt when characters step out of it to sermonize, 146; master of perfect naturalness in mimesis of ordinary conversation, 146: tells how book came into existence, 146–7; high theme incarnated on level of adventure story, 147–8; motives of pilgrims, 148; right way to read his allegory, 149; style compared to that of AV, 149–50; his style, 150–1; premises, 151; narrowness of religious outlook, 152; story required religious momentousness, 152–3; *Pilgrim's Progress*, 139, 140, 146, 147, 148, 149, 150, 151, 152, 153; mentioned, 137, 265

Burke, Edmund: *Philosophical Inquiry into the Sublime and Beautiful*, 166; mentioned, 227

Burnet, Thomas: *Telluris Theoria Sacra*, 165

Burns, Robert, 295

Burton, Robert: *Anatomy of Melancholy*, 131 n. †, 146; mentioned, 5, 134

Bussy D'Ambois (in Chapman), 155

Butler, Joseph, 265

Byron, George Gordon, Lord: *Don Juan*, 193; mentioned, 62, 187, 196 n. 1, 199, 225, 271, 272

Caedmon, *see* Pseudo-Caedmon

Caesar, Gaius Julius: in Jonson, 78; his lines on Terence, 204–5 n. 1

Calkas (in Chaucer), 30

Calvin, Jean, 116

Camelot, 115

Campion, Thomas, 23

Canon's Yeoman (in Chaucer), 170

Canterbury, 15 n. 1

Cantharus, 172

Carbonek, 115

Carew, Thomas: 'When thou, poor Excommunicate', 124; 'A Song', 124; mentioned, 112

Carlyle, Thomas: trans. *Wilhelm Meister*, 90 n. 1; mentioned, 209, 242

Carritt, E. F., xiii

Carroll, Lewis (C.L. Dodgson): *Alice*, 288, 298

Casaubon (in *Middlemarch*), 101

Castle of Otranto, The, see Walpole

Catherine de Bourgh, Lady (in Austen's *Pride and Prejudice*), 181

Catullus, Gaius Valerius, 119, 170, 171

Caxton, William, 58

Cecil, Lord David: *Jane Austen*, 179; mentioned, 213

Ceremonie, the goddess in Chapman, 65, 66, 67

ceremony, 65, 68

Cervantes: *Don Quixote*, 218 n. 1; mentioned, 215

Chapman, George, on his sestiads of *Hero and Leander*: natural to treat poem as two separate works, 58; Saturn dominates his sestiads, 58; question of whether Marlowe asked him to finish poem, 62–3; tells of wasting of joy, 63; moral content, 63; celebration of marriage, 63–4; lines of extravagant sweetness, 64; conceits nearer than Marlowe's to metaphysical manner, 65; his goddess Ceremonie, 65, 66, 67; creation of a new mythology embodying his doctrine, 68; bad writing, 68–9; how conceits differ from Marlowe's, 69–70; imagination stimulated by ideas, 71; ideas and images catch fire from one another, 71–2; midway between allegory of Spenser and poetry of the moderns, 72–3; faults, 73; *Hero and Leander*, 63, 64, 66, 67, 68, 69, 70, 71, 72, 115; trans. of *Iliad*, 141, 275, 311; his Bussy and Clermont, 155; mentioned, 97, 272

Chapman, R. W.: ed. *Novels of Jane Austen*, 175 nn. 1 ff.

Chapone, Hester, 266

Chatterton, Thomas: his imaginary poet, Thomas Rowley, 166

Chaucer, Geoffrey: Rossetti's collation of *Troilus* and *Filostrato*, 27; aim to 'reflect life', 27; medievalization of *Filostrato*, 27; why he chose *Filostrato* for retelling, 28; Gower's hopes for, 28; approached *Filostrato* as poet of courtly love, 28–9; desire to amend and reduce which was amiss in *Filostrato*, 29–30; as 'historial' poet contributing to story of Troy, 30–1; amplified by Troy story, 31–3; as poet of *doctryne* and *sentence*, 33–5; made Troy story more accurate representation of orthodox erotic code and emphasized its didactic element, 35–6; innovations

Scott (cont.)
knowledge in *Gurnal*, 211–12; novels, more than *Gurnal*, represent his settled criticism of life, 212; purpose of novels, 213–14; insufficient seriousness, 214; opposition between his outlook and modern men of letters, 214–15; difference between style of narrative and style of dialogue, 215–17; first taught us feeling for period, 217; novels have own essential rectitude, 218; *The Antiquary*, 212, 215; *Castle Dangerous*, 214; *Count Robert of Paris*, 214; *Guy Mannering*, 214, 215, 216; *The Heart of Midlothian*, 215, 218; *Journal, 1825–26*, 209, 210, 211, 212, 215, 216; *Journal, 1827–28*, 210, 211; *Journal, 1829–32*, 211, 214; *Rob Roy*, 212, 215; *Waverley*, 217; 'Waverley Novels', 7, 11, 211, 217; mentioned, 167, 221, 235, 271, 272, 273, 276

Scriblerus (Club), 154

Seneca, 5, 99

Septuagint, The, 127

Sessions, B. F.: trans. *La Survivance des dieux antiques*, 1 n.*

Seznec, J.: *La Survivance des dieux antiques*, 1 n.*

Shaftesbury, 3rd Earl of, *see* Anthony Ashley Cooper

Shakespeare, William: form of verse, 45; *Venus and Adonis* compared to Marlowe's *Hero and Leander*, 59–61; 'Degree' in, 65, 66; question as to whether he or Milton had drawn more admirable picture of a man, 74–5; descriptive method compared to that of Milton, 74–6; plays variations on a theme that remains the same, 76; his method of variation compared to method of construction, 76–7; method of variation shared by all Elizabethan dramatists, 77; combined imaginative splendour of highest type of lyric and realistic presentation of life and character, 81–3; used variation in earlier work as poetical ornament, 83–4; accepted tradition of variation without much reflection, 87; three schools of *Hamlet* criticism, 88–90; question as to what *Hamlet* is a picture of, 90; critics who consider *Hamlet* a bad play, 91; what Hamlet pronounces

himself to be, 91; goodness of play dependent on character of Hamlet, 91–2; Eliot considers play artistic failure, 92; critics place excellence of *Hamlet* in delineation of hero's character, 93; excellence of play from standpoint of poetry and situation, 93–5; *Merchant of Venice* twisted out of recognition by character criticism, 95–6; *Merchant* about metals, 96–7; Hamlet formula is 'a man who has been given a task by a ghost', 97–8; subject of *Hamlet* is death, 98; in *Hamlet* we think about being dead, 99–100; mistake to assume characters are themselves poets, 101; Hamlet's speeches describe spiritual region through which most of us have passed, 101–2; true hero of *Hamlet* is man with his mind on frontiers of two worlds, 102–3; error to mistake machinery for real play, 103; critics put mystery of *Hamlet* in wrong place, 103–4; on reading *Hamlet* with childlike attention, 104–5; genuine text of *Hamlet*, 105 n. 1; *Antony and Cleopatra*, 75–6, 77, 99; *Hamlet*, 62, 74, 82, 88, 89, 90, 91, 92, 93, 94, 97, 98, 99, 100, 101, 102, 103, 104, 105, 123, 160, 303; *Henry IV*, 102, 161; *Henry V*, 47, 49, 77; *Julius Caesar*, 99; *Lear*, 99; *Macbeth*, 82, 83, 94, 303; *Measure for Measure*, 103, 165; *Merchant of Venice*, 95, 96, 97, 98, 213; *Much Ado about Nothing*, 102, 118; *Othello*, 83, 99; *Richard II*, 83, 94, 95; *Romeo and Juliet*, 99, 118; *Tempest*, 77; *Twelfth-Night*, 95, 213, 274; *Venus and Adonis*, 59, 60, 61; *Winter's Tale*, 118, 224; mentioned, xviii, 10, 43 n .‡, 71, 80, 115, 125, 135, 180, 202, 210, 217, 223, 269, 272, 273

Sharrock, Roger: ed. *Pilgrim's Progress*, 139 n. 1, 146 n. 1

Sheffield, John: 'An Essay upon Poetry', 173, 174

Shelley, Percy Bysshe: suffers from modern dislike of Romantics, 187; offered up by Eliot as sacrifice to fame of Dryden, 187; more masterly, sufficient, and classical poet than Dryden, 188; poetry proper to theme and species of composition, 194; influence of Dante and Plato at least as dominant in thought as that of Godwin, 195–6; is supposed